THE GREEK LANGUAGE

THE GREAT LANGUAGES

Joint General Editors

L. R. PALMER, M.A., D.PHIL., PH.D.
formerly Professor of Comparative Philology in the University of Oxford
A. E. MORPURGO DAVIES, M.A.
Professor of Comparative Philology in the University of Oxford

---

The French Language
A. EWERT, M.A., LITT.D.

The Spanish Language
together with Portuguese, Catalan, Basque
WILLIAM F. ENTWISTLE, M.A., LITT.D., LL.D.

The Chinese Language
R. A. D. FORREST, M.A.

Russian and the Slavonic Languages
WILLIAM F. ENTWISTLE, M.A., LITT.D.
and W. A. MORRISON, B.A., PH.D.

The Latin Language
L. R. PALMER, M.A., D.PHIL., PH.D.

The Sanskrit Language
T. BURROW, M.A., PH.D.

The Romance Languages
W. D. ELCOCK, M.A., L.ES.L., D.DE L'U. TOULOUSE
(revised with a new introduction by
JOHN N. GREEN, M.A., D.PHIL.)

The Scandinavian Languages
EINAR HAUGEN

The German Language
R. E. KELLER, DR.PHIL., M.A.

Other titles are in preparation

THE
GREEK LANGUAGE

Leonard R. Palmer

HUMANITIES PRESS, INC.

Atlantic Highlands, New Jersey

First published in 1980 in the U.S.A.
by Humanities Press Inc.
New Jersey
Printed in Great Britain

Library of Congress Cataloging in Publication Data

Palmer, Leonard Robert, 1906–
The Greek language.
(The Great languages)
Bibliography: p.
Includes indexes.
1. Greek language–History.
2. Greek language–Grammar, Historical. I. Title.
PA227.P3   480'.9   79-26758
ISBN 0-391-01203-7

To Elisabeth

CONTENTS

Part II

Comparative-Historical Grammar

FIGURES IN THE TEXT

PREFACE

In 1954, when *The Latin Language* was published, a companion volume on the Greek Language was already envisaged. Its completion was put off for over twenty years by the decipherment of the Linear B script, which gave us direct knowledge of Greek some five centuries earlier than Homer. Michael Ventris's brilliant discovery provided for two decades the material for a new and highly productive academic industry. Now that there are signs that the seam has been worked out and that, in default of new and rich finds, Linear B studies have virtually reached the end of the road, the time is ripe to incorporate the results into a general work on the Greek language.

Like its predecessor, the book is divided into two parts: the first concentrates on tracing the development and ramifications of the language as the vehicle and instrument of a great culture. After an attempt to site Greek in the network of Indo-European dialects, it considers the complex and debatable problems presented by the entry of the Proto-Greeks into their historical homeland and their linguistic debt to the pre-Greek substratum, whose identity and provenance are also discussed.

A chapter on the Linear B texts and the nature of the Mycenaean 'chancellery' language is followed by one on the Greek dialects of the 'Hellenic Age'. This is the necessary prelude to the core of the book, the chapters on the manifold literary dialects of poetry and prose. The final chapter of the first part is concerned with the coalescence of the ancient dialects into a Common Language and its further development into the various forms of Modern Greek.

The second part is a condensed Comparative-Historical Grammar. Users of *The Latin Language* will doubtless note and regret the absence of a chapter on Syntax. This was envisaged for the present volume; but time, space, and the great rise in costs precluded its execution. The main reason is the mass of material. Latin was considered to end with Charlemagne. Greek has a longer history. Except for a gap of some five centuries in the Dark Age which intervenes between the end of the Mycenaean civilization and the first 'alphabetic' texts of the Hellenic Age, we have direct textual knowledge of Greek from the thirteenth century B.C. down to the present day. Another consideration increased the size of the book. Whereas we felt able to dispense with translations of the Latin examples (this has been deplored and remedied in the Italian edition), we were urged to provide such aid for the Greek. The versions have no pretensions to literary merit. They serve a purely utilitarian aim and are meant simply as aids to construing and analysing the examples.

The bibliography also serves a limited purpose. It lists merely a few works which will help the inquisitive reader and student to find his way into the luxuriant jungle of the specialist literature.

As before, the duty of the contributor to such a series as The Great Languages remains 'to state the *communis opinio* where one exists and elsewhere to set forth fairly the evidence and the divergent views which have been expressed'. In a field so vast as that of the Greek language the reader will not be surprised to discover that there has been ample scope for divergencies and that the author occasionally has views of his own.

The completion of a book so long in gestation would have been impossible without the generous assistance of the relevant departments of the University of Innsbruck: the Institut für klassische Philologie (Professor R. Muth), the Institut für vergleichende Sprachwissenschaft (Professor W. Meid) and the Universitätsbibliothek (Dr O. Stranzinger).

The main debt owed by the author of such a work is to the general body of scholars, only a few of whom could be named. Professor Anna Davies, the joint editor of The Great Languages, in particular gave generously of her time and learning with the result that the book shed many of its imperfections.

My wife, as always, has been of constant support and infinite patience throughout the many vicissitudes of composition, typing, checking, proof reading and index making. Undaunted by the loss in the post of the finally processed typescript she set to work with speed and efficiency to reduce the delay to a minimum. To her this book is dedicated *quinquagesimo anno*.

Sistrans, Tyrol   L. R. Palmer

PART I

AN OUTLINE HISTORY OF THE OF THE GREEK LANGUAGE

I

THE PREHISTORY OF THE
GREEK LANGUAGE

---

1. Greek and Indo-European

The Greek language, spoken today by between nine and ten
million people in Greece itself and abroad, is one of the best
documented languages of the world, for we have direct knowledge of it over a time span of some 3,000 years. It appears first
in the syllabic Linear B inscriptions of Mycenaean Greece and
Crete, dated to not later than the thirteenth century B.C. (see
pp. 27–56). Then, after a Dark Age following the destruction
of the Mycenaean civilization, the language reappears in a new,
written guise, an alphabetic script (based on a North Semitic
script), the earliest text being dated roughly to the last quarter
of the eighth century B.C. From this time on there is an unbroken chain of written testimony for the history of the language
down to the present day.

The use of the comparative method enables us to reach
farther back in time than the date of the earliest texts. In the
first place, ancient Greek is presented to us in the form of a
number of dialects and this enables us to devise a hypothetical
ancestral form, 'Proto-Greek'. The dating of this and the entry
of the 'Proto-Greeks' into the land which their descendants now
occupy requires the assessment of archaeological and other data
which will be examined below. For the time being it will suffice
to say that in all probability the Hellenization of the Balkan
peninsula took place in the first half of the second millennium
B.C. and that the invaders imposed themselves as conquerors on
an indigenous population whose language(s) became extinct,
but has (have) left traces in place-names and in the vocabulary
of Greek.

The history of Greek may be carried a stage farther back
thanks to the fact that it is a member of the Indo-European
family, which comprises languages stretching from Celtic in
Western Europe to the Indo-Aryan languages of present-day

India. Comparison of these languages enables us not only to reconstruct an ideal grammar of the parent Indo-European (IE), but also to group them in major sub-families. The siting of Greek in this network of relationships is arrived at by assessment of the peculiarities which it shares with certain other languages of the family. By this means some guesses may be made about the history of the Greeks in the intermediate period between proto-Indo-European and their entry into their historical habitat.

We have said 'comparison of languages', but in fact what the comparatist does is to compare linguistic descriptions comprising lists of words (lexicons) and the rules by which these are formed into sentences (grammars). It follows that the first step is to attempt at least a summary description of Greek based on the earliest available texts (see Part II). This description will provide the necessary basis for assessing its Indo-European relationships. That task performed, it will then be possible to trace the history of Greek, starting with the first invasions which are believed to have brought about the Indo-Europeanization of Greece. There is, however, a possibility that the Greeks had been preceded by another Indo-European people, just as the Anglo-Saxon peoples imposed themselves on a Britain occupied perhaps a thousand years earlier by the Celts, both Celtic and Germanic being IE languages. This is a delicate problem involving the assessment not only of the elusive evidence bearing on the languages of pre-Greek populations and the contributions they made to the vocabulary of Greek, but also the archaeological evidence, which reveals in the first instance patterns and movements of cultures, but not necessarily of peoples.

2. The Greekness of Greek

We first turn to the identity of Greek, that is the delineation of its linguistic physiognomy which, while affirming its family relations, at the same time sets it apart from all other members of the Indo-European group. This physiognomy is statable as a set of features which, taken as a whole, provides the investigator with a criterion which enables him to decide that a given text is written in Greek and no other Indo-European language. The separate features which make up this unmistakable identity may be stated as equations between the reconstructed IE and the corresponding Greek representatives. They comprise points of phonology and morphology. An illustration is the word for 'seven', IE *septm̥ > ἑπτά, which exemplifies two sound changes diagnostic of Greek: the aspiration of initial antevocalic *s (p. 235) and the treatment of the sonant nasal (p. 217). Other phonological features are the changes of initial *j to the aspirate or to ζ (*jos > ὅς, *jugom > ζυγόν, p. 224), the unvoicing of the aspirated plosives (*bherō > φέρω, p. 229), the loss of all plosives in word-final position (*galakt > γάλα, p. 228), and the change of final *m to n (p. 223). A prosodic feature is the limitation of the accent to one of the three final syllables of the word (p. 244). In the morphology of the noun the most striking innovation of Greek was the reduction of the eight cases of IE to five (p. 277). In the declension there was mutual influence between the o- and the ā- stems, and both were influenced by the pronominal inflexions (e.g. the replacement of the nominative plural *-ōs, *-ās, by -οι and -αι). Conversely, the noun inflexions have replaced most of the endings peculiar to the pronominal declension, so that Greek no longer shows the IE difference between the two systems (still apparent for instance in Latin istius, istud, etc.), with the exception of the neuter singular in -d (*tod > τό with loss of final d, p. 285). The pronominal stems were strengthened by combination and addition of deictic particles (e.g. ὁ-ὗ-τος, ἐ-κε-ενο-ς, pp. 285 f.). In the adjective a new superlative in -τατος was developed (pp. 281 f.). In the verbal system the IE present stem formations survived only in fossil form, and a new set of productive formants developed, based largely on the inherited type in *-jō (pp. 261 f.). The originally independent aspectual stems were organized into regular conjugations (pp. 293 ff.), notable features being the perfect in -κ- (p. 306), the aorist passive in -(θ)η- (p. 302), and a number of future formations (pp. 310 ff.). The development of the infinitive was a relatively late phenomenon, for the forms differ from dialect to dialect (pp. 314 f.).

To this reconstructed Proto-Greek we must assign features which no longer figure in the texts of the post-Mycenaean dialects. Vocalic hiatus was prevalent and the intervocalic aspirate (< *VsV) still survived (for Myc. see p. 41). It is also likely that the clusters -*sm*-, -*sn*- remained unchanged (e.g. **selasnā*, **usme*, etc., p. 41). On the evidence of Mycenaean (p. 42), Proto-Greek may well still have possessed the phoneme **-j* (p. 224) not only in the positions *jV*- and -*VjV*-, but in many of the clusters *Cj* (e.g. *kjāwetes, aljos, phulakjō*, etc.). It is likely that the sonant liquids **ṛ* and **ḷ* were also retained since their dialectal treatment varies. That the labio-velar consonants still survived is clear not only from their different representation in the dialects but also from the Linear B evidence (p. 40). It has also been argued that the dissimilation of the aspirated plosives (Grassmann's Law) had not yet taken place, but see pp. 230 f. Morphology will also have remained at a more archaic stage (e.g. the survival of athematic verbs such as *kteimi*, later κτίƷω).

To site Proto-Greek in a network of IE relations we simply list shared innovations. Shared archaisms carry little weight for they may be merely accidental independent survivals left untouched by the continuous and random process of linguistic renewal. One such survival is the preservation of the palatal plosives in the so-called *centum* languages as opposed to the change to fricatives in the *satəm* languages. The latter comprise Indo-Iranian, Balto-Slavonic, Armenian and Albanian, and it is plausibly deduced that the change took place within the Indo-European period before their dispersal, that is to say it was a common isogloss of a group of Indo-European dialects. The absence of this change, on the other hand, has no relevance for the grouping of the *centum* languages Celtic, Italic, Germanic, Greek, Hittite and Tocharian. Below we shall see that Greek, though a *centum* language, has close affinities with certain *satəm* languages. Thus while it makes sense to speak of a *satəm* group characterized by the change of **k* to a sibilant, there was no corresponding *centum* group.

A special type of innovation is the exclusive selection of one possibility from a number of alternatives: e.g. the inflexions of the dative, ablative, and instrumental plural have a characteristic -*bh*- in Indo-Iranian, Armenian, Greek, Italic, and Celtic as against -*m*- in Germanic and Balto-Slavonic. Within Greek, the dialects select as terminations of the first person plural active of the verb either -μες or -μεν, both of which may be attributed to Proto-Greek (p. 297). Such 'selection' is a valid

criterion for affinity. By assessment of such criteria scholars are
generally agreed that Greek has closest affinities to Armenian
and Indo-Iranian. In the first place all three share a remarkable
morphological feature—the augment (ἔλιπε, Skt. áricat, Arm.
elikʻ, p. 292). Common vocabulary items add some weight:
e.g. a common expression for 'old man' (γέροντ-, Skt. járant-,
Arm. cer), the replacement of IE *man by *mr̥to-, a back-
formation from *n̥-mr̥to- 'immortal' (βροτός, Skt. márta-, mr̥ta-,
Av. marəta-). Greek shares with Armenian the prothetic vowel
as in ἀστήρ, Arm. astł, ἀνήρ 'man', Arm. ayr, and especially
the word for 'nine' ἐννέ(ϝ)α, Arm. inn (p. 221), and items of
vocabulary such as the verb 'to grind' ἀλέω, Arm. alam, cf.
ἄλευρον 'flour', Arm. alewr, the bird-name ἰκτῖνος, Arm. çin,
Skt. śyená-, and the adjective 'empty' κεν(ϝ)ός, Arm. sin. Add
further the prohibitive particle μή, Skt. mā, Arm. mi, though
this also occurs in Tocharian and Albanian. Indo-Iranian also
has important connections with Balto-Slavonic, which prompt
the conclusion 'that there did at one time exist a special relation
between early Indo-Iranian and those dialects of Indo-
European which developed into the Baltic and Slavonic
languages'.[1]

The location of the cradle lands of the Proto-Balts and
Proto-Slavs is still under discussion, but it is an important
pointer that Baltic elements occur in the river and place names
in the area between Vilna and Moscow. Study of the hydronyms
of the Upper Dnepr Basin shows a great density of Baltic
elements north of the Pripet river, whereas south of the river
they are much sparser and interspersed with Iranian and
Finnish names. The latter give point to the linguistic connections of Indo-Iranian with Finno-Ugrian, a neighbouring but
non-Indo-European language family, comprising Finnish,
Esthonian, Hungarian and a number of minor languages. This
is regarded as 'conclusive evidence' of early contact and is
another important pointer to the location of Proto-Indo-
Iranian in southern Russia with the Proto-Balts to the north-
west and the Finno-Ugrians to the north-east (the homeland
of the latter being located in the vicinity of the River Oka).

Given these pointers we may arrange the IE languages in a
schematic geographical pattern (Fig. 1). The satəm languages

[1] Burrow, 18.

[Finno-Ugrian]

Celtic   Germanic   *Baltic*

Slavonic

Italic   *Indo-Iranian*   Tocharian

Armenian

Albanian Thracian

Phrygian

Greek

Anatolian

Fig. 1. The Distribution of the Indo-European Languages
in the Third Millennium B.C. (*satəm* languages in italics)

occupy a central position flanked on the west by Germanic,
Celtic and Italic, this group having certain points of contact
with Balto-Slavonic (e.g. the instrumental or dative plural in
-*m*- occurs exclusively in Germanic, Baltic and Slavonic).[1] To
the south lay the Anatolian group (Hittite, Luwian and Palaic),
which was introduced into Asia Minor *c.* 2000 B.C. To the east
lay Tocharian (actually two related dialects, A and B), which is
known to us from texts found in Chinese Turkestan, dating from
between the sixth and tenth centuries A.D.

The striking fact which emerges from the study of this network of interrelations is that Greek, though it is a *centum*
language, has no special connection with the western group. In
particular, despite the close cultural symbiosis of Rome and
Greece in the historical period, Latin and Greek are linguistically, within the Indo-European family, worlds apart. Burrow
(p. 15), noting that the connections between Sanskrit and Greek
far outweigh those with other IE languages (outside Indo-
Iranian), adds that some of the common features involved are
of late IE origin (e.g. the augment). Yet Greek, despite its
affinities with the *satəm* group, did not participate in certain of
the common linguistic innovations of that group. This suggests
that the Proto-Greeks, having participated in certain of the
common linguistic innovations of the central group, separated
before the advent of the characteristic *satəm* sound-changes.

[1] For Italic see my *Latin Language*, 12 ff.

Given the above argued south-Russian siting of the *satəm* group, we may plausibly site the Greeks of this period in the area west of the Black Sea, from which they eventually migrated into their historical habitat.

3. Greek and Pre-Greeks

Greece had long been inhabited before the coming of the new invaders from the north. Archaeological evidence points to an age-long cultural drift from Asia Minor and perhaps actual infiltration of new population elements from the same quarter. Linguistic evidence likewise points to an affinity between pre-Greek speech and that of Asia Minor. On this topic scholars almost unanimously refer to Paul Kretschmer's fundamental work *Einleitung in die Geschicht deer griechischen Sprache* (Introduction to the history of the Greek language), published in 1896. Kretschmer focused on an observation made over forty years earlier: certain place-names of Greece, characterized by the suffix -νθ- (Σύρινθος, Κόρινθος, Πύρανθος, Ἀμάρυνθος, Τίρυνθος, etc.), which also occurs in vocabulary words like ἀσάμινθος 'bath-tub', μήρινθος 'thread', ἐρέβινθος 'pea', ὄλυνθος 'unripe fig', etc., and in the divine name Ὑάκινθος, are ascribable to the pre-Greek population. Another such indicator is the element -σσ-/-ττ-, likewise observable in names and vocabulary words (Καρνησσόπολις, Ὑμηττός, Μυκαλησσός, Παρνασσός, etc.). By analysis of the place and personal names of Asia Minor, Kretschmer supported the following theses:

1. A language characterized by the suffixes -*ss*- and -*nd*- (earlier -*nt*-) was in use particularly in the southern half of Asia Minor—Lydia, Caria, Lycia, Pisidia and Cilicia.

2. People of related language were responsible for the -νθ- and -σσ-/-ττ- names and words of the Greek islands and mainland.

3. The clue to this language lies in the inscriptions of Lycia, where an *s*-suffix is clearly established.

4. Lycian is certainly a non-Indo-European language.

Subsequent research substantiated the soundness of Kretschmer's method (see below). But new sources of information have compelled a different answer to thesis 4: Lycian is an IE language belonging to the Anatolian group. For those who accept Kretschmer's analyses and comparisons (and modern authors are virtually unanimous in doing so) it follows that another group of IE speakers took possession of Greece before the arrival of the Greeks, just as Celts preceded the Anglo-Saxons in the British Isles. We may dub them the 'Parnassos folk'.

4. The Anatolian languages

The discovery and elucidation of this group of languages have constituted the major advance this century in the IE field. In 1906 German archaeologists excavated a site, some 200 kilometres east of Ankara, which was identified as the Hittite capital Khattusha. The archives yielded thousands of tablets written in a cuneiform script in a number of different languages. Best known is Hittite, which was spoken in an area concentrated within the bend of the Halys river. Now, since Hittite names (and a few technical terms) of a distinctly IE character occur in Old Assyrian texts dated to the nineteenth century B.C., it would appear that the Hittite presence in central Anatolia may well go back to the beginning of the second millennium. Two main linguistic stages have been detected: 1, pre-imperial Old Hittite (seventeenth to fifteenth century), and 2, imperial Hittite (fourteenth to thirteenth century), the latter being subdivided into (a) classical Hittite (fourteenth century) and (b) late Hittite (thirteenth century), the last considerably altered and with an abundance of Luwian elements (see below).

North-west of the Hittite area, in what came to be known as Paphlagonia, the related language Palaic was spoken. These two languages form the North-Anatolian branch, both being imposed on a substrate language, Hattic, of which numerous texts survive.

In their expansion south-west the Hittites entered territory occupied by linguistic relatives, the Luwians. Their language is first attested in cuneiform tablets of the thirteenth century. Despite its much less archaic appearance, it is identical in all fundamentals with Hittite; they are sister languages, like Italian and French. Late Hittite tablets of the thirteenth century attest a considerable measure of bilingualism, so much so that scholars speak of a 'Luwian repopulation' of central Hatti.

It was in this last period that the Luwian script also came to be used in purely Hittite territory. This is the script known as 'Hieroglyph Hittite', remarkable as the earliest script invented to record an IE language. The script has been known to scholars since 1870, and the inscriptions are scattered about an area covering northern Syria and the south Anatolian provinces. The protracted process of decipherment, helped by the discovery of a Phoenician–Hieroglyph Hittite bilingual inscription at Karatepe near Adana, has yielded a form of Luwian somewhat different from cuneiform Luwian, though the differences have been lessened by recent advances in decipherment.

The close relationship of Lycian (spoken in south-west Asia Minor) to Luwian has now been established beyond reasonable doubt despite the time gap thirteenth to fourth century B.C.[1] As an illustration of the complex patterning of the facts in the Anatolian group we may choose the representatives of the IE word for 'hand': *ghesr- > O. Hitt. kes(a)r, Class. Hitt. kesera-, Luwianism kisari- > kisri-; proto-Luwian *yesar(i)- (ke- > ye-), Cun. Luw. isari-, Hier. Luw.[2] istri-, Lyc. izri- (instr. izredi < Luw. is(a)radi).

Study of the names of southern Anatolia has shown that Luwian speakers survived along the Mediterranean coast from Caria to Cilicia until Greco-Roman times. To sum up, we may quote the most recent pronouncement on this key topic: 'While Hittite, Palaic and Lydian remain somewhat on one side, Cun. Luwian, Lycian, and the language of the Hieroglyphs share a special relationship which allows us to speak of a Luwian subgroup of Anatolian.'[3]

To return now to the -ss- and -nd- suffixes, it has been shown that the latter comprise -anda and -wanda: 'the Anatolian languages...provide a total explanation of these three suffixes...; the territories over which the names in -anda, -assa, and -wanda occur include the south, south-west, and central Anatolia, but not the north, the north-west, and the east beyond the Euphrates.' This corresponds in the main to the

---

[1] See E. Laroche, 'Linguistique Asianique' in *Acta Mycenaea*, 112–35, Salamanca (1972).

[2] 'Hieroglyph Luwian' is another term for 'Hieroglyph Hittite'.

[3] J. D. Hawkins, A. M. Davies and G. Neumann in *Nachr. Ak. Wiss. Göttingen*, Phil.-hist. Klasse 1973, No. 6 (1974).

Luwian area. A leading authority in the field, E. Laroche, whose results have just been quoted, concludes in another paper[1] that peoples speaking an Anatolian type of IE invaded Greece, bringing with them names of the type *Parnassos* and *Erymanthos*. The Greeks formed a later wave of invaders.

Did the invasion of the 'Parnassos folk' proceed from Asia Minor or did groups of related speech invade Greece independently from the 'Anatolian' cradle-land, presumably north of the Black Sea? Another paper by Laroche gives us a clue. The inherited IE suffixes (such as -*ašša*) were also used to make derivatives from indigenous words which the invaders picked up in their new homeland. The noun *per/parna* 'house' is a case in point. It provides such derivatives as Hitt. *parn-alli-* 'domesticus' and the derived Hier. Hitt. verb *parnawa/i* 'serve?'. Lycian offers another genitival adjective *prñnezi* = οἰκεῖοι 'of the house'. This *z*- suffix, especially productive in Lycian, also occurs in both Cuneiform and Hieroglyph Luwian, and it is conceivable that the Aegean place-names in σσ/ττ are distributed between the *z*- and *ss*-suffixes.

Yet the word *parna* appears in Egyptian *pr*- and Hurrian *purli/purni*, so that it is likely to be an indigenous word of Asia Minor. Laroche posits as the original meaning 'rock dwelling', and in one passage in Hieroglyph Hittite he translates *parna*- as 'temple'. If, then, *Parnassos*, an Anatolian place-name (it is attested in Cappadocia), combines a Hittite-Luwian suffix with an indigenous Anatolian word, and the word recurs as a mountain name in Greece, this speaks for an invasion of Greece from an Indo-Europeanized Asia Minor as against one by linguistic cousins from the northern 'Anatolian' cradle-land.

While the suffixes just discussed are Anatolian in general rather than specially Luwian, the geographical distribution of the languages (see above) favours the Luwians as the carriers of these names to what was later to become Greek territory. Yet another observation points to the presence of Luwians in Crete and the Greek mainland. As a preliminary it will be well to review the methodology. A language is most effectively diagnosed by its morphology, for vocabulary elements easily pass as loan-words from one language to another. What was sound

[1] For Laroche's contributions see my survey in *Atti e Memorie del 1° Congresso Internazionale di Micenologia*, I, 339–54, Rome (1968).

about Kretschmer's method was his concentration on certain suffixes, but from the scanty information then at his disposal he wrongly concluded that Lycian was a non-Indo-European language. But even though a place-name like *Parnassos*, which actually occurs in Asia Minor, is securely established as an Anatolian formation, its transfer to Greece might be due to secondary displacement. It might be argued that Greeks settled for some time in Anatolia, learned the mountain names there, and on their occupation of Greece bestowed it on a mountain of their new territory. To argue the presence of Luwian speakers in Greece must pose the question whether Luwian morphological procedures were productive on Greek territory.

It has long been suggested that the name of the Cretan goddess Δίκτυννα is a derivative from the mountain name Δίκτᾱ. Scholars who made this suggestion were implicitly stating that a suffix -*unna* had been used to make a derivative from a toponym. If we now ask where such an ethnic-forming suffix is known, the answer is Luwian. Here, too, Laroche has made an illuminating contribution. Common Anatolian possessed a suffix *-uwan* which was used to form ethnics. This appears in Hittite in the forms -*uman*-, -*umna*-, -*umana*-, -*umma*- (e.g. *Luiumna*, *Luiumana* 'Luwian'). In Luwian the corresponding suffix is -*wanni*-, which was later contracted to -*unni*-. It was by this process that the inhabitants of Adana came to be known as *Danuna*. Thus this study of the Anatolian suffix satisfactorily accounts for the connection between *Diktā* and *Diktynna*: the goddess will have been so named by Luwian speakers. What is of interest is that on the Greek mainland we find a similar formation: *Delphyna* from *Delphoi*, the religious centre of the Greeks, situated on the slopes of Parnassos. Here two Luwian suffixes consort.

The Luwian connections of the name *Delphyna* have been recently strengthened by convergent philological and mythological research. It recurs as the name of a dragon in a mythical context which clearly reveals its Anatolian background. Typhon was a monster, borne by Gaia the Earth, who fought with Zeus for dominion over the world. In the struggle he severed the sinews of Zeus's hands and feet and carried him to Corycus in Cilicia. There he hid the sinews in his cave under the guard of the dragon Delphyna. The Cilician connections of this strange story long ago suggested to scholars an oriental origin, and this was confirmed by the emergence of Hittite texts about the dragon Illujankas and his struggle with the Weather God. The link with Cilicia is strengthened by Hesiod's story (*Theog.* 306) that Typhon married the dragon Echidna, half woman, half serpent, who lived in a cave 'among the Arimoi'.

Corycus, which figures in the myth, was the site of a famous sanctuary of the Weather God and we are fortunate in possessing inscriptional evidence which shows plainly the Luwian background.[1] This is to be found in a list of the priests of Corycus which covers a period of over two hundred years, starting about the middle of the third century B.C. Study of the names has shown a large number of indigenous Luwian names based on divine names. These reveal that the most prominent gods worshipped in the sanctuary were the Weather God *Tarhunt-* and a tutelary deity *Runt-*, who was a protector of wild animals. The following conclusions have been drawn:

1. The most important gods of Corycus were the leading characters in the first version of the Illujankas myth, which was probably a cult myth of Corycus.

2. Throughout the first millennium B.C., the sanctuary of Corycus continued to be a very important Luwian shrine.

3. In this way the sanctuary kept alive Luwian traditions going far back into the second millennium B.C.

In general 'it is becoming more and more evident that large groups of Luwians lived on the south coast of Asia Minor until well into the Hellenistic period'. For our thesis, the occurrence of the name Delphyna 1, for a serpent conquered by Apollo in the context Delphi/Parnassos and 2, for a dragon monster in a clear Luwian context must surely carry weight, particularly when added to the testimony of *Dictynna*.

The occurrence of a name of Luwian formation in a Greek myth traced by scholars to Luwian Asia Minor has an interest that goes beyond the immediate question being discussed here. It may be briefly noticed because of its relevance to our argument, for once again we find ourselves in the presence of important Oriental contributions to the Mycenaean world which lead us straight to Delphi and Parnassos.

[1] See Ph. H. J. Houwink ten Cate, *The Luwian Population Groups of Lycia and Cilicia Aspera during the Hellenistic Age*, Leiden (1961), for references.

The struggle of Zeus with the monster Typhon, sited in southern Asia Minor, is merely one episode in the great Succession Myth that forms the backbone of Hesiod's *Theogony*. It seems to be firmly established that the myth relating to the divine succession Ouranos–Kronos–Zeus came to Greece from the East for 'it is closely paralleled by myths known to the Phoenicians, the Babylonians, the Hurrians, and the Hittites, and in the case of the last three peoples we can show that these myths were current in the second millennium B.C.' (M. L. West, Hesiod, *Theogony*, 28). West comes to the conclusion that this myth was already known to the Mycenaean Greeks. The mechanism of its transmission from the Orient to Greece is left open: 'Exactly where in the eastern Mediterranean the Minoans or the Mycenaeans learned of it, we cannot be sure.' If, however, the Minoans were in fact Luwians, then they would have been the most likely vehicle for the transmission of this complex Mesopotamian Succession Myth to the Mycenaeans. This is supported by another observation: one curious feature of this myth brings us back once again to Delphi and Parnassos. Kronos swallows the children borne to him by Rhea, but she hides the youngest, Zeus, and gives Kronos a stone to swallow instead. Later Zeus forces Kronos to disgorge the stone along with his brothers and sisters and he plants it in the earth 'in holy Pytho, down in the vales of Parnassos'. West is clear about the significance of this detail: 'It cannot be doubted that the myth was related at Delphi in connexion with the stone'. It will be clear that this exploration of the names *Dictynna* and *Delphyna* fits comfortably into the general framework of an Hellado-Asianic symbiosis which in recent years has gradually emerged from scholarly researches. West formulates it thus: '…the great civilisations lay in the East, and from the first, Greece's face was turned towards the Sun. Greece is part of Asia; Greek literature is a Near Eastern literature.' Our own thesis is that the invading Greeks did not need to look to the Sun: they found an Asianic people already in possession of their new homeland. That this was so is suggested by the name *Dictynna*, a Luwian formation on Cretan soil. The suffix *-wanna/-unna* will reappear when a synthesis of the linguistic and archaeological evidence is attempted. Of interest to pre-historians is Laroche's finding that the *-umna-* formations belong to the northern branch of Anatolian and the -*unna*- type to the southern branch. This enables us to add names like *Larymna* (Boeotian Locris, and Caria), *Methymna* (Lesbos, where we also have the mountain *Lepetymnos*), and *Kalymna* to the possible Anatolian elements in Greek toponymy. They carry with them the implication that speakers of different Anatolian dialects were involved in the occupation of Greece, just as Angles, Saxons and Jutes took possession of Britain.

There is one striking linguistic phenomenon linking Greek and Luwian that deserves mention, though its significance is difficult to assess. It concerns a point of phonemic structure. The word-final plosive consonants were lost in Greek (e.g. *γαλακτ > γάλα, p. 228), while final *-*m* > -*n*. Consequently the only consonants which occur in a final position are *r*, *s* and *n*. In Luwian, too, the only word-final consonants are *s*, *n*, *r*, along with *l*. Again, as in Greek, nearly all words originally beginning with *r*- have developed a prothetic vowel (p. 223). There are a number of theoretical possibilities of explaining this striking resemblance in phonetic structure (e.g. a substratum common to Greek and the Luwian parts of Anatolia). However, if the morphological features discussed above favour the prior occupation of the country by Luwians, then the said transformation of the phonemic structure of Greek may well be ascribed to the Luwian substratum.

5. The Coming of the Greeks

A preliminary note of warning is needed before approaching the much disputed problem of the entry of the Greeks into their historical home. Aegean prehistory is the concern of both philology and archaeology. When two different sciences are forced into partnership, prudence suggests that each discipline should in the first place operate independently with its own techniques on its own material. For the linguist this is all the more imperative in the present instance because the *Cambridge Ancient History* offers him two mutually exclusive historical reconstructions based on the same archaeological material. He will naturally choose the version more easily reconcilable with his own analyses and conclusions, for a satisfactory answer must match the linguistic and the archaeological evidence. This is no more than an application of the law of the economy of hypotheses.

Now 'Greek' and 'Luwian' are primarily linguistic concepts, and both sides agree that prior importance attaches to the pre-Greek elements just examined. This is stressed by the Aegean archaeologist J. L. Caskey, the author of one of the two accounts between which we have to choose:[1] 'the final criterion [is] that of language'.

The prior task thus falls to Anatolian linguistics. It has firmly established that 1, the suffixes -anda, -wanda, and -ašša are common to both (a) Luwian and (b) Hittite and 2, they can be added to stems that are (a) Luwian or (b) Hittite or (c) Common Anatolian. Thus the Anatolian languages provide a complete explanation of these three suffixes. In order to 'dock' successfully with his partner in the Anatolian field, the linguist will next seek to find an answer to the key questions of geographical distribution and date. The crucial importance of the latter is evident: a chronological specification of the name-giving process in Anatolian toponymy will provide a *terminus post quem* for the transference of these place-names to Greece. The geographical specification has already been provided, and the concentration of the key place-names in the southern half of Asia Minor implies a dense pattern of settlement. This evidently rules out a period in which the Anatolian archaeologist deduces from his evidence a sparse population and nomadic conditions in the area in question.

We may next turn to the chronological determination of the Luwian settlement of Asia Minor. For geographical reasons, as we have seen, they are the more obvious candidates for the transfer of the place-names to Greece than the Hittites, whose homeland lay to the north-east within the bend of the Halys river. It has, however, been maintained that the Luwians preceded the Hittites by many centuries, so that a third millennium date could be upheld for their invasion. Laroche dismisses this thesis. His first point concerns the unity of the Anatolian group: all the languages have an unmistakable 'Anatolian' stamp, and they give the impression of having differentiated within a linguistic continuum. There are no linguistic indications that there was any 'staggering' of the

[1] *CAH*, 3rd edn., II 1, iv (a), 137; see below.

invasions by the Anatolian-speaking peoples. On the contrary, in a linguistic sense, the Luwians of history are for us the most 'recent' of the Anatolians: their language has evolved further than Hittite from proto-Anatolian. However, the question of 'modernity' of a language has little relevance for relative chronology: it is a commonplace of linguistics that closely related languages exhibit different rates of change.

It will be more profitable to address ourselves to the linguistic evidence[1] for the earliest appearance of Luwians and Hittites in Anatolia. Here we have the good fortune to have witnesses for a period as early as the twentieth century B.C. Assyria, in the course of commercial expansion, established trading colonies (*kārum*) in Asia Minor, the local princes becoming vassals of the Assyrian kings. One of these was in the city of Kanesh (at Kültepe, near Kayseri), and here thousands of clay tablets were found, covering the period *c.* 1910–1780 B.C. These make it clear that some of the princes were either Hittites or Luwians, and the same is true of the natives mentioned in the documents. Of outstanding historical importance are texts containing references to the prince Pitkhana and to Anitta, the commander of the fortress, for they are identifiable with the Pitkhana and his son Anitta, mentioned on a Hittite inscription, the latter having made great conquests and destroyed Khattusha, which subsequently became the capital of the Hittite empire. This dynastic family changed its seat from Khushshar to Kanesh. The importance of Kanesh as a power base in early Hittite history is underlined by the fact that the Hittite designation for their own language is a derivative from the place-name Kanesh: *kanešumnili*, *nešumnili* (also *našili*, *nišili*). As O. R. Gurney[2] has written: 'A more strict terminology would therefore use "Neshian" rather than Hittite as a name for the official language.'

The Old Assyrian texts thus give us a glimpse of the beginnings of the Hittite presence in Asia Minor before they established their capital at Khattusha. We also have a reasonably close date: Pitkhana was contemporary with the first generation of Assyrian merchants at Kanesh while his son Anitta and his

---

[1] See H. Lewy, *CAH*, 3rd edn., I 2, xxiv (*b*).

[2] *CAH*, 3rd edn., II 1, 229. Gurney embraces the view that Kültepe was destroyed by the Hittites, but Mellaart discounts this (*op. cit.* p. 703).

conquests fell within the second generation. At this early period
Luwians were also present, presumably as traders from their
own area of occupation. The western connections of Kanesh are
underlined by the fact that the patron god of the city was the
West Semitic deity, Anna. In the course of time the flag
followed trade, and the Luwian areas were incorporated into
the Hittite empire.

The general geographical, chronological, and historical
picture now having been established as far as is possible from the
linguistic evidence, we may turn to the evidence afforded by
Anatolian archaeology. Here two points of crucial importance
may be made at once. The first is that our chief consultant,
James Mellaart,[1] is aware of and fully accepts the linguistic
evidence: 'Hittitologists are now agreed that both Luwians and
Hittites were already present at Kültepe II [i.e. Kanesh] in the
twentieth century B.C.' The second is that there was a continuous cultural development with no breaks between the early
Bronze Age 3 period and the following Middle Bronze Age, just
as there are none between the Middle and Late Bronze Ages.
The whole period from c. 2300/2200 to 1200/1100 B.C. is a
cultural entity.

For our problem the focus must be on the concentration area
of the distinctive place-names, the south and south-western
parts of Asia Minor. Here, at the end of EB 2, Mellaart has
detected[2] a widespread invasion accompanied by extensive
destruction which resulted in a virtual abandonment of settled
occupation throughout the entire Konya plain and the
southernmost part of south-west Anatolia. Recovery is
not observed in the Konya plain until c. 2000 B.C., but
the Aegean coast south of the Troad remains an archaeological blank until the appearance of a Middle Bronze Age
culture, datable to c. 1900 B.C. Mellaart ascribes this destructive
invasion to Indo-Europeans and in particular to the Luwians.
The cultural recovery in the Luwian area, e.g. in the plain of
Konya, is consistent with the appearance of Luwian traders at
Kanesh in the late twentieth century. Of great significance, as
we shall see, is the evidence provided by excavation at Beyce-
sultan, which Mellaart identifies as the capital of the Luwian

[1] *CAH*, 3rd edn., I 2, xxiv(a), 703.
[2] *CAH*, 3rd edn., I 2, xviii, § vi.

state of Arzawa. This site was totally destroyed *c.* 1750 B.C., a date close to the beginning of the Old Hittite Kingdom.

In this general account we single out 'the virtual abandonment of settled occupation throughout the entire Konya plain', for this offers a crucial phase in comparing the linguistic picture. We again adduce the suffix -*wanna*. Konya (ancient Iconium) is situated in the province of Lycaonia. This name patently goes back to *Lukkawanna-, an ethnic adjective based on *Lukka*. The *Lukka* lands are known from Hittite texts, and though their exact location is disputed, they were certainly in the south-west part of Asia Minor, and some authorities would include Lycaonia. But that their territory extended to the sea is evident from references to piratical raids on Cyprus and sea trade with Ugarit.[1] Whatever the truth about this may be, the fact essential to our argument is clear: the territory in which Konya is situated bore a Luwian name and formed part of the lands where the -*assa* and -*anda* names were most concentrated: (from east to west) central Cappadocia, Lycaonia, Isauria, Pisidia, and Lycia. If these firmly established linguistic and geographical facts are given due attention and weight, there is little difficulty in arriving at an historical synthesis which harmonizes the findings of Anatolian linguistics with those of Anatolian archaeology.

An invasion of the late third millennium B.C., accompanied by widespread destruction, is followed by a revival which re-populates the area of our characteristic place-names. These names imply, of course, dense settlement. As noted above, they cannot be attributed to a phase described by Mellaart as 'a relapse into nomadic conditions'. In other words, these places were founded and named not earlier than the recovery in the Middle Bronze Age from the devastations of Early Bronze Age 3. This gives us our *terminus post quem* for the invasion of Greece by the 'Parnassos folk'. We may now turn to the archaeological history of Troy, for this will be the stepping-stone to the world of Middle Helladic Greece.

The site of Troy was occupied by a series of settlements beginning *c.* 3000 B.C. The period relevant to the present discussion is that known to archaeologists as Troy VI, when the most powerful of the successive citadels was built. There are

[1] See Houwink ten Cate, *op. cit.* 195–6.

many signs that this phase was due to newcomers, and it is significant that the horse now makes its first appearance. The period was a long one, 1900–1300 B.C., and some eight strata have been distinguished. In the earlier levels the predominant pottery was that known as grey Minyan. This is a type of ware that is also found in Middle Helladic Greece, and it was so named by Heinrich Schliemann because it first turned up at Boeotian Orchomenos, the legendary founder of which was Minyas. It is because of this common ceramic element that Aegean archaeologists believe[1] that 'both areas [i.e. the Troad and Middle Helladic Greece] were overrun at about the same time by invaders in the same folk-movement and probably of Hellenic stock'. It would, however, be wiser to view the grey Minyan pottery first in its given Anatolian context.

James Mellaart comments[2] that this type of pottery 'is now known to have been in use long before in neighbouring areas', which 'suggests rather a peaceful acquisition than a foreign intrusion'. With other Anatolian scholars he stresses 'the persistently Anatolian character of the Troy VI culture', and deprecates conclusions 'based on an estimate of the finds which is limited to the site of Troy itself or, at most, the Troad'. If one views the phenomenon of grey Minyan in its proper context, then what seem to be Troy VI innovations 'prove to have been for a long time familiar features of contemporary culture'. He concludes 'It is understandable, therefore, that scholars as yet unaware of recent discoveries in the interior of West Anatolia, when faced with the simultaneous appearance of grey "Minyan" on the Greek Mainland and at Troy, should have wrongly located its common source or even suspected its arrival at Troy from Greece. This view must certainly now be corrected.' Mellaart's general historical interpretation is that there was a general movement of peoples or groups in Anatolia from east to west which culminated with the arrival of Middle Helladic people bringing grey 'Minyan' pottery to Greece. Whatever the initial impulse of this great shift of population may have been (Mellaart moots Hittite expansionism), the implicit con-

[1] C. W. Blegen in *A Companion to Homeric Studies* (eds. A. J. B. Wace and E. H. Stubbings), 377.
[2] *CAH*, 3rd edn., I 2, xxiv(a), 682.

clusion is that there was an Anatolian invasion of Greece shortly after 2000 B.C.

To turn now to the alternative historical reconstruction: the chapter in the *Cambridge Ancient History* which deals with the 'Minyan' ware problem from a Greek point of view (written by the Aegean specialist J. L. Caskey)[1] still maintains the orthodox 'parochial' conclusion. It demands close examination, all the more because even historians of the Greek language refer to 'Middle Helladic Greek'. Seeing that an acceptable solution must harmonize the linguistic and the archaeological evidence and that Caskey favours the Anatolian origin of the *-inthos* and *-assos* place-names, it is surprising that the discussion shows no awareness of recent advances in our knowledge of Luwian and in particular there is no reference to Laroche's fundamental articles on the suffixes, which are the key to the problem. His argument is in fact purely archaeological and of notable simplicity. The Bronze Age cultures of Mainland Greece fall into three main periods, with subdivisions marked by distinctive pottery: Early, Middle and Late Helladic. Excavations at Lerna in the Argolid showed that a major break occurred at the end of EH II and that soon after there was an incursion of kindred settlers who inaugurated the very long Middle Helladic period, which lasted from *c.* 1900 B.C. until the onset of Late Helladic with the Shaft Grave period at Mycenae early in the sixteenth century B.C. Late Helladic is synonymous with 'Mycenaean', and this period lasts until the end of LH III C, *c.* 1100 B.C. Now the first indubitable evidence for the presence of Greeks is the occurrence of Linear B tablets in the ruined palaces of LH III B, *c.* 1200 B.C. If we work back from this point, there is no perceptible cultural break until we reach the beginning of Middle Helladic, or rather, on the Lerna evidence, EH III. Ergo, EH III/MH is Greek.

So early an entry of the Greeks, however, is hardly reconcilable with the linguistic and archaeological evidence from Anatolia since, as all sides agree, we must find time for an occupation by the 'Parnassos folk' originating in Asia Minor before the coming of the Greeks. To put this event back into EH III would entail an impossibly high date (well back into the third millennium B.C.) for the invasion of Asia Minor by the

[1] See note 1, p. 17.

Anatolian-speaking peoples. The settlement history of southern Asia Minor in the concentration area of the key place-names, as we have seen, also offers difficulties.

At this point it will be pertinent to examine another archaeological argument which seeks to show that the -*inthos* and -*assos* places were so named in the Early Bronze Age of Greece.

C. W. Blegen and J. B. Haley[1] noted that the distribution of these names coincided with that of Early Helladic sites, many of which were subsequently abandoned. This coincidence they regarded as significant and their conclusion has been endorsed in downright terms by Caskey (*loc. cit.*): 'they must belong to the Early Bronze Age and not any other.' The fallacy in this argument has already been pointed out:[2] 'Names, like all linguistic evidence, are transmitted from generation to generation by word of mouth. Thus if they were bestowed in the Early Helladic period and survived into Hellenic times, this means that they must have been also on the lips of men during the intervening Middle Helladic generations. What significance can there be, therefore, in the apparent coincidence of distribution with Early Helladic sites? Once such sites had been abandoned, how would Middle Helladic men have found occasion to refer to them and perpetuate their names for after-generations? In other words, even if the names had been bestowed by the EH people, the only ones which could have survived would refer to sites which remained in occupation later. Thus we should also observe a no less significant correlation with Middle Helladic sites and, of course, with Late Helladic sites, because in their turn the Mycenaean people relayed these ancient place-names and passed them on, to be eventually recorded in the documents of Hellenic and even Byzantine times. One must, therefore, reject the distribution argument as having any bearing on the attribution of the names to this people or that.'

To turn now to the purely archaeological argument in favour of so early a dating of the Greek immigration, the weak link in the chain of deduction connecting the Greekness of the Linear B tablets with an archaeological phase some seven or eight hundred years earlier, lies in the explicit dogma 'no cultural break—no intrusion of new people'. There are, on the contrary,

[1] *American Journal of Archaeology*, 32, 1928, 141–54.
[2] *Mycenaeans and Minoans*, 2nd edn., 346.

numerous instances where the invaders have introduced a new language or a new dialect without any perceptible break in the material culture (see below on the 'Dorian invasion'). But is it true that there is no noticeable change between Middle Helladic and the onset of the Late Helladic in the early sixteenth century, the most impressive witness to which are the Shaft Graves at Mycenae? Emily Vermeule writes:[1] 'Speaking honestly, there is nothing in the Middle Helladic world to prepare us for the furious splendor of the Shaft Graves.' In particular 'there are no horses yet, no chariots, no swords and precious little metal...', so that 'it is hard to believe that the Shaft Graves represent simply a mild progress from Middle Helladic cists'. Another important cultural feature points to Asia Minor. In Middle Helladic Lerna (Lerna V a) 'one finds new kinds of local pottery and tools, new imported goods, and, most notable, intramural burials in large numbers.'[2] Emily Vermeule also notes that this intramural burial is an unusual feature, 'a habit new to Greece though old in the East'.

To sum up, in choosing between the opposing cases presented in the *Cambridge Ancient History* by the Anatolian and the Aegean advocates, the latter cannot be preferred for the following reasons. While it accepts the Anatolian origin of the Parnassos place-names, it shows no awareness of the evidence firmly established by experts in Anatolian linguistics. Further, it does not attempt to take the obvious step of linking the admittedly Anatolian names with the findings of Anatolian archaeology. In particular, it neglects the settlement history of the concentration area of the said place-names and dissociates Troy VI from its Anatolian background. Finally, the basic principle of the logical deduction 'no cultural break—no intrusion of new people' is also questionable.

On the other hand, the linguistic and the archaeological evidence can be reconciled by assigning the Middle Helladic culture to the Anatolian 'Parnassos folk' and crediting the Greeks with the 'furious splendor' of the Shaft Graves. But not even this is wholly satisfactory. A general study of the 'Aegean' loan-words in the Greek vocabulary suggests that the Greeks encountered an advanced and elaborate civilization, and this does not fit an archaeological picture of the Middle Helladic

[1] *Greece in the Bronze Age*, 81.   [2] Caskey, *op. cit.* 136.

world which refers to the 'extreme poverty and sense of marginal existence' (E. Vermeule, *op. cit.* 73). The same author writes (p. 75) of the Middle Helladic people 'One feels that they had only recently emerged from a real Neolithic stage.'

The difficulty is apparent in a cultural sphere where the matching of philological and archaeological findings should be easiest. This is architecture. Vermeule writes that the 'Minyans', while clever at pottery, were still behind their predecessors in other techniques of civilization. This was especially true of architecture: 'There were no palaces yet, or even spacious houses, though excavators are always hopeful.' Yet it has long been pointed out by linguists that the Greeks must have learnt the art of building in stone from the subjugated population, the reason being that the technical vocabulary is largely non-Indo-European (e.g. γεῖσον 'cornice', θριγκός 'coping', θάλαμος 'chamber', etc.). It seems hardly conceivable that the Greeks picked up a complete vocabulary of stone building from their Early Helladic predecessors late in the third millennium and, after they had lapsed into a quasi-Neolithic stage, preserved it for something like half a millennium until the time when Middle Helladic 'ends as a broadly civilized era though beginning in a dark age and a mystery'. The plain lesson of the architectural terms used by the Greeks is that their immediate predecessors were masters of a complex technology of stone building so that the archaeological *terminus post quem* for the adoption of the terms cannot be earlier than the re-emergence of elaborate architecture after the sad decline at the beginning of Middle Helladic.

So a number of scholars have argued for an even later date for the advent of the Greeks, some putting it as late as LH III B. This would be quite reconcilable with a conservative assessment of the linguistic evidence from the Linear B tablets, to which we turn in the next chapter. This would mean identifying the 'Mycenaean' Greeks with the 'Palace Age': the great palaces were not built until the time of the latest 'tholoi' (i.e. the 'beehive' tombs like those of 'Atreus' and 'Clytemnestra' at Mycenae) in the thirteenth century.

The uncertainties in the absolute chronology do not affect our overall picture of the Indo-Europeanization of Greece. Speakers of an Indo-European dialect, who had remained in contact with the central group of dialects and in particular with Indo-Iranian, during the second millennium moved south into their historical homeland (possibly as highly mobile warrior bands) and wrested the country from their Anatolian linguistic cousins, who had left the Indo-European cradle-land at a considerably earlier date and had crossed into Greece and Crete after establishing themselves in Asia Minor.

II

THE EARLIEST TEXTS: THE
LINEAR B TABLETS

1. The Aegean Scripts

Until 1952 the oldest written record in the Greek language was believed to be an alphabetic inscription written on an Attic jug (dated to *c.* 725 B.C.). In this year Michael Ventris deciphered the Linear B script and showed that the clay tablets thus inscribed were written in an early form of Greek.

Linear B is one of a family of scripts in use in the Aegean during the second millennium B.C. They were discovered and described by A. J. (later Sir Arthur) Evans in the last decade of the nineteenth century. His studies started with an inscribed bead brought to him when he was Keeper of the Ashmolean Museum at Oxford. Further study of similar objects enabled him to set up (in 1893) an Aegean system of hieroglyphs distinct from the Egyptian and the 'Hittite'. Indications of provenance led Evans to Crete, where he secured large numbers of the inscribed objects. It became clear that the script had a history: a first stage of conventionalized pictographs (hieroglyphs) had been succeeded by another where the 'pictures' were reduced to simple linear outlines with quasi-alphabetic values. Two stages of this linear script could be distinguished, Linear A and Linear B. Both the hieroglyphs and the Linear A stages are attested in the earliest palace at Phaistos and both forms are widely diffused through Crete. Linear B, on the other hand, was long thought to have been confined to the site of Knossos, and there it appears only in the Last Palace, the construction and destruction date of which is of particular importance to philologists and must be discussed later.

In 1900 Evans's brilliant deductions about the Aegean script were confirmed. In that year he started excavations at Knossos and almost immediately began to find large deposits of tablets inscribed in the Linear B script. In successive campaigns their number increased to several thousands. Evans was convinced that some form of writing must also have been in use in the Mycenaean palaces of the Greek mainland. Stirrup jars with inscriptions in Linear B came to light first at Orchomenos (in Boeotia), Mycenae and Tiryns; then in 1921 twenty-eight specimens were found in a store room at Thebes. Subsequent research, however, was to make it likely that most of these Mainland inscribed vessels had been imported from Crete not long before the destruction of the Mycenaean palaces in the thirteenth to the twelfth century B.C.[1] Evans's intuition, however, found decisive confirmation when C. W. Blegen in 1939 found the first linear B tablets on a Mainland site at Pylos in the western Peloponnese. Their number increased in renewed excavations after the 1939–45 war, while Mycenae and Thebes also yielded their quota.

Other branches of this Aegean script were in use in Cyprus. Yet other important material exhibiting this script has been found at Ugarit (Ras Shamra). While the signaries are difficult to equate (virtually every document has a unique inventory), the varieties have a distinct family resemblance which justifies a common appellation such as Cypro-Minoan.

Another syllabic script was used in Cyprus between the seventh and third centuries B.C. Two varieties are known: 1, in central and eastern Cyprus and 2, in the south-west ('Paphian'). Most of the inscriptions are in the Cypriot dialect of Greek (see below), but others are in an unidentified language known as Eteo-Cypriot. While it is clear that the Cypriot syllabary is related to Linear B, there is no direct line of descent. The most plausible inference is that both derive from an ancestral script which was similar to Linear A. There is a number of quasi-identical signs with the same or a similar value, and the number is high enough to justify the positing of ancestral forms; it also encourages us to believe that it is justifiable to use the Linear B values, at least as a working hypothesis, for the 'decipherment' of Linear A (see below).

The material used for making the tablets was clay, and they were prepared for use by pressing a lump of clay on a flat surface. They were inscribed with a stylus while the clay was still damp and later merely dried in the sun. There

[1] This has been recently confirmed by analysis of the clay and study of the handwriting.

are two distinct types of tablet. One is an elongated slip of clay (the palm leaf shape) with the text running from left to right parallel with the long sides. The other is the page type in the form of a rectangle with its height greater than its width. There is evidence that tablets of the first type were sometimes used for preliminary notes which were later combined in records of the page type. To the right of the text we find ideograms followed by numerical indications in a decimal system.

The Linear B tablets were not meant for long keeping. Being merely sun-dried, they would soon have disintegrated under the action of moisture. Moreover, the only indications of time are month names and expressions such as 'this year', 'last year', and 'next year'. However, certain texts imply that less ephemeral texts were also kept, but on material that was more perishable. The archives show that the central administration of Pylos collected and kept an immense amount of detailed information relating to the population of the dependent territories. In particular, occasion arose to specify the parentage of groups of adults, such as textile specialists and rowers. Such data relating to the 'marriages' of the parents and the birth of their children must have been preserved for many years, in fact until the children had already become trained industrial workers. It would seem to follow that long-term records were compiled on less bulky and more permanent material than unfired clay tablets. They will have perished in the flames to which we owe the preservation of the ephemeral tablets. Thus these texts give information about the last months of the first European high civilization.

The Linear B script (see Fig. 2) is a most inadequate instrument for rendering the phonemic system of Greek. In essence the script takes account of the vocalic nucleus of the syllable and the immediately preceding consonant if there is one. In the consonants the vital distinctions of voice and aspiration (e.g. κ, γ, χ) are ignored, the system being skew in that there is a special series only for the voiced dental plosive (*da, de, di, do, du*). As for the vowels and diphthongs, the script ignores the distinctions of length and, in the main, the second elements of diphthongs:[1] *i, l, m, n,* and *r,* the only exception being *u*. Finally,

[1] Particularly at Knossos *i*-diphthongs are occasionally rendered, e.g. *kotoina* = *ktoinā*, *woikode* = *woikonde*.

1 da	23 mu	46 je	68 ro₂
2 ro	24 ne	47 ?	69 tu
3 pa	25 a₂	48 nwa	70 ko
4 te	26 ru	49 ?	71 dwe
5 to	27 re	50 pu	72 pe
6 na	28 i	51 du	73 mi
7 di	29 pu₂	52 no	74 ze
8 a	30 ni	53 ri	75 we
9 se	31 sa	54 wa	76 ra₂
10 u	32 qo	55 nu	77 ka
11 po	33 ra₃	56 pa₃	78 qe
12 so	34 ?	57 ja	79 ?
13 me	35 ?	58 su	80 ma
14 do	36 jo	59 ta	81 ku
15 mo	37 ti	60 ra	82 jai?
16 qa	38 e	61 o	83 dwo?
17 za	39 pi	62 pte	84 ?
18 ?	40 wi	63 ?	85 au
19 ?	41 si	64 ?	86 ?
20 zo	42 wo	65 ju	87 ?
21 qi	43 ai(a₃)	66 ta₂	89 ?
22 ?	44 ke	67 ki	90 dwo
	45 de		91 two

Fig. 2. The Linear B Syllabary

syllabic-final *s* is ignored[1] as are all word-final consonants. These rules reduce Greek to a bewildering mass of homograms: *ako* can stand for ἄγω, ἄκος, ἄλγος, ἀργός, ἄρχων, ἀσκός,* ἄγκος, etc., and only the context, if it can be established, guides our choice. Consonant clusters are treated as in the Cypriot syllabary. Gemination is ignored, but all members of non-homogeneous clusters receive the immediately following vowel: *konoso* = *Knōsos*, *tekotone* = *tektones*, *atoroqo* = *anthrōq^{w}ōi*. While the system thus fails to match the phonemic system of Greek, it makes distinctions superfluous for Greek: between (a) plain, (b) palatalized, and (c) labialized consonants. Examples of (b) are: *66 ta$_2$* = *tja*, *76 ra$_2$* = *rja*, *68 ro$_2$* = *rjo*; of (c) *71 dwe*, *90 dwo*, *48 nwa*, *87 twe*, *91 two*, to which we may add the labio-velars, conventionally transcribed with *q*, *16 qa*, *78 qe*, *21 qi*, *32 qo*. The phonological oppositions thus reflected in the syllabary are foreign to Greek, and this suggests that the ancestral form of the script was created for a language of a different type. This impression is reinforced by the failure to distinguish between *r* and *l* and the rendering of the later *labyrinthos* as *dapu$_2$rito*, if this identification is correct.

The series conventionally transcribed as *za*, *ze*, *zo* presents a special problem vital for Mycenaean phonology. Some scholars assume an affricate value [tsa], etc., while others regard them as palatized plosives [kja], etc. The certainly identified words like *topeza* = *torpeza* 'table' < *-pedjə*, *mezoe* = *mezo(h)es* 'bigger' < *megjoses*, *zeukesi* = *zeugessi* 'for pairs' < *jeuges-si* show that IE *dj*, *gj* and *j-* had already converged. On the other hand identifications like *suza* standing both for *sukiai* 'fig trees' and *sukia* 'figs', *kaza* = *khalkia* 'bronze' (adj.), *kazoe* = *kakjohes* 'inferior', *a$_3$za* = *aigia* 'goat (skin)' show that *z* also corresponds to later *ki* and *gi*. To interpret *suza* as [sutsa] is to assume changes unparalleled in later forms of these Greek words. These are 1, synizesis reducing *sukiai* and *sukia* to disyllables and 2, affrication of *kj* > *ts*. Moreover, there are numerous examples of spelling alternations *ze/ke* (*aketirija/azetirija*, *keijakarana/zeijakarana*, etc.) but none involving *ze/se*. The orthographic alternations thus suggest quasi-equivalent values for *ze* and *ke*, *zo* and *ko*, etc. Ventris originally used the transcriptions *ke$_2$*,

---

[1] With the exception of *sm* (*dosomo* = *dosmos*).

ko_2, etc., and there has recently been a shift of opinion back to the view that the z series represents palatalized plosives.

In arriving at a value for the conventional transcription with z we must make a distinction between 'values' and 'equivalents'. The identified words containing these signs lie between the ancestral Proto-Greek (and the much earlier IE) and the alphabetic texts. If both these poles present plosives as 'equivalents', then the onus of the proof is on those who argue an affricate 'value' for the intermediate Linear B. Now, all the alphabetic dialects show -κ- in the word for 'fig' and all its derivatives (σῦκον, συκέα, συκία, etc.). The word is presumably of Aegean origin and -k- also appears in Latin *ficus*. The same applies to the 'equivalents' of a_3za, *kaza*, and *kazoe*: both poles show plosives.

The improbability of [ts] has been increased by new word identifications. It has been shown that *aketirija*/*azetirija* stands for *askētriai* '(cloth) finishers', from the verb ἀσκέω. A phonetic form [*astsetrjai*] could hardly be also written *aketirija*. The same difficulty attaches in a greater degree to the ox-name transcribed a_3zoro. All these names are ordinary Greek adjectives: a_3woro = *Aiwolos* 'chequered, variegated', *kerano* = *Kelainos* 'black', *kosouto* = *Ksouthos* 'golden, yellow', etc. A_3zoro has hitherto resisted interpretation, but the name becomes less baffling if we return to Ventris's original transcriptional conventions and follow the semantic prescription suggested by the other names: the word is likely to be a Greek adjective appropriate as a name for an ox. Then $aiko_2ro$ is easily recognizable as *Aiskhros* 'ugly' (this word-family in later Greek names includes *Aiskhulos*). Evidently this new identification involves even greater difficulties for giving zo the phonetic value [tso]: a form [aistsros] lacks all phonetic plausibility.

Thus there are strong grounds for positing the values *kja*, *kje*, *kjo* for the signs conventionally transcribed *za*, *ze*, *zo*. Since they are used not only for the products of *kj, *khj, and *gj but also for the representatives of *dj and some instances of *j-, it is evident that these last two sounds must also have evolved to *gj.

There is one peculiarity about the use of the z-series which is of phonemic significance: there are a number of instances where the k is preceded by s: *asketria*, *aiskhros*, and possibly *zeto = skheto*, though *gento* 'he got' is also possible. This suggests that the phoneme /k/ had a palatalized allophone when it was preceded by *s*. The exact value of the phoneme represented by *z* is a matter of guesswork. If we posit a compromise between *dj* and *gj*, this would point to a prepalatal plosive [ɟ] or its voiceless counterpart [c]. The later developments in the different Greek dialects will be discussed below (pp. 59 ff.).

The phonetic values of the Linear B syllabary may be conveniently arranged in a table which brings out the oppositions of plain, palatalized, and labialized consonants.

8 a	43 ai (a_3)	38 e	28 i	61 o	10 u
3 pa		72 pe	39 pi	11 po	50 pu
56 pa_3?		62 pte < *pje?			29 phu
1 da		45 de	7 di	14 do	51 du
		71 dwe		90 dwo	
59 ta		4 te	37 ti	5 to	69 tu
66 tja		87 twe		91 two	
77 ka		44 ke	67 ki	70 ko	81 ku
17 kja		74 kje		20 kjo	
16 kwa		78 kwe	21 kwi	32 kwo	
80 ma		13 me	73 mi	15 mo	23 mu
6 na		24 ne	30 ni	52 no	55 nu
48 nwa					
60 ra	33 rai (ra_3)	27 re	53 ri	2 ro	26 ru
76 rja			68 rjo		
31 sa		9 se	41 si	12 so	58 su
? sja					
57 ja	82 jai (?)	46 je		36 jo	65 ju
54 wa		75 we	40 wi	42 wo	
25 ha					

There are two signs having a diphthongal value (*C*)*ai*: *43 *ai* (only in initial position) and *33 *rai*. It is possible that *82 has the value *jai*, but this is *sub judice*. *85 is also anomalous: it has the value *au* and, like *ai*, occurs only initially. The form of the sign transcribed as *sja* is uncertain. It occurs in a damaged form in the place-name *a-?-ta*, the usual orthography of which is *asijatia*.

2. Personal Names

Mycenaean grammar must be based primarily on securely established vocabulary words, but most of the words occurring in the tablets are names of persons and places, not unexpectedly in documents which are largely concerned with the registering and control of the population. However, the personal names are not only of interest linguistically, since they often preserve fossilized phenomena, but, as will be shown below, they carry implications for the history of the Homeric Epic. By way of preliminary some remarks on their morphology must be made.

The abundance of securely-identified personal names in the Linear B tablets shows that Mycenaean had already evolved the categories familiar in later times. We may first cite an example of the stately combination of full name and patronymic adjective: *Alektruōn, Etewoklewehios* (spelt *arekuturuwo etewokereweijo* 'Alektryōn son of Eteoklēs'. The father's name is a word with two components, a type familiar also from other IE peoples. Of particular interest are the names in which one of the components is a verbal stem. Where it is the first component there are three main types: (a) *Ekhe-dāmos* 'holding the people', (b) *Orti-nāwos* 'urging on the ships' and (c) *Philo-wergos*[1] 'loving work'. In (b) the *-ti* also occurs in the assibilated form *-si*: *manasiweko* = *Mnāsi-wergos* 'mindful of work'.

Such full names may be shortened (e.g. *Tēlemos* for *Tēle-makhos, Ekhelos* for *Ekhelāwos, Patroklos* for *Patro-klēs* (**-klewēs*), and certain characterizing suffixes may be attached, particularly *-eus*: e.g. *Menestheus* for *Mene-sthenēs*. This is a fact which will be of importance in the analysis of *Akhilleus*. The same suffix can also be added to a full name: e.g. *tatiqoweu*, which is interpreted as *Stati-gʷoeus* 'he who steads the oxen'.

It was natural that scholars should have looked for the names of the Pylian dynasty, and in particular for *Nestōr*, in the Linear B tablets recovered by Blegen from Pylos. The search led to results which revealed what may be called the *leitmotiv* principle operative in the dynastic names of the Heroic Age. *Nestōr* is an example of a familiar type, an agent noun in *-tōr* attached to a verbal root, in this case *nes-* 'bring back safely', 'save'. Others of the same type are *Mentōr, Kastōr, Hektōr*, etc.

[1] With compositional vowel *-o-*.

Now the parallels of *Mentōr*: *Menelāwos*, *Hektōr*: *Ekhelāwos*, *Aktōr*: *Agelāwos* open up the possibility of a name **Nese-lāwos*, in which the intervocalic *-s-* would become *-h-*: the form *Nehelāwos* in fact accounts for the name *neerawo*, which occurs in a list of notables in a Pylian tablet. It also includes *akireu* (dat. *akirewe*) = *Akhilleus*, on which, see below. The element *nes-* also occurs in the type *-ti-*, i.e. with component *Nesti-* in the name *netijano*, dat. *netijanore* = *Nestianōr*. We may compare *Kas-tōr*: *Kasti-aneira*. The root *kas-* 'excel' would also undergo the aspiration of *-s-* intervocalically, and this insight suggested an answer to the puzzle presented by the name *Nausikaā*, the Phaeacian girl whose brother was called *Kluto-nēos*, a name combining the themes 'renowned' and 'ship'. The girl's name is simply the feminine form of *Nausi-kahos* 'excelling in ships'.

We may now turn to Nestor's father *Nēleus*, again a long-standing puzzle, not only linguistically but also in Greek proto-history: why do so many of the earlier generation of heroes have non-Greek and even non-Indo-European names? One of these was allegedly *Pēleus*, the father of *Akhilleus*, but here the solution is not far to seek: it is a shortened form, characterized by the suffix *-eus*, of a name which has as its first component the adverb *qʷēle-* 'from afar' that is also found in *Tēlemakhos* 'fighting from afar', but with the Aeolic treatment of the labio-velar consonant *qʷē-* > *pē-* (see p. 60). A later form *Tēleus*, with the Attic-Ionic phonological development, is also attested. This opens up a similar solution for *Nēleus*: it is explicable as the shortened form of *Nehe-lāwos* 'saving the folk'. This full form would regularly develop in Attic-Ionic to *Neileōs*, and this is the name given to the son of Kodros, who in the tradition was the Pylian saviour of Athens from the onslaught of the Dorians.

In *Nēleus/Nestōr*, both based on the verbal root *nes-*, we have an example of the *leitmotiv* principle: the habit of giving the son a component of his father's name. This is particularly frequent in Cyprus, an island which preserved so much of Mycenaean tradition: thus *Onāsilos* (short for *Onāsi-lāwos* 'he who helps the people') is the son of *Onāsi-kupros*. We have a striking example of the same principle in the names of the Atreidai, the descendants of *Atreus*. The name of his younger son is transparent: *Mene-lāwos* 'he who makes the folk stand fast', with *men-* in the sense 'abide', 'cause to abide'. This occurs more obscurely also in the name of his brother *Aga-memnōn*, which has been analysed as *Aga-men-mōn* with a metathesis; but it is also possible that the characterizing suffix -*ōn* has been added to *memn-*, a reduplicated form of the root *men-*. With both analyses the meaning remains the same: 'he who stands fast exceedingly'. The *leitmotiv* is detectable semantically in the father's name, but there it is given different linguistic expression. *Atreus* is clearly a shortened form of a name whose first element was *a-tres-* 'not running away', for the root *tres-* has the meaning of 'panic-stricken flight'. In Sparta *tresās* was the term for a deserter.

There is no name in the tablets which bears any resemblance to *Odysseus*, but morphological analysis opens up a possible explanation. We may note first that the name of his father *Laertās* is transparent and is of interest because it preserves an obsolete verbal root *er-* 'urge on' which is preserved by Hesychius, the Alexandrian lexicographer of the fifth century A.D. *Lāw-er-tās* means 'he who urges on the folk'. A name made of the same two components actually occurs in the Pylos tablets, but it is of a different morphological type. The verbal component comes first and it is of type (b) *erti-lāwos* written *etirawo*. Another observation is necessary before venturing on a suggestion for *Odysseus*. In some of the -*eus* names the suffix is added directly to a verbal stem: e.g. *epekeu*, equivalent to *Epeigeus* (the name of a Myrmidon in the Iliad), which is made directly from the present stem *epeigō*, meaning 'drive on', 'press hard in pursuit'. If we set up a morphological schema verbal prefix (*epi*) + present stem + -*eus*, this will provide the framework for a possible analysis of *Odysseus*. In the first place there is evidence for a prefix *o-* 'on to', 'in to' as in *o-trūnō* 'urge on', 'cheer on' (which may occur in the short form *Otreus*), *o-kellō* 'run a ship aground'. In view of the predominance of martial themes in the name-giving, natural in a heroic context, we should seek in this semantic sphere for a present stem which also consorts well with the directional significance of the prefix *o-*. The root *deuk-* 'lead' is an obvious possibility. There is some evidence for an ancient present stem *dukj-*, with zero-grade and suffix -*j-* (see p. 264): **odukjeus* would regularly develop to Odysseus, but as has been argued above, at the time of the tablets the cluster -*kj-* was still retained and was written with the *z*-series. If the name should ever turn up in a Linear B tablet, the expected spelling would be *oduzeu*.

Finally, because of its implications for the Homeric epic, we may turn to the name of its central hero *Akhilleus*. First a morphological observation. Neuter *s*-stems, when used as first components, appear in what is known as the 'Caland-form', with a stem vowel -*i*: examples are *Kallilāwos* (*kallos*), *Oidipodās* (*oidos*), *Kūdianeira* (*kūdos*), *Thersilokhos* (*thersos*), etc. Such names have short forms, e.g. *Penthilos*, etc. In such short forms, expressive doubling of the consonant is often observed, e.g. *Kurillos*, the components of which are the neuter *s*-stem *kūros* 'supreme power', 'authority' and *lāwos* 'the folk'. Finally, the -*eus* suffix may be attached to such short forms. Given this morphological schema, the name *Akhilleus* readily resolves into the component parts *akhos* 'pain', 'distress' and *lāwos* 'the folk'.

The word *lāwós* must now be given new precision. In the epic it refers to the body of warriors, the army. It might be objected that no one would think of giving his son a name meaning 'one who causes distress to the army'. There is, of course, a parallel in the transparent *Penthilos* with the components *penthos* 'grief' and *lāwos*, cf. the short form *Pentheus*. However, the point has been taken up in a recent study by Gregory Nagy. He writes[1] that the proposed morphological analysis, plausible as it is, 'will not carry conviction unless we can show that the meaning of *'Aχί-λαϝος* is intrinsic to the function of Achilles in myth and epic.' His study brings out that the central theme of the *Iliad* is the pain and distress (*algea, pēmata, stonakhai*, etc.) caused to the *lāwos* by the wrath of Achilles. The word *akhos* itself also occurs in a number of passages such as the verse describing the plight of the Achaeans during the Battle of the Ships: τοῖον γὰρ ἄχος βεβίηκεν 'Aχαιούς 'for such an ἄχος has beset the Achaeans' (16. 22). Thus, from the fact that the central hero of the Iliad is given a name appropriate to his role, we have an easy counter to the objection that in real life no son would be given so inauspicious a name by his father. Certainly there is no dynastic *leitmotiv* principle at work here. As was shown above, his father's name *Pēleus* was no more than a shortened form of *Qʷēlemakhos*. *Akhilleus* is thus evidently a 'speaking name' invented for the purpose of the story and inseparable from it.

[1] 'The Name of Achilles: Etymology and Epic', in *Studies Palmer*, 209-37.

If this conclusion is valid, then the occurrence of the name *akireu* in the list of Pylian notables referred to above has an implication of interest to students of the Homeric Iliad. If such a name was already in ordinary use in aristocratic circles at the end of the thirteenth century B.C., this is because its intrinsically inauspicious meaning had been masked by its use as an heroic name. The conclusion may seem bold and we give it an interrogative form: is this an indication that the central theme of the Wrath of Achilles was already current at the time of the Pylos tablets? The chronological perspective will be given greater depth for those who believe in an early fourteenth century date for the Knossos Tablets: *akireu* occurs on a text from the Room of the Chariot Tablets. But here the archaeological context for a low dating is particularly clear.

3. Mycenaean Grammar

The sketch of Mycenaean Grammar which follows is a distillation from the words securely identified by rigorous textual philology. Morphology depends also on the establishment of syntactical function. As has been said, most of the material consists of personal and place-names. The example (p. 32) of *a₃zoro* = *Aiskhros* illustrates the hazards and difficulties that the philologist and grammarian faces in extracting 'grammar' from the Linear B tablets. Still more unreliable than personal names, it need hardly be said, are proposed identifications of place-names. The place-name *matoropuro* (once written *matopuro*) may serve as an illustration, since it figures repeatedly in arguments bearing on the representation of syllabic *γ in Mycenaean. It has been etymologized as *mātropulos* or *mātorpulos* and given the meaning 'mother city of Pylos'. However, sober textual philology shows that this place is a sheep station, for which the tablet records one missing sheep. Moreover, the later μητρό-πολις is no true parallel: we should require exemplifications like †Μητροκόρινθος, 'mother city of Corinth'. In addition, such a designation could not have been coined until after the founding of the 'daughter city' Pylos. Finally, the proposal would also carry historical implications. We should have to assume that 'Mother Pylos', having received this honorific title, subsequently dwindled to an insignificant sheep station, figuring in the Palace records only to the extent of one missing sheep and an unknown quantity of linen.

Place-names even more than personal names are thus suspect in that they elude the control and discipline imposed by the prior necessity to establish meaning by textual and contextual analysis. We are on surest ground with complete sentences, but these are a great rarity. A few may be quoted.

One set of texts, which is of unique historical importance since it records dispositions of men in defence of the territory of Pylos in the last months of its existence, is introduced by the preamble:

ouruto opia₂ra epikowo = *hō(s) wruntoi opihala epikowoi* 'How (thus) the watchers are guarding the coastal areas.'

Another preamble refers to an inspection by the prominent functionary Alxoitas:

owide akosota toroqejomeno aroura a₂risa = *hō(s) wide Alxoitas stroqʷhejomenos* (or *troqʷejomenos*) *arouran* Halisa- 'What (thus) A. saw on an inspection tour of the ploughland of H.' (the last word, taken here as a place-name, is not surely diagnosed or identified).

The set of tablets forming a 'book' that records land-holding arrangements on the temple estate of the goddess Potnia contains an entry that throws light on the status of the *dāmos*, for it appears as a collective contesting the status of certain holdings.

erita ijereja eke euketoqe etonijo ekee teo damodemi pasi kotonao keke-menao onato ekee = *erita hijereia ekhei eukhetoiqʷe etōnion* (?) *ekhehen theon dāmos de min phāsi ktoināōn kekeimenāōn onāton ekhehen* 'E. the priestess holds and makes solemn declaration that the goddess has an *etōnion* (a type of land holding), but the *dāmos* says that she has a lease (?) of shareland plots.'

The sense of emergency that pervades the whole Pylian archive is reflected in the preamble to a text recording levies of bronze from the sixteen main districts of the Pylian kingdom.

jodososi koretere dumateqe . . . kako nawijo patajoiqe ekesiqe a₃kasama = *hō(s) dōsonsi koretēres dumatesqʷe . . . khalkon nāwion paltaioihiqʷe enkhes(s)iqʷe aiksmans*, 'how (thus) the *k.* and *d.* (types of office holder) are to give temple bronze as points for arrows (or javelins) and spears.'

PHONOLOGY

VOWELS

Because of the inexact script little can be said about the vowel/
diphthong system, but in view of far-reaching retention of the
IE system in alphabetic Greek, the same is likely to have been
a fortiori true of Mycenaean. *$\bar{a}$* is, of course, retained as in all
non-Attic-Ionic dialects: *damo* = *dāmos*, *mate* = *mātēr*.

There are a number of examples of the interchange *e/i*:
atemito/atimite = *Artemitos/Artimitei*. The phenomenon appears
to be restricted to non-Greek words, which may originally have
had a vowel midway between the two. *Dipa* = *dipas* 'a jar' (cf.
δέπας) is particularly instructive since the Hieroglyphic Hittite
'rebus' ideogram for *tipas/tepas* 'heaven' appears to be a bowl
or cup. So *dipas/depas* may well be a Luwian loan-word in
Mycenaean (see above). The example of *i/u* in *moriwodo* rests on
the false attribution of the meaning 'lead (metal)' to this word
and its equation with *molubdos*. Nor is there an interchange of
o/u: *apu* is a different word from *apo* (see below).

Mycenaean was largely tolerant of hiatus: there are no certain
examples of vowel contraction.

CONSONANTS

That the voiced aspirates had already become voiceless is shown
by the use of the *t*-series to represent both τ and θ (*tukate* = *thu-
gatēr*, *tekotone* = *tektones*, *teo* = *theos*) as against the *d*-series for δ.
The existence of a series of syllabograms, conventionally transcribed *qa*, *qe*, *qi*, *qo*, distinct from the labials and dentals in
words containing IE labio-velars (e.g. *-qe* = the enclitic *-q^we*
'and') is proof that these were still phonemically distinct. The
same signs are used for the reflections of *kw, e.g. *iqo* = *hikwos*.
What the actual pronunciation was is a matter of surmise
unless the word *ikuwoipi* is an alternative spelling of *iqoipi* (see
below). The general opinion is that the phonemes were still
phonetically labio-velars. There are a few examples of a development to a labial (e.g. *ipopoqoi* = *hippophorg^woihi* 'ostlers' (dative
plural), and the names *pereqota/qereqota* and *opeqa/oqeqa*).

Unfortunately among these the only vocabulary word whose
etymological identification is secure is *ipo-* (*hippo-*) for *iqo-*

(*$hikwos$), and this involves not a labio-velar but the cluster kw. In any case, it is open to two explanations: 1, regressive dissimilation kw—$g^w > pp$—g^w or 2, regressive assimilation kw—$ph > pp$—ph. The other two examples are personal names; but if *opeqa* can be etymologized as $ophēg^wā(s)$ (cf. ἔφηβος < *epi+ $jēg^wā$), then *oqeqa* will be the product of assimilation; and the same explanation could hold good of *qereqota/pereqota* if the first element is *phere-* and not $q^wēle$-. *Non liquet*!

The dissimilatory loss of the labialization in the environment of *u* (p. 232), common to all Greek dialects, is illustrated in *qoukoro* = $g^woukolos$ 'cowherd' < *g^wouq^wolos, and *kunaja* = *gunaia*. Words like *qouqota, suqota, ouqe*, etc., are either combinations post-dating this sound change or have the labiovelar analogically retained or restored.

Important for classificatory reasons is the assibilation of $t(h)i$ > si: *pāsi* < *$bhāti$, *rawakesijo* = *lāwāgesios*, cf. *lāwagetās*, *epikorusijo* = *epikorusios*, cf. *koruto* = *koruthos*, *ekosi* = *ekhonsi* < *ekhonti*, *korisijo* = *korinsios*, cf. *korito* = *korinthos*, *zakusijo* cf. *Zakunthos*. The last two illustrate the assibilation of the pre-Greek suffix -νθος (see above, and cf. Attic Προβαλίσιος < Προβάλινθος). Among the proper names there are a few instances of hesitancy between *ti* and *si*, which may be due to the competition between a conservative and a more recent phonetic spelling: *tutijeu/tusijeu, tinwasija/tinwatijao*. We may compare *Ortilochos* (*Il.* 5. 546), the grandfather of *Orsilochos* (*Il.* 5.542). The implication that the change *ti* > *si* was comparatively recent is supported by names like *otinawo* = *Ortināwos*, *etirawo* = *Ertilāwos* (cf. *Laertēs*), *tatiqoweu* = $Stātig^woweus$. Unassibilated ethnics like *ratijo* = *Lātios* are due to analogical retention or restoration like Κορίνθιος, etc.

Mycenaean, of course, exhibits the pan-Greek aspiration of initial antevocalic and intervocalic *s. That the aspirate was retained intervocalically is clear from the use of a_2 in plurals of neuter *s*-stems: $pawea_2$ = *pharweha* 'woollen cloths', $kerea_2$ = *skeleha* 'legs', $mezoa_2$ = *megjoha* 'greater', $tetukowoa_2$ = *tetukhwoha* 'finished'. The far greater frequency of the spelling *-a* at Knossos may reflect the loss of the aspirate in this position (see below on *qetea, qeteo* as against $qetea_2/qetejo$). The cluster *sm* survives in $a_3kasama$ = *aiksmans* 'tips'; in alphabetic Greek the *s* has been aspirated: αἰχμή. The treatment of certain other consonant clusters deserves notice. Assimilation is apparent in *popi* = *pop-phi* < *pod-phi, *ekamapi* = *ekhmap-phi* < *ekhmat-phi, *korupi* = *korup-phi* < *koruth-phi, *rewopi* = *lewom-phi* < *lewont-phi. On the other hand, *erapemena* is usually interpreted *er-raphmena* 'sewn' and *araromotemena* as *ararmotmenā* 'fitted out', both without assimilation, but these spellings may be due to the tendency of scribes to preserve a constant form of the stem in declension and conjugation.

SONANTS

IE *j. Mycenaean exhibits the double treatment of initial *j- discussed on p. 224, but the problem is complicated by un-certainty over the sign values. Where later Greek has an aspirate, the conventional transcription presents the alternatives *o*/*jo* (*jodososi*, *odoke*, *ote* = ὅτε < *jo-).[1] It may be that the syllabo-grams transcribed as *j* in fact were neutral as to voice and encompassed the values [ç/j] and so were available as occasional renderings of the aspirate, which may have had the value [x] closer to [ç] than [h]. This would explain the alternation *jaketere*/*a₂ketere*, but the identification of the two words is dubious. Intervocalically, however, there is supporting evidence 1, that -*j*- may stand for the aspirate and 2, that -*a₂*- may be used instead of the glide -*j*-. For 1, we have the adjective describing perfumed oil with the meaning 'garment-anointing' *wearepe* (so twice) = *wehaleiphes* < *wes-aleiphes (with neuter *s*-stem *aleiphos/-*es*-); but this is also written *wejarepe* (four times), though the -*j*- cannot be a glide (the first element being *wes-), cf. also *wea₂noi* = *wehanoihi* 'for garments' (dat. plur.). For 2, we may quote the forms of the word for 'coriander': *korijadana* twice in MY, *korijadono* (constantly in KN), *koria₂dana* (once each in PY and MY). The distribution of the forms of the transaction term meaning something like 'to be exacted' (see below), is interesting: PY has *qetea₂* and *qetejo*, whereas KN has *qetea*/*qeteo*. We shall argue that these gerundival forms are based on verbal nouns in *-*ti*-/-*tei*-, the invervocalic -*j*- first developing to an aspirate which was subsequently lost. The alternative

---

[1] The alternation *o*-/*jo*- might reflect the distinction between the demon-strative pronoun *so- and relative *jo-.

spellings are most easily interpreted as reflections of this aspirate, which was preserved at PY (a_2 = *ha* and *jo* = *ho*), but already lost in KN. It should be added that the -*j*- spellings are no more evidence for the survival of intervocalic **j* than a_2 is for the presence of -*h*- in the word for 'coriander'.

The other treatment of initial **j*- is evidenced by *zeukesi* = *gjeugessi* < **jeug*-, *zesomeno* = *gjessomenŏi* < **jes*- 'boil'. The phonetic value of *z*- [gj] has just been discussed. For the similar development of **dj*, **gj* cf. above on *topeza* = *torpeza* 'table' < **tr̥-pedjə*, *mezoe* = *mezohes* < **meg-jos-es*.

There is one piece of evidence which suggests that the change *j* to *gj* was comparatively recent. Two Pylian texts list components of buildings such as *pirijao taranuwe* = *phliāōn thrānues* 'cross-beams of door jambs'. Among these components are *epi*65ko* (singular) and *pe*65ka* (plural). The common element is evidently **65ko/ka*, a neuter *o*-stem. This is compounded with the preposition *epi* in the first example, which suggests that *pe*- also stands for a preposition and so points to a form *per*65ka*. Now there is a strong probability that **65* has the value *ju*. The test of any value is the yield of vocabulary words plausible in the given context, and here we are fortunate in having a later equivalent which fits: ἐπίζυγος, used of tiles, cf. ἐπιζύγιον 'cross-beam', a word also glossed by Hesychius as 'part of a ship'. No such technical sense is attested for the later περίζυξ, but the component in question will also have been a 'joining' piece. If these identifications are correct, then two points of phonological interest emerge: 1, **j* is preserved under the influence of the preceding vowel of ἐπί and περί; 2, *perijugo-* > *peŕŕugo-* (with palatalized geminate). This anticipates a phenomenon observable in the later Aeolic dialects: e.g. Thess. κυρρος < κυριος, Lesb. περροχος < περιοχος, etc.

*kj- in alphabetic Greek was represented differently even in the closely-related Attic-Ionic (e.g. τῆτες/σῆτες), and this is evidence that these changes are later than A-I. The Mycenaean *zawete*, in our view, represents a stage virtually identical with the ancestral **kjā-wetes* 'this year' (see p. 225).

*tj > *s(s)*: *toso* = *tos(s)os* < **totjos*, *pasa* = *pansa* < **pant-jə*, *operosa* = *ophelonsa* < **-ontjə*.

*pj in alphabetic Greek > *pt*. That this change was recent in Mycenaean Greek has been argued from analysis of the sylla-

bary: there is a sign *pte* which fits into the system better if we assume an ancestral $*pj$, one of the palatalized consonants.

$*w$ was retained in all positions: *watu* = *wastu* 'town', *wirinijo* = *wrinijos* 'of leather'; *kakewe* = *khalkēwes* 'bronze-smiths', *karawiporo* = *klāwiphoros* 'key-bearer', *widwoijo* = *Widwohios* (a man's name), *kesenuwija* = *xenwia* 'for guests', *dowejo* = *dorweios* 'wooden', *kowo* = *korwos* 'boy', 'youth'.

The cluster *wj* is rendered in two ways: *mewijo/meujo* = *meiwijo(s)* or (-*n*) 'smaller', *diwija/diuja* = *Diwja*, a goddess.

The sonant nasals and liquids have all been vocalized in Mycenaean. In initial position $*n̥ > a$- before a consonant and $> an$- before a vowel: *akitito* = *aktitos* 'uncleared, uncultivated', *anamota* = *anarmota* 'without wheels (undercarriage)', a_2tero = *hateron* < $*sn̥tero$-; in other positions the vowel may be *o* under the influence of a labial consonant: *enewo*- < $*en(n)ewn̥$ 'nine', *pemo* = *spermo* 'seed' < $*spermn̥$ (but *pema* also occurs), *anowoto* = *anowotos* 'without handles' < $*n̥-ousn̥to$-.

The evidence for the sonant liquid $r̥$ is confused and disputed. The most certain vocabulary words are: *opawota* 'attachments' < $*-awr̥ta$, *qetoropopi* = $*q^wetropopphi$ 'quadrupeds' < $q^we-t(w)r̥$-, *topeza* = *torpeza* 'table' < $*tr̥-pedjə$ (but the identity of the first element is doubtful), *woze* = *worgjei* 'he works' < $*wr̥gj$-. At Mycenae we appear to have examples of *ro/ar*: *woroneja* (contrasting with *ouka* = *owika* 'sheep's (wool)') is interpretable as *wroneia* 'lamb's (wool)' < $*wr̥n$-. It is also possible that a form *worn* < $*wr̥n$- 'lamb' is the basis of the Pylian term *wonewe* 'young sheep', for it denotes a class of sheep contrasting with *parajo* = *palaioi* 'old'. Another Ablaut form of the same root occurs in *wereneja* = *wrēneia*, an adjective describing leather; *wrēn*- (cf. Hom. πολύ(ϝ)ρηνος) will have been a sheep of a different age class from a lamb.

On the other hand, *tukatasi* (also MY) may be *thugatarsi* (dat. plur.) 'daughters' < $*-tr̥si$. We should then have to regard the first example as due to the influence of preceding *w*. That *wodowe* = *wordowen* 'rose (perfumed)' is clear, but *wordon/ (w)rodon* fits into the pattern θόρνος/θρόνος so that it need not be < $*wr̥do$-, a hypothesis which in any case requires the assumption that ῥόδον in all dialects is a Mycenaean survival.

MORPHOLOGY

NOUNS

Owing to the defects of the script the few distinct case-endings must be interpreted in the light of comparative evidence.

A preliminary word must be said about the case-ending (or perhaps 'postposition') -*phi*. Words that require interpretation as instrumentals are frequently distinguished by this ending and they are in parallel with singular forms, e.g. *ekamate/ekamapi* 'support(s)', *ponike/ponikipi* 'palm tree(s)', *adirijate/adirijapi* 'statue(s)'. The suffix appears in the instrumental plural of all noun classes except the *o*-declension, the solitary exception being at Knossos, *erepatejopi omopi* 'with ivory *omo*-'. This corresponds to what is presumably the ancestral distribution: in Sanskrit -*ais* appears in the *o*-nouns and -*bhis* elsewhere. The opposition appears clearly in the phrase *erepatejo adirijapi rewopiqe = elephanteiois andrian(t)phi lewon(t)phi qʷe* 'inlaid with ivory figures of men and lions'. The -*phi* is added directly to the stem and there is assimilation of the stem consonants except the dorsals: *popi = popphi < *pod-phi*, but *ponikipi = phoinikphi* 'with palms'.

In the dual there is the disputed example (*epi*) *ikuwoipi* (see above), where '(in honour of) the Two Horses' makes excellent sense in its context. The form, thus diagnosed, may be interpreted as *hikwoiin-phi*, with strengthening 'postposition' -*phi* added to the case-ending.

Another postposition is the 'allative' -*de* added to accusatives of direction: *posidaijode = Posidahion-de*, *dikatade = Diktān-de*, *woikode = woikon-de*. Particularly striking is the pronominal form *ude* 'hither' (cf. Cret. οπυι, υι, τυι, Aeolian ἀλλυι, etc.). The origin will be sought in Proto-Greek forms of the interrogative *qʷū* (cf. Skt. *kūcid* 'everywhere', Avest. *kū* 'where'). We may perhaps adduce *ἀλλυ-δε which lies behind Hom. ἄλλυδις. But the interpretation of the Linear B word is dubious: *ude* could be a man's name.

In the *o*-stems -*os* -*on* -*oio* -*ōi* are assumed, but only the genitive is distinct. Locatives in -*ei* are *woke = woikei* and *didakare = didaskalei* (?). In the plural -*oi* -*ons* -*ōn* are presumed (all written -*o*). The dative is -*o-i* e.g. *teoi*, and this is plausibly interpreted *theoihi < *theoisi*. The instrumental plural -*o* presumably conceals -*ois*: *opoqo* = *opōqʷois* 'with blinkers'. On the -*phi* suffix in *erepatejopi* and *ikuwoiphi* see above.

The feminine *ā*-stems have the dual in -*o*, which is usually taken to stand for -*ō*, but could be -*oi* (*kotono* = *ktoinō*, *iqijo* = *hikwiō*, *topezo* = *torpegjō*). A dative dual has been proposed for *wanasoi* = *wanassoiin* 'to the two Queens'. The genitive plural ends in -*ao* = -*āōn*, and the dative plural ends in -*ai* = -*aihi* or -*āhi* (e.g. *aketirijai*). That the nominative plural ended in -*ai* is certain because of the use of ra_3 = *rai* in $kutera_3$, etc.

The masculine *ā*-stems have the regular Greek declension with genitive singular in -*āo* (*akosotao* = *Alxoitāo*). We cannot determine whether the nominative singular ended in -*s*. Noteworthy is the dual nominative *eqetae*, apparently a borrowing from the consonantal stems.

The consonantal stems appear to have the normal Greek inflexion, as far as the orthographic system allows us to see, except for the dative singular in -*e* = -*ei* (*atimite* = *Artimitei*, *diwe* = *Diwei*, cf. Διϝείφιλος, *pomene* = *poimenei*), which predominates over -*i*. In the texts from Mycenae -*i* is usual, but there are also sporadic examples from Pylos (*posedaoni* = *Poseidāoni*). Neuter *s*-stems in all Linear B archives show a preference for -*i*: *wetei* = *wetehi*. In the dual we have nom./ accus. in -*e* (*dipae* = *dipahe*, *mezoe* = *megjohe*, *qisipee* = *qʷsiphehe* 'two rapiers').

The plural shows the usual Greek endings -*e* = -*es*, -*a* = -*as* (*pakijanade* = *pakijanasde*, cf. nom. *pakijane* = *pakijanes*), -*o* = *ōn*, -*si* = -*si*. In the dative plural of *r*-stems the expected reflection of zero grade *$r̥$ appears in *tukatasi* (= *thugatarsi*, but the last two signs are dubious); but elsewhere they appear to have full grade: *pirietesi* = *prietērsi* 'sawyers'. But this is perhaps illusory, and the form may be due to the scribal tendency to keep the stem form constant: a good example is *wanakate*, *wanakatero* = *wanaktei*, *wanakteros*. The written stem form is simply that of *wanax*, which is written according to the rules *wanaka*, just as *wonoqo* = *Woinoqʷs*. The 'regular' spelling *wanakete* = *wanaktei* occurs once. In the neuter *s*-stems the forms *pawesi*, etc. are doubtless to be interpreted *pharwessi*, etc.

For the *i*-stems we have only the form *potipi* = *portiphi*, on which see below. For the *u*-stems we have the plural *taranuwe* = *thrānues*. The stem alternation -*u*/-*eu* is perhaps exemplified in the word for 'son': *iju* = *hius*, dat. *ijewei* = *hiewei*. On the relations of these forms to υἱύς/υἱός, see p. 276. The frequent *eu*-stems show the normal declension with *-ēw-* in the oblique cases and *-eusi* in the dative plural: *kakeu* = *khalkeus*, *kakewe* = *khalkēwes*, *kakeusi* = *khalkeusi*. For the diphthong-stem *Djeu-* we have genitive singular *diwo* = *Diwos*, dative singular *diwe* = *Diwei*. The word $g^w\bar{o}us$ occurs in the compounds *qoukoro* = g^w*oukoloi*, etc. The form *qoo* appears to be accusative singular = $g^w\bar{o}n$ (the plural $*g^w$*ouns* > g^w*owos* would presumably be written *qowo*), the second vowel being a scribal device for avoiding a mono-syllabic writing.

The word for 'head' has a remarkable heteroclitic declension (see p. 278). The simple word occurs in the instrumental plural *karaapi* (decorated with lions) 'heads', which may stand for *karaa(t)phi* or *krāa(t)phi*. The use of *a* and not a_2 precludes the derivation from $*k\bar{r}s\underline{n}$-*phi*, which underlies Skt. *śīrṣabhis*. We have further the compounds *quokara* 'having a bull's head', *seremokaraore* and *onokara(ore)* (both instrumental singular). Later Greek also has *r* extensions of the word for 'head' (p. 279), particularly in compounds: *-krāōr/-krāor-* is thus posited for the Mycenaean forms. The instrum. plur. in *seremokaraapi* is indistinguishable from that of simple noun. The nominative *qoukara* presumably contains *karā* (not < *karasa*, since *karaha* would be written $karaa_2$), or the zero grade *krā*: g^w*oukarās* or g^w*oukrās*.

COMPARISON OF ADJECTIVES

The sole attested type is the inherited suffix *-jos-*, *-tero-* being confined to its original use of 'dual-oppositive', e.g. *wanakatero* 'belonging to the Wanax', *zawetera* 'this year'. In the nom. sing. the spelling rules do not allow us to decide whether the ending was *-jōs* or *-jōn*, but the former is more remote from the unanimous testimony of alphabetic Greek, so the interpretation *-jōn* should perhaps be preferred. Examples are masc.–fem. nom. sing. *mezo* = *megjō(s)(n)* 'bigger', *mewijo/meujo* = *meiwjo(s)(n)* 'smaller', dual *mezoe*, *mewijoe* with ending *-e*, plur. *mezoe*, *mewijoe*, *kazoe* (= *kakiohes* 'of inferior quality'), all with *-es*. In the neuter we have nominative singular *mewijo* = *meiujo(s)(n)*, dual aro_2e = *arjohe* 'of superior quality', *mezoe*, plural $mewijoa_2$, *meujoa₂*, all with *-joha*, but *aro₂a* (six times at Knossos!) with no indication of *-h-*.

PRONOUNS

An anaphoric enclitic form corresponding to Homeric μιν occurs in *demodemi pasi = damosdemin phāsi* 'but the *damos* says that she...' and *akitito ekedemi a₂kumijo* 'uncultivated, but A₂. holds it (a plot of land)'. *Pei* is evidently third person plural instrumental-comitative in the phrase *meta pei* 'with them...'. The rigorous application of the spelling rules requires interpretation as *sphehi* rather than connection with Arcadian σφεῖς (see further pp. 288 f. for the stem *sphe-*). The form *autojo*, obviously genitive singular, occurs in a tablet of uncertain reading, while *auto-* occurs as the first element in proper names, e.g. *autoteqajo = Autothēgʷaios*. Of the demonstrative forms the only certain example is *toi ereutera = toihi* '(so much is) remitted to them'. On the alleged locative forms *toe, tome* see below. A reduplicated form *toto* (for the dubious occurrence in an early Attic inscription, see p. 286) occurs in the phrase *totoweto* 'this year'.

The only instances of the relative pronouns are the proclitic *o-/jo-* in the introductory formulae *jodososi* (see above). The conjunction *ote* occurs and we may also have *oqe* with possible future reference in the phrase *oqe erase* 'when he drives' (see below). A form *joqi = jo(d)qʷi(d)* (?) occurs in a phrase *joqi wotomo pere = jo(d)qʷi(d) W. pherei* (?), 'what W. is bringing'.

The pronominal adjectives *toso-/tosode* are presumably to be transcribed *tossos/tossosde*. At Mycenae *tosone* may be a demonstrative with the same appended particle as Thessalian ὄνε, but the diagnosis is uncertain.

NUMERALS

The dative *eme = hemei* shows that the word for 'one' *hems* < *sems still retained the *-m-* in the oblique cases (on the origin of *-n-* in the neuter ἕν < *ἕμ, see p. 289). Two forms for 'two' are attested: *dwo* and the locative/instrumental *duwoupi*. The Mycenaean form of the nominative seems to have been monosyllabic, as in Attic δώδεκα (< **dwō-*, Ved. *d(u)vā*); the genitive–

dative, on the evidence of the Arcadian duals like διδυμοιυν, may well have been *dwoun, and possibly -phi was added to form the instrumental or locative;[1] alternatively the stem form may have been *dwou-. For 'three' there is only the dative *tirisi = trisi*. A compositional *tri-* occurs in *tirijowe = triōwes* 'with three handles' and *tiripo = tripōs* 'tripod cauldron'. There are also compositional forms for 'four' (*qetoropopi = q^wetro-popphi* instr. plur. 'quadrupeds', *qetorowe = q^wetrōwes* 'with four handles'), 'six' (*wepeza = wespegja < *wekspedjə*) and 'nine' (*enewopeza = en(n)ewopegja* 'with nine feet').

THE VERB

The augment is absent with the one exception *apedoke*, as against *apudoke*, *doke = dōke*, *dekasato = deksato*, *epidato = epidasto*, *qirijato = q^wriato*, *teke = thēke*, *wide = wide*, *zeto = skheto* or *gento* (?). Reduplication shows no peculiarities in the perfect: *dedemeno = dedemenō*, *dedomena = dedomena*, *epidedato = epidedastoi*, *eeto = (h)ehentoi* 'have been sent'. Examples in the present are *didosi = didonsi*, *didoto = didontoi*; the personal name *pepitemenojo = pepithmenojo* may be either aorist or perfect middle participle of πείθω.

The third person singular middle endings, singular and plural, of the present and perfect are written *-to*, and this is interpreted as *-(n)toi*, which recurs in Arcado-Cypriot (see pp. 298 f.): *euketo = eukhetoi*, *(o)uruto = wruntoi*, *epidedato = epidedastoi*, *qeqinoto = g^weg^winōtoi* 'it is carved (with patterns)', *-didoto = dido-(n)toi* 'they are given'.

The thematic verbs in the active appear to have the normal endings: *eke = ekhei*, *ekosi = ekhonsi*, *operosi = ophēlonsi/ophellonsi*. The athematic verbs show the usual Ablaut alternation: *kitijesi = ktiensi* (< *ktei-/kti-*), later κτίζω. There is a verb *ije- = hiē-* (*isē-/isə-*) 'sacrifice, etc.', homophonous with *hiē-* 'send' (< *jijē-*); known forms are *(jo)ijesi = hiensi*, *ijeto* (which may be aorist middle) and *apieke = aph-iēke* 'he made offering' (later ἀφιέρωσε). The verb *tereja* third person singular (with infinitive *terejae*, see below) is an athematic vowel stem like Hom. δάμνᾱ.

Future formations are *dose = dōsei*, *(jo)dososi = dōsonsi*, *ze-*

---

[1] Cf. *hikwoiin-phi* above.

someno = *gjessomenōi* 'for him to boil'. Of great interest is *ewepesesomena* = *ewepsĕsomena* 'to be woven', a future with the expected *e*-grade < $*H_1webh$-, a verb replaced later by the denominative ὑφαίνω (< $*H_2ubh$-$n̥$-j-). A parallel formation with suffix -*sē* is *asesonsi* = *assēsonsi* 'they are to fatten up' < $*H_2es$- 'sate with liquid food'. Another type of future (p. 311) is *demeote* = *demehontes* 'going to build'.

Active aorist formations are *doke* = *dōke*, *teke* = *thēke*, *apieke* (see above), (*jo*)*oporo* = *ōphlon* 'they owed' or 'I owed'. Strangely, there are no certain sigmatic forms[1] (but see below on *erase*). Sigmatic Middle forms are *dasato* = *dassato*, and *dekasato* = *deksato*; other types are *qirijato* = $q^{w}riato$ 'bought', and possibly *zeto* = *gento* or *skhento* 'get'.

The following finite forms of the perfect can be quoted: *epidedato* = *epidedastoi*, *qeqinoto* = $g^{w}eg^{w}inōtoi$ (denominative verb from $*g^{w}inos$ 'a graving tool', see above), *eeto* = (*h*)*ehentoi* 'have been sent'.

The thematic infinitive shows the uncontracted form -*ee* = -*ehen*: *ekee* = *ekhehen*, *anakeι* = *anagehen*, *wozee* = *worgjehen*, *eree* = *erehen* 'to row' (primary verb < $*H_1erH_1$-, later replaced by the denominative ἐρέσσω). The form *terejae*, alternating with the indicative *tereja* (see above), is an athematic vowel stem; a similar type of infinitive occurs in Lesbian κέρναν, etc. (see below).

Participial formations are frequent. Present: active *ekote* = *ekhontes*, *ijote* = *iontes*, *operota* = *ophēlonta*/*ophellonta*, *operosa* = *ophēlonsa*/*ophellonsa*, *wozo*/*wozote* = *worgjōn*/*worgjontes*; middle *reqomeno* = $leiq^{w}omenoi$, *toroqejomeno* = $stroq^{w}heiomenos$, *kitimena* = *ktimenā*, *oromeno* = *horomenos* 'watching', *wozomeno* = *worgjomenō* 'under construction'. Future: *zesomeno* = *gjessomenōi*, *ewepesesomena*, *demeote* (see above). Aorist: active *akera₂te* = *agerjantes*;[2] middle in numerous personal names *kurumeno* = *Klumenos*, *pirameno* = *Philamenos*, etc. Perfect: in the active the sigmatic suffix *-wŏs-* appears throughout and there is no trace of *-wot-*: *araruwoa* = *ararwo*(*h*)*a*, *araruja* = *araruia* 'joined', *tetukowowoa₂* = *tetukhwoha* 'finished', *keketuwoe* = *kekēthwohes* (? < κηθεῖν

---

[1] Perhaps the aorist interpretation of *ereuterose* = *eleutherōse*, 'he has excused' is to be preferred to the fut. *eleutherōsei*.

[2] The spelling with *ra₂* suggests that *-rs* in *ager-sa-* had developed to a palatalized *-ŕŕ-*.

'help'). The personal name *widowoijo* = *Widwohios* is derived from *widwŏs-*, the masculine perfect participle of *weid-/wid-* 'know', with zero grade of the root. The form *dedikuja* = *dedikuiai* 'having finished their apprenticeship' (the etymological connections of the root *dik-* are obscure; an error for *dedi⟨ka⟩-kuja* is suspected). Middle forms are frequent: *dedemeno* = *dedemenō* 'bound', *kekaumeno* = *kekaumenos* 'burnt', [*pe*]*pu₂temeno* = *pephut(ē)menō* 'planted', *araromotemena* = *ararmot(ē)menā* 'fitted out' (others interpret *ararmotmenā*), *ajameno* = *aiaimenō* 'inlaid' (?) (there is an agent noun *a₃tere* = *aitēres*). Augment for reduplication appears in *erapemena* = *erraphmenā* 'sewn'.

The following verbal adjectives in -*to*- occur: *akitito* = *aktitos*, *aneta* = *an(h)eta* 'remitted', *kakodeta* = *khalkodeta* 'bound (riveted) with bronze'. Surprising is what appears to be a gerundive form *qeteo*/*qetejo*/*qetea₂*/*qetea* contrasting with *ono* and so presumably a transaction term. Cypriot evidence (*tesata* = θεστά) favours Ventris's first interpretation[1] *gʷheste(ja)* (< *gʷhedh-* 'miss', 'long for', see p. 235) rather than *qʷeite(j)a* 'to be paid', see p. 314 for the gerundive formation).

The following forms of the verb 'to be' are found: *eesi* = *ehensi* 'they are', *eo*/*eote* = *ehōn*, *ehontes* ptcp., and perhaps *esoto* = *essontoi* 'they will be' and -*ape* = *apēs* 'he was absent'. The alleged *eni* = *enesti* is a proper name.

Possible modal forms are obscured by the ambiguous spelling rules. If *ekeqe* is a prospective form with the particle -*qe* distinct from -*qe* 'and' (which makes no sense in the context, see below), then *eke* may stand for subjunctive *ekhē*. The same may be true of *toe* = *thōē* 'he is to pay'. Another possible example is *oqe erase*, the final item in a list of 'missing' herdsmen and animals: this is open to interpretation as *hoqʷe(n) elasē* (the man and his animals will be absent) 'when he drives'.[2] For the further connections of the particle *qe* distinct from -*qʷe* 'and', see pp. 67 f. Of relevance to the phonological history is the fact that a combination with the negative *ouqe* also occurs, which cannot be translated 'and not', 'nor'. Thus *ouqe akerese* is also likely to be a

---

[1] This is also favoured by contextual analysis, yielding a meaning 'not issued, to be demanded'.

[2] But *hoqʷē* (cf. ὅππη) is equally possible: this would be an instrumental form equatable with Thessalian ὅπει (and possibly also with Cypriot ὅπι) and hence of interest for the affinities of Linear B Mycenaean.

modal form 'he will not...'. Note that in this combination the rule relating to the development of the labiovelar has not applied (see above on *qoukoro, suqota*).

Important for the assessment of dialect relations is the construction of the preposition *paro*. Expressions like *eke onato paro...pomene* are most easily translated 'he has a lease (?) from the shepherd' (*pomenei*, dative), but a sense '*chez* the shepherd' has been argued. Decisive is PY Un 138 *qetea₂ paro dunijo* if the gerundive is identified as g^w*hesteha* 'to be demanded (from D.)'.

MISCELLANEOUS

Patronymic adjectives are used instead of nouns in the genitive: *etewokereweijo* = *Etewoklewehios* 'Son of Eteocles'. The material adjectives alternate between -*ejo/a*- and -*ijo/a*-: *raeja* = *laheia* 'stone', *weweea* = *werwe(h)e(h)a* 'woollen', *kakejapi/kakijo* = *khalkeiāphi/khalkiō* 'of bronze', etc. Adjectives in -*went*- are frequent, and the feminine has the analogical full grade -*wessa* (for the expected *-*wn̥tjə* > *-*wassa*). The suffix is added directly to the stem-consonant: *pedewesa* = *pedwessa* (with zero grade *ped*- of *pod*-), *toqidewesa* = *torq^widwessa* 'with spirals'(?), *odatuweta* = *odatwenta* 'having teeth' (of wheels) (< **odn̥t-went*-, with zero grade of root), etc. A strange form is *potinijawe(i)jo* 'belonging to Potnia', perhaps with a suffix -*weio*- parallel with the -*meio*- attested in ἀνδρόμεος.

Prepositions (verbal prefixes) worthy of comment are *ano* (only in compounds like *anoqota, anomede*), which possibly owes the final vowel to its opposite ὑπό; final *o* occurs also in *paro* (elsewhere *para*); *apu* (*apu kekaumeno, apudosi*, etc.); *peda* (*peda watu* = *peda wastu*); *opi* 'on', 'over', 'in the charge of', 'at the head of' (also in compounds like *opoqo* = *opōq^wois* 'with blinkers', *opidamijo* 'man in charge of, at the head of, the *dāmos*', *opia₂ra* = *opihala*; cf. later ὄπιθεν, ὀπώρα). The word *posi* may stand either for *posi* or *porsi* (see below); it is used adverbially as in *ouqe anija posi* 'nor are the reins attached'.

A surprising omission from the Linear B texts is any form corresponding to καί/κας 'and', though enclitic -*qe* is common. The negation *ou* is always written as a proclitic.

4. Dialect Variation and Chronology

The Mycenaean language, attested in so many widely separated places, is of a striking uniformity. The only differentiations of any note are 1, the occasional dative in -*i* instead of -*ei* and 2, the occasional representation of *-*m̥*- as -*a*- instead of -*o*- even after a labial consonant. These aberrations from 'normal Mycenaean' are confined to a few scribes and hardly deserve the positing of a 'special Mycenaean' dialect. Such uniformity suggests that 'Linear B' is a 'chancellery language', though it was doubtless originally based on a living dialect, the affinities of which will be discussed below. Such a fossilized language will surely have been more archaic than the spoken language of the scribes, and occasionally this will have intruded into their written work. At all events the dative in -*i* had superseded -*ei* by the time of 'alphabetic' Greek except for survivals in proper names.

The uniformity of language (and administrative practices) would be all the more impressive if it was extended not merely in space but in time, for it was long believed that the Knossos tablets (*c.* 1400 B.C.) were some 200 years earlier than those of the Mainland (*c.* 1200 B.C.). The evidence for the centuries-long unity and tenacity of such an administrative language deserves the attention of philologists. However, in 1958 C. W. Blegen, the excavator of Pylos, questioned the chronology of the Knossos tablets and suggested 1, that the Throne Room at Knossos was inserted in the 'Minoan' Palace in the LM III B period and 2, that the Linear B tablets belonged to the end of that period. (Here it is relevant to recall that the tablets were sun-dried and would soon have disintegrated if they had not been accidentally baked in the fire that accompanied the final destruction.) A point that had escaped notice gave strong support to the thesis: Evans and his later assistant J. D. S. Pendlebury both stated that the East Wing (the Domestic Quarter) had been cleared of debris after the destruction of *c.* 1400 B.C. and reoccupied in the subsequent LM III B period. Evidently the deposit found by the excavators must in that case have belonged to this 'Reoccupation'; it contained large numbers of Linear B tablets, giving cross-references to deposits in other parts of the palace. This 'unity of the archives' was later reinforced by a study of the scribal 'hands'.

Blegen's thesis focused attention 1, on Evans's evidence for dating the construction of the Throne Room and 2, on the evidence submitted bearing on the chronology of the tablets. It is now established 1, that the sub-floor sherd material referred to, but not published, by Evans was of LM III A 2/III B type, which supports the LM III B construction date, and 2, that the elaborate stratigraphy presented by Evans as 'decisive' for the LM II date of the tablets was wholly invented by him to support his 'Reoccupation' theory. The tablets and pots assigned by him to the room in question and sited on different floor levels had been found in different widely-separated parts of the palace, while the three floor levels had also not been observed in the said room. Evans, however, stated that tablets found in the Little Palace belonged to the later Reoccupation Period. This has been confirmed by recent excavations in the adjacent area which brought to light an inscribed stirrup jar of LM III B date, a fact which must be interpreted in the light of the view shared by virtually all Linear B scholars that use of the script implies a Palace administration. Furthermore, excavations at Khania have also produced inscribed jars together with fragments of Linear B tablets, and it has been shown that Khania was the source of some of the inscribed jars found at Thebes. In general, it is now firmly established that Crete, so far from lapsing into isolation and poverty after the alleged destruction of Knossos c. 1400 B.C., remained literate and an exporter to the Mainland palaces until shortly before their destruction c. 1200 B.C.

Philologists, therefore, have no solid archaeological grounds for believing that a fossilized administrative language was in use in the Mycenaean world for something like two centuries. The new results will also have their impact on ideas about the genesis of the Linear B script in Crete as early as the fifteenth century B.C. As mentioned above, it was evolved in all probability from the 'Aegean' parent script independently of Linear A. The latter is overwhelmingly a Cretan script, whereas Linear B is widespread in the Mycenaean Greek mainland in the LM III period. Since it is attested also in Crete only during the same period,[1] the simplest hypothesis is that Linear B

[1] Not one single piece can be securely assigned to any phase of the Palace of Knossos earlier than the 'Last Palace', which recent archaeological work has shown to be of thirteenth-century construction and destruction.

evolved on the Greek mainland independently of Linear A and was introduced into Crete when the Mycenaean Greeks took possession of the island at some time after the beginning of the LM III B period. Considerable numbers of sherds of this ceramic phase, many showing signs of severe burning, were found in the sub-floor deposits of the Last Palace.

Another historical fact of importance to the philologist will be more conveniently discussed in the next chapter, but it deserves mention in the present connection. In post-Mycenaean times Crete was occupied by Dorian speakers, but the presence of Mycenaean elements in their dialect suggests that there was no gap between the Mycenaean and Dorian occupation. The evidence for continuity is further supported by tribal names. Peculiar to Dorian states is the organization into three tribes, Hylleis, Dymanes and Pamphyloi. These appear also in Crete, but there are in addition names attributed by historians to the pre-Dorian settlers. Units with such names are believed to have comprised elements of the Mycenaean population who were subjugated by the Dorians. One of these is *Aithaleis*; it is interesting that a locality in the Pylos Linear B tablets has the name a_3*tareusi* = *Aithaleusi*, dative plural of *Aithalēwes*, which must have been a tribal name meaning 'people of Aithalos'. Evidently historians who discern Mycenaean tribal organizations incorporated into the Dorian states of Crete can hardly posit a centuries-long gap between the expulsion of the Mycenaeans (by a native revolt) and the Dorian seizure of Crete.

This question of substrate elements will arise later in the discussion of the Doric dialects of the Peloponnese. They are, however, of relevance to the nature and status of the 'Mycenaean' presented in the Linear B tablets. It will appear that the Doric dialects of Corinth and Argos contain datives in -εσσι that are an important characteristic of the Aeolic dialects and that this evidence is strengthened by ancient tradition that Corinth was an Aeolic settlement before the coming of the Dorians. If, then, on such evidence we may posit the presence of a dialect exhibiting an important innovation of Aeolic in the northern Peloponnese at the end of the Bronze Age, this would be additional reason for believing that the 'Mycenaean' of the Linear B tablets is a standard chancellery language which masks the contemporary spoken dialects. It is noteworthy that -εσσι datives occur in the Argolis, for it is in Mycenae that we should expect *a priori* the chancellery language to have originated. That there was such a single origin has been underlined by the recent finds of tablets at Thebes. The Linear B scholar finds himself in a familiar world with the same scribal conventions and administrative practices. The administrative language was learned by the scribes as part of their general training. This makes it unlikely that any future accretion of Linear B tablets will enable the linguist to break out of this magic circle. For our knowledge of the dialects of the Mycenaean Age we shall still have to rely on inferences suggested by a comparative study of the later dialects, to which we turn in the next chapter.

III

THE GREEK DIALECTS

1. Introductory

The Mycenaean civilization came to a violent end during the twelfth century B.C. The Linear B script was the instrument of a centralized palace-based economy, and there is no evidence for its use outside the narrow circle of palace scribes. Thus the script was bound up with the activity of the palace as the brain and nerve centre of a vulnerable, over-organized society. Consequently when the palace was destroyed, society fell apart and the script ceased to have a function. After the collapse there ensued an illiterate 'Dark Age', greatly reduced in population, wealth and resources, that lasted something like four centuries. When literacy dawns again as the gift of the Phoenicians,[1] the linguistic picture of Greek is totally different. Instead of the rigid uniformity of the Mycenaean 'Kanzleisprache', a supra-regional administrative language, we find a congeries of local dialects, some characteristics of which may be gathered from the inscriptional evidence. These developments were the result of historical forces and events which must largely be deduced from the linguistic evidence itself. While political disunity is matched by an extreme dialect fragmentation, each centre having its own individual dialect, nevertheless the plethora of patois evidently falls in the first instance into four distinct groups[2] with a geographical distribution which is particularly instructive in the primary 'colonial' area of Asia Minor and the offshore islands (see Fig. 4 and pp. 64–82 for the historical implications and the differerent colonial periods).

I. Arcado-Cypriot. The dialect of Cyprus has an unmistakable affinity to that of Arcadia in the central highlands of the

---

[1] On the Greek alphabet, see Chapter VII.

[2] The gaps in our knowledge must be stressed. We have few early inscriptions and, by the time that they become numerous, they exhibit the influence of the 'Common Language' (the κοινή, see below). The fact remains that we can list clusters of diagnostic features which suffice for the establishment of family groups.

[57]

Peloponnese and of Triphylia, the southern canton of Elis. The relation of this group to Mycenaean will be discussed below, but the significant geographical fact is that Arcadian in the alphabetic period is completely surrounded by speakers of Doric (see next group).

II. West Greek. This comprises two sub-groups (a) Doric and (b) North-west Greek. The Doric area in Asia Minor is restricted to the coastal region facing the southern Sporades, which extend from Rhodes to Cos and Calymna. A series of island stepping-stones—Carpathos, Crete and Cythera—leads back to the mainland source of this colonial area, the south and east Peloponnese comprising Messenia, Laconia, Corinth and thence eastwards to Megara, where it impinges on Attic territory. The main concentration of the North-west Greek dialects is in Aeolia, Locris and Phocis (Delphi), while Elis offers a bridge-dialect between NWG and Doric.

III. Proceeding northward in Asia Minor we next enter Ionic territory, which extends from Halicarnassus as far north as Smyrna.[1] This area, including the off-shore islands (the northern Sporades and Chios), is the region of East Ionic. To the west we have the Ionic of the Cyclades, with West Ionic in Euboea and Oropus (in north-east Attica). Closely related to Ionic is Attic, essentially the language of Athens, and the whole group is known as Attic-Ionic.

IV. The coastal area north of Ionia, stretching from Smyrna to the Hellespont, was occupied by speakers of a dialect known as 'Lesbian', since our main sources for the dialect come from the offshore island of Lesbos. This dialect shares important characteristics with the dialects of Thessaly and Boeotia and the whole group is known as 'Aeolic'.[2] The two mainland representatives are strongly infused with West Greek features (see below).

---

[1] According to Herodotus (I. 150) Smyrna was wrested from the Aeolians by exiled Ionians from Colophon. On the Aeolic features of the dialect of Chios, see p. 87. Again according to Herodotus, Doric had once been spoken in his native city of Halicarnassus.

[2] Linguists use the term in this purely technical sense. For the ancients 'Aeolic' meant the dialect of Sappho and Alcaeus (see below). It was also used in a much wider sense to designate what was neither Attic-Ionic nor Doric. For this 'residual' group comprising Aeolic and Arcado-Cypriot the term 'Achaean' is widely used today (see below).

2. Dialect Characteristics

I. ARCADO-CYPRIOT

Phenomena shared exclusively by Arcadian and Cypriot:

1. The labiovelars usually > dentals before front vowels, but important are occasional examples of assibilation. In Mantinea a special sign (σάν, transcribed σ̱) is used, which suggests a sibilant (perhaps cerebral or palatal) distinct from that represented by sigma: σ̱ις = τις, εἰσ̱ε = εἴτε. In north Arcadia a spelling ὀзις = ὅτις occurs, and this recurs in the glosses зέρεθρα = βάραθρον and зέλλειν = βάλλειν. Corresponding examples from Cyprus are σις and σι. Note, however, the divergence between Arc. (ἀπυ)τεισατω and Cypr. πεισει 'he will pay'.
2. Nominatives like ἱερης for ἱερεύς.
3. The genitive singular of the masculine ā-stems in -αυ: Arc. Μιλτιαδαυ, Cypr. 'Ονασαγορᾱυ.
4. The pronoun ὀνυ for ὅδε.
5. The preposition πος for ποτί, πρός.
6. The syntactical innovation of constructing ἀπύ and ἐξ with the dative/locative.
7. The conjunction κας for καί.
8. The third person middle ending -τοι (elsewhere -ται, see p. 64); also Arc. second singular κειοι < *keisoi.

Further important characteristics are:

9. Athematic infinitives in -εναι (-ναι also occurs in Attic-Ionic, see below).
10. ἀπύ for ἀπό (this is not a phonological change).
11. ὀν (ὐν) = ἀνά.
12. μι- inflexion of contracted verbs (e.g. ποιενσι, ἀδικημενος).

A notable difference between Arcadian and Cypriot is the conditional particle, εἰ and ἠ respectively, the former being perhaps due to the influence of Attic. On the potential particle (κ)αν/κε and the treatment of the sonant nasals and liquids, phenomena of importance in dialect classification, see below. For the Arcado-Cypriot words in Homer, see p. 90.

II. West Greek

The physiognomy of this dialect group is characterized by a constellation of archaic features:

1. -τι resists assibilation: διδωτι, ποτι, Ποτειδαν, etc.
2. ϝῑκατῑ 'twenty' < *wī-kn̥tī (p. 290).
3. τριακατιοι, etc. (elsewhere -κοσιοι).
4. Article τοι, ται (elsewhere οἱ, αἱ).

Other points are:

5. ἱαρος (= ἱερός).
6. κᾱ (= ἄν, κε, see below).
7. Temporal adverbs in -κα (instead of -τε): ποκα, τοκα.
8. First plural active -μες (φερομες, etc.).
9. Future in -σεω.
10. Future passive with active endings: ἀποσταλησεῖ.
11. Athematic infinitive in -μεν (see p. 315).
12. τυ 'thou' (= σύ).
13. τηνος (= κηνος, κεινος).
14. A point of word order: the modal particle follows the pronoun in αἰ τις κα.

West Greek innovations are:

1. The development of *qʷetwores to τετορες.
2. The aorists in -ξα from -ʒω verbs < *-dj- and *-gj- alike, see p. 302.

North-west Greek peculiarities are:

1. ἐν = εἰς (this is the retention of an archaism).
2. Present participle middle in -ειμενος (e.g. καλειμενος).
3. Dative plural of consonant stems in -οις (e.g. παντοις).
4. Accusative plural of consonant stems in -ες (e.g. τετορες).

III. Aeolic

Characteristics common to Lesbian, Thessalian and Boeotian are:

1. *qʷ > π even before a front vowel: πεσσαρες, πεμπε, πηλε, etc. (p. 232).
2. The perfect participle active in -ων, -οντος: κατεληλύθοντος, etc.
3. Patronymic adjective instead of genitive of father's name.
4. ἰα = μία.

5. Dative plural of the 'third declension' in -εσσι: ἄνδρεσσι, πολιεσσι, etc.

To these may be added:

(a) Characteristics common to Lesbian and Thessalian:

6. Gemination of liquids and nasals instead of compensatory lengthening of the preceding vowel in the reflexes of the clusters -sm- and -sn-, etc. (pp. 236f.): ἔμμι, ἄργεννος, μηννος, etc. Here belongs also -sw- > -ww-, e.g. Lesb. ναυος < *naswos (see p. 238).

7. Athematic inflexion of contracted verbs: καλημι, etc.

8. ἀπυ for ἀπό.

9. ὀν for ἀνά.

10. κε for ἄν/κᾱ.

(b) Common to Lesbian and Boeotian:

11. στροτος for στρατός.

12. -σσ- in future and aorist of verbal stems ending in a short vowel: ἐκαλεσσα (by analogy from τελέω: ἐτελεσ-σα).

13. πεδα for μετά (this a positive characteristic despite the fact that it is a 'selection' from *peda* and *meta*, both present in Linear B).

Found only in Lesbian but still probably Aeolic are:

14. Athematic infinitive in -μεναι: ἔμμεναι, etc. (see above).

15. *-sw- > -ww-: ναῦος, etc. (see above).

16. ὀτα, etc. for ὄτε.

17. Possibly also infinitives of the type διδων, κερναν (see above on Linear B *terejae*).

Elements common to Thessalian and Boeotian are not necessarily Aeolic since both these dialects were strongly infused with West Greek elements. The most important are:

1. Retention of -τι (but see below).

2. (ϝ)ικατι 'twenty'.

3. ἰαρος for ἰερός.

4. -ξ- aorists of -3ω verbs.

5. τοι, ται for οἱ, αἱ (this an archaism).

The extension of the athematic infinitive in -μεν to thematic verbs (φερεμεν, etc.) is a common innovation of the two Mainland Aeolic dialects and it is also found in Homer (see below).

IV. ATTIC-IONIC

1. ᾱ > η (p. 214): δῆμος, μήτηρ, etc.
2. *v-ephelkustikon*: ἔλυσε(ν), etc.
3. Quantitative metathesis (see below): λεώς < λᾱϝος, etc.
4. Aorist third plural active in -σαν: ἔθε-σαν for ἐ-θεν(τ) (p. 298).
5. ἄν for κε/κᾱ (see below).
6. In the personal pronouns nominative ἡμεῖς, accusative ἡμέας/ἡμᾶς (as against ἅμες/ἅμε or ἀμμες/ἀμμε, see p. 288).
7. ἦν 'he was', ἦσαν 'they were' (for ἦς < *ēs-t, ἦεν < ēs-ent, p. 298).

Ionic is distinguished from Attic by:

1. The thoroughgoing change of ᾱ > η, whereas in Attic this is 'inhibited' (see below) after ε, ι and ρ: χώρη, οἰκίη, etc.
2. Absence of 'Attic' contraction (p. 239) in εα, εο, etc.
3. The compensatory lengthening in ξεῖνος, κούρη, etc. (< ξενϝος, κορϝᾱ, p. 227).
4. σσ for ττ (p. 225).
5. -εω in genitive singular of masculine *ā*-stems (< ᾱο > ηο > εω; Attic substitutes -ου p. 270).

A chronological note on the change ᾱ > η will be relevant to the discussion below on dialect interrelations. Since the change is common to Attic and Ionic, the change must have been at least initiated in the proto-Attic-Ionic period (*A-I). An intermediate stage *ǣ*- before merger with η [ε:] is posited because in some islands η was used for the sound < *ā, whereas the original *ē was represented by ε. The relative chronology may be deduced from a variety of samples:

(a) νεώς 'temple' < *naswos implies the succession 1, nahwos (p. 238), 2, nāwos, 3, nǣwos, 4, nǣos, 5, neōs. The last change, 'quantitative metathesis', being peculiar to Attic and Ionic, is also *A-I. Since the effects are visible in Homer, this is further evidence of its early date (p. 85). Further, since the change in words like λᾱϝος requires the loss of intervocalic digamma, this loss must also be *A-I.

(b) παρε(ι)ά 'cheek', cf. Aeol. παραυα < *par-ausā 'cheek', lit. 'alongside the ear' (with compositional lengthening of the initial vowel of *aus- 'ear') > *parāwā. The subsequent stages are 1, parǣwǣ; 2, parǣǣ; 3, parǣǣ (for shortening in hiatus, see p.239); 4, *pareā*.[1] The word shows that at stage 2 the inhibiting effect of *r* was not yet operative, for the later ε implies at least the initial step *ǣ*. The 'inhibition' is thus a prevention on the further development of *ǣ* to [ε:]. This forces us to conclude that Attic χώρᾱ is due to the reversion of *ǣ* to *ā*, just as the final *ǣ* reverted to *ā* under the influence of the preceding ε, as in the next example.

(c) νέᾱ 'new' < **newā*: 1, *newǣ*, 2, *neǣ*, 3, *neā*.

(d) κόρη < *korwā*: 1, *korwǣ*, 2, *korǣ*, 3, *korē*. This shows that the 'reversing' influence of preceding *r* had ceased before the loss of post-consonantal *w*. That this change is post-*A-I is shown by the contrast of A κόρη I κούρη (pp. 227f.).

(e) κόρρη 'temple' (of head) < **korsā*: 1, *korsǣ*, 2, *korrǣ*, 3, *korrē*. The reversing influence of *r* had ceased before -*rs*- > -*rr*-, which is also post-*A-I (cf. Ionic κόρση). For the late merger of *ǣ* and η, see below.

The examples where the *ā* is not original but due to the peculiarly Attic 'vowel contraction' need separate discussion.

(f) πλήρη (acc. sing.) 'full' < **plēres-ṃ* > proto-Greek **plēreha*: 1, *plērea*, 2, *plērǣ*, 3, *plērē*. Thus the reversing action of *r* had ceased before the contraction of *ea* > *ǣ*.

(g) ὑγιᾶ (acc. sing.) < **su-gʷijes-ṃ* (p. 233) > proto-Greek *hugieha*: 1, *hugiea*, 2, *hugiǣ*, 3, *hugiā*.

(h) ἐνδεᾶ (acc. sing.) 'deficient' < **deu(s)-* > Proto-Greek **endeweha*: 1, *endewea*, 2, *endeea*, 3, *endeǣ*, 4, *endeā*. These two examples show that the reversing action of the preceding *e* and *i* persisted after the contraction.

An important point of relative chronology emerges from the adjective πηλίκος 'how big, how old' < **qʷāli-kos*. The stages are 1, *pālikos*, 2, *pǣlikos*; i.e. the change of the labiovelar to labial before a non-front vowel preceded the change of *ā* to *ǣ* and will have belonged to an early stage of A-I. Similarly the characteristic change exemplified in Boeot.-Thessalian πετταρες, Lesb. πεσυρες belongs to Proto-Aeolic.

One dialect, Pamphylian (on the name see below), is difficult to place within the above major grouping, and it is best treated as *sui generis*. Archaic features are the absence of the article and the retention of -τι, and in particular the numeral φικατι

---

[1] The other Attic form παρειά is difficult; possibly < **parāw-iā*.

'twenty'. But this may be a West Greek feature (the city of Aspendos is stated to have been a colony of Argos), and this is also true of ἱαρός. The medial endings -ται and -νται are common to all dialects except the Arcado-Cypriot group. Points of affinity with Cypriot are ἰν < εν, -ᾱο > αυ, the verb Ϝεχω (this, however, is an archaism, cf. Myc. *woka* = Ϝοχᾱ 'chariot'), the infinitive in -ναι and, most important, ἐξ with the dative.

3. Dialect Interrelations and Historical Interpretation

The historical interpretation of this network of dialect inter-relations will best begin with the most evident and least-disputed case. From the virtual identity of Cypriot and Arcadian, together with the 'island' position of the latter in a sea of Peloponnesian West Greek, it emerges that Cyprus was colonized from the Peloponnese at a time when the ancestral dialects occupied the Peloponnesian coastal regions. The isolation of Arcadia is evidently due to a movement of West Greek speakers into the Peloponnese, the original pre-Dorian dialect surviving only in the mountain fastness. This raises the question of the affinities of Mycenaean.

After long debate scholars have generally returned to the first intuitive judgement that Mycenaean is most closely related to Arcado-Cypriot. A major factor in this earlier opinion was doubtless the conclusion long proposed and accepted that 'Arcado-Cypriot' was spoken in the Peloponnese before the coming of the Dorians. Most striking points first seized on were the middle endings in -τοι and the datival construction of *paro*. Certainly it has been argued that -τοι carries little weight in the calculus of dialect relations since it is merely a retained archa-ism, but the fact that -ται is found in all other dialect groups is surely evidence that this was an early isogloss from which A-C was excluded.

An important methodological point must now also be stressed. 'Arcado-Cypriot' is a linguistic construction: this is merely the name given to a set of linguistic features common to the Iron Age dialects Arcadian and Cypriot, features so peculiar that we are justified in attributing them to a group of dialects spoken in the Bronze Age Peloponnese before the coming of the Dorians. This construction does not imply, however, a com-pletely uniform language in the Mycenaean Peloponnese. The dialect inscriptions of Arcadia and Cyprus themselves show local differentiations; for instance there is evidence both for ἀν (ἀνά) and ὀν (ὐν), whereas Mycenaean has the peculiar form *ano*.

In Mantinea the labiovelars are represented by σ̱, but elsewhere by τ (rarely (τ)ζ as in Tegea). In Mycenaean they are still retained. The infinitives at Tegea end in -εν, but in -ην (< -εεν) at Lycosoura. Mycenaean has -ε(h)εν. Consequently, we may expect to find in Mycenaean features which did not occur in the dialect(s) from which Arcadian and Cypriot are descended. Thus both have analogical nominatives of the type ἱερης, and this resemblance is too peculiar to be attributed to independent development after the separation. Yet Linear B has abundant nominatives in -ευς.

Such examples raise two problems. Was the 'Linear B' language (the term is preferred to the question-begging 'Mycenaean') an archaic supraregional administrative language which gives us no direct evidence of the contemporary local dialects of Pylos, Mycenae, Thebes, Knossos, etc.? Or did the pre-Dorian Greeks continue to occupy the Peloponnese after the great collapse and have a common linguistic development before sending out colonists to Cyprus?

This raises a chronological problem on which archaeologists have firmly pronounced. H. W. Catling writes:[1] 'The proposal to locate Aegean colonies in Cyprus during the fourteenth and thirteenth centuries B.C. has never surmounted the obstacle of missing evidence.' On the other hand, the city of Enkomi was replanned and rebuilt 'after the destruction at the end of the thirteenth century B.C., which coincides with the arrival of Achaean colonists from Greece.' Another disaster took place in Mycenaean III C 1, and this has been attributed to the 'Sea Peoples' defeated by Rameses III in 1191 B.C. New waves of fugitives from the Aegean appeared in Cyprus (associated with 'Granary' style pottery, i.e. not earlier than 1150 B.C.). There is also evidence that this flight from Greece to Cyprus continued until the beginning of the Iron Age. Catling concludes (p. 213): 'It fell to Cyprus to shelter the remains of Mycenaean civilization, including its political structure, aspects of its language,

[1] *CAH*, 3rd edn., II 2, xxii (*b*), 200 'Cyprus in the Neolithic and Bronze Age Periods'.

traces of its writing and much of its visual art long after its complete disappearance from the Greek mainland.'

This archaeological evidence pointing to a progressive exodus from the Greek mainland extending from the fall of the palaces until the beginning of the Iron Age may be supported by a linguistic observation concerning the semantic development of the Linear B word *qasireu*, if this is correctly identified as $g^w asileus$ = βασιλεύς 'king'. In early post-Mycenaean times the Basileus was at the heart of the 'political structure'. In Cyprus he functions also as the priest of the goddess Wanassa. Yet *qasireu* in the Linear B tablets is the title of a minor functionary: he appears simply as the local headman of a royal (that is 'non-temple') establishment of craftsmen. In Homer the βασιλεῖς are at least petty kings who enjoy the same title as Agamemnon, though graduations are implied by the comparative and superlative βασιλεύτερος, βασιλεύτατος. It was as a consequence of political fragmentation and local autonomy that the former local 'manager' of the king's industrial establishments could rise to his new status. If, then, *qasireu* (always supposing that the generally accepted equation with βασιλεύς is correct) was taken to Cyprus with the meaning 'king' (perhaps already in the form *basileus*), we should have to postulate a quite lengthy period of political and linguistic development to bridge the semantic gap.

It was perhaps during this period that 'Arcado-Cypriot' innovations, like *ἱερης, developed. Still more cogent evidence for a post-palatial 'Achaean' occupation of the Peloponnese is provided by the potential particle, which will be discussed in detail below. Arcadian presents a striking innovation (κ)αν in agreement with Attic-Ionic ἄν against Cypriot κε, agreeing with Aeolic. This common innovation, implying contact, must have developed before the Dorians isolated the Arcadians. Thus the linguistic evidence is compatible with the archaeological thesis that a considerable time elapsed between the destruction of the Mycenaean palaces and the intrusion of the Dorians (see below).

The linguistic and archaeological evidence bearing on the Mycenaean settlement of Cyprus is also in broad agreement with the traditions preserved in Greek literature. Paphos is said to have been founded by the Arcadian Agapenor (Hdt. VII. 90, Paus. VIII, 5. 2), while Kurion, Golgoi and Lapethos were settled by colonists from Argos, Sicyon and Laconia respectively (Hdt. v. 113, Steph. Byz., *s.v.* Γολγοί, Strabo xiv. 682). Place-names also point in the same direction: on Cyprus we find Λακεδαίμων, while the town-name Κερύνεια has a counterpart in Achaia (town and mountain). If the promontory name Ἀχαιῶν ἀκτή (Strabo xiv. 682) is ancient, then it follows that the colonists brought their national name with them, and it would be correct to speak of the 'Achaean' settlement of Cyprus.

In Homer Ἀχαι(ϝ)οί is the name for the Greeks generally, and it may be reflected in Hittite records. References to the country of Ahhiyawā begin in the reign of Suppiluliumas (1380–1340 B.C.) and continue with Mursilis II (1339–1306)and it is evident that friendly relations existed. Either Mursilis II or his son Muwatallis (1306–1282) wrote a letter in connection with the operations by a Hittite renegade in the *Lukka* lands (see p. 20) from a base in Millawanda (Miletus?) asking the king of Ahhiyawā to intervene, the impression being that the latter has merely influence there but is not in control. Since the culprit escaped by ship, Millawanda will have been on or near the sea. That Ahhiyawā was a considerable power is shown by a (deleted) reference in a treaty of the time of Tudhaliyas IV (1250–1220), and during his reign we hear of operations by Attarisiya of Ahhiyā, which included an attack on Alasiya (Cyprus). The resemblance of *Ahhiyawā* to *Akhaiwia* is seductive, but even if the equation is accepted there is uncertainty over its location, and guesses include the kingdom of Mycenae or some local 'Achaean' kingdom situated on one of the offshore islands, like Rhodes.

There is also the possibility that the *Akhaiwoi* called themselves after a locality which had a pre-Greek name (cf. 'British' for the English nation and its extensions). Quite a number of Anatolian place-names end in -*wa* and this ending characterizes a large number of Linear B place-names.

Philologists use 'Achaean' in a narrower technical sense as a term embracing the two dialect groups Arcado-Cypriot and Aeolic, which share a number of important isoglosses.

1. In the first place we have the potential particle κε in Cypr., Thess. and Lesb. Arcadian has (κ)αν and this links up with Attic-Ionic ἄν. This isogloss is of primary importance in the classification of the Hellenic post-Mycenaean dialects. It is

unaffected by the possibility that they all have a common etymological origin. It has been suggested that all forms go back to adverbial forms of the demonstrative pronoun *ke-*, with Ablaut alternation *ken/kn̥*. The latter would have developed before consonant and vowel respectively to κα/καν. In the combination ουκαν false division resulted in the A-I ἄν, while in Arcadian the original form is visible in εἰκαν. The status of Mycenaean (*eke*)-*qe* is disputed. But if this is also a potential particle, then overall unity can be established only by postulating $*q^we(n)$, with a post-Mycenaean development of $ouq^we(n)$ to *ouke*(*n*). The particle q^wen might be an adverbial form of the indefinite pronoun with the meaning 'at some time, ever, etc.' The full grade is mirrored in Skt. -*cana* (*ná ékaś cana* 'not anyone')[1] and in the Germanic *-ʒin*, e.g. OE *hwerʒen* 'somewhere', OHG *iowergin* 'somewhere', cf. Gmc *irgend*. The -*hun* appended in Gothic to indefinite pronouns or adverbs (*ni ains-hun, ni hvas-hun* 'no one') is traceable to the zero grade $*q^wn̥$.

If this etymology holds for the Greek potential particle, then Doric *kā* goes back to a separate adverbial form $*q^wā$. Whether from this or from $*kā$, this form of the particle sets West Greek apart from the other Greek dialects, just as ἄν is an unmistakable feature of Attic-Ionic.

2. The second isogloss arises out of the treatment of the sonant liquids $*r̥$ and $*l̥$. Many of the examples are from literary and grammatical sources or culled from proper names in the epigraphic sources. Among the words concerned are στροτος (for στρατός), βροχυς (for βραχύς < $*mr̥ghu$-) and θροσυς (for θρασύς < *dhr̥su*-). Further, Cypriot has the aorist κατέϝοργον (< $*wr̥g$-) and the glosses κορζα (= κραδία < $*kr̥d$)-, εὐτρόσ-σεσθαι· ἐπιστρέφεσθαι (< $*tr̥q^wj$-), and perhaps στορπα (Arc. στορπᾶ, Στροπαιος). Homer adds the presumably Aeolic aorist ἤμβροτον (< $*amr̥t$-), and ἄμβροτος (< $*n̥-mr̥to$-).

Ingenious attempts have been recently made to dispose of these examples by *ad hoc* hypotheses, but they remain curiously concentrated in the sphere of A-C and Aeolic, a distribution which has been given new point by the Linear B evidence (see above), to which we must now add the name *tosita* = Θορσιτᾶς

[1] It is of interest that in Latin after a negative the indefinite pronoun also has an appended adverbial form of the same stem, *quisquam*, the full meaning of which would have been '(not) anyone anyhow'.

(with zero grade *dhr̥s- as opposed to full grade *dhers- in Thersites).

3. The pronoun ὄνε occurs in Thessalian and Cypriot and possibly also in Linear B.

4. The athematic conjugation of contracted verbs.

5. Vocabulary items like πτόλις in Thess., Arc., Cypr., and Linear B (it has been plausibly argued that πτόλεμος also once had a similar distribution); δαυχνᾱ (= δάφνη), Thess. and Cypr.; ἀπυ Thess., Lesb., Arc. and Linear B (this is not due to a change of o > u).

The Linear B evidence has confirmed and increased the earlier conclusions about the affinity of Thessaly and Boeotia with the Mycenaean Peloponnese. For instance, q^wetro- (qetoro-popi) finds its counterpart in E. Thess. πετρο-. The dual of ā-stems in -ō has its parallel only in Hesiod's καλυψαμένω, while the infinitive terejae echoes the Lesbian type κερνᾶν. If qeromeno is taken more plausibly as g^wēlomenoi 'willing', this form of the verb again links up with Boeotian βειλομαι and Thessalian βελλομαι rather than A-C βολομαι. The fact that Lesb. has βόλλομαι with the same vowel as A-C but the typical Aeolian gemination (as in Thess.), suggests a complex dialect patterning of *g^wel(s)-, g^wol(s)- in Mycenaean Greece.

Again, suza = sukiai 'fig-trees' finds an echo in Lesb. συκια (contrast A-I συκέα/συκέη). Another vocabulary item has an interesting distribution: the word for 'willow' is εἰτέα in most Greek dialects. But Mycenaean has erika = helikās 'of willow', and ἑλίκα is ascribed to Arc. by Theophrastus while Ἑλικοῦς is the name of an Arcadian town. The mountain name Ἑλικών attests the one-time presence of the word in Boeotia while Ἑλίκη is a town in Achaea, the name of which is testimony to a pre-Dorian 'Achaean' population.

An example of decisive importance is unfortunately doubtful and disputed. It concerns the morphological pair toe/tome that occur in the Pylian land texts. However, if methodological considerations give second place to 'solutions' which simply dismiss toe as a scribal error and grant preference to the proposal which accounts for both forms, then the interpretation θωη (subj.) 'is to pay' and θῶμεν (inf.) 'must pay' provides us with a criterion which links Linear B with Boeot.-Thess. and separates it from A-C (infin. in -εναι).

Finally, there is evidence that before the coming of the Dorians, Aeolic and Arcado-Cypriot formed a geographical continuum, with Aeolian stretching into the territory of Corinth and Argos. Both these dialects show examples of the typically Aeolic dative plurals in -εσσι, while the Argive pronoun ὄττινες recurs in the literary Lesbian of Sappho and Alcaeus. Dorian operations against an Aeolic Corinth are attested by Thucydides (IV. 42. 2) (Δωριῆς τὸ πάλαι...τοῖς ἐν τῇ πόλει Κορινθίοις ἐπολέμουν οὖσιν Αἰολεῦσι).

To conclude, the constellation of cross-connections seems strong enough to support the long proposed setting-up of a major unit embracing A-C and Aeol. It has been called variously 'Central Greek' or 'Achaean', with subdivisions 'North Achaean' = Aeolic and 'South Achaean' = Arcado-Cypriot.

A more recent suggestion, which has enjoyed considerable vogue, makes a north–south division in the Greek dialects and links 1, Aeolic with West Greek and 2, Arcado-Cypriot with Attic-Ionic. This involves the re-drawing of what has always been regarded as a major isogloss in Greek dialectology: the assibilation of τι > σι (δίδωτι/δίδωσι), which was basic to the old division between West and East Greek. It is, of course, true that -τι is found in Boeotian and Thessalian (as opposed to Lesbian -σι), but this has been explained as one of the many West Greek intrusions into these dialects (see further below, pp. 72–3). That there was a movement of 'Doric' speakers from the north-west into 'Achaean' territory is evident from the dialect map (Fig. 4). Of the occupation of the Peloponnese and the isolation of Arcadian we have already spoken. In Thessaly the concentration of West Greek elements diminishes from west to east, so that scholars have set up two divisions: 1, Thessaliotis in the south-west, 2, Pelasgiotis in the north-east. Important isoglosses separating the two are (a) -ō/-oi as genitive singular of o-stems and (b) -ēn/-εμεν as the infinitive of thematic stems. Typical West Greek elements of Thessalian are 1, ἴκατι, 2, -ξα aorists of -3ω verbs with original dental stem, 3, ἱαρος for ἱερός.

Boeotian is still more heavily contaminated since, in addition to the above, it has 4, the article τοι/ται for οἱ/αἱ, 5, κᾱ for κε/ἄν, 6, πρᾱτος for πρῶτος. Common to Thessalian (Pelasgiotis and Boeotian) are the thematic infinitives of the type φερεμεν (see above). There is thus no difficulty in ranging the non-assibilation of -τι among the West Greek intrusions into the Mainland Aeolic dialects, for ϝικατι is in any case to be so classified. Those who would rearrange the isogloss explain away Lesbian -σι as an Ionic borrowing; this done, they posit -τι as a feature of the proto-Aeolic regions from which Lesbos was colonized. Since Linear B has overwhelmingly -σι (see above), the assibilation is regarded as a major north–south division. However, we have seen that there are signs that even in Linear B the assibilation was comparatively recent, and so slight a phonological change must be weighed against the complex cross-relations discussed above. In any case, if -τι in Thessalian and Boeotian is a proto-Aeolic feature, this does not constitute a link with West Greek, for it is a generally accepted principle in the calculus of dialect relations that the retention of archaisms has little or no significance. The preservation of -τι is precisely such a non-change. For the pre-Dorian innovations of proto-Aeolic, see below.

Considerable difficulties also arise in coupling Attic-Ionic with Arcado-Cypriot and deriving both from a hypothetical 'South Greek'. Certainly they share the important isogloss -ναι characterizing the athematic infinitive. But Linear B shows that in the development of ϝ their paths had already divided: or/ar, ra. Cypr. κε again is a major isogloss separating A-C from A-I with its striking innovation ἄν (on Arc. (κ)αν see above). The A-I fronting of ā (pp. 62 f.) is also an early phenomenon, as was shown by the development of *naswos to νεώς, for this involves 1, change to nāwŏs, 2, loss of digamma, 3, ā > ǣ, 4, quantitative metathesis ǣo > eō. Even the Homeric poems exhibit the last stage in the development of āo with synizesis: Πηληϊάδεω, etc. This shows incidentally how early in A-I the loss of intervocalic digamma was. Against this the proponents of the new theory have urged a low date for the change of ā > ǣ by adducing the example of Ionic Μῆδοι < Pers. Māda- since this ethnic name would not have become known to them until their settlement in Asia Minor. But the argument is fallacious: if the Ionians had already changed ā to fronted ǣ, then they would have substituted this for the foreign ā. Such sound substitution is a commonplace phenomenon of 'languages in contact'.

All the indications are that A-I was a separate dialect already

in the Mycenaean age: there is no linguistic road leading from
torpeza to τράπεζα. Again, A-I ἀπό is distinct from A-C ἀπυ
(also Linear B) as A-I πρός is from A-C πος. The latter pair
involves two points of difference: the basic element of πο-ς is
different from that of προ-ς. Each of these elements may be
extended by the endings -*s* or -*ti* so that the Greek dialect map
offers us four different words for 'towards': πος, ποτί: πρός,
προτί. The primary division is into πο- and προ- regions, and
from this point of view A-I and A-C belong to different linguistic worlds. The geographical patterning is also an obstacle
in linking A-I with A-C to the exclusion of Aeolic. We mentioned above the distinctively Aeolic datives in -εσσι as substratum elements in the Doric dialects of Corinth and Argos.
These forms are especially important: since they are innovations
and indicate not only that Aeolic was a distinct dialect in the
Bronze Age but also that it extended into the Peloponnese,
where it presumably linked up with the Arcado-Cypriot group.[1]

We now pass to the still more formidable obstacles in the way
of positing a North Greek dialect group comprising West Greek
and Proto-Aeolic. To make this even plausible we require a
constellation of shared *innovations* not found in other dialects. It
has just been pointed out that retained -τι cannot be accepted as
such evidence. On the contrary, the featural constellations of
West Greek and Proto-Aeolic are remarkably different. The
latter presents such striking innovations as the third declension
dative plural in -εσσι and the perfect participle in -ων/-οντος.
To this we may add another point of verbal morphology—the
extension of the athematic infinitive -μεν to thematic verbs
(φερέμεν, etc.) which, as we saw, is common to Thess. and Boeot.
and is also Homeric. Significant is also the occurrence of forms
like προϝειπεμεν in Cretan Doric, where they must be ascribed
to the Achaean substratum. The conclusion imposes itself that
the thematic infinitives in -μεν are yet another feature that must
be ascribed to the pre-Doric Peloponnese. But Homer also uses
athematic infinitives in -μεναι, which is the Lesbian form. The
explanation is that Proto-Greek had a number of competing

[1] We quote the verdict passed by Householder and Nagy (1972), 62:
'...there are strong arguments in favor of positing the penetration, in the
Late Mycenaean era, of Aeolic or North-Mycenaean elements into such
South Mycenaean dialectal areas as the Peloponnese'.

infinitives from which the dialects selected (selection being also an 'innovation', like that between πεδά and μετά). We conclude that Proto-Aeolic possessed two athematic infinitive forms -μεν and -μεναι; that the extension of the former to thematic verbs (an important innovation) was ancient is shown by the agreement of Homer and the two mainland dialects of Aeolic. The gulf between this group and West Greek is highlighted by the contrast of Thessaliotis -ēν with Pelasgiotis -εμεν, paralleled by the dative plurals -σι and -εσσι, the latter being, as we saw, another characteristic innovation of Aeolic (see further below). We may add yet another to the Aeolic elements in the Peloponnese. This is the Homeric masculine form ἰός 'one', which recurs also in the Doric of Messenia and Crete.

To turn now to West Greek: what is notable about this dialect group is the rich set of features which mark it off from all other groups, yet with a distribution over the whole territory from north-west Greece to Crete and Rhodes that reveals their pre-migration date. For methodological reasons we mention first the 'selection' of -μες as the ending of the first person plural active of the verb. Again, the futures in -σεω are another striking example which can hardly be discounted as 'surely a recent innovation'. On the contrary, they must find their place in the dialect patterning now enriched by the Linear B futures *ewepsesomena* and *aseso(n)si* (p. 50).

That Proto-West-Greek, characterized by these exclusive innovations, must be pushed back some considerable time before the 'Dorian' migrations is indicated by its dialectal split. For the NWG dialects also are distinguished by a remarkable innovation—the third declension dative plural in -οις (ἀγωνοις, ἀρχοντοις, etc.). What is of special interest is that these datives, common to all the dialects of this sub-group, appear to have been ancient in the NWG heartland (Aetolia and West Locris) but were introduced relatively late (possibly as a consequence of the Aetolian League, fourth century B.C.) to the eastern Locrians and Phocaeans (Delphi), where they replace the earlier -εσσι type of the 'Achaean' substratum.

A similar picture appears in Elis, where we find a kind of bridge-dialect between NWG and Doric. Elis was divided into three cantons 1, Elis, 2, Pisatis and the Alpheus and 3, Triphylia in the south. The occupation seems to have been least effective in the last: according to Strabo, VIII. 333 Triphylia was originally inhabited by Arcadians, who still claimed it as their territory in the fourth century B.C. While the regular NWG datives in -οις appear, there is an example of -εσσι (φυγαδεσσι). This important isogloss, third declension -οις, and the dialect stratification, imply that the so-called 'Dorian' migrations involved West Greek tribes speaking dialects which, though closely related, were clearly differentiated into two main branches. One of these had already introduced striking innovations into the Proto-West-Greek which their unmistakable common physiognomy compels us to postulate. How implausible and remote from the observed facts the postulated 'North Mycenaean' is emerges from the genealogical tree of Fig. 5, which is discussed below, pp. 99 ff.

In conclusion, it may be said that neither the new material provided by the decipherment of Linear B, nor the recent reassessment of the dialect material have, in our opinion, seriously shaken the long-established picture of Greek dialect relations. So far from there being an impressive constellation of shared innovations between West Greek and Proto-Aeolic, there is a deep gulf between the two groups which goes back to the Late Bronze Age.[1] On the other hand, the shared features of Arcado-Cypriot and Aeolic have, if anything, been increased, and the geographical continuum of their respective territories has been reinforced by the distribution of the -εσσι datives as substratum elements in the West Greek dialects to the north of the Corinthian gulf and in the Peloponnese.[2] There is thus a strong case for the old view, now regaining support, that the four major groups had already evolved considerably before the great Dorian migrations. Their geographical siting may be schematically represented as in Fig. 3.

It now remains to attempt an historical interpretation. The self-evident event that emerges from the comparison of Fig. 3 and Fig. 4, particularly from the parallel west–east bands

---

[1] This is also the view expressed by Householder and Nagy (1972), 61: 'The most plausible conclusion, then, is that the prehistoric phases of Arcado-Cypriot, Aeolic, and Attic-Ionic were already differentiated in the late Bronze Age...'

[2] An evident substratum element in Laconian is the divine name Ποhοιδαν (cf. Arc. Ποσοιδαν, by vowel assimilation < Ποσειδαν).

Fig. 3. The Distribution of the Greek Dialects *c.* 1300 B.C.

spanning the Aegean in the latter, is in the first place the colonization of the littoral of Asia Minor and the intervening islands by Aeolic and Ionic settlers, with a corresponding 'South Achaean' settlement of Cyprus. All this accords with the traditions handed down in Greek as folk-memory. This is also true of the events which caused the major change in the dialect pattern: there can be no serious doubt about the reality of the 'Dorian' migrations. A point of interest emerges from the distribution of the Dorian colonies in the islands and the littoral of Asia Minor. They form a wedge between Cyprus and Ionia and it is evident that when the overseas thrust took place, the central and northern Aegean were barred to the Dorians by strongly-held Ionic and Aeolic settlements. This is particularly clear with Ionic which occupies the whole of Euboea, and the

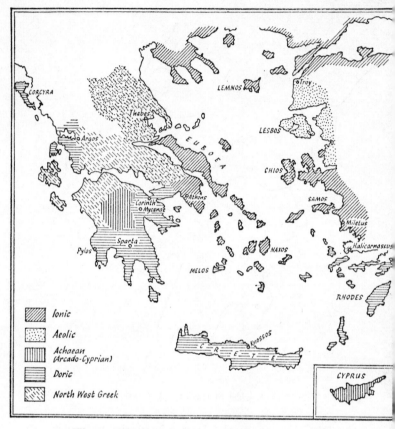

Fig. 4. The Distribution of the Greek Dialects
in the Alphabetic Period

greater part of the Cyclades, only Melos, Thera, Carpathos,
Cos and Rhodes falling to the Dorians.

A 'Dorian' migration is the only way of accounting for the
distribution and stratification of the West Greek dialects.
North-west Greeks moved along the north side of the Gulf of
Corinth and also into the north-west Peloponnese, while
Dorians took possession of the rest of the Peloponnese (excepting
the fastness of Arcadia) and subsequently moved to Crete,
Carpathos and Rhodes. This conclusion is in full accord with
the traditions of Greek folk-memory. N. G. L. Hammond[1]

[1] *History of Greece to 322 B.C.,* 79.

observes: 'The distribution of these dialects conforms with that of the invading peoples, as portrayed in the literary tradition. The pattern of Doric coincides precisely with the traditions of Dorian settlement. The pattern of north-west Greek enlarges on the meagre traditions which survive of the other invading peoples. It indicates that the Thessaloi, the Boeotoi, and the followers of Oxylus [the leader of the Aetolians who occupied "hollow" Elis] spoke the same dialect and therefore flowed from a common source into south-west Thessaly, Boeotia, and Elis. This common source can hardly have lain elsewhere than in southern Epirus.' As for the Dorians, with their closely-related dialect, this 'is explicable only on the hypothesis that before the time of the invasions the speakers of the two dialects lived in contiguous areas. These areas were probably West Macedonia and Epirus. For, according to the literary tradition, the Dorians were situated first in south-west Macedonia and then in Doris, and the Thessaloi came from Thesprotia in Epirus.'

Yet there is nothing in the archaeological record which matches the striking uniformity of the West Greek settlement. This has led some archaeologists to deny the reality of the 'Dorian invasion', but this is a dispute about a word. It may well be that the collapse of the Mycenaean civilization was the work of other forces and that the Dorian expansion was a later step-by-step infiltration, extending perhaps over a century or so. This would fully accord, as we saw, with the archaeological and linguistic evidence for the continuation, at a much lower cultural and economic level, of the 'Achaean' occupation of the Peloponnese. But the indubitable fact which we have to interpret is the change in the dialect pattern, reinforced by sociological facts, such as the tribal organization into Hylleis, Dymanes and Pamphyloi.

The disparity between the linguistic and archaeological evidence is particularly clear in Crete. Here I follow in the main the account of Vincent Desborough.[1] After the mainland disasters of *c.* 1200 B.C. Crete appears to have received an access of Mycenaean refugees signalized by the sudden appearance of locally-made Mycenaean III C pottery, particularly noticeable at Knossos and Phaestos. These followed a brief period of revival in the Central Aegean characterized by the Central

[1] *The Greek Dark Ages*, London (Benn, 1972), especially 112–29, 221–39.

Aegean Octopus Style, which originated in Crete. Cretan influence has also been argued for the Argive Style of much the same date. During the second half of the twelfth century there are signs of a further accession of Mycenaean elements, while at the end of that century some Cretans appear to have migrated to Cyprus.

All this is consistent with the view that Crete remained in close contact with the Mainland palaces until their destruction (see above on the inscribed stirrup-jars) and remained a centre of Mycenaean influence during the twelfth century.

For the eleventh century the available material is 'exceedingly meagre' and, in particular, west Crete is 'completely blank'. However, Desborough writes of 'a clear continuity with what went before and what came after'. Still more striking is his general conclusion. 'At the middle of the eleventh century we can identify with certainty only two regions that were comparatively stable and undisturbed, the one being Crete...'. Until this time, it would seem, there is no evidence for the arrival of the Dorians. What of the tenth century? In the more purely Dorian west the material 'is confined to a single cemetery of uncertain date'. Throughout central Crete, on the other hand, we find a clear influence of the Late Geometric Style of Athens (which was never occupied by the Dorians!) with actual imports of such vases. As for the general picture of Cretan relations during this century—'probably the most significant feature of Crete...is precisely the links with the east Mediterranean'. In fact there was probably continuous contact with Cyprus at least from *c.* 1100 B.C. On the other hand the only evidence adduced for contact between Crete and the regions to the north is of dress pins and fibulae (safety-pins) and it is concluded 'neither area had any effect on the other'.

In his general summing-up Desborough concludes with a series of questions 'with fact heavily outweighed by hypothesis'. Who evicted the Mycenaean refugees who fled from the mainland overseas? Were they aggressors from north-west Greece? Did they spread into the Peloponnese during the late eleventh and some of the tenth century 'constituting a somewhat isolated and backward block of population?'

Henri van Effenterre[1] is more forthright. The dialect distri-

---

[1] *La seconde fin du monde,* 180 ff. (1975).

bution is basic and essential, but it is supported by certain
sociological institutions and practices, among which we may
mention certain details of the calendar. Why, then, he asks, is
there no such widespread scepticism about the importance of
the Dorian invasion? It is because the Dorians have been a
serious disappointment to the archaeologists. Effenterre agrees
with the historian Moses Finley that there is no archaeological
feature which enables us to identify the Dorians. In the face of
such archaeological agnosticism it will be well to recall the
indubitable Dorian character of Iron Age Crete and the
'Achaean' substratum elements in the dialect (to say nothing
of the preservation of tribal designations) that argue a symbiosis
of the two Greek population elements. That the material studied
by archaeologists gives no hint of this drastic reshaping of the
political and linguistic map of the Mycenaean world is a lesson
to be remembered when dealing with the remoter events that
brought the Proto-Greeks into Greece.

According to a theory which was launched by Paul Kretschmer
and remained canonical for a long time, the Greek invasion
comprised three waves stretching over the greater part of the
second millennium: 1, Ionians, 2, Aeolians and 3, 'Dorians'
(West Greeks). The distinction of 1 and 2 was due to the belief
that there had been an Ionian occupation of certain parts of
the Peloponnese, which was later overlaid by Aeolians. The
evidence for the widespread belief in a 'Middle Helladic'
invasion has been considered above. Now with the acknowledged archaeological silence about the coming of the Dorians,
the keystone in this construction ('no archaeological break—
no invasion') will be regarded with increased scepticism. If we
keep to the linguistic evidence, two facts must be stressed:
1, Linear B, our first evidence for 'Greekness', is exclusively an
LH/LM III B phenomenon; 2, the differences between the four
Bronze Age dialect groups are slight. The second point affects
our estimate of the time required for such differentiation.
Modern dialectological studies have shown that major developments which lead even to mutual unintelligibility may take place
within a comparatively short time. For instance, Ernst Risch
has pointed out that in the Middle Ages there was no Schweizer-
deutsch really distinct from Swabian or Alsatian. Thus, purely
linguistic considerations would not require us to put the

beginning of 'Linear B Greek' further back than the beginning of LH III B, when the Last Palace at Pylos was constructed, and it is quite possible that the change from τι to σι occurred towards the end of this period. As for the changes that led to the dialect break-up of 'Proto-Greek' (on this concept see above), they could easily have been accomplished wholly within the LH III period.[1] Any earlier date for Proto-Greek is a departure from the minimum hypothesis. Consequently the onus is on those who speculate about 'Middle Helladic' (or even 'Early Helladic III') Greek. These are constructions that rest on archaeological silence. It is curious that such silence should on the one hand justify a hypothetical Proto-Greek people virtually a millennium before our earliest records and on the other prompt a denial of the reality of an event virtually within the historical period and vouched for by language, institutions and folk-memory. If the drastic transformation of the Greek world by the West Greek invasions could take place without archaeological reflections, it is difficult to accept the validity of the principle that archaeological continuity implies ethnic continuity (see above pp. 23f.).

4. The Second Colonial Period

A. Meillet has observed that to write the history of the Greek dialects is to write the history of Greek colonization. Above, the colonial movements of the sub-Mycenaean and the Dark Ages have been largely deduced from the dialect map. A second colonial period began in the eighth century B.C as a consequence of which Greek dialects and Hellenic culture were spread to the Black Sea, the Libyan coast of Africa and the countries and islands lying to the west of Greece by the implantation of colonies. The effective agents were the now-flourishing Greek city states. The colonists took with them not merely the dialect of the mother city but its institutions, cults, calendar and alphabet.

[1] It is pertinent to recall the dictum of Antoine Meillet (*Aperçu d'une histoire de la langue grecque*, p. 17) on the date of Proto-Greek: '...the differences [between the Greek dialects] concern only details that developed at a recent date, a short time before the historical period; all known Greek dialects go back to one and the same common language'. In the light of the new evidence we can rephrase this conclusion 'a short time before the end of LH III B'.

The colonists in due course developed their own dialectal idiosyncrasies, but these fall outside the framework of the broad sketch attempted in this chapter. The present section is concerned simply with the spread of Greek in the Mediterranean as a consequence of this second wave of colonial expansion. The lead was taken by Miletus to exploit the resources of the Black Sea areas. It founded colonies on the south shore in the first half of the eighth century and on the other shores during the seventh century. These colonies, together with their secondary foundations, came to number close on a hundred. Other colonies in the same area were founded by other Ionian states, while Dorian Megara also took a hand, notably with Chalcedon and Byzantium, both in the first half of the seventh century. In Italy the earliest colony was established by the Euboean cities Chalcis and Eretria (together with some from Asiatic Cyme), first on the island of Pithecusae (Ischia) and subsequently at Cymē (Cumae) on the opposite coast. The Chalcidians also founded Rhegium at the toe of Italy. The Achaeans were active with Sybaris, Croton, Metapontium, and Caulonia (but these were later Doricized), while the Spartans founded Taras (Tarentum).

The Chalcidians were again the first in Sicily with Naxus (with a contingent from the island of Naxos), Leontini and Catana. Zancle, too, was colonized jointly by Chalcis and Cumae on the Sicilian side of the passage opposite Rhegium.

South-east Sicily was secured by the Dorians. Syracuse, founded by Chalcis, was taken by Corinthians, who also dislodged the Eretrians from Corcyra and founded colonies controlling the entry to the Gulf of Corinth, followed by others at Leucas and Ambracia. A force of Dorians from Megara, who had assisted the Corinthians at Syracuse, later founded a colony at Selinus close to the Phoenician settlements in the south-west of the island. Between this and Syracuse, Gela was founded by Cretans and Rhodians early in the seventh century and over a hundred years later Gela planted a daughter colony at Acragas (Agrigentum).

In the west the Phocaeans founded Massilia (Marseilles) at the end of the seventh century, with later offshoots along the coasts of France and Spain.

The Dorians of Thera first settled on the island of Platea and later founded Cyrene (*c.* 630 B.C.) on the coast of Libya.

In conclusion one should stress what one might call the sovereignty of the Greek local dialects in the pre-Hellenistic age. They were not subject to the relentless pressure of an ever-present standard language like the dialects of modern Europe in centralized states. This development had to await the extinction of Greek political freedom and the institution of a central power under the Macedonians (see Chapter VI). What is peculiar to Greek is the emergence of standard literary languages which found acceptance outside the dialect area in which they originated. Here the motive force was cultural prestige. Their development is the subject of the next chapter.

IV

THE LITERARY LANGUAGES: POETRY

1. Homer

It was argued above that the language of the Linear B tablets was a widespread administrative *koine* which, though once based on a living dialect, conceals from us the everyday speech current in the various regions of the Mycenaean world; this implies that it may well have been archaic at the time of the destruction of the palaces. Nothing could be more flat, terse and bald than these earliest specimens of Greek prose; functionally determined as they are, being the concise, severely practical memoranda of the palace scribes, they may conceal not only the local dialects, but a highly developed and sophisticated Mycenaean poetical language. The evidence for this is indirect: the possibility emerges from the analysis of our earliest specimen of Greek poetry—the Homeric Epics.

At first glance the Epic language betrays not only its artificial and conventional character but also that it is the product of a long and complex history. The conclusions which emerge from the analysis may be stated at once: while the language of 'Homer' is basically Ionic, it has incorporated elements of widely different date and dialect origin reaching back into the Mycenaean age. There is a reasonable measure of agreement among scholars that the long process of linguistic and poetical evolution reached its culmination in the work of the 'monumental poet(s)',[1] datable to the latter half of the eighth century for the Iliad and the early part of the seventh century for the Odyssey. They lived and worked in the Ionian 'New World' in Asia Minor, the settlement of which began *c.* 1050 B.C.

The predominantly East Ionian character of the epic dialect is immediately obvious from the treatment of ᾱ (> η even after ρ, ι and ε), and this first impression is supported by the presence

---

[1] The author shares the view that the Odyssey is later than the Iliad and of different authorship.

of all the other major features; quantitative metathesis (Πηληϊά-δεω, etc.), *nu ephelkustikon* (ἔλυσε(ν)), athematic infinitives in -ναι, third singular ἦν for ἦς, third plural in -σαν, the pronouns ἡμεῖς and ὑμεῖς, and the potential particle ἄν. The distinction from Attic is marked not only by the consistent change of ᾱ > η, but also by the contracted form ἤν = Attic ἐάν, ἄν, by the absence of contraction in εα, εο, εω, by the treatment of digamma in the clusters -νϝ-, -ρϝ- (ξεῖνος, κοῦρος, see p. 62), and by the genitive singular -εω for Attic -ου in masculine *ā*-stems.

This overall picture is distorted, however, by the presence of certain unmistakably Aeolic features. First, there are words with the typically Aeolian change *q^w > π before front vowels: πίσυρες, πελώριον, πέλομαι, etc. More important are the morphological features, notably the dative plurals in -εσσι and the infinitives in -μεν, -μεναι, the former appearing also in thematic verbs (p. 61). There is only one example of an Aeolic perfect participle in -ων, κεκλήγοντες, but there are also certain artificial forms in -ῶτες which are suspected of concealing earlier -οντες. We also find third plural endings like ἤγερθεν for ἠγέρθησαν and the athematic conjugation of contracted verbs (φορήμεναι).

The complex dialect problems which the epic language presents may be illustrated by the Homeric forms of the preposition 'towards', προτί, ποτί and πρός, which have figured largely in arguments about the chronology and dialect distribution of the change τι > σι (see above). In view of the importance attached to the pre-Dorian elements in Crete and the fact that they are concentrated in central Crete, a fact of Cretan dialect geography may be relevant to this problem. It is in central Crete (Gortyna, Knossos, Vaxos, etc.) that we find πορτι as against ποτι in the east and west (ποι before dentals in Kydonia). C. D. Buck presents the overall dialect picture thus: [Central] Cretan πορτι, Attic-Ionic, Lesbian πρός; ποτί in the West Greek dialects (except [Central] Crete), as well as in Thessalian and Boeotian; A-C πός. He comments '...the relation of πρός, πός to προτί, ποτί can hardly be the same in origin as that of δίδωσι to δίδωτι'.[1] E. Schwyzer, for his part, regards the -τι forms as 'archaisms which prove nothing'. In

---

[1] *The Greek Dialects*, 2nd edn. 100; in the 3rd edition, p. 58, he writes: '...It is a question whether the -ς of πρός, πός comes from -σι by elision and apocope or is a different ending, original -ς'.

assessing the bearing of the dialect evidence on the provenance of the different Homeric forms the first point to be seized on is that προτί finds the closest analogue in Central Cretan πορτι. Arcado-Cypriot πος does not appear in Homer. It is unfortunate that Linear B *posi* is ambiguous, for it may stand for *posi* or *porsi*. In either event if, as appears likely, the Central Cretan form πορτι is an 'Achaean' survival, this would add to the evidence that the Linear B administrative *koine* masks the real dialect situation in the Mycenaean Peloponnese. What is essential to the picture of the Epic language is that Homer presents forms from the two different nuclei προ- and πο-, the combinations of which with -τι and -ς span the whole Greek dialect world (see above). If we exclude any Doric participation in the formation of the Epic language, the combined evidence of Homer and the inscriptions suggests that we must attribute to the pre-Dorian, pre-migration Mainland the whole set of forms just discussed. It is significant that only the exclusively A-C form πός is excluded from Homer.

With this we approach the question of Arcado-Cypriot elements in Homer. They consist in the main of vocabulary items: αἶσα (A-C), δῶμα (Arc.), (ϝ)άναξ (A-C, Myc.), κέλευθος (Arc.), ἦμαρ (Arc.), οἶος (Arc., Cypr.), ἀσκηθής (Arc.), ἀνώγω (Cypr.), ἠπύω (Arc. ἀπύω), χραύω (Cypr.), δέαμαι (Arc.), λεύσσω (Arc.), and the particles αὐτάρ, ἰδέ and νυ. To these may be added elements culled from the glossographers which also recur in Linear B: φάσγανον, δέπας and ἄρουρα. The evidence will be discussed below.

We may now turn to the presence of forms of different date (the terms 'early' and 'late' are correlative; they have no implications of absolute date and certainly do not mean 'genuine' *v.* 'intrusive'). The treatment of digamma is illuminating. By way of preliminary it is necessary to distinguish the positional variants, for these disappeared at widely different times. As was shown above (p. 71), intervocalically the loss of this sound in Attic-Ionic must be attributed to pre-migration times. On the other hand the divergent treatment of καλϝος (κᾰλός/κᾱλός), ξενϝος (ξένος/ξεῖνος), etc. shows that in these clusters the change was post-migration and later than the completion of the evolution ᾱ > η, the inception of which must also be placed in pre-migration times (see pp. 62 f.). What concerns us most is initial digamma. The texts of Homer (see below) lack any indication of this sound, but its presence in the epic language emerges from metrical considerations. Hiatus of a short final vowel is very rare before a word beginning with a vowel, whether aspirated or not. But over 2,000 examples have been counted where this word originally began with ϝ (or *sw-), so that we can remove the hiatus by inserting this sound: Ἀτρείδης τε ϝάναξ, μάλα ϝειπέ, οἴσετε ϝάρν' ἕτερον, etc. In other verses an apparently short syllable receives the required length if the digamma is inserted. Most instructive are examples like φίλε ϝϝεκυρέ and πατέρι ϝϝῷ, where the anomalous hiatus and apparent lengthening of the short vowels is due to the *ww*- which developed from *swekuros and *swos respectively (p. 238). But this treatment is by no means constant for there are numerous examples of elision and non-lengthening before words that originally began with digamma: ἠδ' ἄρν' ἐκέλευον, μένος καὶ θυμὸν ἑκάστου.

One reflection of the digamma is of interest in that it shows how evidently artificial forms occurring in late passages may nevertheless go back to ancient formulas. We recall that the adjectival suffix -*went*- in Linear B is added directly to the stem-consonant in third declension words (e.g. *pedwessa* 'footed'). In Homer we have reflections of φοινῑκ-ϝεντ- 'purple', 'crimson'. Later a thematic vowel was inserted; but then φοινικόεις – – ∪ – became unusable in hexameter verse. The relevant passages are: ἀπὸ δὲ χλαῖναν θέτο φοινῑκόεσσαν (ξ 500), ἥ, καὶ ἀπ' ὤμοιιν χλαῖναν θέτο φοινῑκόεσσαν (φ 118); ἀμφὶ δ' ἄρα χλαῖναν περονήσατο φοινῑκόεσσαν (Κ 133), said of Nestor, who also appears in Νέστωρ δ' ἐν χείρεσσι λάβ' ἡνία φοινῑκόεντα[1] (Θ 116); σμώδιγγες...αἵματι φοινικόεσσαι ἀνέδραμον 'the weals red with blood sprang up' (Ψ 716–17).

While φοινῑκόεσσα with its false quantity ῐ is evidently an artificial form, the connection with χλαῖνα 'cloak' and its verse-final position suggests that it goes back to a genuine ancient formula which still preserved the Mycenaean φοινικϝεντ-. The last example (from the Games) is the only one where the adjective has freed itself from the formulaic position and connection with χλαῖνα and so belongs to a later phase in the evolution of the Epic language.

[1] Another reading is σιγαλόεντα.

The example quoted above, θυμὸν ἑκάστου, leads to another feature which reveals the presence of earlier and later elements. This is the contraction of vowels, and we have in ἑκάστου an example which cannot be resolved. This ending of the genitive singular is the last stage in the Greek development of *-osjo (p. 238): -oio, -oo, -ou. Homer offers examples of all these forms (on -oo see below); Linear B shows -oio, and this form appears in an apocopized form in the Thessalian (Pelasgiotis) -oi. In Homer the contracted forms are much in the minority: the Iliad has only 20 per cent and the Odyssey only 24 per cent of all o-stem genitive singular forms. In general, contraction of vowels is comparatively rare in Homer if we count only those examples which are metrically protected. For instance, ἀ(ϝ)έκων 'unwilling' appears both as ἄκων and ἀέκων but the former can everywhere be resolved. Similarly, only one example of κοῖλος < κο(ϝ)ιλος resists resolution, while ἔ(ϝ)ιδον can be scanned as trisyllabic in all but five instances. Adjectives in -ϝεντ- from feminine ā-stems are usually uncontracted (αὐδήεντα, ὑλήεις, etc.), but there are a few contracted forms: τιμῆντα Σ 475, τεχνῆσσαι η 110 (on καιροσέων for καιρουσσέων, see below). The word 'to wash' is of interest because in Linear B the verbal stem is lewo- as opposed to later λο(ϝ)ε-. Homer has λόεον, λοέσσαι, λοέσσατο (also the derived λοετρόν), and in many instances the reading λοῦσεν can be replaced by λόεσεν. But there are examples where the contracted form must stand: λούσατε, ἀπολούσομαι, λούσῃ, λοῦσθαι.

We now turn to the problem of how such a linguistic amalgam comprising forms of different dialect and date came about. One suggestion may be ruled out at once: the notion that such a mixed dialect represents the spoken language of any historical Greek community. It is true that we have testimony for the northward advance of the Ionians in Asia Minor and their occupation of the originally Aeolic town of Smyrna, while the inscriptions of Chios present Lesbian features, such as πρηξοισι or πρήξουσι. As we have seen, the dialects of Boeotia and Thessaly present a striking mixture of Aeolic and West Greek elements. But there is no parallel for the type of mixture observed in the Epic language. It is hard to imagine a living dialect which possessed simultaneously three different genitive forms, such as -οιο, -οο, -ου or so many different forms of the personal pronouns as ἄμμες/ἡμεῖς, ὔμμες/ὑμεῖς, etc., or would use a form ἐλέλιχθεν in one sentence and ἐλελίχθησαν in the next. The first line of the Iliad contains the name Πηληϊάδεω with a quantitative metathesis[1] followed by Ἀχιλῆος, where this change has not taken place. A similar collocation of different forms is observed in πολυφλοίσβοιο (Aeolic) and θαλάσσης (Ionic). So, too, Aeolic κύνεσσιν (Aeolic dative with Ionic movable ν!) is followed by πᾶσι. Not long after we encounter ἀγορήνδε (Ionic) καλέσσατο λαόν (Aeolic). In the speech of Achilles (A 59ff.) there occur the Aeolicisms ἄμμε, κε, ἱερῆα, τόσσον, but it ends with the Ionic infinitive ἀμῦναι.

The presence of features of different date is merely emphasized by the suggestion that forms like -οιο may be early Ionic and not merely Aeolic. If this strategy is applied consistently to all the typically Ionic features and it is supposed for instance that forms like ἱκέτᾱο belonged to Ionic before the change of ᾱ to η and the subsequent quantitative metathesis, this procedure would drain the term 'Ionic' of its content, for it simply designates a group of characteristic features. Quite apart from that, the explanation breaks down in the face of typical Aeolic innovations like the datives in -εσσι and the perfect participles in -ων, -οντος, to say nothing of the presence of the characteristic forms of the potential particle ἄν/κε(ν).

There remains no other choice than to accept dialect mixture and chronological mixture as a characteristic of the language in which the Homeric poems were actually composed. There is general agreement about the process of its genesis: the Epic language was the product of a long tradition of oral poetry in which the 'singers' (aoidoi) operated with a large stock of memorized formulas. These were repeated groups of given metrical patterns, the building-blocks of the hexameter, each regularly (and to a large extent with mutual exclusion) employed to express a given notion. This stock was built up from generation to generation, and in the course of time it passed from an 'Achaean' to an Ionian milieu via the 'colonial' Aeolic which is mirrored in the Lesbian inscriptions. As a consequence certain 'Achaean' elements, preserved in stereo-

---

[1] In over 90 per cent of the examples it is possible to substitute the Aeolic ending -ᾱο for -εω; e.g. Πηληϊάδα' Ἀχιλῆος. But over twenty instances resist substitution.

typed formulas, became part of the repertory of the Ionian school of oral poetry which culminated in the works of the two 'monumental' poets known collectively as 'Homer'. How comparatively late in the tradition Homer must be is shown by the linguistic analysis of what surely must be a constitutive characteristic of the Iliad and Odyssey: the rich offering of brilliant and elaborate similes which adorn these works of genius shows an exceptionally strong concentration of 'late' linguistic features.

This picture of the genesis of the Epic language was challenged soon after the decipherment of Linear B. Ventris and Chadwick[1] wrote: 'Should we not conclude that the "Aeolic" stratum, which so obviously underlies the text of Homer, is not the Aeolic of Lesbos, but a much older Achaean form which had already set the conventions of epic verse within the second millennium B.C.?' This formulation, however, does not pose the question correctly. Scholars have posited Proto-Aeolic, and not the Aeolic of Lesbos, as one of the sources of the epic amalgam. They have rightly pointed to Aeolic innovations like the datives in -εσσι, and this cannot be countered by interpreting the -εσσι forms in the Doric dialects as 'Achaean' substratum elements in the West Greek Peloponnese. The fact remains that these are specifically 'Aeolic' forms. That Arcado-Cypriot stands apart in this respect is underlined by the absence of these dative forms in Linear B. The same is true of the thematic infinitives in -μεν, for which in any case we have to cite Mainland dialects and not the Aeolic of Lesbos.

On the other hand, the potential particle κε, on the evidence of Cypriot, might well be common 'Achaean'. Other features commonly classified as Aeolicisms might equally well belong to 'Achaean' in general: genitives in -ᾱο and -οιο, initial πτ- in πτόλις (A-C, Myc. and Cret. πτολίοικος), and πτόλεμος (Cypr., Myc. and Cret.). The origins of the -φι case (see p. 45) in Homer, which was brought into connection with Boeotian ἐπιπατρόφιον, have now been revealed by the Linear B inscriptions, but the new evidence shows how far the evolution had progressed since the Bronze Age. In Homer -φι appears both in the singular and the plural whereas in Linear B it is used only in the plural and is restricted to the non-thematic

[1] *Journal of Hellenic Studies*, 73 (1953), 103.

declensions, with only one example (Knossos) of the *o*-declension.[1] In Linear B the functions are instrumental and locative, with only one prepositional example (*opi qʷetropopphi oromenos* 'watching over the cattle...'). In Homer more than half the examples are prepositionally governed. Chantraine concluded[2] that while Mycenaean confirms the antiquity of the -φι forms, it presents a more archaic stage of their morphology with syntactical uses which are different and more authentic. He regards this as a further indication of the artificial character of the epic dialect.

It remains to assess the significance of the Arcado-Cypriot words in Homer. It is commonly said that the Linear B inscriptions have increased the number of such words, e.g. φάσγανον. What the new evidence shows is merely the genuine Mycenaean origin of such words. It does not prove that they found their way into the epic vocabulary direct from Arcado-Cypriot sources. This is an *argumentum ex silentio* until we have direct evidence that the northern Mycenaean world used, say, a different word for φάσγανον. What is involved may be no more than retained archaisms, evidence of little value in establishing exclusive connections. A common fund of words used in an ancestral language wastes away along different lines in its descendant dialects, so that they present different patterns of survival. The fact that Cheshire gardeners happen to use the word *delve* for the common English *dig* has little relevance for the origin of poems containing this word. In the same way there is no reason why we should not attribute φάσγανον, etc., to the Mycenaean world as a whole.

The general verdict, therefore, must be that the new Linear B evidence has done little to modify the long-accepted views on the genesis of the Epic dialect. Basically East Ionic, it nevertheless contains well-established Aeolicisms of frequent use. Chantraine concludes:[3] 'The Aeolic features of the Homeric language thus appear less important than was believed in the time of Fick, but all the same they remain well established on certain points.' We should add that the previous discussion has

[1] We cannot be sure that the Pylian place-name *maropi* (locative) is an *o*-stem.

[2] *Op. cit.* 501.

[3] *Op. cit.*, 2nd edn, I, 512.

shown that the most important elements, the -εσσι datives and the thematic infinitives in -μεν, could possibly date back to Mycenaean times and that we cannot exclude the Peloponnese as the place of origin.

There is a reasonable consensus that while an unbroken tradition of formulaic diction reaches back into the Mycenaean age, Ionic features predominate even in the earliest strata of the Homeric poems. If we consider the criteria of post-Mycenaean and post-migration composition, such as neglected digamma and irresolvable contractions, it becomes clear that many of the best-established formulas of the Homeric repertory evolved in post-migration times. Other formulas, though possibly pre-migration, must be denied on linguistic grounds to the South Achaean represented by the Linear B inscriptions. To take one interesting case: a poet using the Linear B dialect could not insert *wōrdŏdāktulos* (cf. Myc. *wodo-* = *wordo-* 'rose') in an hexameter line; the 'rosy-fingered dawn' must have originated in a dialect which used *wrodon* for 'rose'.

The linguistic evidence has featured largely in discussions of the artistic unity or multiplicity of Homeric Epics. What linguistic analysis has achieved is to illuminate the history and provenance of the different ingredients which make up the Homeric palette. Their results might be thought to have little relevance to the pictures painted with such resources. But, if we accept the view that this linguistic palette was virtually complete by the end of the eighth century and that 'Homer' was free to choose any 'colour', 'early' or 'late', whatever the dialect provenance, according to his pleasure and convenience, then it would be reasonable to expect an even scatter of 'early' and 'late' elements on the pages of our Homeric texts. That this is not so was shown by the researches of G. P. Shipp, who made a systematic study of the distribution in the Iliad of forms classified by Chantraine as 'late'. He found that they occur predominantly in similes, digressions, and 'comments'. This uneven distribution of the late features, concentrated as they are in the similes, one of the most characteristic and brilliant features of the poems as we know them, suggests that the 'monumental poets' responsible for the similes constructed their great masterpieces from earlier material.

M. Leumann approached the question of such stratification

from a different angle. In the course of a centuries-long poetical tradition the inherited formulas preserve words and phrases which had been lost from everyday speech and so were liable to misinterpretation by the later bards. A grotesque and notorious example is the use of στήτα 'woman' in the pseudo-Theocritean *Syrinx* 14, which is due to the misinterpretation of διαστήτην ἐρίσαντε (A 6) 'they parted in strife' as 'having quarrelled over a woman' (διὰ στήτην). If such examples could be plausibly established within the Homeric poems it would be reasonable to conclude with Leumann that the correct use cannot be attributed to the same author as the incorrect.

A good example involves a technical word which has the additional interest of possible Anatolian origin: κύμβαχος 'crown of a helmet' (cf. Hittite *kupaḫḫi*). In O 536 κύμβαχον ἀκρότατον νύξ' ἔγχεϊ ὀξυόεντι 'he struck the top of the helmet with his sharp spear', the word is used authentically. But in E 585–6 ἔκπεσε δίφρου...κύμβαχος ἐν κονίῃσιν 'he fell from the chariot head first in the dust' the sense of the word is completely misunderstood. Opinions may differ over the 'lateness' of the grotesque elaborations which follow; Mydon the charioteer remains upright with his head buried in the sand until the horses kick him over.

Another example of the same kind concerns the use of another technical word παρήορος, literally 'what is attached alongside' (cf. Linear B *opāworta* 'attachments' (of a corslet)), used of an extra horse in a chariot team. It is used apparently in its proper technical sense in Π 470 f.; this horse is wounded and confusion results ἐπεὶ δὴ κεῖτο παρήορος ἐν κονίῃσι 'since the παρήορος lay in the dust'. Here we appear to have an authentic technical detail of Mycenaean chariot-fighting. Quite different is the use in H 154f., where Nestor boasts of an early exploit: 'He was the tallest and strongest man I ever slew' πολλὸς γάρ τις ἔκειτο παρήορος ἔνθα καὶ ἔνθα 'for there he lay a sprawling bulk this way and that'. Evidently the composer of this passage has completely misunderstood the κεῖτο παρήορος of the first. The phrase πολλὸς...τις is also indicative: it is common in Herodotus, but this is its only occurrence in Homer. The fact that the hero on this occasion is Nestor is also significant: there are numerous indications that much of the Nestorian material is late. For instance Ψ 602 f. uses παρήορος in yet another sense. Menelaus says 'I will yield to you, angry though I am, for you were not previously παρήορος or ἀεσίφρων' ('feckless or foolish'). Here the person addressed is Antilochus, the son of Nestor.

With these examples we approach the question of the accretions and distortions that can be detected in the history of our Homeric texts. These reproduce in the main the best available manuscript, Venetus A, which goes back in the last instance to the canon established by Alexandrian scholarship, notably by Aristarchus of Samothrace (c. 215 to c. 145 B.C.), the head of the library at Alexandria. Here the divisions are schematic and somewhat arbitrary. It is reasonable to suppose that the bardic traditions remained fresh, vigorous, and authentic until their culmination in the monumental poems, though of course misunderstandings and creation of entirely artificial forms may have arisen at any stage in the history of this oral poetry. G. S. Kirk[1] distinguishes two critical stages in the transmission of the text of the poems, which we may presume to have been virtually complete by 700 B.C. The first period ends with what is known as the 'Peisistratean recension'. According to the pseudo-Platonic dialogue, the *Hipparchus*, it was Hipparchus, younger son of the Athenian tyrant Peisistratus, who first brought the poems of Homer to Attica and compelled the reciters (the rhapsodes) at the Panathenaic festival to perform them in relay (ἐξ ὑπολήψεως) continuously (ἐφεξῆς). This rule evidently implies the existence of some authoritative text to which officials could refer and competitors would defer. In this first period we may surmise that the texts were liable to corruption from two main influences: first from the later 'singers' (ἀοιδοί) who, with diminishing competence and skill, continued to practice the traditional craft, and secondly from the professional reciters (ῥαψῳδοί), pure performers, whose natural leanings towards virtuosity and display were stimulated by the existence of regular competitions. As J. A. Davison has written: 'Thus the very nature of epic style made it easy for the skilled rhapsode deliberately or insensibly to revise the texts which he recited and even to insert "cadenzas" of his own composition.'[2]

[1] *The Songs of Homer*, 310 ff., Cambridge (1962).
[2] A. J. B. Wace and F. H. Stubbings (eds.), *A Companion to Homer* (1962), 218.

As a result of these activities we may suppose that many divergent texts of the poems were in circulation, and it was doubtless because of these that Hipparchus procured what was recognized as an authoritative version. There is little evidence from the poems themselves to support the statement which appears first in Cicero (*de Oratore* III. 137) that the poems were arranged in their present state by Peisistratus, having been previously in a disorderly state (*confusos ante*). In fact what is of interest is how few and slight the Attic features of the text are. The optative in μαχέοιντο (A 344) is not merely Attic but even late Attic, since the ending -οιντο competes with the original -οιατο (* < =-oịạto, see p. 297) throughout the fifth century. The true reading will have been μαχεοίατ' or μαχέοντας. However, ἥατ' cannot be substituted for ἦντ' (Γ 153). Again, ὅτε... σταίησαν (P 732–3) is the only example of this formation in Homer, and there is no suggestion of repeated action, which is the function of the optative in such temporal clauses. The optatives φοροίη (ι 320) and φιλοίη (δ 692) are peculiar to Attic and they will have replaced the athematic type (Aeolic conjugation of contracted verbs) *φορείη, *φιλείη.

Some further distortion of the original text was occasioned at a later stage when the texts were transcribed (μεταγραμματισμός) into the reformed alphabet. Greek inherited from Indo-European two *e*-sounds (p. 213), exemplified in the first two vowels of ἔθηκα. The same is true of the *o*-sounds. The early alphabet of Attic used E and O for both varieties, the closed short vowel and the open long vowel. The Ionic alphabet developed distinct signs for the long vowels, H and Ω; a further refinement was the use of the digraph EI to represent the lengthened ε, a new sound in Greek arising from contraction or compensatory lengthening (e.g. εἰμί = ẹ̄mi < *es-mi), and OY for lengthened o. In transcribing E and O into the new orthography the scribes will have experienced no difficulty in choosing between ε/ει/η and o/ου/ω as long as they could get guidance from their own speech. Elsewhere they could easily go astray. For instance, our texts read καιροσέων 'closely woven' (η 102), though the original doubtless was pronounced καιρουσσέ̥ων (with synizesis). Similarly ΘΕΟΔΕΣ, to be scanned ∪ – –, goes back to θεοδϝής (< *θεοδϝεhής). The scribe has transcribed θεουδής, not knowing the original metrical effect of the lost

digamma, which is seen in other derivatives from *dwei- 'fear':
e.g. ἔδδεισεν < *e-dwei-sen. The apparently present form δείδω
'I fear' is actually a perfect δέδϝω < *δε-δϝοι-α; the corresponding plural form is written δείδιμεν, which conceals the true
δε-δϝι-μεν.

Similar misinterpretations occurred when quantitative metathesis occasioned metrical difficulties. Evidently ἕως cannot
stand at the beginning of a verse, unlike the earlier ἧος. If ΕΟΣ
stood before a vowel and had to be scanned – ∪, the scribe
wrote εἷος (e.g. εἷος ἐγώ, δ 90); but before a consonant the
scribe could come closer to the Attic ἕως and wrote εἵως (e.g.
εἵως Πηνελόπειαν, δ 800). Similar embarrassment was caused by
the short-vowelled (athematic) subjunctives like θήομεν, which
later changed to θέωμεν. Here ΘΕΟΜΕΝ – ∪ ∪ was wrongly
transcribed as θείομεν. Other unauthentic forms were occasioned
by the contraction of vowels (see above). In -άω verbs traditional
forms like ὁράεις, ὁράοντες, etc., were contracted in Attic to
ὁρᾷς, ὁρῶντες, etc. As long as the poems were recited and not
committed to writing, the rhapsodes could have made con-
cessions to contemporary pronunciation without metrical difficulties by distributing the contracted sounds over two syllables.
When, however, the poems came to be written down, metrical
integrity was established by writing ὁράᾳς, ὁρόωντες, etc. This
is what is known as 'epic diectasis' ('distension'). Similar is the
spelling φόως, which is a re-expansion of φῶς, the contraction of
φάϝος.

Other contractions were also misunderstood. Important are
the different forms of the genitive singular of the o-stems. Homer
presents both -οιο and ου. But some verses with the contracted
form will not scan: e.g. in βῆν εἰς Αἰόλου κλυτὰ δώματα Κ 60
the impossible cretic – ∪ – is removed if we read Αἰόλοο.
Sometimes the intrusion of the contracted forms into the text
occasions consequential alterations. For instance, in ἐπιδη-
μίου ὀκρυόεντος Ι 64 and κακομηχάνου ὀκρυοέσσης Ζ 344, the
intrusive prothetic vowel in the word κρυοεντ- is due to the
false division of ἐπιδημίοο and κακομηχάνοο. Again, ἀδελφειοῦ
κταμένοιο Ε 21 probably conceals the correct ἀδελφεόο κταμένοιο, a phrase which is a good illustration of the artificiality
of the language in that it combines two historically different
forms of the genitive. In the same way ὅου κλέος Β 325 should be

read ὄο. That this artificial language evolved according to its own laws is shown by the fact that, on the analogy of οὗ:ὄο, ἧς was expanded to ἕης Π 208. Exigencies of scansion, again, were responsible for the dative ἐπέεσσι in χειρὸς ἑλοῦσ' ἐπέεσσι προσηύδα Ε 30, which probably goes back to ἑλοῦσα ϝέπεσσι. However, datives of s-stems in -εεσσι are elsewhere secured by the metre (νεφέεσσι, βελέεσσι, ξιφέεσσι, etc.) and these hyper-Aeolicisms are one more illustration of the artificial nature of the Homeric *Kunstsprache*. It developed according to its own laws.

Finally, a peculiarity of spelling is a clue to a comparatively late insertion in the text. It concerns the verb ὀφείλω. The Odyssey presents the Aeolic form ὀφέλλω with the geminated consonant (< *ὀφελ-νω, p. 241), whereas the Iliad shows examples of the Ionic form ὀφείλω, all forms in book Λ. This distribution has puzzled grammarians, but the Iliadic examples are all from Nestor's account of the Elean war. The aberrant spelling must date from after the alleged metagrammatism. Before that there would have been no difference of spelling, for both dialect forms would have been spelt ΟΦΕΛΟ (archaic writing did not indicate double consonants). In Attic fifth-century inscriptions ΕΙ is used for the inherited diphthong while ē is written Ε, the spelling ει becoming regular from about the beginning of the fourth century, though there are sporadic earlier examples. The orthographic oddity of the Nestorian episode is explicable if this was a later insertion into our text of the Iliad.

With the μεταγραμματισμός (the Ionic alphabet was made official in Athens in the archonship of Eucleides 403–402 B.C., see p. 204), we have moved into the second critical period in the history of the text, beginning with the Panathenaic 'canon', which in any case would have been authoritative only in Athens. During the following centuries the text again fell increasingly into a chaotic state until the edition by Aristarchus. This is the point at which we can first speak of a standard text. As J. A. Davison[1] points out 'Henceforth "wild" papyri (i.e. those which differ in length, or materially, in wording from the text on which our editions are based) are the exception rather than the rule.' Its orthography shows that it had come to Alexandria by way of Athens.

---

[1] *Op. cit.* 223.

Linguistic arguments have again figured largely in recent discussions among classical scholars about the genesis of the Homeric Epics, which have naturally been stimulated by the decipherment of Linear B and the new thesis about the inter-relations of the Greek dialects. Speculation has been especially busy on the existence of nuclear versions of the Iliad and the Odyssey in the Mycenaean Age and their further development in the Dark Age which followed the collapse of Mycenaean civilization.

Of particular relevance is the name of the central hero of the Iliad, Akhilleus, which was analysed and made the basis of an argument (Chapter II above) to the effect that some version of 'The wrath of Akhilles' must have been known in Pylos and Knossos in the thirteenth century B.C. The importance of this may now be underlined since acceptance of a 'Wrath' of this date evidently implies transmission in some form or other through the Dark Age which intervened between the destruction of the Palaces and the time of the monumental poet who composed the Iliad as we know it. Some further clarification is now required, all the more so since the most recent authoritative work on Homeric word-formation[1] still regards Akhilleus as a pre-Greek word.

The first point that must be made is that such a diagnosis is not based on any positive evidence. This may be brought out by considering once again the parallel case of pre-Greek place-names. With these, ample testimony was forthcoming not only for the Asiatic occurrence of place-names with certain suffixes, but actual names like Parnassos could be located in Asia Minor and explained by the languages known to have been used in the same localities. Nothing of this kind has been adduced to support the ascription of Akhilleus, Pēleus, etc., to a pre-Greek language, although we are no less amply informed about personal names than place-names. The suffix -eus was extremely productive even in ordinary words already in Mycenaean Greek (pp. 34 ff.), and we should require strong evidence to show that it was taken over from a pre-Greek language. The current view is thus void and ex nihilo. It is simply a confession of failure: scholars who label these formations 'pre-Greek' really mean 'non-Greek', and by this they are in effect saying that they do

[1] Ernst Risch, *Wortbildung der homerischen Sprache*, 2nd edn, Berlin (1974).

not yield to a known process of Greek morphological analysis. But in fact Risch lists all the morphological procedures necessary for the analysis of *Akhilleus*: 1, Caland-form ἀχι- corresponding to the neuter *s*-stem ἄχος, e.g. *Kudi-aneira/kūdos* (the procedure goes back to IE); 2, short forms characterized by *-eus*, e.g. *Eury-sth-eus* short for *Eurysthenēs*; and 3, expressive gemination, e.g. *Ekhemm-ōn* short for *Ekhe-mēdes* (with characterizing suffix *-ōn*), which appears in Linear B *ekemede*. Thus the analysis of *Akhilleus* as the short form of *Akhi-lāwos* is morphologically unimpeachable. We now add the semantic factor which is vital. To reject this solution it would have to be argued 1, that a pre-Greek name merely happens to conform to the known morphological procedures established on the basis of Greek names and 2, that this happens to yield a combination of words appropriate to the role of the hero in the *Iliad*, as demonstrated by Nagy.

We are not so well placed with the central figure of the Odyssey. But here, too, Risch cites (p. 158) an example which yields, as we saw (p. 36), a morphological schema that fits *Odysseus*: *Epeigeus* is made directly from ἐπείγω 'press hard (in pursuit, etc.)'. As shown above, the combination of elements verbal prefix + present stem + *-eus* suggests the analysis *o-dukj-eus*. No Linear B text has so far produced *oduzeu*, but morphological and lexical facts speak for a formation of great antiquity. The IE root **deuk-* is widespread (Lat. *dūco*, Engl. *tug*, etc.), and the present stem *dukj-* with zero grade is of a well-known type represented in Greek by βαίνω < **gʷm̥-j-*, with zero grade of the root **gʷem-* 'go, come'. In Linear B we have *woze* = *work-jei* < **wr̥g-j-*, the zero grade of **werg-* 'work'. What is of further significance in the present connection is that Greek replaced the root **deuk-* by ἄγω and ἐλαύνω. Thus in *odukjeus* we have an example of the preservation in a personal name of a linguistic element which was later discarded from ordinary speech. The name could, however, only have been coined when the present stem with its likewise archaic prefix *o-* was still in current use, and that points to a date long before the Linear B tablets.

Our belief in the Mycenaean ancestry of the Iliad and the Odyssey does not alter the fact that little or nothing was preserved by the bardic tradition of the complex bureaucratic society so surprisingly revealed to us by the Linear B tablets. As we wrote soon after the decipherment: 'Homer would have been astonished.' Both the Iliad and the Odyssey (as G. Kirk, *op. cit.* p. 140, has written), 'are in an important sense *Ionian* poems made by eighth-century singers out of material that has passed for generations through a primarily Ionian tradition.' Nevertheless, we repeat, to accept the existence of Mycenaean tales having Achilles and Odysseus as their central characters inescapably involves the continuation of the story-telling through the so-called Dark Age (the eleventh and tenth centuries), however dismal and impoverished they may appear to have been from the archaeological record.

This raises the problem of detecting possible 'Dark Age' elements in the Iliad and the Odyssey. The stumbling-block is that we know little or nothing about this period, and this is particularly true of the things which of their nature do not appear in the archaeological record, such as institutions and forms of society. The very darkness of the age in such matters as land-tenure confines us to uncontrollable speculation. As for language, certain features can be diagnosed as lying between the Linear B tablets of the thirteenth century and the alphabetic inscriptions so many centuries later. An obvious instance is the deduced genitives in -oo. Another is the obsolescence of the -φι case. The post-Mycenaean development of the labiovelars at least allows us to trace the path of dialectal descent in the Achilles–Peleus legend. If our analysis of the name *Pēleus* is correct, then the form of the story which became canonical will have evolved in a dialect in which $Q^w\bar{e}leus$ > *Pēleus* and not > *Tēleus*, that is in Aeolic. But this does not add greatly to our knowledge, since the Iliad locates the kingdom of Peleus in what was later known as Thessaly. In any case, none of these linguistic developments can be dated with sufficient accuracy, and the difficulties increase if our view of the Linear B language is correct, with the consequence that we know nothing about the dialects actually spoken in Mycenaean Greece in the thirteenth century B.C., to say nothing of the century or so which elapsed before the influx of refugees to Cyprus and the Aeolic and Ionian migrations.

This whole complex of problems may be further illustrated by a final simple concrete example which will incidentally also clarify the terms North Mycenaean and South Mycenaean

which Homeric scholars have taken over from the new school
of dialect geographers (pp. 70 ff.) and are being used in debate.
Originally the demonstrative pronoun which later became the
definite Greek article had the stem forms masculine ὁ, feminine
ἁ (> ἡ) in the nominative singular, but τοί, ταί in the corresponding plural forms. Later the aspirated forms οἱ, αἱ were
introduced into the nominative plural by all Greek dialects
except West Greek (the examples in Boeotian and Thessalian
could also be West Greek). Yet Homer presents a few examples
of the archaism τοί, ταί. Since there is little or no trace of West
Greek influence on the Epic language, the Homeric forms are
plausibly ascribed to some pre-migration Mainland dialect.
Now both Arcadian and Cypriot present the new forms, and
this would appear to rule out the dialect of the Peloponnese,
what may be called 'South Mycenaean'. This conclusion is
supported by the occurrence of the new aspirated forms in the
Doric dialect of Crete, where scholars are inclined to regard
them as intrusions from the dialect of the Creto-Mycenaeans
reflected in the tablets of Knossos. This would leave pre-
migration Mainland Aeolic as the probable source of the
Homeric forms, with the consequence that this would have
differed from Arcado-Cypriot in retaining the archaic forms.

Now the Proto-Aeolic which is reconstructed by comparison
of Thessalian, Boeotian and Lesbian sums up all we know about
the language of Mainland Aeolis before the coming of the West
Greeks. It is on a par with the reconstructed Arcado-Cypriot,
which together with the Linear B tablets from Pylos and
Mycenae provides us with data about the language of the
Mycenaeans of the Peloponnese in the thirteenth century B.C.
It would, therefore, be natural to distinguish these two varieties
as 'South Mycenaean' and 'North Mycenaean' respectively.
Some confusion in scholarly discussion is caused, however, by
the use of 'North Mycenaean' in another sense. The newer
school of thought about Greek dialect relations (not accepted by
us) links Aeolic and West Greek and derives them both from a
common ancestor, which, of course, long antedated the South
Mycenaean dialect of the Linear B tablets, and the ancestral
Arcado-Cypriot. The proposed dialect genealogy is set forth in
the following diagram (Fig. 5), in which the asterisks represent
different orders of abstraction from the textual data. Seeing that

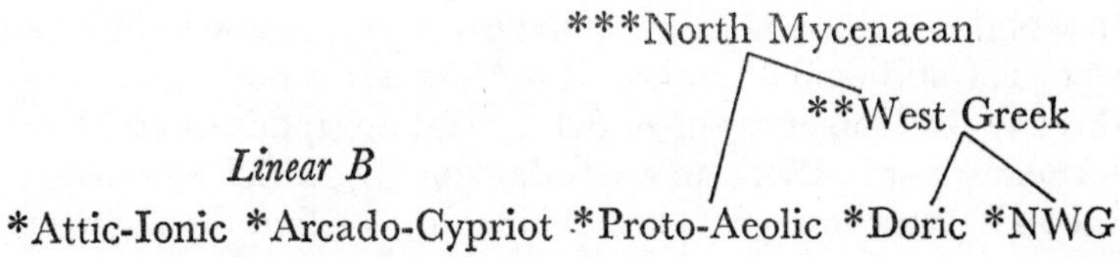

***North Mycenaean

**West Greek

Linear B

*Attic-Ionic *Arcado-Cypriot *Proto-Aeolic *Doric *NWG

Fig. 5. A Proposed Genealogy of the 'North Mycenaean' Dialect

the ancestral 'North Mycenaean' in this sense by definition antedates both Proto-Aeolic and West Greek, Homeric scholars who accept this thesis but exclude West Greek influence from the Epic cannot attribute any feature to 'North Mycenaean'. In general, seeing that Arcado-Cypriot (supported by Linear B) is of the same order of abstraction as Proto-Aeolic, if the former is regarded as South Mycenaean then it would be sensible to apply the correlative term North Mycenaean to the latter. However, little is gained by coining new terms for entities long familiar to scholarship as North Achaean (Proto-Aeolic) and South Achaean (Arcado-Cypriot).

2. Hesiod

The Epic language in a sense was formed by its chosen metre, the hexameter. The generally held view that this verse in its turn is a stylization of the dactylic rhythms of natural speech is borne out by the very first specimen of Mycenaean Greek which emerged from the soil of Blegen's Pylos: ἐρεται Πλευρωναδ(ε) ἰοντες 'rowers going to Pleuron' ($\cup \cup - - - \cup \cup - -$). It is a peculiar fact of the Greek literary scene that all hexameter poetry from Homer on, whatever its theme and however diverse the dates and origins of the poets were, was bound up with the artificial Epic language described above. Hesiod's father was an Aeolian from Cyme who migrated with his two sons to mainland Greece and settled at Ascra in Boeotia. After the father's death, following a dispute about the inheritance with his brother Perses, Hesiod composed the *Works and Days* (*Op.*) which combines moral admonitions with an account of a year's farm operations. In the *Theogony* (*Th.*) the poet systematizes ancient traditions and beliefs about the gods. For all their difference of theme (and that of the *Works* is more remote from the heroic Epic) the language of both these poems is patently the same as that of the Iliad and Odyssey, and the poet uses much the same stock of traditional formulas. That Hesiod to some extent draws directly on Homer is suggested by certain applications of the formulas. For instance, in the Catalogue (B), which enumerates the Achaean contingents and their ships, we find the recurrent phrase τοῖς δ' ἅμα τεσσαράκοντα μέλαιναι νῆες ἕποντο 'them forty black ships accompanied'. Hesiod has occasion to prescribe the advantages of a forty-year-old ploughman and writes, *Op.* 441, τοῖς δ' ἅμα τεσσαρακονταετὴς αἰʒηὸς ἕποιτο 'them (the pair of oxen) a stout slave of forty years should accompany'. An additional point of interest is that he uses as a noun αἰʒηός, which in Homer is an adjective 'vigorous, lusty'.

More grotesque is the application of another recurrent phrase. In the Iliad it is a standard feature of a heroic duel that one warrior hurls his spear and misses: ἐτώσιον ἔκφυγε χειρός (Ζ 407, etc.) 'fruitless it sped from his hand'. This is adapted in *Th.* 182 to the castration of Uranos by Cronos: ἐτώσια ἔκφυγε χειρός 'fruitless sped the genitals (μήδεα) from his hand'. There can be little doubt which use is original and which is derivative.

That the language of Hesiod comes at a later stage in the evolution of the Epic language is further suggested by a number of indicators. The proportion of -ου to -οιο genitives is higher than in Homer, and this is especially so in the *Works*. This general pattern is repeated with other indicators: in Homer the ratio of -āo to -εω genitives is 9 : 1, whereas in Hesiod they are fairly evenly balanced, and much the same is true of the genitives -āων/-εων. The overall figures are given further point if we distinguish between traditional phrases and new invention or adaptation of old material to new uses, for in these Hesiod sometimes substitutes the later endings.

In Homer, as we saw, intrusion of such later forms can most readily be explained from the contemporary speech of the Ionian *aoidoi*. But Hesiod spoke a dialect which retained -āo and -āων. The same picture emerges from a study of the non-observance of initial digamma. Here, too, a Boeotian poet, whose native dialect preserved initial digamma, might well be expected to show greater metrical respect for this sound than the Ionian singers whose dialect had lost it. Not only is the contrary true but neglected digamma features in Hesiod's own innovations, e.g. *Op*. 524 ὅτ' ἀνόστεος (ϝ)ὸν πόδα τένδει 'when the boneless one (cuttlefish?) gnaws his foot'.

From the general pattern of the evidence it emerges 1, that Hesiod was trained in a school of Ionian poetry where digamma was preserved in traditional phraseology, but could be neglected in newly-coined phrases and 2, that he continued to behave, Boeotian of colonial Aeolic extraction though he was, like a neo-Ionian *aoidos*. Yet it must be emphasized, both with Homer and Hesiod, that observed digamma is still preponderant. This brings out the force of tradition in the Epic language and the stubborn conservatism inherent in bardic schooling and practices. The accumulated literary capital of centuries was not lightly to be discarded.

There are features of Hesiod's language which cannot be accounted for simply as a choice between earlier and later elements in the traditional hexameter language. For instance, in *Op*. 564 neglected digamma is associated with an accusative plural of the *ā*-declension in -ᾰς: εὖτ' ἂν δ' (ϝ)ἑξήκοντα μετὰ τροπὰς ἠελίοιο 'when sixty [days have elapsed] after the solstice'. There are nine examples of such accusatives in *Th*. and *Op*. The short vowel originated in the loss of *n* where *Vns* occurred before a consonant. This resulted in doublet forms -ανς/ᾰς before vowel and consonant respectively, the original distribution still being preserved in Cretan and Argolic. In most dialects *n* was later lost before *s* with compensatory lengthening or diphthongization (p. 237). The different dialects 'selected' and generalized one or other of the two forms: the short vowel occurs in Arcadian, Thessalian, and some West Greek dialects. Three possible explanations have been put forward for the Hesiodic forms: 1, that this is a West Greek element in his language, 2, that Hesiod is drawing on a Mainland tradition of poetry to which 'Achaean' dialects had contributed and 3, that these are artificial 'metrical' shortenings. A recent study of the metrical distribution of the short-vowel forms favours the first explanation. The difficulty is that precisely Boeotian lacks such accusatives.

Much has been written about the Doric elements in Hesiod. What makes a decision difficult is that most of the alleged West Greek features are retained archaisms, a fact which makes it possible to assign Hesiod's examples to archaic poetical diction:

e.g. third plural ἔδον and ἦν. The sole example which seems incontrovertibly West Greek is the numeral τέτορα, since Homer uses πίσυρες where he requires this metrical pattern and τέσσαρες elsewhere. In the dialects the forms are Ionic τέσσερες, Attic τέτταρες, Boeotian and Thessalian πέτταρες, West Greek τέτορες. On the other hand the dual feminine καλυψαμένω, *Op.* 198, which on the evidence of the archaic Elean τὸ κατα-στατὸ 'the two restorers' was *prima facie* also a West Greek feature, can now, in the light of the Linear B evidence, be classified as an 'Achaean' survival. The upshot is that one single vocabulary element is all that remains of the supposed West Greek features in Hesiod's language.

It remains to consider possible Attic constituents. In *Op.* 63 κᾰλὸν (ϝ)εῖδος, neglect of initial digamma is combined with absence of compensatory lengthening in καλ(ϝ)ος, a pheno-menon which distinguishes Attic from Ionic (p. 62). Similar is the double neglect in *Op.* 752 δυωδεκάμηνὸν ἴσον (< ϝισϝος, p. 238). However, other sources are possible: Homer has analogous short forms from μονϝο-, ξενϝο-, etc., and the Lesbian poets Sappho and Alcaeus offer examples which include καλος and ἰσος. Still, at least λαμπράν τε Σελήνην, *Th.* 19, 371 seems to have been taken over as a complete phrase from an Attic source. Similar are the names Θείᾱν and Ῥείᾱν, *Th.* 135. The perfect ἔᾱγε *Op.* 534 has also been explained as an Atticism. But another form of the same verb καυάξαις *Op.* 666, 693 = καϝϝαξαις < *κατ-ϝαξαις, is evidently Aeolic and is of additional interest in that it does not occur in Homer. This is also true of αἴνημι, which illustrates the athematic conjugation of contracted verbs. There remains a small number of features which recur in Lesbian Aeolic: δείκνυ *Op.* 526 and the declined numeral τριηκόντων *Op.* 696.

Certain general conclusions emerge. First Hesiod is enmeshed firmly, both as regards dialect and formulaic expression, in the same oral tradition as Homer. What is surprising is how few and unimportant the un-Homeric elements in the poems are. There is still dispute about Hesiod's date, and some scholars would place his poems between the Iliad and the Odyssey. What is central to the understanding of the Greek attitude to the language of literature is his whole-hearted submission to the linguistic conventions of hexameter poetry. The point has been

made that only an exceptional flowering of the Ionian Epic,
such as Homer represents, can account for the pre-eminence of
Ionic as the language of hexameter poetry in Hesiod's time. We
may add that the skilled adaptation for his own purposes of this
highly complex and sophisticated language, with its undeniable
East Ionic stamp, by a poet speaking a Mainland non-Ionic
dialect is unthinkable without a long and arduous training. It is
not necessary to suppose that Hesiod acquired his skill in Ionia.
It is equally thinkable that he attached himself to one of the offshoots of the schools of oral poetry which had established themselves in the principalities of the Mainland.

That the flow of ancient poetical tradition had branches
partially independent of that which culminated in Homer is
suggested by an analysis of the *Homeric Hymns*. On the whole the
language of these poems is more 'recent' than that of the Epic,
but they present a small but significant number of features
which are more archaic than those used by Homer. Thus
χρυσάορα 'with golden sword' (*h. Apoll.* 123) has an athematic
stem contrasting with the more recent thematic stem of χρυ-
σάορον (Ο 256). Of interest is κατάκειαι (*h. Hermes*) < *-keisai*
with regular loss of -*s*-, which at a later stage was restored
analogically, hence Homeric κεῖσαι. Yet another archaism not
found in Homer is the athematic first plural perfect form
ἄνωγμεν 'we command' (*h. Apoll.* 528). These archaisms evidently cannot be derived from our Iliad and Odyssey, and they
have been regarded as 'proof' that the Hymns 'must have
stemmed from an Epic phase when the Epic *Dichtersprache* was
not moribund (i.e. before the onset of fixed texts)...'[1]

3. Elegy and Iambos

That poetry in dactylic hexameters should conform closely to
the Homeric model needs no explanation: it had taken centuries
of experiment and practice to bring this linguistic instrument to
so high a pitch of perfection and economy of expression. What
is striking, however, about Greek literature is that compositions
in other genres and metres should be, in different degrees, so
unmistakably Homeric in language. In Ionia, where the new
genres first make their appearance, Homer was not only the
stock-in-trade of the *aoidoi* who provided the bulk of literary

[1] Householder and Nagy, 23 (1972).

entertainment; the epic poems, we may surmise, were also the instrument of education. The cultural air the Ionians breathed was Homeric. It was thus, seemingly, inevitable that poets working in such a milieu should use the given linguistic medium, sensitively blended in various degrees as genre and theme dictated.

This fact is all the more noteworthy in that with Archilochus, with whom these new developments begin, we move from the heroic grandeur and the conventional virtues of Homer and from the high moral earnestness of Hesiod into a new world, the colonial New World of seventh century Ionia. The very note of his poetry is individualism, and self-expression with cynical and flippant rejection of heroic ideals, unconcealed surrender to erotic passion, ferocious attacks on enemies and gross obscenity.

Archilochus was born into an aristocratic family of the island of Paros in the second decade of the seventh century B.C., and his poetical activity can be dated to c. 660–640 B.C. It is a sign of the new times that, poet of genius that he was, he turned not to the traditional school of epic but to songs appropriate to an entirely different social context. Though he is the first of the poets of the archaic age, the technical perfection of his production is such that we must suppose a long period of development, going back to origins beyond our ken on which it would be idle to speculate. His poetry exhibits a great variety of metre but the bulk of it falls into two main categories. We shall first consider poems in 'elegiac' couplets, a verse form with evidently close affinity to the dactylic hexameter, for it combines such an hexameter with a shorter verse—a pentameter, having the metrical structure $-\cup\cup-\cup\cup-\,|\,-\cup\cup-\cup\cup-$. It so happens that the word ἔλεγος is attested later than the derivative ἐλεγεῖον. Etymological speculation connects it with the Armenian *elegn* 'pipe', 'reed', which may have been a loan-word from Phrygian. The Greeks are said to have taken over the flute from the Phrygians, and at least at one stage the elegy was accompanied by the flute (Theognis, 533 ὑπ' αὐλητῆρος ἀείδων). The argument is finely spun.

The analogy of ἰαμβεῖον:ἴαμβος::ἐλεγεῖον:ἔλεγος certainly suggests that at one stage of its development ἔλεγος denoted poetry characterized by the 'elegiac' metre. In fact there is evidence that such an association between the genre and its characteristic metre existed in the Peloponnese in the sixth century B.C. There the predominant theme was lamentation, and the performance was accompanied by the flute.

Strangely, the first attestation of ἔλεγος in Attic literature is in Euripides, who in four examples also uses it with reference to a lamentation. It is thus clear that the term ἔλεγος by the fifth century had come to denote a genre of poetry predominantly threnodic in character, elegiac in metre and accompanied by the flute. But that this was a restriction of a once more general application is suggested also by Euripidean usage. In two of the examples (*Hel.* 185, *I.T.* 146) his use of the adjective ἄλυρος shows that for him the accompaniment was normally played on the lyre. That the theme could be other than lamentation emerges from his use of ἔλεγος to refer to the music which Orpheus played on his lyre to keep the oarsmen of the ship Argo in time (*Hypsipyle* 62, Page). An examination of the elegiacs of Archilochus, meagre and fragmentary though they are, shows quite clearly that lamentation is only one thematic possibility and that this type of verse was merely one of a number of media for expressing his views and sentiments on a variety of themes. What needs stressing is that, whatever the subject matter, for its linguistic expression he remained largely within the ban of the traditional school of Epic. His faithfulness to the manner and matter of oral poetry becomes less surprising if we reflect that Greece had remained illiterate until less than half a century before Archilochus's birth, and that no more than half a dozen specimens of writing can be dated to the first quarter of the seventh century. The most rapid survey of the fragments of his poetry suffices to show that Archilochus, too, whether by formal training or otherwise, had absorbed the poetical culture of the traditional school. A great many fragments which have survived derive their sentiments ready-made from Homer and the expression is a structure of re-used blocks from the epics. A good illustration is Fr. 7 Diehl:

> κήδεα μὲν στονόεντα, Περίκλεες, οὔτε τις ἀστῶν
> μεμφόμενος θαλίῃς τέρψεται οὐδὲ πόλις·
> τοίους γὰρ κατὰ κῦμα πολυφλοίσβοιο θαλάσσης
> ἔκλυσεν.

'Mourning grievous misfortunes, O Pericles, none of the citizens will have delight in feasting nor the city either, for such are those whom surge of the roaring sea has whelmed.'

κήδεα στονόεντα is taken from 1 12; for θαλίηις τέρψεται compare τέρπεται ἐν θαλίηις λ 603; and πολυφλοίσβοιο θαλάσσης is a familiar Epic formula.

More original in sentiment and vernacular in expression is Fr. 5 A D. with the theme 'We may be on guard, but that is no reason for staying sober'.

ἀλλ' ἄγε σὺν κώθωνι θοῆς διὰ σέλματα νηός
φοίτα καὶ κοίλων πώματ' ἄφελκε κάδων.
ἄγρει δ' οἶνον ἐρυθρὸν ἀπὸ τρυγός· οὐδὲ γὰρ ἡμεῖς
νήφειν ἐν φυλακῇ τῇδε δυνησόμεθα.

'Come now, with your cup stride through the benches of the swift ship and wrench the lids from the hollow jars and take red wine down to the lees; for neither shall we be able to stay sober on this watch.'

We must first single out the technical vocabulary: κώθων is a cup used by men on campaign; κάδος, of which this is the first occurrence, is a wine jar but here provided with a formulaic epithet—κοίλων 'hollow', just as the ship is θοῆς 'swift'. The phrase ἀπὸ τρυγός 'off the lees' must surely mean 'down to the dregs'. The imperatives raise a problem: φοίτα normally has a frequentative meaning 'go often, habitually, etc.'; ἄφελκε 'drag off' is seemingly a violent word in this context, but Linear B provides a more humdrum derivative from this root in *poro-eketerija* = *prohelktēriā*, which appears to mean 'ladle'; ἄγρει in Homer is merely exclamatory, serving to introduce another imperative, but ἀγρέω is simply the ordinary Aeolic word equivalent to Attic αἱρέω 'take'. There may be one simple explanation of all these phenomena: violence of expression is everywhere a mark of colloquial and vulgar speech, so perhaps in φοιτάω 'go', ἀφέλκω 'prise off', ἀγρέω 'take' Archilochus is consciously turning his back on traditional vocabulary and drawing on *Kraftausdrücke* from contemporary vocabulary.

With the ἴαμβοι (comprising iambic and trochaic metres) we should expect to encounter not merely a different metre but also a different genre. Iambic verse is certainly of venerable antiquity. It was associated with, and possibly originated in, the ritual of the cults of Dionysos and Demeter, ingredients of which were mockery and insult. Proverbs and maxims, too, universal expressions of folk-wisdom, were couched in iambic trimeters. Finally, one of the earliest Greek inscriptions, on the Ischia vase (*c.* 700 B.C.), has a rough iambic trimeter preceding two hexameters. Contrary to what we should expect from the popular associations and the later development of iambic verse, it has been observed as regards the ethos of Archilochus's *iamboi* that 'every note which is struck in the elegiac fragments is struck also in the ἴαμβοι' (K. J. Dover). The same scholar observes that there is little or no linguistic differentiation either. Both alike 'give an epic colouring to a predominantly vernacular phonology and morphology'.[1] D. L. Page concurs that the style and tone do not vary with subject matter: 'it is always a blend of Homeric phrase with modern vocabulary'.[2]

That the older elegists, for all their dependence on Homer, felt that Ionic was the dialect appropriate to their genre, is revealed by a curious fact. They tend to exclude the Aeolic elements detected in the epic dialect although these were admitted by later practitioners. Thus phonological developments exemplified in πίσυρες, ἀργεννός, ἄμμες are absent from Archilochus; he uses ἄν and not κε(ν) (with one exception), genitive plurals in -εων not -άων, dative plurals in -σι and not -εσσι(ν) (e.g οὓς ἔμαρψεν ποσίν 61 Diehl contrasted with its source Φ 564 μάρψῃ ταχέεσσι πόδεσσιν); he avoids infinitives in -μεν, -μεναι, though the papyrus reads νηφεμεν in 5 A D. and unaugmented preterites (except in 117 D. where there is a special effect).

One feature, which is a symptom of great modernity, distinguishes the iamboi from the elegiacs. This is crasis: ὦναξ, κἄνεμον, κἀπί, θἠτέρηι, etc. In one detail Archilochus perhaps shows an aversion to local Ionic peculiarities. Whereas his contemporary Callinus of Ephesus uses κοτ', κως, κοτε, Archilochus has πῆι, πω, που, ποῖον. However, since he also uses ὁκοίην and ὁκοίοισ' (68 Diehl), it may be that his usage reflects the original confinement of the forms with kappa to the words beginning with ὁ-.

Remarkable are a certain number of Atticisms, the presence of which is difficult to explain. One is the phrase ἐν δορί used

---

[1] See *Entretiens sur l'antiquité classique* (Fondation Hardt), 10 (1964), 183–222, at pp. 185 and 183.

[2] *Ibid.* 117–79, at p. 160.

three times in 2 D. (the Ionic form being δουρί), the Attic echo being reinforced in the phrase ἐν δορὶ μέν μοι μᾶζα μεμαγμένη 'in the spear is my bread kneaded', for μᾶζα is included in the *Attic Words* of Moiris. The feminine δέκτρια (15 Diehl) is likewise Attic, contrasting with the epic formations in -τειρα and the Ionic in -τρις; but it is combined with ξείνων, exhibiting the characteristic Ionic phonology. In the *Hymn to Demeter* (119 Diehl) the Attic form κόρη is simply taken over from cult, but the verse also presents the active σέβω, an Attic feature instead of the middle σέβομαι. More striking and inexplicable is the occurrence of three examples of ἄρα in the sense of ἄρα, a usage which is virtually confined to Attic. Yet in 81 Diehl the previous verse contains the Ionic form μοῦνος.

That elegiac poetry in Mainland Greece is an importation from Ionic is shown by the example of Tyrtaeus, a poet of the seventh century B.C., who made a speciality of hortatory themes in a military context, their ostensible aim being to fire and enhearten the Spartans during the stresses of the Messenian Wars. His birthplace is disputed and claims are made for Laconia, Miletus, and Athens. The essential fact is that, whatever his origins, he was active in Sparta, and his poems are addressed to a Spartan audience. Despite this his chosen dialect is Ionian, and his practice has been neatly demonstrated by his adaptation of a passage of Homer (X 71ff., where Priam foresees what awaits him if Hector is killed) to elegiac verse.

> νέῳ δέ τε πάντ' ἐπέοικεν
> ἀρηϊκταμένῳ, δεδαϊγμένῳ ὀξέϊ χαλκῷ,
> κεῖσθαι· πάντα δὲ καλὰ θανόντι περ, ὅττι φανήῃ·
> ἀλλ' ὅτε δὴ πολιόν τε κάρη πολιόν τε γένειον
> αἰδῶ τ' αἰσχύνωσι κύνες κταμένοιο γέροντος,
> τοῦτο δὴ οἴκτιστον πέλεται δειλοῖσι βροτοῖσιν.

Fr. 7 D. 21 ff.

> αἰσχρὸν γὰρ δὴ τοῦτο μετὰ προμάχοισι πεσόντα
> κεῖσθαι πρόσθε νέων ἄνδρα παλαιότερον
> ἤδη λευκὸν ἔχοντα κάρη πολιόν τε γένειον
> θυμὸν ἀποπνείοντ' ἄλκιμον ἐν κονίῃ,
> αἱματόεντ' αἰδοῖα φίλαις ἐν χερσὶν ἔχοντα—
> αἰσχρὰ τά γ' ὀφθαλμοῖς καὶ νεμεσητὸν ἰδεῖν—

καὶ χρόα γυμνωθέντα· νέοισι δὲ πάντ' ἐπέοικεν,
ὄφρ' ἐρατῆς ἥβης ἀγλαὸν ἄνθος ἔχῃ.

'A foul thing is this, that an older man should fall in the van and
lie before the younger, his hairs already white and beard grey,
breathing forth his valiant soul in the dust, holding his bloodied
parts in his hands—a foul thing to the eyes and an affront to the
beholder—and his naked flesh. But all is seemly with a young
man so long as he has the bright bloom of lovely youth.'

In his adaptation of νέῳ δέ τε πάντ' ἐπέοικεν Tyrtaeus is
inhibited by the elegist's avoidance of the peculiarly Homeric
use of τε in combination with other particles (ἀλλά τε, γάρ τε,
καί τε and μέν τε); the omission leaves him with a missing short
syllable, which he supplies by substituting the plural νέοισι δέ;
but this plural chimes awkwardly with the singular subject of
ἔχῃ in the following line. A similar inconsistency occurs in the
parenthetic αἰσχρά ... καὶ νεμεσητόν, an expression which has a
strange origin. Homer always uses νεμεσσητός except in Λ 649
αἰδοῖος νεμεσητὸς ὅ με προέηκε πυθέσθαι 'awesome and prone
to anger is he who sent me forth to inquire'. It looks as though
the word αἰδοῖα in Χ 75, which was Tyrtaeus's direct model, has
also activated in his mind the collocation αἰδοῖος νεμεσητός. But
why did he not say νεμεσητὰ ἰδεῖν with Homeric observance of
the digamma, a licence all the easier because his audience was
Laconian and still possessed this sound in their everyday
speech? This brings out the tyranny of the genre: he conforms
to the practice of the Ionian elegists who were his model. As a
consequence he is forced to use the awkward singular νεμεσητόν
to avoid the hiatus.

Little more need be said about Tyrtaeus's language than that
he wrote elegiacs in the Ionian manner. One detail deserves
mention: his verses contain examples of short-vowel accusative
plurals, which also appear in Hesiod (see above): δημότας 3a, 5,
δεσπότας 5, 4 and κακκείμενος 8, 19 (with Homeric apocope of
κατα- to κατ- and assimilation to κακ-).

The same general statement is true of the elegiacs of Solon,
the Athenian statesman and poet (c. 640/635–c. 561/560 B.C.),
whose verses served political purposes. Like the inventor of the
genre he avoids the non-Ionic constituents of the epic language
such as -αο and κε. In the sole example of the dative plural

-εσσιν, δῆμος δ' ὦδ' ἂν ἄριστα σὺν ἡγεμόνεσσιν ἔποιτο (5, 7),
'so best would the people follow their leader', he follows closely
ἅμ' ἡγεμόνεσσιν ἔποντο M 87. Genitives in -οιο are embedded in
the formulaic flosculi πόντου πολυκύμονος ἀτρυγέτοιο 1, 19,
ἠελίοιο μένος 1, 23, both in a simile of distinctly Homeric
flavour. There are some striking Attic features: while the MSS
waver, the verses quoted in the papyrus containing Aristotle's
Constitution of the Athenians make it likely that Solon used the
characteristic -ρᾱ, -εᾱ and -ιᾱ instead of the Ionic forms with η,
except in words confined to Epic, ἡμετέρᾱ 3, 1, etc. (but
Homeric ὀβριμοπάτρη three lines later in the cultic description
of Pallas Athena containing 'Ιαονίας, ὑπερηφανίαν, etc.). On
the other hand he opts for the traditional case forms like
πολυτέχνεω, 'Αΐδεω, σεῦ, Μουσέων, ἡμέων, etc., even where the
Attic equivalents offered no metrical difficulties. It is, however,
possible that the poems have undergone processes of Ioniciza-
tion. The forms -ευ- for -εο- appear first in Ionic inscriptions
from the fourth century B.C. on. Yet νοεῦμεν 1, 33 and φορεύ-
μενος 1, 45 figure in our texts, as against the Attic forms like
ἀδικοῦσι 3, 22 and κυπρογενοῦς 20.

The poems attributed to Theognis of Dorian Megara, whose
floruit was the middle of the sixth century B.C., are in fact a
collection of elegiac verses and sympotic songs from various
hands, and there appears to be no way of sifting out what is
authentic. The language conforms to the conventions of Ionian
elegy but with greater receptivity to non-Ionic Homerisms. A
few Doricisms have been detected: genitive Εὐρώτᾱ, παιάνων
779, the infinitives φεύγεν 260 and ἦμεν 960. Doric words are
λῆι, 'wishes', 'wants' 299 and μῶσθαι 'covet' 771.

Above it was noted that linguistically little or nothing distinguishes the elegiacs of Archilochus from the 'iamboi'. More
clearly separated are the two genres in Semonides of Amorgos
(second half of the seventh century B.C.) if it is correct to
attribute to him the elegiacs Fr. 29 Diehl (ascribed by Stobaeus
to Simonides) which offer the Aeolic Homerisms ἔειπεν,
γηρασέμεν and ποτί. His iambics adhere closely to the Ionic
dialect (there are no genitives in -οιο, datives in -εσσι, etc.) and,
unlike Archilochus, he uses ὅκου, κοτ(ε), ὅκη, and ὅκως.

Archilochus and Semonides are linked by Lucian (*Pseudol.* 2)
with Hipponax of Ephesus (sixth century B.C.), another writer

of 'iamboi', who gave the iambic trimeter a twist by making
the last foot into a spondee, thus inventing the χωλίαμβος ('lame
iambos'), also called σκάζων ('limping'). His language comes
closer to the everyday speech of the Ionians who had imposed
themselves on a mixed native population with various ethnic
elements such as Lydians, Carians, and Maeonians. Hipponax
betrays some knowledge of Maeonian in Fr. 3:

> ἔβωσε Μαίης παῖδα Κυλλήνης πάλμυν
> Ἑρμῆ κυνάγχα Μηονιστὶ Κανδαῦλα.
> φωρῶν ἑταῖρε, δεῦρό μοι σκαπαρδεῦσαι

'He called upon (ἔβωσε, with Ionic contraction of ἐβόησε) the
son of Maia, the Lord of Cyllene, "O dog-strangling Hermes,
called Kandaulas in Maeonian, Companion of Thieves, come
back me up".'

Here σκαπαρδεύω is evidently a native word having some such
meaning. The Greek epithet κυνάγχα ('dog-strangler') appears
to be a translation of *Kandaulas*, which is open to etymological
interpretation as a compound of *kan*- 'dog' and an *l*-derivative
from the root **dhau*- 'strangle' that is reflected in O. Sl. *daviti*
'strangle'. Another foreign intruder is πάλμυς 'king', this time
from Lydian, as is καύης 'priest', 'soothsayer' (cf. *kaveś* on a
Lydian inscription from Sardis). The last occurs in Fr. 4 Masson
in a verse which gives an idea of the tang of this linguistic hotch-
potch: Κίκων ὁ πανδάλητος ἄμμορος καύης, 'Kikon the broken-
down, luckless priest'. Κίκων is a Thracian ethnic, and two
epithets in the grand manner qualify the Lydian καύης:
πανδάλητος links up with δηλέομαι (cf. φρενοδαλής Aesch. *Eum.*
330), while ἄμμορος is taken straight from Homer.

   Little survives of Hipponax, but indirect light on his language
is thrown by a later imitator, Herondas (of Cos?, third century B.C.), who wrote mimes (μιμίαμβοι) in the same metre
depicting scenes from everyday life.

4. Melic Poetry

SAPPHO AND ALCAEUS

The μέλος was a monodic song accompanied by the flute or
lyre. As a literary genre it came into existence on the island of
Lesbos and so became linked with the local dialect, which has,

on the evidence of extensive papyrus material, been surprisingly well preserved in the manuscript tradition. Sappho uses the vernacular in most of the surviving fragments but certain features of the Epic language appear in some genres. What has been called the 'abnormal' dialect of Sappho appears in pieces which have a celebratory or ceremonial character, such as the epithalamia ('nuptial chamber songs') and wedding songs, the so-called hymeneal poems, in which Sappho's dactylic hexameters of the Epic type occur almost exclusively. The Epic elements are more evenly scattered in the surviving verses of Alcaeus.

We list the chief features of the Lesbian dialect (pp. 60 f.) which appear in the poets. Initial aspirates are lost: the accent recedes as far as possible ('barytonesis'); ε + ε > η (κῆνος, φέρην), ο + ο > ω; ορ/ορ appears for αρ/ρα (βροχέως, στρότος); ο for α also in κόθαρος, μόλθακος, ὀνία for ἀνία; ο is raised to υ, especially before labials (ὔμοι = ὁμοῦ, στύμα = στόμα, ὑπίσσω = ὀπίσω; ερ appears for ρι and ιρ (τέρτος for τρίτος, κέρνατε, Περράμω for Πριάμω). Before the cluster νσ the preceding vowel was diphthongized (ταλανς > τάλαις, λιπονσα > λίποισα, Μονσα > Μοῖσα, ἐλεφαν(τ)ς > ἐλέφαις); note that εἰς before vowels has a real diphthong, which contrasts with ἐς before consonants. The clusters σν and σμ > νν and μμ (σελάννα, ἄμμες, etc.) and ρσ > ρρ (χέρρα). Zeta appears initially (Ζεῦς), but internally the sound is written σδ (νομίσδεται, φροντίσδην; note ζεύξαισα/ ὑπασδεύξαισα). Initial δι- > ζ- in Ζόννυσσον = Διόνυσσον, ζα- = δια-(ζάλεξαι). In ὄππατα = ὄμματα we appear to have an assimilation *-q^wm- > *πμ > ππ. The Aeolic = *q^we- > πε- = appears rarely: πέμπων (genitive), πεμπεβόεια, πήλοι, and the epic forms φῆρα and πέλοντ'. Initial digamma is nowhere written and is also metrically neglected except in the pronouns Ϝοῖσι, Ϝοι, τὸν Ϝόν and Ϝέθεν. The sound was preserved in the dialect before ρ, and the poems present βρόδα, βραδίνοις, Ϝρῆξις (attested for Alcaeus by the grammarian Tryphon, first century B.C.). Internally σϜ > ϜϜ as in ναῦος. In the clusters with liquids and nasals digamma was lost without compensatory lengthening (καλϜος > κάλος, γονϜα > γόνα). Note Lesbian δέρᾱ contrasting with Epic-Ionic ποικιλόδερροι.

In the morphology accusative plurals of the first and second declensions appear as -αις and -οις < -ανς and -ονς, while the datives are regularly -αισι, -οισι (except for the article ταις, τοις). The third declension has the expected -εσσι (ὀππάτεσσι, etc.). The personal pronouns are typically Aeolic, ἄμμες/ἄμμε, ὔμμε, etc., while the double inflexion of τωνδέων is to be compared with Homeric τοίσδε(σ)σι(ν) and the Thessalian τουν-νεουν. The interrogative τίς is declined like an o-stem: τίῳ = τίνι, τίοισιν = τίσιν. Noteworthy are the adverbs in -οι for Attic -ου (πήλοι, ἄλλοι, ὔμοι = ὁμοῦ, ἴψοι = ὑψοῦ), the form τυίδε (for the Linear B evidence, see p. 45), and those in -τα (τότα, πότα, ἀτέρωτα, ἄλλοτα).

In the verb the contracted stems are treated as athematic: κάλημμι, ὄρημμι, πώλενται (third plural of πώλημμι). The infinitive of -κα perfects ends in -ην: τεθνάκην, while the perfect participles have the suffixes -ων/-οισα: ἐκγεγόνων, παρεστάκοισαν. In two instances sigmatic aorists have short-vowel subjunctives: χαλάσσομεν, ἐρύσσομεν (but φαρξώμεθ'). The verb 'to be' has third singular imperfect ἦς.

Characteristic are the prepositions πεδά and ἀπύ, the apocope in ὀν = ἀνά, κάτ and πάρ, and the modal particle κε(ν).

The Homeric elements of Sappho's abnormal 'formal' dialect are the lengthening of the first vowel of ἀθάνατος, genitives in -οιο (Περάμοιο, ἐρχομένοιο), in -αο ('Αΐδαο), the characteristic Old Ionian genitive πόληος, the inflexion of certain names in -ευς ('Αχίλλεα, Πήλεος), and the dative plural παῖσι for παίδεσσι. In the verb we have unaugmented preterites ἀνόρουσε, γέννατο (Aeolicized from Homeric γείνατο), κάτ-θανε, and ἔλε (= εἶλε), and the third plural ἔδοσαν. These are the purely grammatical indicators of the formal style which appear only in Sappho. For their vocabulary both poets draw largely on the rich resources of the Epic language.

The text in its history has evidently been 'Aeolicized' at some stage. This emerges from 'hyperforms' like Αἰολίδαις and Κρονίδαις, which are due to the analogical extension of the relationship πᾶσα : παῖσα (< *πανσα < *pantjə). Other examples of the wrong application of ᾱ : αι are ἐπτόαισεν and μέμναισ'; in μειδιαίσαισ' 'having smiled' the second αι is authentic but the first is not. Conceivably the consonant gemination in κάλημμι, ἀσυννέτημμι come under this heading; forms with single consonant also occur: κάλημι, οἴκημι, etc.

Sappho, Fr. 1 Lobel–Page

> ποικιλόθρον' ἀθανάτ' 'Αφρόδιτα,
> παῖ Δίος δολόπλοκε, λίσσομαί σε,
> μή μ' ἄσαισι μηδ' ὀνίαισι δάμνα,
> πότνια, θῦμον
> ἀλλὰ τυίδ' ἔλθ', αἴ ποτα κἀτέρωτα
> τὰς ἔμας αὔδας ἀίοισα πήλοι
> ἔκλυες, πάτρος δὲ δόμον λίποισα
> χρύσιον ἦλθες
> ἄρμ' ὑπασδεύξαισα...

'Immortal Aphrodite of the ornate thrones
Daughter of Zeus, wile-weaving, I beseech you
Do not subdue with anguish and love-pangs,
Lady, my spirit.
But come here if ever in the past
Hearing my cries from afar
You gave ear and, leaving your father's house,
You came, your golden
Chariot having yoked.'

Alcaeus, Fr. Z2 Lobel–Page

> ἀσυννέτημμι τὼν ἀνέμων στάσιν·
> τὸ μὲν γὰρ ἔνθεν κῦμα κυλίνδεται,
> τὸ δ' ἔνθεν, ἄμμες δ' ὂν τὸ μέσσον
> νᾶϊ φορήμμεθα σὺν μελαίναι
> χείμωνι μόχθεντες μεγάλωι μάλα·
> πὲρ μὲν γὰρ ἄντλος ἰστοπέδαν ἔχει,
> λαῖφος δὲ πὰν ζάδηλον ἤδη,
> καὶ λάκιδες μέγαλαι κὰτ αὖτο.

'I understand not the strife of the winds;
One wave rolls from this side,
Another from that, and we in their midst
Are borne along with the black ship
Toiling in the violent storm.
The bilge covers the masthold,
The whole sail now lets the light through
And there are great rents along it.'

ANACREON

Personal poetry was written in other dialects than Lesbian. Anacreon of Teos (mid sixth century B.C.) took service with Polycrates of Samos and was later invited to Athens by Hipparchus. In addition to 'iamboi' and elegies he wrote lyrics (μέλη) including hymns, love-songs and convivial poetry. Grammatically the language is basically Ionic with a few standard Homerisms (πτερύγεσσι, ὀχάνοιο, δακρυόεσσαν, etc.), but the vocabulary has the unmistakable stamp of the Epic school with its rich store of compound epithets, e.g. χρυσοκόμης, ποικιλο-σαμβάλω, εὐκτίτου in the following poem, allegedly addressed to Sappho (5 D.):

σφαίρῃ δηὖτέ με πορφυρέῃ
βάλλων χρυσοκόμης Ἔρως
νήνι ποικιλοσαμβάλῳ
συμπαίζειν προκαλεῖται·
ἡ δ’, ἐστὶν γὰρ ἀπ’ εὐκτίτου
Λέσβου, τὴν ἐμὴν κόμην,
λευκὴ γάρ, καταμέμφεται,
πρὸς δ’ ἄλλην τινὰ χάσκει.

'Once again with a purple ball striking me
Golden-haired Eros invites me to play
With the girl of the embroidered slipper.
But she, being from well-ordered Lesbos,
Scorns my hair, for it is white,
And gapes after another—a girl.'

Note the contracted νῆνις < νε(ϝ)ηνις; cf. Attic νεᾱνίας.

CORINNA

The lyric poetess Corinna of Tanagra wrote in her native Boeotian dialect on themes of local interest and so was not known to the wider Greek literary world. Our first knowledge of her poems comes in the shape of citations used by writers of Imperial times in illustration of metrical or linguistic points. However, thanks to a Berlin Papyrus found in 1906 we have substantial parts of two of her poems. Her date is disputed: she may have been a contemporary of her more famous fellow-countryman Pindar of Cynoscephalae (see below), but another possibility is the third century B.C.

The chronological point is of importance for orthographical reasons. The Boeotian vowel system underwent important changes which are reflected in inscriptions from the fourth and third centuries B.C. on. The change will be discussed systematically below (pp. 176 f.). Two processes are involved. Certain vowels are raised: ε > ι before vowels (already fifth century), η > ει (c. 400 B.C.). Some diphthongs become monophthongs: αι > η, ει > ι (both c. 400 B.C.), οι > υ, presumably pronounced [ö] (c. 250 B.C.). Boeotian retained the unfronted pronunciation of υ [u] unlike Attic [y] and this came to be represented as ου: δουῖν = δυεῖν, κρατούνι for κρατύνει, Κούπρις for Κύπρις, κρουφάδαν for κρυφάδην. From about the mid third century B.C. a front glide developed after dental stops and λ and ν, and this was written ιου. The effect of these changes appears in such spellings as πήδων for παίδων, κή for καί, ἐλέσθη for ἐλέσθαι, ἔχι for ἔχει, πεντείκοντα and πατείρ for πεντήκοντα and πατήρ, τύ and ὑκτρῶς for τοί and οἰκτρῶς, οὐψόθεν and δάκρου for ὑψόθεν and δάκρυ. If the earlier date for Corinna is accepted, it follows that the text as we know it must have had its Boeotian orthography modernized. The following specimen (1 Page = 4 + 5 Diehl) comes from a poem in which the seer Akraiphes gives the Boeotian river god, Asopus, news of his daughters:

> τᾶν δὲ πήδων τρῖς μὲν ἔχι
> Δεὺς πατείρ, πάντων βασιλεύς,
> τρῖς δὲ πόντω γᾶμε μέδων
> Ποτιδάων, τᾶν δὲ δουῖν
> Φῦβος λέκτρα κρατούνι,
> τὰν δ᾽ ἴαν Μήας ἀγαθὸς
> πῆς Ἑρμᾶς. οὕτω γὰρ Ἔρως
> κὴ Κούπρις πιθέταν, τιὼς
> ἐν δόμως βάντας κρουφάδαν
> κώρας ἐννί᾽ ἐλέσθη.

'Of the daughters Father Zeus, the King of all, has three
And three were wed by Poseidon, ruler of the sea,
Of two Phoebus has mastery of their bed,
One, Hermes, goodly son of Maia (possesses).
For thus did Eros and the Cyprian persuade them,
Going secretly into your house, to take the nine girls.'

5. Choral Poetry

ALCMAN

Sparta in the seventh century B.C. was not the grim, xenophobic, military state of later times, but an aristocratic society of liberal culture, open and receptive to art, music and poetry from abroad. A school of music was founded by Terpander of Lesbos, and we hear of other musicians and poets from Crete, Magna Graecia, Argos and Colophon who were active in Sparta. Nothing has been preserved of the productions of these men, but the earliest work of Spartan poetry that has come down to us was also the work of an immigrant. This was Alcman, who certainly came to Sparta from abroad, and was possibly a Lydian from Sardis, but more probably an Ionian. He flourished in the second half of the seventh century B.C.

His poetry belongs to the genre of choral lyric, which from the beginning was bound up with the cult of the gods and so also became a major component of tragedy (see below). Choral poetry was technically μολπή, that is a combination of music, poetry and dance. It was developed especially among the Dorians, and for this reason Doric became the conventional dialect of this genre. There was an Alexandrian edition of Alcman's poetry, but until 1855 all that was preserved were brief quotations. In that year a papyrus, written probably in the first century A.D., was found which contained about 100 verses of one of his Partheneia, 'Maiden Songs'. The text is evidently a scholarly edition and is provided with accents and other 'prosodies' and notes.

The dialect is 'abstractly' Doric and lacks local Laconian peculiarities. In common with all poets Alcman owes much to Homer. It has been argued that he draws to some extent on the language of Lesbian poetry, and he also shows the influence of the Mainland branch of the Epic school discussed above under Hesiod. The following key features may be singled out. The accentuation in the papyrus is evidently Doric: παῖδα, πάντῶν, γεραίτάτος, etc. The contraction of α plus an e-sound is η and not ᾱ as in Attic-Ionic: ὁρῆς, ποτήσθω, κῆν, κῆπί (= καὶ ἐν, καὶ ἐπί). The nominative plural of the article is ταί; among the personal pronouns distinctive are first plural ἁμές, ἁμέων, ἁμίν,

nominative singular ἐγών, ἐγώνγα, the third singular dative τίν,
etc. The first plural active ending of the verb is -μες, e.g. παρή-
σομες, and that of the third plural active is -ντι, e.g. αἰνέοντι,
ἐντί 'they are'. Further points of verbal morphology are ἦς 'he
was', the infinitive εἶμεν (or ἤμεν), and the participle ἐντ- in
παρέντων; the ξ-aorist ἁρμόξατο and the Doric future φασεῖς
(as against the normal Greek type in δώσω, ἀείσομαι, etc.).

Little that is more narrowly Laconian must be added to this
general Doric physiognomy. One prominent feature of our texts
must be due to the manuscript tradition. This is the late
Laconian θ > σ, as in σιός = θεός, παρσένος = παρθένος, etc.,
for the early inscriptions still regularly show θ, the first example
of σ (ἀνέσηκε) being dated to the beginning of the fourth
century B.C. Another Laconian feature is the comparative
κάρρων < *κάρσσων < κράσσων < *κρατιων, as opposed to
Attic-Ionic κρείττων/κρέσσων < *κρέτιων. On the other hand,
there is no example in Alcman of the characteristic change -σ- >
-h-, as in ἐνικαhε, while digamma is very rarely written in the texts
although this sound was particularly tenacious in Laconian.

Preservation of digamma is too widespread to serve as a sensitive indicator of dialect except negatively to exclude Attic-
Ionic. Though it seldom appears in our texts, it is clear that
Alcman took account of it in an initial position. Intervocalically
the occurrence of contracted forms like ἅλιον and φῶς argues its
loss, so that αὐειρομέναι = ἀϝειρομέναι will come from an Epic
source. On the dual treatment of λϝ, ρϝ, and νϝ (κᾱλόν, κόρα:
δουρί, γούνατα), see below.

That the text of Alcman has been modified, in all probability
by the Alexandrian editors of his works, is suggested by another
phenomenon pointed out by the Swiss scholar Ernst Risch.
Alcman's dialect, though lacking in notable Laconisms, shows
remarkable similarities to the dialect of Cyrene, which was a
colony of Thera (p. 82): notable points of resemblance are
the thematic infinitives in -εν, short-vowel acc. plur. like τὰς
κολοσός and τὸς ἱαρές, with the same phonological change as
occurs in the nominative singular of participles like κοιμαθές.
Add the 'Aeolic' treatment of -νσ- in the participles ἐκοῖσα and
καθάραισα, the change of -λθ-, -λτ- > -νθ-, -ντ-, in ἔνθη, τένται
(< *τέλται < τέλεται). But these are not ancient characteristics of Cyrenian, and so the resemblance cannot be explained

by supposing that Alcman was using a particularly ancient form of Laconian that has been preserved in the dialect of Cyrene. Risch concludes that our text of Alcman does not yield an authentic picture of his dialect but that it was modified by Alexandrian scholars, for whom Cyrene was the nearest Doric city. On the other hand certainly authentic features of his dialect are non-Laconian. Thus the ă of τροπάς is metrically guaranteed. Moreover, though no such authentication secures the short-vowel infinitives in -εν (they could all be replaced by -ην), the fact that later choral poets like Pindar and Bacchylides also have -εν infinitives indicates that this was traditional in the genre and so in all probability goes back to Alcman.

Risch poses the problem of the source and origin of phenomena like Αἴᾱς, τροπᾱ̆ς, and ἀείδεν. Αἴᾱς is an epic name and τροπάς, as we saw (p. 103), actually occurs in Hesiod. In all likelihood Alcman was here drawing on the Mainland literary language, his immediate source being perhaps Tyrtaeus (see p. 111).

A Lesbian source is possible for participles like φέροισα, but the phonological treatment contrasts with Μῶσα, and since there is little or nothing else which is indisputably Lesbian, the -οισα forms in the text are presumably due (see above) to the later editors who held that Alcman was 'constantly Aeolicizing' (συνεχῶς αἰολίζων). More important are the Homerisms, which may be either Ionic or Aeolic. Thus the potential particle appears both as ἄν and as κ' (which may stand for either κε or κᾱ). Alongside the Doric adverbs like ὄκα, ὄκκα and ποκά we also have ποτ', probably ποτ(έ) though Lesbian ποτα is not impossible. Dative plurals end in -σι(ν) and -εσσι (e.g. ἀλκυόνεσσι) for the third declension and in -αισι/-οισι for ā- and o-stems, though the short forms are predominant. In the verb third plural active forms in -ουσιν (ἔχουσιν, εὔδουσιν) are attested besides those in -οντι. There is one example of the -μεναι infinitive: ἔδμεναι. The familiar Aeolic treatment of -sm-, -sn- occurs solely in the name Φαέννα. The adjective κλεννός is likely to be an intrusive false Aeolicism based on κλεινός, for the true Aeolic product of *κλεϝεσνος is κλεεννος. In clusters ending in digamma δουρί and γούνατα must be regarded as Epic forms. As in Homer, all three versions of the preposition 'towards', ποτί/προτί/πρός, occur in Alcman.

Such grammatical abnormalities tend to occur where metre or theme are Heroic (thus D. L. Page). But it is in matters of diction and phraseology that in Alcman as in other poetry the pervasive influence of Epic is most apparent, whether by imitation or wholesale borrowing: e.g. ἵππον παγὸν ἀεθλοφόρον καναχάποδα, cf. Hom. I 123–4 ἵππους πηγοὺς ἀθλοφόρους; ϝέργα πάσον κακὰ μησαμένοι, cf. Hom. ω 199 κακὰ μήσατο ἔργα.

Partheneion (23 Bergk, 1 Diehl = 1 Page, col. ii, 2–14):

> ἔστι τις σιῶν τίσις·
> ὁ δ᾿ ὄλβιος, ὅστις εὔφρων
> ἀμέραν διαπλέκει
> ἄκλαυτος· ἐγὼν δ᾿ ἀείδω
> Ἀγιδῶς τὸ φῶς· ὁρῶ
> ϝ᾿ ὦτ᾿ ἄλιον, ὅνπερ ἄμιν
> Ἀγιδὼ μαρτύρεται
> φαίνην· ἐμὲ δ᾿ οὔτ᾿ ἐπαινῆν
> οὔτε μωμήσθαι νιν ἁ κλεννὰ χοραγὸς
> οὐδ᾿ ἁμῶς ἐῇ. δοκεῖ γὰρ ἤμεν αὔτα
> ἐκπρεπὴς τὼς ὥσπερ αἴ τις
> ἐν βοτοῖς στάσειεν ἵππον
> παγὸν ἀεθλοφόρον καναχάποδα
> τῶν ὑποπετριδίων ὀνείρων.

'There is a vengeance of the gods. Blessed is he who in gladness weaves his day to the end unweeping. I sing of the radiance of Agido. I see her as the sun which Agido summons to shine as our witness. But the illustrious chorus-leader utterly forbids me to praise or blame her; for she thinks she herself is pre-eminent as if one set among the grazing herds a sturdy, thunderhoofed, prize-winning steed, one from wingèd dreams.'

It was Alcman who apparently established the dialect canon for his successors in the genre of choral lyric. First among these are two poets from the colonial world of Magna Graecia— Stesichorus of Himera (632/629–556/553 B.C.) and Ibycus of Rhegium, who was born in the first half of the sixth century B.C. and was active at the court of the tyrant Polycrates of Samos (538–522 B.C.). Little has survived of their work but the dialect shows much the same mixture of Doric, Lesbian, Aeolic and

Epic. That a gradual watering-down of the Doric element with a corresponding increase in epicisms took place in the development of choral lyric has been made clear by siting Stesichorus and Ibycus in their chronological position between the Mainland poets Alcman and Pindar. The two island Ionians Simonides and Bacchylides will be considered separately below.

PINDAR

Pindar of Cynocephalae near Thebes in Boeotia (518–438 B.C.) was the greatest of the writers of Greek choral lyrics. He came of a well-connected family and as a youth was sent to Athens. He became a professional poet of international reputation with patrons throughout the Greek world—Thessaly, Aegina, Athens, Magna Graecia, Rhodes and Cyrene. He wrote religious poetry, processional songs (προσόδια), maiden songs, encomia, dirges, and songs celebrating victories in the games (ἐπινίκια). Only the last have survived complete, but enough has been preserved of the other works to show that the epinicia may be taken as representative of the whole.

What is characteristic of the language of choral epic has emerged from the study of Alcman. Its essential feature is what we may call its polymorphism: the poetic repertoire includes a number of alternative dialect forms on which he may draw at his convenience for particular effects (see below). In view of certain recent theories, to be discussed at the end of this section, the point must be made that this is an artificial language, modelled on the first literary language of the Greeks, the Epic language, towards which it gravitated in the course of its development. This emerges clearly from a study of certain diagnostic alternative forms.

In Homer the conditional particle εἰ occurs over four times more often than αἰ, which is confined to the combinations αἴ κεν, αἰ γάρ and αἴθε. Whereas εἰ is never used by Alcman, it is the sole choice of Simonides. In Pindar and Bacchylides αἰ rarely appears, but Stesichorus and Ibycus remained close to the practice of Alcman. Of the three Epic alternatives ποτί/προτί/πρός the last becomes increasingly dominant over the combined figures of the first two in the progression Iliad, Odyssey, Hesiod and Homeric Hymns. After Homer προτί drops out from the literary language (it is conjectured once in Alcman but the weight of the evidence favours ποτί). Stesichorus has a number of examples of ποτί including the compound ποταύδη (also with Doric αε > η) but only one certain occurrence of πρός. The figures for Ibycus are too small to be of significance (ποτί and πρός once each), but in Pindar πρός is two to three times more frequent than ποτί.

The dative plurals -οισι/-ησι versus -οις/-αις provide another valuable indicator. In Homer the longer forms are predominant and this is also true of Hesiod, despite a considerable increase (especially in the *Works and Days*) in the proportion of shorter forms. In choral lyric, despite the fact that the Doric dialects on the whole have the shorter forms, the disyllabic endings occur in great abundance. In Alcman and Stesichorus they still outnumber the shorter forms. Ibycus is exceptional, for with him the shorter (presumably epichoric) forms are now preponderant, the disyllabic type occurring in prepositional phrases of the pattern ῥοδέοισιν ἐν ἄνθεσι. In Pindar about 56 per cent of the clear examples are short forms.

A similar progression emerges from the figures relating to the alternative typified by καλός/κᾰλός. Alcman and Stesichorus still remain faithful to Epic in their large preponderance of forms with compensatory lengthening, but Pindar has some 70 per cent of the short-vowel forms (always κᾰλός).

It is in the use of the potential particles by the choral lyricists that the strength of the Homeric tradition and the insulation from the local dialects is most apparent. There is no example in this genre of the characteristic Doric κᾱ, but both κε(ν) and ἄν occur. Stesichorus has a 'free Homerism' in that he ventures εὖτέ κεν though in the Epic only the combination εὖτ' ἄν is found. As in Homer, κε(ν) outnumbers ἄν in all representatives with the exception of Bacchylides. Increasing dilution of the Doric element is shown in the use of the alternative forms of the temporal adverbs typified by ὅτε/ὅκα. The Doric forms predominate in Alcman, while Stesichorus and Ibycus use them even in adaptations of Homeric material. On the other hand only -τε forms are used by Pindar, Simonides and Bacchylides.

The next feature to be considered involves the possibility of three dialect alternatives: the type example is the third plural active endings -οντι (Doric)/-ουσι (Ionic)/-οισι (Lesbian). The material from the earlier lyricists is meagre but both forms are attested for Alcman, and he is the first of the choral lyricists to present analogous forms in the aorist participles -σαις and -σαισα. There is a clear difference between Pindar, who prefers Doric forms, and Bacchylides, with whom they are extremely rare.

The Aeolic alternative with -οισ- < *-ons- recurs in the present participle -οισα < *-ontjə and in the dative plural of -nt- stems -οισι < *-ont-si. It is a peculiar fact that Alcman's text, Doric in character though it is, constantly offers the Aeolic participles in -οισα, and the same is true of Stesichorus. Here again we find a sharp contrast between Pindar with whom -οισα greatly predominates and Bacchylides, who has only one such form. How restricted this phonological Aeolicism is in the whole of choral lyric is shown by its non-occurrence in dative plurals and in the word πᾶσα < *pant-jə. The different poets vary in their choice of form for the 'Muse'. Alcman keeps to the Doric Μῶσα whereas Pindar prefers the Aeolic Μοῖσα, once again in contrast to Bacchylides for whom Ionic Μοῦσα is overwhelmingly attested.

One point must be made in connection with the 'Ionicisms' of the choral lyricists. There is in fact no Ionic feature which is not also Epic. In other words, the Ionian features should be ascribed to the influence of Epic. This is brought out by Bacchylides' use of unaugmented preterites. He is the only poet in the genre with whom such forms predominate, as they do in Homer (about 60 per cent). They occur in all choral lyrics from Alcman on, but their proportion increases progressively in the order Stesichorus, Ibycus, Pindar and Simonides. In the observance and non-observance of initial digamma, too, the example of Epic is unmistakable. Once again Bacchylides represents the culmination of a general tendency. His practice reveals that he was simply, at his convenience, availing himself of certain metrical licences founded in the Epic tradition. This is no less true of Pindar who, despite the fact that digamma was preserved in the Boeotian of his day, freely makes his choice between ϝιδεῖν/ἰδεῖν, ϝάναξ/ἄναξ, etc.

If the influence of Epic made itself increasingly felt in the minutiae of phonology and morphology, the flesh and blood of poetry, vocabulary and phraseology remained overwhelmingly Homeric. There remains this limited but curiously persistent Aeolic, or rather Lesbian, colouring. Pindar strengthens this to some extent, for he is the first of the choral lyricists to add aorist participles in -σαις and -σαισα to those in -οισα, etc. Was this done haphazardly or was there some hidden effect in the choice between the alternatives? That Lesbianisms were a conscious poetical device is suggested by *Pythian* II, which is outstanding in Pindar's work for its Aeolic colouring. It is an oddity that the best MS presents ἐν τ' ἄρματα although elsewhere we have ἀφ' ἀρμάτων, etc. This points to a source in a psilotic dialect. The spelling λακτισδέμεν (with an Epic infinitive form) again points to Lesbian, and this is consistent with the patronymic ὦ Δεινο-μένειε παῖ 'O son of Deinomenes'. This archaism is, of course, common Aeolic, but Pindar normally uses the genitive of the father's name. The Lesbian connection is stronger in ἀλλά νιν ὕβρις εἰς αὐάταν ὑπεράφανον / ὦρσεν, 'But Hybris drove him into arrogant delusion '(l. 28). Not only is αὐάταν a Lesbian form but the diction is clearly a reminiscence of Alcaeus...τάν τις 'Ολυμπίων / ἔνωρσε, δᾶμον εἰς αὐάταν ἄγων '(civil strife) which one of the Olympians has sent, leading the folk to blind folly'. Yet another Aeolic form occurs in εἰνάλιον πόνον ἐχοίσας βαθὺ σκευᾶς ἑτέρας 'while the rest of the tackle has labour in the sea deep down' (ll. 79–80). Yet in general the poem has the same Doric character as the other odes: dative plural in -οις (e.g. στεφάνοις), -αις (χορδαῖς), third plural active in -οντι (τελέθοντι) with epicisms like ὅταν (contrasting with Lesbian ὅτα κε). Why then these echoes of Lesbian poetry, which were apparently deliberate? They will have had some point and purpose to which the poet obscurely alludes in the passage (67–71) 'This song is sent over the grey sea like Phoenician merchandise...τὸ Καστόρειον δ' ἐν Αἰολίδεσσι χορδαῖς θέλων / ἄθρησον χάριν ἑπτακτύπου / φόρμιγγος ἀντό-μενος 'this Castor song on Aeolian strings regard kindly for the sake of the seven-toned lute when you receive it'. What Pindar may be saying is that as a good Dorian Hieron of Syracuse (whose victory is being celebrated) will expect a good Spartan martial song (the Καστόρειον is said to be a Spartan war tune) but that what is sent has been given an Aeolic twist. *Pythian* IV is outstanding among Pindar's work not only for its size but also for the great proportion of the whole devoted to myth, for the bulk of the poem treats of the voyage of the Argonauts. Here Pindar demonstrates the lyric treatment of an Epic theme, and

in language this is among the most Homeric of his poems. Thus
it is no accident that he here used aorist forms in -ας instead of
the Aeolic -αις (καταβάς 22, παπτήνας 295 and ἀπούρας 149),
the first two actually occurring in Homeric quotations with
Ionic η in the second, while ἀπούρας is a well-known Epic
Aeolicism (= ἀπό-ϝρας).

From what is Pindar's outstanding masterpiece (*Pythian* IV)
we choose our illustrative specimen (188–98):

ἐς δ' Ἰαολκὸν ἐπεὶ κατέβα ναυτᾶν ἄωτος,
λέξατο πάντας ἐπαινήσαις Ἰάσων. καί ῥά οἱ
μάντις ὀρνίχεσσι καὶ κλά-
    ροισι θεοπροπέων ἱεροῖς
Μόψος ἄμβασε στρατὸν πρόφρων· ἐπεὶ δ' ἐμβόλου
κρέμασαν ἀγκύρας ὕπερθεν,
χρυσέαν χείρεσσι λαβὼν φιάλαν
ἀρχὸς ἐν πρύμνᾳ πατέρ' Οὐρανιδᾶν ἐγ-
χεικέραυνον Ζῆνα, καὶ ὠκυπόρους
κυμάτων ῥιπὰς ἀνέμους τ' ἐκάλει νύ-
κτας τε καὶ πόντου κελεύθους
ἄματά τ' εὔφρονα καὶ φιλίαν νόστοιο μοῖραν.
ἐκ νεφέων δέ οἱ ἀντάϋσε βροντᾶς αἴσιον
φθέγμα· λαμπραὶ δ' ἦλθον ἀκτῖ-
    νες στεροπᾶς ἀπορηγνύμεναι.

'And when that flower of seafarers had come to Iolcus, Jason
reviewed them all and approved them. And the seer Mopsus,
prophesying from birds and holy lots, embarked the host with
glad heart. And when they had hung the anchors above the
ram, their leader, taking in his hands a golden cup, at the stern
called upon bolt-hurling Zeus, father of the Ouranidae, and the
thrust of the waves and winds that speed voyage and the nights
and the paths of the sea and fair days and sweet portion of safe
return. And from the clouds a propitious peal of thunder roared
in reply to him, and bright came the lightning flashes bursting
forth.'

SIMONIDES AND BACCHYLIDES

Pindar, because of his genius and the sheer bulk of his surviving
poetry, is of particular importance in showing what Doric,
Epic and Aeolic colouring was regarded as appropriate for the

genre of choral lyric. Simonides (born *c.* 556 B.C.) and his
nephew Bacchylides (*flor.* 467 B.C.), both Ionians from Ceos,
mark a turning-point. In their choral poetry they are content to
make a formal bow to the established convention that the Doric
dialect is proper to the genre. In limiting their Doric in the main
to a few standard features they anticipate the practice of the
Attic tragedians in their choral odes. These are the use of ᾱ for
η, the genitive of the *ā*-declensions, i.e. singular -ᾱ and plural
-ᾶν, and the accusative of the third personal pronoun νιν. Apart
from these there are isolated Doricisms such as τίν 'to thee',
some third plural active endings in -οντι, infinitives in -εν and
aorists in -ξα from dental stems. Of the now familiar Aeolicisms
like Μοῖσα and κλεεννός enough will have been said. Doubtless
of Lesbian origin is the imperative ἕλλᾱθι 'be gracious' < *se-
slā-dhi* with Aeolic psilosis, λλ < *sl*, and retention of ᾱ (which
here is analogical). Further Aeolicisms are the athematic forms
ἐπαίνημι and δίνηντο. The standard Homerisms make their
appearance: genitives in -οιο, datives in -εσσι(ν), aorists in
-σσαι, omission of the augment, infinitives in -μεν/-μεναι, and
the particle κε(ν). Epic also is the compensatory lengthening in
ξεῖνος, μοῦνος, κᾱλός, and ἷσος.

The practice of the two Ionian poets marks the establishment
of an elaborate and artificial pan-Hellenic literary Doric,
bound up with the genre of choral lyric, devoid of provincial-
isms, its dialect colouring reduced to a few salient features, a
kind of rough linguistic make-up which suffices to give the
general impression of Doric. The artificiality emerges from a
single word in the above passage of Pindar: ὀρνίχεσσι has an
Epic-Aeolic inflection added to a Doric stem ὀρνιχ-. In the same
line we have two different datives for the *o*-stems: κλάροισι...
ἱεροῖς. Later the genitive νόστοιο consorts with πόντου.

It is *a priori* probable that poets were active in all Greek
communities and that there was a Mainland stream of tradition
at least partly independent of that which led to the Homeric
Epic, so that the poetry of Alcman and his successors in the
genre of choral lyric may well have incorporated 'heirlooms
from its own ancestry'.[1] Recently attempts have been made to
remove this question from the realm of pure speculation and to
discount the unmistakably Doric components of choral lyric as

[1] D. L. Page, *Alcman*, 133.

later accretions. In his attempt to show that Alcman was heir
to a traditional language going back to a North Greek Mainland source, the Russian scholar N. S. Grinbaum has examined
a key feature of all Greek literary language discussed above,
namely the nominal compounds. Pindar is particularly prolific,
300 of the examples occurring first in his odes, while others are
attested only in Homeric proper names. Further, certain verbal
stems which occur as the first element in some Pindaric compounds are not found in Homer but appear in the Linear B
texts. The Mycenaean inscriptions also present compounds
which appear for the first time, or uniquely, in Pindar. From
his comparison of the Pindaric material with the Homeric
proper names and their Linear B analogues Grinbaum concludes that, at least in the domain of the nominal compounds,
choral lyric preserved, along with the common tradition, its own
peculiar tradition which goes back to the Mycenaean Age and
possibly even further.

This is largely an *argumentum e silentio*. By chosen examples it is
possible to link the Homeric Epic language directly with
Linear B. Thus Λαέρτης < *Lawo-er-tā* preserves in the second
component the verbal root *er-* which is attested only in
Hesychius ἔρετο, ὠρήθη, etc. This was replaced by the extended
forms ἐρέθω and ἐρεθίζω. Thus *Laertes* means 'he who urges on
the folk'. The same combination of elements in a different type
of compound occurs in the Linear B name *etirawo* = *Ertilāwos*
(p. 36). A number of observations may be made. First, proper
names often preserve elements that have passed out of ordinary
use: second, the available components may be combined freely
within a few types of nominal composition, so that at any time
new compounds may be created by any poet. Thus Stesichorus
coins δακέθυμος (cf. Hom. θυμοδακής) and περσέπτολις (cf.
Hom. πτολίπορθον); third, the absence of a given element or
given combinations from Homer does not mean that they were
not used in the Homeric Epic tradition. It must not be for-
gotten that these poets could draw on a fund of traditional Epic
poetry besides the Iliad and Odyssey. For instance, Ibycus uses
ξειναπάτας 'deceiving one's host' with reference to Paris. We
now know that this word was used earlier by Alcaeus in a
similar connection, but from the Ionic form of the first component we may be sure that the ultimate source was Epic

hexameter poetry unknown to us. If we add to these uncertainties the notorious hazards in securely identifying
Linear B proper names, it will be evident that the comparisons
adduced are too slight and uncertain to support the new
thesis.

What tells further against it is the progressive creativity
evinced in the successive choral lyricists. If they were drawing
on non-Homeric sources of compounds, we might reasonably
expect that this Mainland material would be more prominent
in the early poets and would be progressively diluted with the
acknowledged growing supremacy of the Homeric school of
Epic, as has just been demonstrated by the gradual reduction of
the Doric characteristics. But precisely the opposite is the case.
It is the latest poets who show the largest proportion of non-
Homeric creations in their compounds: with Pindar it is 65 per
cent and with Bacchylides 55 per cent. The earlier poets are
content to take the majority of their compounds ready-made
from Homer, many of them in the same collocations as Homer.
But even their new compounds are often simply new combinations of familiar elements.

The long-accepted conclusion must stand. Choral lyric
resembles Epic and the personal lyrics of the Lesbian poets in
employing a linguistic medium which is not the vernacular of
any Greek community but an artificial composite language
with conventions of its own. These languages are varieties of
literary formal dress: in Epic the warp was Ionic, in the
Lesbian poets the Aeolic of their island, in choral lyric a neutral
pan-Doric, but all three warps were woven through with other
dialect threads.

6. Tragedy

The literary genres considered hitherto originated and flourished
on the one hand in the colonial world of Ionia and Lesbos and
on the other in the Dorian Peloponnese and its colonies to the
west. With tragedy we turn to a genre which reached its fullest
flowering in Athens. Yet its composite origin is linguistically
evident at first glance. There is a clear distinction between the
Attic of the spoken parts, in iambic trimeters, and the Doric
colouring of the choruses. The origin of tragedy, perhaps the
greatest and most enduring creation of Greek literary genius, is

a disputed question, but there seems no really cogent reason for not accepting, at least in outline, Aristotle's account.

The chorus was originally the heart of the matter. Tragedy originated in cult songs sung by performers playing the part of satyrs and dressed as goats (hence τραγῳδία 'goat song' < τράγος 'he-goat'). Such songs, of an orgiastic character, were sung in honour of the god Dionysus and were known as 'dithyrambs'. The Greek word διθύραμβος resembles θρίαμβος, which was also a song sung in honour of Dionysus, and ἴαμβος. All three words, which have a similar morphology, are technical words from the semantic sphere of song and dance. They are in all probability foreign loan-words in Greek, and the first two were conceivably introduced along with the worship of Dionysus which (according to W. K. C. Guthrie, *The Greeks and their Gods*, 31) 'descended upon Greece from Thrace in post-Homeric times as a foreign intrusion'.[1]

According to Herodotus (I. 23) the development of the dithyramb to a distinct literary genre was the work of the poet Arion, who was active at the court of Periander of Corinth (c. 628–625 B.C.) though he came from Lesbos. It is to be noted that the Corinthian choirs whom he trained to perform his compositions were dressed up as satyrs. The dithyramb was later introduced to Athens and became a subject for competition at the festivals of Dionysus. According to Aristotle, the germ of the non-choral element of tragedy is to be sought in the ἐξάρχοντες, those who 'gave the lead' to the choir in the performance of the dithyramb. The word ἐξάρχειν occurs along with the earliest example of the word διθύραμβος: Archilochus (fr. 77 Diehl) boasts that in his cups he has the gift of starting up (ἐξάρξαι) the lovely song of Dionysus. It is conceivable that this 'leader' explained the subjects of the successive songs for the benefit of the audience. It was the Athenian Thespis who was given the credit for inventing the prologue and spoken parts (ῥῆσις), which were all the more necessary when complex stories from myth and saga provided the theme of dithyrambs.

The next stage, we may surmise, was the introduction of dialogue between this speaker and the chorus leader. It was Thespis who is recorded as being the first to present a tragedy at

---

[1] This was written before the decipherment of Linear B, but the occurrence of *diwonuso(jo)* on fragmentary Pylian tablets is difficult to evaluate.

the Great Dionysia in Athens in the 61st Olympiad (536/35–
533/32 B.C.). Aeschylus introduced a second actor, and he also
curtailed the choral odes, giving predominance to the spoken
parts. Sophocles increased the actors to three. As for the plots,
according to Aristotle they were originally short and the language
facetious, but they achieved dignity at a later stage, once
tragedy had grown out of its 'Satyr' origins. It was at this stage
that iambics were substituted for trochaic tetrameters, the latter
being a metre appropriate to the 'satyric' and to dancing. It
was nature herself who hit upon the appropriate metre once
dialogue had developed. For the iambic measure is the one most
appropriate to speaking, as can be seen from the fact that in
ordinary conversation we (i.e. Greeks of Aristotle's time) fall
into iambics more frequently than we do into hexameters.

Given such a complex origin, we should expect the dialogue
parts of tragedy to be couched in Attic and the choral lyrics in
Doric. At first glance this seems to be the case. In fact (the
point must be made at once) Attic tragedy is through and
through Attic in dialect, both in the iambics and the choral
parts, with only a slight admixture of Doric, Epic and Aeolic
elements, mostly belonging to the general poetic language. As
Gudmund Björck (*Das Alpha Impurum*, 181) has written, 'On the
orchestra speech had to be Attic, in metrical form of course, and
stylistically ennobled and enriched.'

We may emphasize that in the choruses, where the genre
demanded Doric colouring, the Doric elements are even more
restricted than in Simonides and Bacchylides (see above). The
main stylistic colour is the use of ᾱ, but even this appears only
in a small basic stock of fixed Doric elements, such as νίκα,
ἄγον, μᾱτηρ, τλᾱ-, φᾱμᾱ and δᾱμο-. Alternation ᾱ/η between
lyrics and dialogue is regular where the word in question formed
part of the Attic vocabulary. Curiously, ᾱ is shunned in compounds and derivatives (e.g. ἀνήκουστος and πανσέληνος), and
this is true of other non-Attic elements (e.g. πτόλις is admitted
but not *πτολίτης). But Atticisms like γῆρυς, ἡδύς and ἦμαρ
occur in choral parts in all three of the major tragedians. We
even find hybrids like φήμᾱ, πηγᾱ and μηχανᾱ, and these high-
light the essentially conventional and decorative nature of the
literary Doricisms: the ᾱ-colouring persists mainly at the end of
the word. On the other hand it is curious to find certain per-

sistent Doricisms. Thus ἕκατι is solely Doric (Homer has ἕκητι), yet it occurs no fewer than forty-one times in dialogue in all three tragedians. Apart from ᾱ the more noticeable Doric features are the genitive singulars in -ᾱ and plurals in -ᾶν, the pronoun νιν and the occasional -ξα aorist of -ζω verbs, and even these might be Homerisms. A single line τιμῆς ὀχυρὸν ζεῦγος Ἀτρειδᾶν (Aesch. *Ag.* 44) shows how conventional and artificial such touches of Doric were. The Aeolic features are few in number and are not direct borrowings from Lesbian personal lyrics but confined to elements which had become part of the general poetic language: e.g. the preposition πεδά in πεδάρσιος, πεδαίρω and the characteristic phonology in words like φαεννός.

Epic elements, occurring mostly in choral odes and in anapaests, are 1, absence of contraction as in ἀείρω, ἀείδω, φάος, and also in material adjectives in -εος, the declension of s-stems, etc.; 2, compensatory lengthening in ξεῖνος, μοῦνος, etc. (see further below for differences in the usage of the three tragedians); 3, metrical lengthening in εἰν, εἰνάλιος, etc.; 4, the case-endings -οιο, -εσσι; 5, personal pronouns ἐμέθεν, ἄμμι, etc.; 6, in the verb the inflexions -ν (for -σαν, see below for Euripides), and first plural -μεσθα; 7, the infinitive ἔμμεν; 8, aorists like ἤλυθον, ἐπιπλόμενος, ἐκέκλετο, etc.; 9, omission of the augment; 10, optatives in -οίατο, -αίατο; 11, comparatives ἀρείων, βέλτερος, μάσσων.

A peculiarity common to all the great tragedians is that Homerisms are particularly frequent in messenger speeches, which is not surprising, seeing that these are in effect spoken arias in the genre of Epic narrative. But Homer is also drawn on with telling effect when other dramatic occasions call for elevated diction. A wonderful example is Clytaemnestra's reply (Aesch. *Ag.* 1551–9) when asked by the chorus who will deliver the funeral laudation over the husband she has just murdered. She retorts 'Iphigeneia the daughter he sacrificed'.

οὐ σὲ προσήκει τὸ μέλημ' ἀλέγειν
τοῦτο· πρὸς ἡμῶν
κάππεσε, κάτθανε, καὶ καταθάψομεν
οὐχ ὑπὸ κλαυθμῶν τῶν ἐξ οἴκων
ἀλλ' Ἰφιγένειά νιν ἀσπασίως

θυγάτηρ, ὡς χρή,
πατέρ' ἀντιάσασα πρὸς ὠκύπορον
πόρθμευμ' ἀχέων
περὶ χεῖρε βαλοῦσα φιλήσει.

'It is no concern of yours to take thought for this duty. At our hands he fell, he died, and we shall bury him, not with lamentations of the household, but Iphigenia, his daughter, as is right, with fond welcome meeting her father at the swift ferry of woe, putting her arms about him, will kiss him.'

Aeschylus is the only tragedian to use the Homeric ἀλέγειν 'care for'; κάππεσε and κάτθανε are both Homeric verbs with apocope of the preposition; κλαυθμός 'wailing' is an epic word and ἀσπασίως an Homeric adverb, both occurring in tragedy only in this passage. Finally περὶ χεῖρε βαλοῦσα is an hexameter ending and clearly a reminiscence of λ 211, where Odysseus vainly attempts to embrace his mother's shade.

So far we have been mainly concerned with grammatical features (phonology and morphology) as dialect pointers, and it is evident that Greek writers consciously applied them as touches of colour appropriate to the different genres. But, as Antoine Meillet stressed (*Aperçu*, 130), the creation of a literary language means almost everywhere the creation of a vocabulary. Aristotle has some sapient and pertinent observations on the practice of Greek poets in their choice of words which amounts to a concise theory of poetic diction. A fundamental distinction is drawn between colloquial and prose speech on the one hand and poetry on the other. Poetic diction is remote from, and raised above, the language of everyday life. What is dignified, elevated and 'remote' is σεμνός. Dionysus in *The Frogs* of Aristophanes (1604) addresses Aeschylus as 'the first who towered up lofty words' πρῶτος...πυργώσας ῥήματα σεμνά. Aristotle, in prescribing the means of achieving such dignity, in fact applies Tacitus's dictum *omne ignotum pro magnifico*. Men feel about words as they do about their fellow men: strangers are more admired than their fellow citizens. So to give dignity to literary diction we must alter the vocabulary of ordinary speech. This will be achieved (while preserving the necessary clarity) by lengthening and shortening and otherwise altering the form of words. Important, too, is the use of ξένα, 'foreign words' drawn from non-Attic dialects. This he demonstrates by substituting the ordinary words μικρός, ἀσθενικός and ἀειδής for ὀλίγος 'small', οὐτιδανός 'worthless', 'feeble' and ἀεικής 'unseemly' in the Homeric line (ι 515) νῦν δέ μ' ἐὼν ὀλίγος τε καὶ οὐτιδανὸς καὶ ἀεικής. The technical term for such a 'foreign' word is γλῶττα, the everyday term being κύριον, and its technical definition is that it is a word used in other regions. Thus σίγυνον was κύριον to the Cypriots but a γλῶττα to the Athenians. Everything that is 'alien' (ξενικόν) and out of the ordinary contributes to the dignity and elevation (σεμνότης) of style. Aristotle, as a good scientist, doubtless based his generalizations on a study of the practice of the tragedians. In the following list of equivalents the first words of the pairs come from normal prose: ἀνήρ/πόσις 'husband', γυνή/δάμαρ 'wife', υἱός/γόνος 'son', ἀδελφός/ὅμαιμος 'brother', σῶμα/δέμας 'body', οἰκία/δόμος 'house', βαδίζειν/στείχειν 'walk', ὁρᾶν/λεύσσειν 'see', ἀκούειν/κλύειν 'hear', σφόδρα/κάρτα 'extremely', στῆθος/στέρνον 'breast'. For the non-present forms of the verb 'to go' tragedy uses a verb which has dropped out of Attic (except in a transferred sense μέλλω 'I am going to...'): ἔμολον, μολεῖν.

Aristotle chose a Cypriot word to exemplify his definition of a γλῶττα, but the main source of poetical expressions was of course the Homeric Epic. But what appear to be dialect words may have been borrowed by the poets from Epic sources unknown to us. This point has already been made with reference to the supposed Arcado-Cypriot elements in Homer. Eduard Fraenkel underlines this apropos of the word ἀνδρολέτειρα 'man destroyer' (Aesch. Ag. 1456): 'The word shows that the vocabulary of Aeschylus in its bolder coinages is sometimes indebted to the language of post-Homeric Epic, a fact for which there is every now and then direct evidence [ἀνδρολέτειρα occurs in an Epic fragment, applied to the Amazon Melanippe], though far more often we have to infer it from what we find in later poets.' Again, the verb θρέομαι, which occurs only in Aeschylus and Euripides, has the Ionic form θρεῦμαι in Aesch. Sept. 28, and this fact 'would suggest that Aeschylus took over the word from the language of (post-Homeric) Epic, to which he seems to be indebted to a large extent.' It may be added at this point that the greater part of the Ionicisms in the language of tragedy is in all probability to be credited to such Epic sources. It was doubtless to the Homeric model that Greek high poetical language owes its most pronounced feature: the abundance of compound words. Aristotle remarks (1459 a) that 'double' (διπλᾶ) words are most suited to the dithyramb. If this is so, then tragedy is true to its supposed dithyrambic origins, for it abounds in compound words. In his effective coinages Aeschylus is supreme. Typical is *Ag.* 146–55:

> ἰήϊον δὲ καλέω Παιᾶνα,
> μή τινας ἀντιπνόους Δαναοῖς χρονί-
> ας ἐχενῇιδας ἀπλοίας
> τεύξῃ σπευδομένα θυσίαν ἑτέ-
> ραν ἄνομόν τιν᾽ ἄδαιτον,
> νεικέων τέκτονα σύμφυτον οὐ δεισ-
> ήνορα· μίμνει γὰρ φοβερὰ παλίνορτος
> οἰκονόμος δολία μνάμων Μῆνις τεκνόποινος.

'I call upon Apollo the Healer
that she [Artemis] shall not contrive for the Greeks
counterblowing, delaying, ship-detaining non-sailings,
bent on another sacrifice, lawless with no feasting,
not husband-fearing; for there
abides a terrible, ever-arising, cunning
housekeeper, an unforgetting child-avenging Wrath.'

Besides 'foreign' elements and compounds there are other pervasive features of tragic diction, the study of which has revealed interesting differences in the practice of the three main tragedians. As an example we may take the word πόρθμευμα 'ferry' in the passage quoted above (p. 134) from the *Agamemnon* of Aeschylus. This word occurs only here and evidently obeys Aristotle's injunction for alteration of the everyday word, which is πορθμός. This device of substituting an abstract in -μα (for the formation see p. 252) for the familiar word is widely used in tragedy. What is notable is that though this type of formation was evidently abundantly used in Old Attic, it is rather rare in Thucydides, while later Attic prose, particularly oratory, uses such forms even less. On the other hand it is extremely frequent in Ionic prose of a technical character. A possible explanation of this peculiar Attic development is that tragedy at an early stage drew on these Old Attic neologisms as ξένα. As a con-

sequence they became in Athens invested with the aura of high
poetry and so unsuitable to sober prose.

In this usage of the -μα nouns Aeschylus and Euripides are
opposed to Sophocles. Their new coinages greatly outnumber
those of Sophocles (134, 134, 48). Further, while Aeschylus and
Euripides often use a -μα formation as an alternative to the more
common word, Sophocles prefers to employ them in periphrastic phrases, e.g. βουκόλων φρουρήματα 'guard objects of
herdsmen' = 'herds'. This is a favourite device of his elevated
poetic style: it occurs in lyric and also gives colour to ornate
spoken passages, such as the messenger speeches. In general
Sophocles' language abounds in abstract nouns. A counterfoil
to -μα formations (which in the main express the result of an
action) are those in -σις which are action nouns. These developed
in the Ionian writers of the late sixth and early fifth century
B.C. But there is little evidence of this in Attic even as late as the
middle of the fifth century, and these new technical words are
rare in Aeschylus. Sophocles, however, was much involved in
the intellectual development of his time. A symptom of this is
the fact that the -σις nouns are more frequent in his latest plays:
all but three of the fourteen -σις nouns peculiar to Sophocles
occur in the *Philoctetes* and the *Oedipus Coloneus*. He also leans
towards the new -σιμος adjectives, which were a development of
philosophical and technical literature. There is in fact a clear
stylistic distinction in Sophocles between the -σις and the -μα
nouns: the former are rare in lyric, are not used with compound adjectives or in elevated contexts and the periphrases
have a prosaic character. With -μα it is precisely the opposite.
But it should not be thought that the -σις nouns have a 'prosaic'
character in Sophocles. On the contrary, his practice conforms
to the Aristotelian injunction that common words should be
altered. Consequently he draws on Ionian prose for forms such
as give variety and distinction to his language: e.g. οἴκησις,
ἐλευθέρωσις, δόκησις, etc. An illuminating example is ἄλγησις
in *Philoctetes* 792 with reference to the hero's suppurating foot.
The only other instance of the word reveals its high tragic tone:
it is used by Aristophanes in a parody of the poet Agathon. In
much the same way -μα formations are used by Sophocles to
give dignity to everyday things. A good illustration is the string
of -μα nouns in the list of the household effects (in the cave!) of

the hero (35–7): ἔκπωμα, τεχνήματα, θησαύρισμα. The last word is similarly used by Euripides in a passage with accumulation of -μα nouns: βοσκήματα 'herds' (νεογνὸν) θρέμμα 'lamb', τυρεύματα 'cheeses', θησαύρισμα (*El.* 494–7).

Study of the use of abstract nouns thus leads to a paradoxical conclusion. Scholars have observed that in his latest plays Sophocles approximates more and more to the style that 'seems spontaneous and natural' (A. A. Long, 1968). Such new words as he coins are generally simpler and there is less recourse to metaphor and simile. But such simplicity does not mean closeness to everyday speech. The increased use of abstracts is one of the means whereby the everyday expression is kept at a distance and elevation of style (σεμνότης) is achieved. If we must turn to Thucydides and the technical writers to find a comparable liking for -σις nouns, this is not because Sophocles was aiming at an effect of intellectual modernity. The clue is given by the language of Aristophanes: only a few such stock words had been admitted to everyday speech. For Sophocles (and his audience) these formations, precisely because of their rarity in the colloquial language and Attic prose of his day, could function as ξένα and so contribute to the elevation and distinction of style which Sophocles consistently cultivates. Yet the ease and grace, clarity and smooth elegance of his style are given force and piquancy by discreet rhetoric. An example is offered by the exchange between Neoptolemus and Philoctetes, culminating in a sustained condemnation of evil, hammered home by repetition of the word κακός (*Philoctetes*, 1360–1, 1367–72).

> οἷς γὰρ ἡ γνώμη κακῶν
> μήτηρ γένηται, πάντα παιδεύει κακούς
> ...εἶτα τοῖσδε σὺ
> εἰ ξυμμαχήσων, κἄμ' ἀναγκάζεις τάδε;
> μὴ δῆτα, τέκνον· ἀλλά μ', ὃ ξυνήνεσας,
> πέμψον πρὸς οἴκους· καὐτὸς ἐν Σκύρῳ μένων
> ἔα κακῶς αὐτοὺς ἀπόλλυσθαι κακούς.
> χοὕτω διπλῆν μὲν ἐξ ἐμοῦ κτήσῃ χάριν,
> διπλῆν δὲ πατρός. κοὐ κακοὺς ἐπωφελῶν
> δόξεις ὅμοιος τοῖς κακοῖς πεφυκέναι.

'Those whose mind becomes the mother of wicked things bring up children who are in all things wicked.... Then will you ally

yourself with these [who robbed you of your father's accoutre-
ments] and compel me to do these things? Do not do this, child,
but as you promised, send me to my home. And you yourself
staying in Scyrus, leave wicked men to perish miserably. And in
this way you will earn double thanks from me and double from
your father. And you will not by helping the wicked seem to
have yourself a nature like the wicked.'

Above we drew attention to a feature which unites Aeschylus
and Euripides in opposition to Sophocles. To this we may add
the use of the Ionicisms μοῦνος, ξεῖνος and πολλός. These are
avoided in dialogue by Aeschylus and Euripides whereas
Sophocles admits them as convenient alternative forms. It is
also curious that Aeschylus and Euripides use the Homeric form
πτόλις as a simple noun and in compounds. The sole πτόλις
form which occurs in the text of Sophocles is the compound
ἀγχίπτολις (*Ant.* 970), and there it is only a variant for ἀγχί-
πολις, which is rightly preferred by some editors.

It hardly need be said that despite their common use of
certain linguistic features the styles of Aeschylus and Euripides
are poles apart. This is particularly so in dialogue. Aristotle
(*Rhet.* II 42, 1404) comments that one of the ways of concealing art is to draw on the vocabulary of everyday life, and he
adds that in this Euripides was the first of the dramatists to show
the way. A similar point was made by Dionysius of Halicarnassus (*de imitatione*, p. 206 Usener–Radermacher): Euripides
took delight in truth and closeness to contemporary life. In his
style he chose the middle of the road: it was neither elevated nor
plain. But even in the dialogue parts Euripides uses what is
clearly an artificial literary language: there are merely touches
and splashes of modernity. Only in this sense is it true to say
that he approximated to the language of everyday life. In his
morphology, too, there are modern features. Thus he uses
ἔθηκαν, ἧκαν and ἔδωκαν, whereas the two older dramatists have
ἔθεσαν and ἔδοσαν. Similar are the imperatives ἔστωσαν,
ἴτωσαν, whereas Aeschylus and Sophocles use the forms in
-ντων. On the other hand, the dative plural of the *ā*-stems
presents a puzzle: -αισι is normal in all three tragedians despite
the fact that, with few exceptions, -ᾱσι/-ησι appears in the
inscriptions until *c.* 420 B.C., after which -αις predominates both

inscriptionally and in prose. This touch of modernity is avoided by Euripides.

In the lyrics, where the genre demanded an elaborate and highly coloured language, Euripides avoids the heavy accumulation of epithets which he ridicules in his description of Aeschylus (Ar. *Frogs*, 837–9) as ἄνθρωπον ἀγριοποιὸν αὐθαδό-στομον, ἔχοντ' ἀχάλινον ἀκρατὲς ἀπύλωτον στόμα...κομπο-φακελορρήμονα 'a man, creator of savages, stubborn-mouthed, having a mouth unbridled, intemperate and ungated...empty-bundle-worded'. Precisely in their employment of the ubiquitous compound adjectives there is a pronounced difference between Aeschylus and Euripides. In the latter we miss the bold, the obscurely allusive, but dramatically pregnant, creations of his predecessor. His own new coinages, abundant though they are, lack originality in that they are mostly new combinations of a comparatively small stock of old elements. Yet precisely this transparency contributes to the ease and comprehensibility of ordinary language. How successful Euripides was in his coinages can be gauged from the fact that over 55 per cent of them were used by his successors. Among those who borrowed from his lyrics are not only poets like Aristophanes or the Orphic poets, Lycophron, Apollonius Rhodius, the poets of the Anthology and Nonnus, but also prose writers like Xenophon, Plato, Aristotle, Lucian and Plutarch.

The approximation to ordinary language even in his lyrics is revealed by statistical analysis. Whereas Aeschylus (and Pindar) use a vocabulary which is almost wholly σεμνός, consisting of purely poetical words, it has been calculated that the lyrics of Euripides contain over forty per cent of words shared with ordinary Greek prose. Of the poetical words Epic supplies the largest share, and this might well be increased if we knew more of the lost Epic sources. It has been conjectured that Euripides' Homerisms are in the main those which had passed into the general poetic language and had lost their full Epic flavour. In all this we sense deliberate artistic purpose. Public taste had outgrown what had come to be felt as the archaic dithyrambic bombast of his great predecessor, and Euripides strove to replace it by a more natural and less obscure mode of lyrical expression. In this way he progressed towards what was a necessity for a tragic poet in the late fifth century B.C.: a clear and moderate style which, while respecting the rules of the genre, made it easy for the audience to follow what was being said and done on the stage.

Even so, the arias and monodies which he composed for performance by the actors, thereby reducing the part allotted to the chorus, have a strongly emotional character, with the result that the gap between the spoken and the sung constituents of his plays is greater than in all the other tragedians. What is particularly characteristic of his style is the unrelenting use of rhetorical devices: in this respect he was the product of the Sophistic school (see below). This, more than anything else, separates Euripides' style from the dignity and nobility of Sophocles. How Aristophanes assessed their merit emerges clearly from the *Frogs*: in Pluto's world Aeschylus yielded to Sophocles a place on his bardic throne.

V

THE LITERARY LANGUAGES: PROSE

1. Herodotus and Early Ionic Prose

It is a curious fact of Greek literary history that although a number of highly elaborate poetical languages were evolved at an early date, there is no example of artistic prose before the second half of the fifth century and, in the case of Attica, none until towards its end. That prose was used for practical purposes even in the Mycenaean Age has been revealed by the Linear B inscriptions (see Chapter II); but here, too, it is significant that in all likelihood, as we have argued, this language was of a formal and stereotyped character which had to be learned by the Palace scribes as part of their administrative training. But all this was lost with the destruction of the palaces and long centuries of illiteracy ensued. Even after the introduction of the alphabet in the eighth century B.C. (pp. 201 ff.) it seems likely that for long the Greek states relied not on written records but on specially gifted and trained 'remembrancers' for recording matters and events of public importance, both sacred and secular, for that is the meaning of the word for such recorders— μνήμονες, ἱερομνήμονες.

This feature of Greek civilization is in striking contrast to the habits of its neighbours in Egypt and the Orient. As far as we know there was in Mycenaean times no counterpart to the boastful public records of the exploits of the Egyptian Pharaohs. Even in the alphabetic period 'No early chronicles of events, even in the briefest form, have yet been found in any Greek state.'[1] The Epic language, largely the creation of Ionia, remained firmly established as the natural medium of formal expression even for such pedestrian themes as astronomy, navigation and agriculture. Yet it was again to the Ionians that the Greeks were indebted for another major literary break-through—the creation of the first fully-developed prose style. The gift was two-fold: 1, a mature instrument of scientific

[1] L. H. Jeffery, *The Local Scripts of Archaic Greece*, 21.

analysis and exposition and 2, a rich and sensitive artistic prose such as we find in Herodotus. The Ionians, in close symbiosis with the ancient civilizations of the Orient, learned their empirical sciences such as astronomy and geometry, but gave them that abstract and conceptual form which is the hallmark of the Greek mind. These new sciences found the traditional language of poetry inadequate for their needs. The Muse was forced to descend from her carriage and learn pedestrian ways. The speed of advance must have been remarkable: whereas no epigraphic evidence exists even for the inscribing of name-lists earlier than the sixth century B.C., by the middle of the fifth century a technical prose had been hammered out, adequate for the expression of the precise observations and the abstract theorizing of the scientific treatise (the *hypomnēma*).

This we find fully developed, and in great variety and abundance, in the writings preserved under the name of Hippocrates of Cos, the Father of Medicine (469–399 B.C.). The Corpus Hippocraticum, a collection of medical writings which may go back to the library of a school of medicine, spans a full century (*c.* 440–340 B.C.). The very sparseness and sobriety of the language conceal the long effort required to devise a scientific terminology and style which met the needs of anatomy, surgery, diseases and their treatment, climatology and much else. The works subserve a variety of purposes ranging from technical jottings to lectures for lay audiences. The former have no stylistic pretensions, as can be seen from the specimen taken from *Epidemics* (I, 13–14).

Ἐν Θάσῳ πρὸ ἀρκτούρου ὀλίγον καὶ ἐπ' ἀρκτούρου ὕδατα πολλὰ μεγάλα ἐν βορείοις. περὶ δὲ ἰσημερίην καὶ μέχρι πληϊάδος νότια ὕσματα ὀλίγα. Χειμὼν βόρειος, αὐχμοί, ψύχεα, πνεύματα μεγάλα, χιόνες. περὶ δὲ ἰσημερίην χειμῶνες μέγιστοι...ἐν τῇ καταστάσει ταύτῃ κατὰ χειμῶνα μὲν ἤρξαντο παραπληγίαι καὶ πολλοῖσιν ἐγίνοντο, καί τινες αὐτῶν ἔθνησκον διὰ ταχέων. καὶ γὰρ ἄλλως τὸ νόσημα ἐπίδημον ἦν. τὰ δὲ ἄλλα διετέλεον ἄνοσοι.

'In Thasos, shortly before and during Arcturus, many violent rain-storms with northerly winds. About the equinox and until the (setting of) the Pleiades light southerly rains. Winter northerly, droughts, frosts, strong winds, falls of snow. About the equinox violent storms.... In this climate ('constitution')

during winter one-sided paralyses began and many were
affected and some quickly died. In fact, in general the disease
was epidemic. But in other respects they continued free from
sickness.'

Of greater literary interest are two works assignable to the
second half of the fifth century. One deals with the 'environments' (*On Winds, Waters and Places*) and discusses their effects
on healthy and sick persons.

XXIV, 41-52

ὅκου δ' ἐστὶν ἡ χώρη ψιλή τε καὶ ἄνυδρος καὶ τρηχεῖα καὶ ὑπὸ τοῦ
χειμῶνος πιεζομένη καὶ ὑπὸ τοῦ ἡλίου κεκαυμένη, ἐνταῦθα δὲ
σκληρούς τε καὶ ἰσχνοὺς καὶ διηρθρωμένους καὶ ἐντόνους καὶ
δασέας ἴδοις. τό τε ἐργατικὸν ἐνεὸν ἐν τῇ φύσει τῇ τοιαύτῃ καὶ τὸ
ἄγρυπνον, τά τε ἤθεα καὶ τὰς ὀργὰς αὐθάδεας καὶ ἰδιογνώμονας,
τοῦ τε ἀγρίου μᾶλλον μετέχοντας ἢ τοῦ ἡμέρου, ἔς τε τὰς τέχνας
ὀξυτέρους τε καὶ συνετωτέρους καὶ τὰ πολέμια ἀμείνους εὑρήσεις.
καὶ τἆλλα ἐν τῇ γῇ φυόμενα πάντα ἀκόλουθα ἐόντα τῇ γῇ. αἱ μὲν
ἐναντιώταται φύσιές τε καὶ ἰδέαι ἔχουσιν οὕτως. ἀπὸ δὲ τούτων
τεκμαιρόμενος τὰ λοιπὰ ἐνθυμεῖσθαι καὶ οὐχ ἁμαρτήσῃ.

'But where the country is bare and waterless and rough and
suffers from the winter cold and is burnt by the (summer) sun,
there you will see hard, lean, well-knit, taut and hairy men. In
such natures you will find energy and vigilance, men stubborn
and independent in character and temper, with a greater part of
wildness than tameness, sharper and cleverer in practical crafts
and better in war. And whatever grows in the earth likewise
conforms to the earth. Such is the case with the most sharply
opposed natures and kinds. On the evidence of these things draw
your conclusions as regards the rest, and you will not go astray.'

Noteworthy in the passage are the abstract expressions
formed by prefixing the definite article to the neuter of an
adjective (e.g. τὸ ἐργατικόν 'energy'). This was one of the
essential mechanisms of the intellectual revolution. Nominaliza-
tions are the tools of abstract thought: the intellectual is a
nominalizer. Attention may also be drawn to a non-linguistic
point which will recur later in discussing the Sophists: this is the
scientific method of inferring from evidence (τεκμαιρόμενος <

τεκμήρια 'evidence'). The Ionic dialect was also used by the historiographers who, in the new spirit of empirical enquiry (ἱστορίη) tried to assemble basic historical and geographical facts. Hecataeus of Miletus, who as an elderly man was active in the Ionian Revolt (500–494 B.C.), wrote *Genealogiai*, a rationalistic account, the first of its kind, of the pedigrees of old families including his own. He was also a pioneer in the *Periegesis* 'a tour of the world', which is mentioned by Herodotus (IV, 36) as γῆς περίοδος. In this work he seems to have created a scheme of remarkable tenacity which still persists in certain passages of Thucydides. Little survives of the work of Hecataeus and the few connected passages present a bare and unadorned style.

Ὀρεσθεὺς ὁ Δευκαλίωνος ἦλθεν εἰς Αἰτωλίαν ἐπὶ βασιλείᾳ καὶ κύων αὐτοῦ στέλεχος ἔτεκε. καὶ ὃς ἐκέλευεν αὐτὸ κατορυχθῆναι καὶ ἐξ αὐτοῦ ἔφυ ἄμπελος πολυστάφυλος. διὸ καὶ τὸν αὐτοῦ παῖδα Φύτιον ἐκάλεσε. τούτου δ' Οἰνεὺς ἐγένετο, κληθεὶς ἀπὸ τῶν ἀμπέλων (οἱ γὰρ παλαιοί...Ἕλληνες οἴνας ἐκάλουν τὰς ἀμπέλους). (FHG I F15)

'Orestheus, son of Deucalion, came to Aetolia in search of a kingdom, and his bitch bave birth to a log. And he ordered it to be buried and from it grew a vine with many bunches. Hence he called his son Phytius. Of him Oineus was begotten called after the vines (for the ancient Hellenes...called vines *oinai*).'

This specimen supports the judgment of the ancient critics who spoke of his style as being pure, precise, clear and lacking in ornament and less poetical than Herodotus. Our text has evidently been Atticized (Αἰτωλίαν for -ίην, βασιλείᾳ for -ηίῃ, αὐτοῦ for ἑωυτοῦ and ἐκάλουν for -εον). Hecataeus is also stated to have written an 'unmixed' type of Ionic (ἀκράτῳ Ἰάδι καὶ οὐ μεμιγμένη) as contrasted with the variegated (ποικίλη) dialect of Herodotus.

Herodotus was born just before Xerxes' invasion of Greece (480 B.C.) and he lived till after the outbreak of the Peloponnesian War (431 B.C.). His family had Carian affinities (his father Lyxes and his uncle Panyassis both bore Carian names), but his birthplace was Halicarnassus which had been a Dorian colony and had passed into the possession of the Ionians. After a period of exile as a young man in Samos, extensive travels took him to Egypt and thence via Phoenicia down the Euphrates to Babylon. On other occasions he visited the North Aegean and Scythia. These travels of 'sightseeing' (θεωρίη) provided him with the geographical and ethnological material which he incorporated in his great 'History', the central theme of which was the age-old struggle between Europe and Asia that culminated in the Persian Wars. His boundless curiosity and cosmopolitan outlook are reflected in the foreign words which he picked up in the course of his travels: Egyptian (πίρωμις = καλὸς κἀγαθός 'gentleman', κυλλῆστις a kind of bread, καλάσιρις a garment), Persian (ἀγγαρήϊον posting system, ὀροσάγγαι 'benefactors of the King', ἀκινάκης a short sword), Medic (σπάκα 'dog'), Scythian (ἄσχυ, a kind of fruit juice), Libyan (ʒεγέριες corresponding in meaning to Greek βουνός 'a hill', but applied to a species of mouse) and Phrygian (βέκος 'bread'). He also shows knowledge of technical terms from the Greek dialects. Thus he quotes γαμόροι as the Syracusan word for wealthy landholders, ἱπποβόται as the wealthy class of Chalcis, and he knows that in Achaea Phthiotis the council-chamber or town hall was called λήϊτον (Attic πρυτανεῖον).

More important are the Atticisms, for they reflect a lengthy stay in Athens which was decisive in his development. There he enjoyed the friendship of Sophocles and entered into the stimulating intellectual and artistic life of the Periclean Age. He participated in the settlement of the Panhellenic colony Thurii, organized by the Athenian statesman, and it is not without significance that one of his fellow-colonists was the Sophist Pythagoras, who was commissioned by Pericles to draw up a code of laws. It is in the later historical part of his work where Athens appears as the hero of the resistance to the Persian aggression that a distinct difference of vocabulary has been detected. Attic vernacular source is claimed for such words as καραδοκέω 'wait expectantly', δωροδοκέω 'take a bribe', and ἐπ᾽ αὐτοφώρῳ '(catch) red-handed'. The influence of tragedy is noticeable in such words as δειματόω 'frighten' and δράμημα 'running', 'course'. An Attic technical expression of law is ἀπολογέομαι 'speak in defence', and of seamanship ὀκέλλω 'put into land', with compounds ἐποκέλλω and ἐξοκέλλω (Homer uses κέλλω and ἐπικέλλω).

For the description of the lands and peoples encountered by

the Persians in their imperialist expansion Herodotus uses the plain unadorned style of his predecessors in the genre of the *periegesis*. But for the variety of human themes which his greater subject encompassed he evolved a linguistic instrument of great range and sensitivity. What gives his work its particular charm is its rich store of folk-tales told in an artless style in which participial phrases cluster round the simple syntactical structure of the central theme of the sentence. A good example is the story of an ugly duckling of a girl who is miraculously transformed into the most beautiful woman in Sparta.

VI. 61. 2–5.

τούτῳ τῷ ἀνδρὶ ἐτύγχανε ἐοῦσα γυνὴ καλλίστη μακρῷ τῶν ἐν Σπάρτῃ γυναικῶν, καὶ ταῦτα μέντοι καλλίστη ἐξ αἰσχίστης γενομένη. ἐοῦσαν γάρ μιν τὸ εἶδος φλαύρην ἡ τροφὸς αὐτῆς, οἷα ἀνθρώπων τε ὀλβίων θυγατέρα καὶ δυσειδέα ἐοῦσαν, πρὸς δὲ καὶ ὁρῶσα τοὺς γονέας συμφορὴν τὸ εἶδος αὐτῆς ποιευμένους, ταῦτα ἕκαστα μαθοῦσα ἐπιφράζεται τοιάδε· ἐφόρεε αὐτὴν ἀνὰ πᾶσαν ἡμέρην ἐς τὸ τῆς Ἑλένης ἱρόν...ὅκως δὲ ἐνείκειε ἡ τροφός, πρός τε τὤγαλμα ἵστα καὶ ἐλίσσετο τὴν θεὸν ἀπαλλάξαι τῆς δυσμορφίης τὸ παιδίον. καὶ δή κοτε ἀπιούσῃ ἐκ τοῦ ἱροῦ τῇ τροφῷ γυναῖκα λέγεται ἐπιφανῆναι, ἐπιφανεῖσαν δὲ ἐπερέσθαι μιν ὅτι φέρει ἐν τῇ ἀγκάλῃ, καὶ τὴν φράσαι ὡς παιδίον φορέει. τὴν δὲ κελεῦσαί οἱ δέξαι, τὴν δὲ οὐ φάναι. ἀπειρῆσθαι γάρ οἱ ἐκ τῶν γειναμένων μηδενὶ ἐπιδεικνύναι. τὴν δὲ πάντως ἑωυτῇ κελεύειν ἐπιδέξαι. ὁρῶσαν δὲ τὴν γυναῖκα περὶ πολλοῦ ποιευμένην ἰδέσθαι, οὕτω δὴ τὴν τροφὸν δέξαι τὸ παιδίον. τὴν δὲ καταψῶσαν τοῦ παιδίου τὴν κεφαλὴν εἶπαι ὡς καλλιστεύσει πασέων τῶν ἐν Σπάρτῃ γυναικῶν. ἀπὸ μὲν δὴ ταύτης τῆς ἡμέρης μεταπεσεῖν τὸ εἶδος. γαμέει δέ μιν ἐς γάμου ὥρην ἀπικομένην Ἄγητος ὁ Ἀλκείδεω.

'This man happened to have as wife by far the most beautiful of the women of Sparta—strange to say having become the most beautiful from being the ugliest. Her nurse, seeing that the child was not much to look at, in view of the fact that the ill-favoured child was the daughter of well-to-do parents who thought her looks were a disaster, realizing all this, she hit on the following idea. She carried the child every day into the shrine of Helen. And whenever the nurse so carried her, she would set her in front of the statue and would beseech the goddess to take away her ugliness. And one day when the nurse was leaving the shrine, the story is that a woman appeared, and having so appeared she asked her what she was carrying in her arms. And she said she was carrying a child. And the woman told her to show it to her, but the nurse refused saying that she had orders not to show it to anyone. But the woman kept on insisting that she should show it, and the nurse seeing that the woman set great store on seeing it consequently showed her the child. And the woman stroking the child's head said that she would become the most beautiful woman in Sparta. And from that very day her appearance was transformed. And when she came to the age of marriage Agetus, son of Alceides, married her.'

Characteristic of the 'strung-along' (εἰρομένη) style of the logographers is the device of linking clauses and sentences by repeating key words, e.g. ἐπιφανῆναι, ἐπιφανεῖσαν δὲ....The story of the beautiful wife of Kandaules (I. 8) begins in the same way: οὗτος δὴ ὦν ὁ Κανδαύλης ἠράσθη τῆς ἑωυτοῦ γυναικός, ἐρασθεὶς δὲ ἐνόμιζέ οἱ εἶναι γυναῖκα πολλὸν πασέων καλλίστην. ὥστε δὲ ταῦτα νομίζων.... 'Now this Kandaules was in love with his own wife and being in love he thought his wife was by far the most beautiful of all women. And thinking thus...'.

Difficult to pin down is the unmistakable Homeric flavour of these folk-tales. The author of *On the Sublime* numbers Herodotus along with Archilochus, Stesichorus, and Plato as a writer who is ὁμηρικώτατος. It can hardly be a question of vocabulary. In the above story we might pick out ἐπιφράζεται as a verb frequent in Homer which recurs in poetry. But this does not rule out the possibility that it was also current in the Ionic of Herodotus' day. That the spirit of Homer should breathe in the folk-tales would not be unexpected. There is good reason to believe that from time immemorial there existed a fund of folk-tales in prose which delighted the *demos* no less than the hexameter Epic did the nobles in their palaces. No hard and fast line can be drawn between the logopoios and the rhapsode in the sense that the stories and the diction of the Homeric Epics were doubtless familiar not only to the story-teller himself but also to his audiences. The same would have been all the more true of an educated man of good family like Herodotus. In fact Epic reminiscences and phraseology abound in his work. A direct quotation is used in the retort of Syagrus (VII. 159, cf. Hom. H 125) when Gelon of Syracuse insists on the supreme command as a condition for contributing men and ships to resist the Persians: ἤ κε μέγ' οἰμώξειε (ὁ Πελοπίδης 'Αγαμέμων) πυθόμενος Σπαρτιήτας τὴν ἡγεμονίην ἀφαιρῆσθαι ὑπὸ Γέλωνός τε καὶ Συρακοσίων. 'Truly (Agamemnon descendant of Pelops) would groan loudly if he heard that the Spartans had been robbed of the command by Gelon and the Syracusans.' Of unmistakable Homeric and, indeed, Nestorian flavour is the formula with which the old Lydian King Pythius introduces his reply when asked by Xerxes how rich he was (VII. 28): Ὦ βασιλεῦ, οὔτε σε ἀποκρύψω οὔτε σκήψομαι τὸ μὴ εἰδέναι τὴν ἐμεωυτοῦ οὐσίην ἀλλ' ἐπιστάμενός τοι ἀτρεκέως καταλέξω. 'O King, I shall not conceal from you nor shall I pretend that I know not my own wealth, but in full knowledge I shall speak unerringly.'

How subtly and beautifully contrived such Homeric touches are may be illustrated by a phrase which concludes the episode when Cambyses torments the Egyptian king Psammenitos. He bears with fortitude the sight of his daughter enslaved and his son marching to his execution but breaks down when an old comrade passes by. When questioned by Cambyses he replies (III. 14. 10): Ὦ παῖ Κύρου, τὰ μὲν οἰκήια ἦν μέζω κακὰ ἢ ὥστε ἀνακλαίειν, τὸ δὲ τοῦ ἑταίρου πένθος ἄξιον ἦν δακρύων ὃς ἐκ πολλῶν τε καὶ εὐδαιμόνων ἐκπεσὼν ἐς πτωχίην ἀπῖκται ἐπὶ γήραος οὐδῷ. 'O Son of Cyrus, my own personal sufferings were beyond all lamentation but fit for tears were the woes of a friend who from great wealth had fallen into beggary on the threshold of old age.'

Certain grammatical features of the Epic language are also used with self-conscious artistry. Tmesis, for instance, lends solemnity to Amasis' denunciation of his new Cyrenaic wife when he finds that he is impotent with her alone of his harem: Ὦ γύναι, κατά με ἐφάρμαξας... 'Woman, you have bewitched me (...and you must die)'. The iteratives in -σκ- (p. 263) have an interesting distribution which suggests that Herodotus made original and independent use of this Homeric feature. The greatest concentration is found in Book VII which is regarded as the most highly polished part of his History, whereas they are completely absent from Books V and VIII and almost the whole of Books II and III. Instructive is the use of ἔρδεσκε in the sentence describing the sacrilegious acts of the Persian governor of Sestus whom the Greeks punished by nailing him to a plank (VII. 36) : ὃς καὶ ἐς τοῦ Πρωτεσίλεω τὸ ἱρὸν ἐς Ἐλαιοῦντα ἀγινεόμενος γυναῖκας ἀθέμιστα ἔρδεσκε 'who herded women into the temple of Protesileōs at Elaeus and committed lawless acts', where the ritual solemnity of the final phrase is heightened by the use of the Homeric verb ἀγινέω.

We may now turn to the Attic elements. Herodotus leaves us in no doubt of the deep admiration that he felt for Athens (VII. 139): νῦν δὲ Ἀθηναίους ἄν τις λέγων σωτῆρας γενέσθαι τῆς Ἑλλάδος οὐκ ἄν ἁμαρτάνοι τἀληθέος 'Now if a man were to say that the Athenians were the saviours of Greece, he would not miss the truth.' The Attic elements of his vocabulary have been discussed above. Traces of his influence on Sophocles have been detected, particularly in the *Oedipus Tyrannus*. The influence of the dramatist on the historian is more difficult to prove. That it is apparent in the new moral outlook of the folk-tale is intangible and in any case beyond the scope of this book. As for the suggestion that he was influenced by the language of tragic dialogue, this is also difficult to establish since so little survives of tragedy before 435 B.C.

What is inescapable is the effect on the historian of the new intellectual climate which the Sophists had created in Periclean Athens. This will be discussed more fully in the next section when studying the language of Thucydides. Their influence is reflected in the anachronistic debate (a formal ἀγών) by the three Persians on the merits of the three constitutions, democracy, aristocracy and monarchy. The first speech (III. 80) starts by a destructive survey of the evils of tyranny and then focuses on the key features of Athenian democracy—ἰσονομίη 'equality before the law', appointment to public office by drawing lots, and subsequent accountability of office-holders: πλῆθος δὲ ἄρχον πρῶτα μὲν οὔνομα πάντων κάλλιστον ἔχει, ἰσονομίην. δεύτερα δὲ τούτων τῶν ὁ μούναρχος ποιέει οὐδέν· πάλῳ μὲν ἀρχὰς ἄρχει, ὑπεύθυνον δὲ ἀρχὴν ἔχει, βουλεύματα δὲ πάντα ἐς τὸ κοινὸν ἀναφέρει, 'When the people rules, in the first place it bears the fairest name of all, "equality (before the law)"'; secondly, it does none of the things that monarchs do. Lots are drawn for the public offices, the holders are accountable and all resolutions are submitted to the Commons'. The last sentence has a sophisticated structure. It consists of three clauses (κῶλα, see below) of increasing magnitude (seven, nine and fifteen syllables); the ending of the second echoes that of the first which also has a 'figura etymologica' (ἀρχὰς ἄρχει). Noteworthy, earlier in the speech, is the antithetic parallelism of φθονέει γὰρ τοῖσι ἀρίστοισι περιεοῦσί τε καὶ ζώουσι, χαίρει δὲ τοῖσι κακίστοις τῶν ἀστῶν... '(the tyrant) envies the best men, those that survive and still live, he takes pleasure in the worst of the citizens...'.

A still more elaborate example of sophistic antithesis and parallelism of the κῶλα occurs in the speech of Artabanus (VII. 10 η. 2):

διαβολὴ γάρ ἐστι δεινοτάτη, ἐν τῇ δύο μέν εἰσι οἱ ἀδικέοντες, εἷς δὲ ὁ ἀδικεόμενος. ὁ μὲν γὰρ διαβάλλων ἀδικέει οὐ παρεόντος κατηγορέων, ὁ δὲ ἀδικέει ἀναπειθόμενος πρὶν ἢ ἀτρεκέως ἐκμάθῃ. ὁ δὲ δὴ ἀπεὼν τοῦ λόγου τάδε ἐν αὐτοῖσι ἀδικέεται διαβληθείς τε ὑπὸ τοῦ ἑτέρου καὶ νομισθεὶς πρὸς τοῦ ἑτέρου κακὸς εἶναι.

'Slander is a most terrible thing in that the wrong-doers are two and he who is wronged is one: for the slanderer does wrong by accusing a man who is absent, and the other does wrong by being convinced before he has learnt the full truth. Thus the man absent from the conversation is doubly wronged by them, being slandered by the one and believed by the other to be bad.'

It is no accident that much of the exposition in the last book of the History, which recounts what we may call the *aristeia* of the Athenians, takes the form of speeches. In the negotiations with Gelon of Syracuse the Athenian insists (VII. 161) that they alone of the Greeks are autochthonous. Since this claim was a regular feature of orations at Athens, it can hardly be an accident that Herodotus inserts (VII. 162) in Gelon's reply a figure of speech (...ἀγγέλλοντες τῇ Ἑλλάδι ὅτι ἐκ τοῦ ἐνιαυτοῦ τὸ ἔαρ αὐτῇ ἐξαραίρηται 'announcing to Greece that the spring has been taken from its year') which has a significant echo. In fact this splendid image finds its appropriate place in the funeral oration said to have been delivered by Pericles over the men who had fallen in the Samian War (440 B.C.): ...τὴν νεότητα ἐκ τῆς πόλεως ἀνηρῆσθαι ὥσπερ τὸ ἔαρ ἐκ τοῦ ἐνιαυτοῦ εἰ ἐξαιρεθείη 'the youth has been taken from our city as though the spring had been wrested from the year'. The probability that we have here an authentic echo of early Attic oratory will assume its importance in the next section.

The language of Herodotus has been described as a mosaic to which Homer, the folk-tale, the Sophists, Ionic and Attic contributed. It was perhaps this kaleidoscopic quality that prompted its characterization by the ancient critics as ποικίλη. In its grammatical features the language of Ionian prose is that reflected in the inscriptions (discussed above, pp. 62–4). On numerous points of detail it is difficult to form a judgment since we are at the mercy of the manuscript tradition which presents a medley of forms including pseudo-Ionicisms and hyper-Ionicisms. The details of such inconsistencies and vacillations in the dialect picture are irrelevant to a work of this general character (see Bibliography).

2. Thucydides and Early Attic Prose

The first literary language was the creation of the colonial Greek world. Epic, for all its beginning in the 'Achaean' sphere, had been brought to perfection by the Ionians. Personal lyrics originated in Aeolian Lesbos, while the earliest writer of choral lyrics at Sparta, Alcman, was an immigrant and in all probability an Ionian (see p. 119). Now we have seen how the flourishing Ionian civilization of the eastern colonial world also brought forth a rich and sensitive instrument of literary prose. In 494 B.C., however, Ionia succumbed to the pressure of imperialist Persia, and the intellectual hegemony of the Hellenic world passed to Athens, the saviour of Greece. Yet it was not until towards the end of the fifth century that Thucydides, the author of the first masterpiece of Attic prose, wrote the opening words of his history of the Peloponnesian War. The ancient critics also believed in a late date for the development of artistic Attic prose: they traced its beginnings to the visit of the Sophist Gorgias to Athens in 427 B.C. But there is ample evidence that points to the existence of elaborate techniques long before this date. Curiously enough, this conclusion emerges from a comparison of Thucydides' prose style with certain features of the plays of Sophocles and Euripides, but first it will be necessary to say something about the Sophists, with the main emphasis on points of interest for the history of artistic prose.

The word *sophistēs* originally had the meaning of 'skilled

craftsman' and more generally, 'a sage'. It acquired its deroga-
tory sense 'paid teacher' (in Plato's words, 'paid hunter of the
young') in connection with the itinerant purveyors of 'wisdom'
whose activities were a response to the new developments in the
Greek political world. What the 'Sophists' offered to the sons of
rich and influential Greeks was a practical training in the
management of their own affairs and in the pursuit of political
power. Of outstanding importance in the management and
manipulation of one's fellow men is the power of effective
speaking. It was precisely training in oratory, both forensic and
deliberative, that figured prominently in the wares offered to
their prospective clients. But oratory requires more than skill in
the tricks of the trade. Management of men requires knowledge
of man, and the Sophists offered what was in effect a broad
humane education—a *paideia* aimed at instilling *aretē* 'virtue' in
the sense of an all-round capability. In the Platonic dialogue
named after him Protagoras says (317 b) 'I admit that I am a
Sophist and educate men.' The background to this broad
education was a philosophy of life; in fact the Sophists represent
a turning-point in philosophy in that, unlike the earliest Ionian
philosophers who theorized abstractly and deductively about
nature and the cosmos, they turned their attention to the study
of man in all his aspects. Another Sophist, Prodicus, is quoted
(Plato, *Euthydemus* 305 c) as having sited the best products of
Sophistic education 'on the borderline between a philosopher
and a statesman'.

The first and the most important of the Sophists was Protagoras (*c.* 484–415 B.C.), a native of Abdera, an Ionian colony in
Thrace. His travels as a professional teacher brought him to
Athens at the height of Pericles' power. The great Athenian
statesman showed his confidence and esteem by commissioning
the Sophist to draw up the constitution of the new Panhellenic
colony of Thurii and also entrusting him with the education of
his two sons. Protagoras also seems to have enjoyed the friendship of Euripides, in whose house he is said to have read his
work 'On the Gods', for which he was prosecuted for impiety,
escaping condemnation by flight. In the Athens of his day he
was a well-known personality, thanks to his instruction of the
young and the public lectures he gave. The fascinating personality of Protagoras comes out in Plato's brilliant picture of the

Sophist (*Protagoras*, 314e–315b) as he walks up and down in the portico with pupils on either side and the throng of foreigners behind, 'whom Protagoras gathered from every city he passed through, bewitching them with his voice like Orpheus'.

Of special interest in the present connection is the importance he attached to training his pupils in the techniques of disputation. He held that on any theme it was possible to hold and defend two contradictory positions and he wrote model compositions to demonstrate this. In Plato's *Protagoras* (335a) he tells Socrates that he has engaged in verbal contests (ἀγῶνες λόγων) with many opponents. The popularity and influence of such contests is reflected not only in Herodotus (see above), but also in the plays of Sophocles, Euripides, and Aristophanes. Protagoras' professional thoroughness in training his pupils to make the fullest use of the power of words is suggested by the fact that he not only wrote works on grammar and correctness of diction (ὀρθοέπεια) but gave them a background of humane education including the analysis of poetry.

Unfortunately, very little has survived of Protagoras's own works. Of interest is the passage in which he expressed his admiration of Pericles's fortitude when his two sons were killed within a space of eight days:

τῶν γὰρ υἱέων νεηνιέων ἐόντων καὶ καλῶν ἐν ὀκτὼ δὲ τῇσι πάσῃσι ἡμέρῃσι ἀποθανόντων νηπενθέως ἀνέτλη. εὐδίης γὰρ εἴχετο ἐξ ἧς πολλὸν ὤνητο κατὰ πᾶσαν ἡμέρην εἰς εὐποτμίην καὶ ἀνωδυνίην καὶ τὴν ἐν τοῖς πολλοῖσι δόξαν. πᾶς γάρ τίς μιν ὁρέων τὰ ἑωυτοῦ πένθεα ἐρρωμένως φέροντα μεγαλόφρονά τε καὶ ἀνδρήιον ἐδόκεε εἶναι καὶ ἑωυτοῦ κρέσσω, κάρτα εἰδὼς τὴν ἑωυτοῦ ἐν τοιοῖσδε πράγμασι ἀμηχανίην.

'For when his sons, fine young men, died within the space of eight days, he bore it without grief. For he maintained his serenity, which was of great service to him every day both for his well-being and freedom from pain and for his public esteem. For everyone who saw him steadfastly bearing his sorrows thought him a great-hearted and brave man and better than himself, knowing full well his own helplessness in such a plight.'

The major point to be made is that Protagoras wrote in the Ionic dialect and did not eschew poetical words such as νηπενθέως and εὐδίης in the sense of 'tranquillity' (literally 'fair weather'). Prose still moves within the orbit of poetry. But the history of artistic Attic prose consists precisely in the emancipation from the Ionicizing poetical language and the enfranchisement and ennoblement of the natural speech of Athens. Strangely, it was two immigrant Sophists, one from Sicily and the other from Asia Minor, who rank as the founders of Attic prose.

Gorgias of Leontini seems to have been born c. 483 B.C. and to have lived to be over a hundred years old. In 427, when he led an embassy of his city to Athens, the speech he made astonished and delighted the Athenian assembly by its stylistic novelties. This firmly established his reputation as a public speaker and he was in great demand as a teacher of rhetoric. He was the author of a rhetorical handbook, but this seems to have consisted largely of model speeches, and Aristotle criticizes him for his non-theoretical and unsystematic methods. Some of the passages which have come down to us may come from this handbook: the *Encomium of Helen*, which is a specimen of epideictic oratory, and *The Defence of Palamedes*, which belongs to the genre of forensic oratory. In illustration of his style we quote a passage from his *Epitaphios*, a funeral oration delivered over the Athenian dead:

μαρτύρια δὲ τούτων τρόπαια ἐστήσαντο τῶν πολεμίων, Διὸς μὲν ἀγάλματα, αὑτῶν δὲ ἀναθήματα, οὐκ ἄπειροι οὔτε ἐμφύτου ἄρεος, οὔτε νομίμων ἐρώτων οὔτε ἐνοπλίου ἔριδος οὔτε φιλοκάλου εἰρήνης. σεμνοὶ μὲν πρὸς τοὺς θεοὺς τῷ δικαίῳ, ὅσιοι δὲ πρὸς τοὺς τοκέας τῇ θεραπείᾳ, δίκαιοι μὲν πρὸς τοὺς ἀστοὺς τῷ ἴσῳ, εὐσεβεῖς δὲ πρὸς τοὺς φίλους τῇ πίστει. τοιγαροῦν αὐτῶν ἀποθανόντων ὁ πόθος οὐ συναπέθανεν, ἀλλ᾽ ἀθάνατος ἐν οὐκ ἀθανάτοις σώμασι ζῇ οὐ ζώντων.

'As monuments of these things they set up trophies over the enemy, statues of Zeus, votive offerings of themselves, being not untried in civil strife or lawful passions or armed conflict or refined peace, reverent towards the gods by their righteousness, pious towards their parents by their tendance. Just towards the citizens by their fairness, reverent towards their friends by their trustiness. Therefore, though they are now dead, our yearning did not die with them but deathless it lives on in the undying bodies of them that live not.'

What is characteristic is the breaking-up of the sentence into very short *cōla* and their subdivision into smaller pieces (*kommata*), which are arranged in matching or antithetic pairs or sets, the formal parallelism being contrived often by forced and unnatural combinations of words. The commata become in fact the basic elements of the sentence and their groupings are brought out by all manner of sound effects such as identical length (*parisōsis*) and rhyme (*paromoeōsis*). The diction itself is mannered, pretentious and even outlandish, and his compositions have been rightly called prose dithyrambs. Perhaps this was why Plato, in parody of Gorgias's style (*Symposium* 195a–197e), introduces the poet Agathon, who delivers a speech hitting off Gorgias so exactly that Socrates fears that Agathon was going to end up by sending a 'Gorgias's head' to petrify him into speechlessness. Typical of the dithyrambic eulogy of Eros is the following passage (197d):

οὗτος δὲ ἡμᾶς ἀλλοτριότητος μὲν κενοῖ, οἰκειότητος δὲ πληροῖ, τὰς τοιάσδε συνόδους μετ' ἀλλήλων πάσας τιθεὶς συνιέναι, ἐν ἑορταῖς, ἐν χοροῖς, ἐν θυσίαις γιγνόμενος ἡγεμών, πρᾳότητα μὲν πορίζων, ἀγριότητα δ' ἐξορίζων· φιλόδωρος εὐμενείας, ἄδωρος δυσμενείας.

'He (Eros) rids us of alienations and fills us with fraternization, having established that all such gatherings as the present should come together, being our leader at feasts, at dances, at sacrifices, injecting gentleness, ejecting wildness, open-handed in benevolence, empty-handed in malevolence...'.

Despite their initial success, the Gorgianic mannerisms soon palled, and Aristotle dismisses this poetical style as appealing in his day only to the uneducated, making the point that the style of prose is not the same as that of poetry (*Rhet.* III 1. 9). For effective speaking and writing clarity is the prime virtue, and this demands the natural diction of current speech. Further, to enable the hearer to follow the complex exposition and to grasp it as a whole without losing the thread, not only must the sense of each successive *colon* be immediately apparent, but lucidity will depend on making clear the part each one plays in the syntactical structure of the whole sentence.

It was another Sophist immigrant to Athens, Thrasymachus

of Chalcedon, a colony of Megara on the Asiatic side of the Bosphorus, who in antiquity was given the credit for giving a decisive impulse to the development of artistic Attic prose. He appears as the creator of the elaborate periodic style (κατε-στραμμένη), as opposed to the 'strung-along style' (εἰρομένη). It was the purity of his diction allied to the clear ordering of the syntactical relations within the sentence that made the Thrasy-machean period a superior vehicle for complex exposition and argument. Gorgianic preciosity has this fatal defect when it comes to the persuasion of men, whether as juries in the courts or as voters in the assembly—it diverts attention from the matter in hand to the personality of the speaker. The early audiences may have admired and marvelled at the technical fireworks of a Gorgias. Though these continued to have their place in exhibition oratory (ἐπιδεικτική), in deliberative (συμ-βουλευτική) and forensic (δικανική) speeches the impression of vanity and insincerity is self-defeating.

Yet Thrasymachus, too, was not without artifice. In parti-cular, it is to him that Greek prose owed an effective technical device: he imposed on his syntactically complex sentences some of the rhythms of dithyrambic poetry. Chief of these was the use of the paean. Aristotle remarks (*Rhet.* III 8. 4) that in his day only one kind of paean was used, both at the beginning and the end of a sentence. However, in his opinion, the rhythm $-\cup\cup\cup$ is more appropriate for the beginning, while $\cup\cup\cup-$ suits the end, for a final short syllable results in a truncated effect.

By such means Thrasymachus became the creator of what was called the middling style (μέση λέξις), which steered a course half-way between the elaborate excesses of a Gorgias and the simple and bare straightforwardness of a Lysias (see below). Though Thrasymachus was a copious writer, chiefly on themes connected with the technique of rhetoric, little of his work has survived. We quote from a long passage reported by Dionysius of Halicarnassus (*On the Style of Demosthenes*, c. III) which takes the form of a prooemium to a public harangue but in fact was part of a political pamphlet expressing oligarchical views. Its date was about 411 B.C. The speech starts with a conventional *captatio benevolentiae*—I would have preferred to remain silent as was considered proper for a young man in the good old days, but things have reached such a pass that I must speak:

ἐβουλόμην μέν, ὦ ἄνδρες Ἀθηναῖοι, μετασχεῖν ἐκείνου τοῦ χρόνου τοῦ παλαιοῦ καὶ τῶν πραγμάτων ἡνίκα σιωπᾶν ἀπέχρη τοῖς νεωτέροις, τῶν τε πραγμάτων οὐκ ἀναγκαζόντων ἀγορεύειν καὶ τῶν πρεσβυτέρων ὀρθῶς τὴν πόλιν ἐπιτροπευόντων. ἐπειδὴ δ' εἰς τοιοῦτον ἡμᾶς ἀνέθετο χρόνον ὁ δαίμων ὥστε ⟨τὰς μὲν εὐπραξίας⟩ τῆς πόλεως ἀκούειν, τὰς δὲ συμφορὰς ⟨ἰδεῖν⟩ αὐτοὺς καὶ τούτων τὰ μέγιστα μὴ θεῶν ἔργα εἶναι μηδὲ τῆς τύχης ἀλλὰ τῶν ἐπιμεληθέντων ἀνάγκη λέγειν.

'Men of Athens, I should have preferred to belong to the good old days and affairs when it sufficed for the younger men to remain silent, when affairs did not compel them to speak and when our seniors governed the city wisely and well. Now seeing that the deity has set our lives in such times as the present, so that the prosperity of the city we know only by hearsay, but see with our own eyes her misfortunes and, what is more, the greatest of these being not the work of the gods or of luck but of those who have charge of affairs, this makes it necessary to speak.'

The antithetic character of the style comes out well in the following passage: καὶ τοὺς μὲν ἄλλους τὸ πλῆθος τῶν ἀγαθῶν ὑβρίζειν τε ποιεῖ καὶ στασιάζειν, ἡμεῖς δὲ μετὰ μὲν τῶν ἀγαθῶν ἐσωφρονοῦμεν, ἐν δὲ τοῖς κακοῖς ἐμάνημεν... 'With others it is the abundance of good things that makes them arrogant and factious. We showed good sense in the midst of blessings and lost our senses when things went badly...'

Noting that these two foreign immigrants seem to have written excellent Attic as contrasted with Protagoras, who remained faithful to his native Ionic, so that the passage quoted will probably date long after their first arrival in Athens, we may now turn to an early native writer of artistic prose.

Antiphon of Rhamnus in Attica (c. 480–411 B.C.) composed speeches to be delivered by others in court. His Tetralogies are model rhetorical exercises in the form of double *agones*: each set falls into two pairs of opposing speeches (ἀντιλογίαι) on imaginary themes, the speech of the prosecutor being followed by that for his defence. There is a contemporary namesake, Antiphon the Sophist, from whom we have fragments of a work *On Truth* and another *On Concord*. These two literary personalities may well be different facets of one person, for the differences of style could be accounted for as differences of genre. This is, in any case, true of the works ascribed to the Rhamnusian Antiphon. The *Tetralogies* have Ionic forms such as ἀπελογήθην (for ἀπελογησάμην), οἴδαμεν (for ἴσμεν), πράσσειν (for πράττειν or δρᾶν), ἀναγκάζειν (for βιάζεσθαι), etc. Another explanation for stylistic differences is of a chronological character. Attic prose was developing at a rapid rate during Antiphon's lifetime and in his later years he must have been exposed to the influence of Gorgias and Thrasymachus. Thus Orations I and V are archaic in flavour in their studied antithetic structure and their diction, but the influence of Gorgian figures is already apparent. Oration VI is clearly more Thrasymachean. Above all, there is greater sophistical influence in the syntax of the period, with less reliance on the archaic participial expressions, while the vocabulary is purer and more restrained.

The first specimen is from the second Tetralogy (IIα 1–3), which deals with the case of a boy accidentally killed by a javelin:

ὁπόσα μὲν τῶν πραγμάτων ὑπὸ τῶν ἐπιτυχόντων ἐπιβουλεύεται, οὐ χαλεπὰ ἐλέγχεσθαί ἐστιν. ἂν δ' οἱ ἱκανῶς μὲν πεφυκότες, ἔμπειροι δὲ πραγμάτων ὄντες, ἐν δὲ τούτῳ τῆς ἡλικίας καθεστῶτες ἐν ᾧ κράτιστοι φρονεῖν αὐτῶν εἰσίν, πράσσωσι, χαλεποὶ καὶ γνωσθῆναι καὶ δειχθῆναί εἰσι. διὰ γὰρ τὸ μέγεθος τοῦ κινδύνου ἐκ πολλοῦ τὴν ἀσφάλειαν ὧν ἐπιβουλεύουσι σκοποῦντες οὐ πρότερον ἐπιχειροῦσιν ἢ πάσης ὑποψίας φυλακὴν ποιήσωνται.

'Such crimes as are plotted by just anyone are not difficult to convict. But what is done by men who are of fair natural endowments, have experience in court proceedings, and are at a time of life when they have the greatest power of taking thought for themselves, these things are difficult to detect and to be shown up. For, because of the magnitude of their danger, they look far ahead to the security of what they are plotting and do not take action until they have taken precautions against all suspicion.'

We enumerate once again the recurrent features of this archaic Attic prose: poetical colouring, forced and strange expressions, bold new coinages and substantivized neuters of participles and adjectives (e.g. II γ 3 τοῖς δὲ ὅ τε κίνδυνος ἥ τε αἰσχύνη μείζων οὖσα τῆς διαφορᾶς, εἰ καὶ διενοήθησαν ταῦτα πρᾶξαι, ἀρκοῦσα ἦν σωφρονίσαι τὸ θυμούμενον τῆς γνώμης. 'For them their danger and their sense of shame, being greater than their hate, even if they had intended to commit this crime, was sufficient to restrain the anger of their spirit.'). We may add the abundance of participial expressions: an extreme example is εἴτε γὰρ προσιόντας τινὰς προϊδόντες οἱ ἀποκτείναντες αὐτοὺς ἀπολιπόντες ᾤχοντο φεύγοντες πρότερον ἢ ἀπέδυσαν. 'For either the killers, seeing some persons approaching, leaving them (their victims), made off in flight before they had despoiled them.'

The stiff antithetic arrangement with its mechanical symmetries is tricked out with the usual phonetic devices:

IV δ 9
εἰ δέ τις κοινὴν μὲν τὴν πρᾶξιν, κοινὴν δὲ τὴν ἀτυχίαν ἡγούμενος εἶναι μηδὲν ἀπολύσιμον μᾶλλον ἢ καταλήψιμον ἐκ τῶν λεγομένων γιγνώσκει αὐτὸν ὄντα, καὶ οὕτως ἀπολύειν μᾶλλον ἢ καταλαμβάνειν δίκαιός ἐστι. τόν τε γὰρ διώκοντα οὐ δίκαιον καταλαμβάνειν, μὴ σαφῶς διδάξαντα ὅτι ἀδικεῖται, τόν τε φεύγοντα ἀνόσιον ἁλῶναι μὴ φανερῶς ἐλεγχθέντα ἃ ἐπικαλεῖται.

'And if one, deeming the action and the misfortune to be shared by both parties, concludes from what has been said that he is neither to be acquitted nor condemned, in this case it is right to acquit rather than condemn him. For it is not right that the plaintiff should succeed when he has not clearly proved that he has suffered wrong or that the accused should be convicted of impiety when he has not been clearly proved guilty of the charges brought against him.'

The great progress that artistic prose has made will be brought out by contrasting Antiphon's work with what is the oldest specimen of Attic prose. This is the anonymous pamphlet (written by the 'Old Oligarch' possibly before the outbreak of the Peloponnesian War) on *The Constitution of Athens*, which has been preserved among the works of Xenophon. The author states at the outset that he is no democrat, but then goes on to dispel possible illusions about the internal weaknesses of democratic Athens. On the contrary, what the Athenian *dēmos* does is based on rational calculation of what is profitable to the masses as against the richer few. The untidy arrangement, the awkward syntax, and above all the monotonous diction make it difficult to maintain that the Old Oligarch had gone to school with the Sophists. The opening paragraph, where we might expect the greatest polish and elaboration, immediately gives the impression of an untutored and unpractised hand: περὶ δὲ τῆς Ἀθηναίων πολιτείας, ὅτι μὲν εἵλοντο τοῦτον τὸν τρόπον τῆς πολιτείας, οὐκ ἐπαινῶ διὰ τόδε, ὅτι ταῦθ' ἑλόμενοι εἵλοντο τοὺς πονηροὺς ἄμεινον πράττειν ἢ τοὺς χρηστούς. διὰ μὲν οὖν τοῦτο οὐκ ἐπαινῶ. 'Concerning the constitution of the Athenians, that they chose this form of constitution, I do not approve for this reason, (namely) because thus choosing they chose that the base citizens should fare better than the good. For this reason I do not approve.' The literary inexperience is shown up by the constant verbal repetitions. For instance, the word εὔνους 'well disposed' in the passage justifying the intervention of the Athenians in favour of the masses in faction-ridden states, (III. 10) ἐν οὐδεμιᾷ γὰρ πόλει τὸ βέλτιστον εὔνουν ἐστὶ τῷ δήμῳ ἀλλὰ τὸ κάκιστον ἐν ἑκάστῃ ἐστὶ πόλει εὔνουν τῷ δήμῳ. οἱ γὰρ ὅμοιοι τοῖς ὁμοίοις εὐνοί εἰσι. 'For in no city is the upper class favourable to the *dēmos*, whereas the lower class in each city is favourable to the *dēmos*. For like is favourable to like.'

Although Aristotle (*Rhet.* III 12. 2, 1413 b 17) recommends such repetition (πολλάκις τὸ αὐτὸ εἰπεῖν) as a device in oral compositions, this author neglects the injunction to vary the expression. The third section of the work provides a particularly crass illustration. In the first place it begins καὶ περὶ τῆς Ἀθηναίων πολιτείας τὸν μὲν τρόπον οὐκ ἐπαινῶ, which echoes the beginning of the first section. Then he goes on to deal with complaints about delays in securing justice at Athens. In comparatively few lines we encounter in the following order διαδικάζειν, διαδικάσαι, διαδικάσαι, διαδικάσαι, δικάσαι, ἀδίκημα, διαδικάζειν, διαδικάζεσθαι, διαδικάζειν, δικάζοντες, δικάζειν, δικάζειν, δικαστήρια, δικαστηρίῳ, δικαστάς, δικαίως, δικάζειν, ending with the sentence πρὸς δὲ τούτοις οἴεσθαι χρὴ καὶ ἑορτὰς ἄγειν χρῆναι Ἀθηναίους, ἐν αἷς οὐχ οἷόν τε δικάζειν. 'In addition to this one must needs bear in mind that the Athenians need to celebrate festivals during which it is not possible for the courts to sit.'

The impression of a long rambling conversational tone is heightened by the sudden direct appeals to the reader: e.g. φέρε δή, ἀλλὰ φήσει τις χρῆναι δικάζειν μέν, ἐλάττους δὲ δικάζειν.

'Look now, but someone will say judgment there has to be, but fewer should judge.' But, despite these stylistic defects and the often ungainly syntax, the Old Oligarch can make his points forcibly and sometimes with humour. As an example we may quote the passage (I. 10) which explains why it is not the custom in Athens for free citizens to strike slaves:

οὗ δ' ἕνεκέν ἐστι τοῦτο ἐπιχώριον ἐγὼ φράσω. εἰ νόμος ἦν τὸν δοῦλον ὑπὸ τοῦ ἐλευθέρου τύπτεσθαι ἢ τὸν μέτοικον ἢ τὸν ἀπελεύθερον, πολλάκις ἂν οἰηθεὶς εἶναι τὸν Ἀθηναῖον δοῦλον ἐπάταξεν ἄν· ἐσθῆτά τε γὰρ οὐδὲν βελτίων ὁ δῆμος αὐτόθι ἢ οἱ δοῦλοι καὶ οἱ μέτοικοι καὶ τὰ εἴδη οὐδὲν βελτίους εἰσίν.

'Why this is the local custom, I will tell. If it were customary for the slave or the metic or the freedman to be beaten by the free man he (*scil.* the free man) would often strike out, thinking that the Athenian was a slave. For there the common folk is not better in dress than the slaves and the metics and, in appearance, too, they are no better.'

Here the subject of ἐπάταξεν qualified by the participle οἰηθείς has to be supplied from ὑπὸ τοῦ ἐλευθέρου and δῆμος is treated as singular and plural in successive clauses.

We are now in a position to evaluate the language and style of the first Attic prose work of world rank—the History of the Peloponnesian War by Thucydides, who tells us that he began his preparations at the outbreak of the war, a passage written in 404 B.C. or after, when the war was over. Born *c.* 460 B.C., he had reached mature manhood by the beginning of the war (431); he was exiled in 424 and did not return to Athens until twenty years later. The first point to be made, therefore, is that his formative years coincided with the growing influence of the Sophists in Athenian thought and expression. Yet the work as we have it was composed about 404 B.C. The question arises whether its style, particularly in the speeches, is anachronistic. The question may be posed still more precisely. Is Thucydides' style Gorgianic, the finest flower of that first period of artistic Attic prose which, until the coming of the Sophists in 427 B.C., had still been crude and undeveloped? An affirmative answer would imply in particular that the ways of thinking and the modes of expression attributed to the leading speakers in his history were those current in the Athens of the returned exile rather than in the early years of the war. In view of the scanty evidence for pre-war political oratory the approach to the question must be indirect. J. H. Finley has tackled the problem by studying the resemblances between the thought and expression of Euripides and Thucydides.

The first point of importance is that certain leading ideas expressed by the Old Oligarch recur in the speeches of Thucydides and that further resemblances of the same kind can be detected in the early plays of Euripides. Moreover, the influence of Sophistic education becomes manifest through the use of certain stock arguments common to the pamphleteer, the tragic poet, and the historian. Examples are the argument from likelihood (εἰκός), from advantage (τὸ συμφέρον), and from what is right and just (τὸ δίκαιον), which are traceable to the Sicilians Corax and Tisias and were popularized in Athens by Protagoras. Finley's conclusion is that the ideas and modes of argument attributed by Thucydides to his speakers were current at the time of the dramatic date and that both he and Euripides reflect a common rhetorical tradition. How far this reaches back is shown by the accomplished use of opposing pairs of speeches, *antilogiai*, in the earliest extant plays of Sophocles, the *Ajax* and the *Antigone*, for, as we have seen, disputation by this means was a main feature of Sophistic training.

If then there are good grounds for believing that Thucydides in his history conveyed a reasonably accurate picture of Athenian modes of thought and argument at the outset of the war, we may ask whether the same is true of his style. What gives pause is precisely the uniformity of style even though many of the chief characters in his history must have spoken other dialects than Attic. But the trend of our argument is that this personal style of Thucydides was hammered out in his formative years. In other words, it antedates the arrival of Gorgias in 427 B.C. As has been shown, the outstanding feature of the archaic style is its use of antithetical formulations, and while Thucydides uses a plain and matter-of-fact style in the narrative and purely descriptive parts of his exposition, it is in the more philosophical parts, and especially in the speeches, that the antithetical style reaches its pinnacle. The supreme example is the Funeral Oration of Pericles (II. 36–46), from which our illustration is taken (37. 1): χρώμεθα γὰρ πολιτείᾳ οὐ ζηλούσῃ τοὺς τῶν πέλας νόμους, παράδειγμα δὲ μᾶλλον αὐτοὶ ὄντες τισὶν ἢ μιμούμενοι ἑτέρους. 'We live under (literally 'use') a constitution that does not emulate the laws of our neighbours, being ourselves a model for some rather than imitating others.'

39. 3

ἀθρόᾳ τε τῇ δυνάμει ἡμῶν οὐδείς πω πολέμιος ἐνέτυχε διὰ τὴν τοῦ ναυτικοῦ τε ἅμα ἐπιμέλειαν καὶ τὴν ἐν τῇ γῇ ἐπὶ πολλὰ ἡμῶν αὐτῶν ἐπίπεμψιν. ἢν δέ που μορίῳ τινὶ προσμείξωσι, κρατήσαντές τέ τινας ἡμῶν πάντας αὐχοῦσιν ἀπεῶσθαι καὶ νικηθέντες ὑφ' ἁπάντων ἡσσῆσθαι. καίτοι εἰ ῥᾳθυμίᾳ μᾶλλον ἢ πόνων μελέτῃ καὶ μὴ μετὰ νόμων τὸ πλέον ἢ τρόπων ἀνδρείας ἐθέλομεν κινδυνεύειν, περιγίγνεται ἡμῖν τοῖς τε μέλλουσιν ἀλγεινοῖς μὴ προκάμνειν, καὶ ἐς αὐτὰ ἐλθοῦσι μὴ ἀτολμοτέρους τῶν ἀεὶ μοχθούντων φαίνεσθαι.

'No enemy has yet encountered our full forces because of our simultaneous concern with naval matters and our expeditions by land against many objectives. If by chance they engage with some part (of our forces), defeating some of us, they boast that they have repulsed us all, but being beaten, that they have been worsted by us all. And if we choose to take risks by a relaxed way of life rather than laborious training with a courage that springs not so much from legal compulsion but from force of character, we gain the advantage that we are not dismayed in advance by troubles to come and when we are involved show outselves no less courageous than those who so constantly are in hard training.'

40. 1 (This passage is set out so as to bring out the complex antithetic structure.)

Φιλοκαλοῦμέν τε γὰρ μετ' εὐτελείας καὶ
φιλοσοφοῦμεν   ἄνευ μαλακίας·
πλούτῳ τε ἔργου μᾶλλον καιρῷ
      ἢ   λόγου   κόμπῳ χρώμεθα
καὶ τὸ πένεσθαι οὐχ ὁμολογεῖν τινὶ αἰσχρόν,
ἀλλὰ   μὴ διαφεύγειν ἔργῳ αἴσχιον.

'We are lovers of beauty without extravagance (lit. 'with cheapness'). We are lovers of things intellectual without softening of our fibre. Wealth we use more as an opportunity of action rather than boastful words. As for poverty, it is no disgrace for a man to confess it, but quite disgraceful not to take action to escape it.' This passage illustrates the frequent unnatural distortion in the effort to achieve a verbal antithesis. Thus the genitive in λόγου κόμπῳ 'boastfulness of speech' is otiose and put in merely to balance ἔργου καιρῷ 'opportunity for action'.

41. 1–3

ξυνελών τε λέγω τήν τε πᾶσαν πόλιν τῆς Ἑλλάδος παίδευσιν εἶναι καὶ καθ' ἕκαστον δοκεῖν ἄν μοι τὸν αὐτὸν ἄνδρα παρ' ἡμῶν ἐπὶ πλεῖστ' ἂν εἴδη καὶ μετὰ χαρίτων μάλιστ' ἂν εὐτραπέλως τὸ σῶμα αὔταρκες παρέχεσθαι. καὶ ὡς οὐ λόγων ἐν τῷ παρόντι κόμπος τάδε μᾶλλον ἢ ἔργων ἐστὶν ἀλήθεια, αὐτὴ ἡ δύναμις τῆς πόλεως, ἣν ἀπὸ τῶνδε τῶν τρόπων ἐκτησάμεθα, σημαίνει. μόνη γὰρ τῶν νῦν ἀκοῆς κρείσσων ἐς πεῖραν ἔρχεται, καὶ μόνη οὔτε τῷ πολεμίῳ ἐπελθόντι ἀγανάκτησιν ἔχει ὑφ' οἵων κακοπαθεῖ οὔτε τῷ ὑπηκόῳ κατάμεμψιν ὡς οὐχ ὑπ' ἀξίων ἄρχεται.

'Briefly then, I say that our whole city is the school of Greece, and that each individual among us, in my opinion, could in his own person show himself fully competent in the most varied forms with great versatility and grace. And that this is no empty boast on the present occasion but the actual truth, the very power of our city, which we have acquired by these qualities, gives witness. For alone of her contemporaries she is better than her repute when she is put to the test, and alone she causes no vexation to the attacking enemy because of the kind of men by whom he is worsted, and no reproach to her subjects, on the grounds that their rulers are unworthy.'

43. 3

ἀνδρῶν γὰρ ἐπιφανῶν πᾶσα γῆ τάφος καὶ οὐ στηλῶν μόνον ἐν τῇ οἰκείᾳ σημαίνει ἐπιγραφῇ, ἀλλὰ καὶ ἐν τῇ μὴ προσηκούσῃ ἄγραφος μνήμη παρ' ἑκάστῳ τῆς γνώμης μᾶλλον ἢ τοῦ ἔργου ἐνδιαιτᾶται.

'Of famous men the whole earth is the sepulchre, and not merely does an inscription on tombstones in their native land give witness, but in lands not their own, an unwritten memorial, of their spirit rather than their deeds, lives on in every man's heart.'

This is the antithetical style at its finest. With its unremitting search for variation, both of phrasing and of syntax, in the contrasting members, Thucydidean prose is worlds apart from the mechanical matching, the static equilibrium and the wearisome assonances of Gorgias. Examination of the extant works of the Sophist suggests that his essential contribution to the development of artistic prose was to make the *comma* into the functional unit of the sentence and to exaggerate the features of exact balance, word-play and assonances. He cannot be credited with antithesis itself, for this is endemic in Greek thought from the very beginning. It is a reflection of the analytical mind which proceeds to dissect a whole by successive dichotomies into A and non-A. As noted above, the procedure was systematized and given stylistic expression by Protagoras whose influence on the art of debate can be detected at least as early as 442 B.C. in the works of Sophocles, for this is the date of the *Antigone*, while the *Ajax* will be earlier, and may go back to the preceding decade. If so, the *Medea* of Euripides will be fully twenty years later (431), and by then the younger dramatist had brought the antithetical debate to a high pitch of technical perfection with balanced clauses tricked out with the so-called 'Gorgianic' effects, e.g. 408–9:

γυναῖκες, ἐς μὲν ἐσθλ' ἀμηχανώταται,
κακῶν δὲ πάντων τέκτονες σοφώταται

'Women quite helpless for any good ends, but highly skilled contrivers of all manner of evil.'

Antithesis and 'equalization' (*parisōsis*) are also the cardinal figures of Antiphon's style, and he also makes discreet use of *paromoiōsis*, that is assonance achieved by similarities at the extremities of the *cōla*. The conclusion must be that on the evidence available there is little or nothing to justify the key role in the development of artistic Attic prose assigned to Gorgias even in the most recent handbooks, which repeat the statements of ancient critics. But, as has been pointed out by J. H. Finley, there is no evidence that fourth-century Athenians were aware of the crucial importance in their literary history of Gorgias' visit to Athens in 427 B.C. The tradition about its importance goes no further back than Diodorus Siculus and Dionysius of Halicarnassus, both writing in the first century B.C.

The ancient critics characterize the language of Thucydides as archaic and 'glossematic', that is, studded with exotic words.

While he expressed himself in the Old Attic of his youth, he obeyed the convention of Greek literature in making polite bows to the dialect appropriate to the genre, in his case to Ionic. Thus he avoided what might have appeared Attic parochialisms and wrote σσ for ττ (θάλασσα) and -ρσ- for -ρρ- (θαρσεῖν), but apart from such superficial details, there is virtually nothing in his language which can be certainly established as Ionic. He is an Athenian through and through, the exemplar in thought and style of the Sophist-trained generation that grew to manhood in the years of Periclean Athens before the outbreak of the Peloponnesian War.

3. Classical Attic Prose: Peak and Decline

The main lines for the development of prose were laid down and the steps to full fruition may be briefly sketched. The history of Attic prose is a gradual emancipation from its poetical origins, the enfranchisement and ennoblement of ordinary speech. In this the Athenian orators (and Greek prose is through and through oratorical) followed the precept and example of Thrasymachus in preference to Gorgias. The driving force was the adaptation of formal speaking to its function, and this, in a word, was 'persuasion' (πειθώ) whether in the courts or in the assembly.

The prime virtue of effective speaking is clarity (σαφήνεια) and this requires in the first place the vocabulary of everyday speech (Arist. *Rhet.* III 2. 1–2): τῶν δ' ὀνομάτων καὶ ῥημάτων σαφῆ μὲν ποιεῖ τὰ κύρια 'Of nouns and verbs [a phrase meaning collectively the vocabulary] it is the normal ones that produce clarity'. This is plain common sense, for unnaturalness and preciosity of diction not only lack clarity but divert the hearer's attention from the argument to the expression and may prejudice him against the speaker by their pretentiousness and vanity. The psychological effects of diction were pointed out by Aristotle (*Rhet.* III 2. 4): διὸ δεῖ λανθάνειν ποιοῦντας, καὶ μὴ δοκεῖν λέγειν πεπλασμένως ἀλλὰ πεφυκότως · τοῦτο γὰρ πιθα- νόν... 'Hence it is necessary to cover up when doing this [using high-flown language] and not to appear to be speaking in an artificial way but naturally, for this is persuasive...'.

Sentence structure, too, plays a vital part in clarity. It was here that the style of the orators was bound to differ from that of

Thucydides. Intended as it was for oral exposition, the oratorical period, however long and however complex its structure might be, had to make it easy for the hearer to grasp the meanings of the *cōla* as they emerged and to apprehend their relation to the whole and so not only to follow the exposition and the argument but also to experience the intellectual and aesthetic satisfaction given by such a period. As Aristotle puts it, a period is a sentence that has a beginning and an end in itself and is of a size which can be taken in at a glance (εὐσύνοπτον). Such a sentence is pleasant and easy to grasp (εὐμαθής). The style of Thucydides does not conform to this prescription. In the first place the historian packs too much meaning into his *cōla* for ready apprehension by the hearer. Further obscurity results from his constant search for variation in the contrasting members of his antithetic expressions, which results in structural tangles that can be unravelled only by a reader.

There remains a further feature of artistic prose which, we recall, was also initiated by Thrasymachus. This was the construction of periods from rhythmical *cōla*. Aristotle, in requiring that a period should be above all easily apprehended, notes that this follows from being easily remembered (εὐμνημόνευτος), and this quality is enhanced if the period is rhythmical.

Such was the linguistic orchestra that emerged after half a century of experiment in the writing of artistic prose. With the ingrained Greek sensitivity to the distinctions of genre and their appropriate styles it is not surprising that the different writers should differ in their instrumentation, or that one and the same writer should write in different styles in generically different parts of his compositions. This is above all true of Plato, the 'Homer of prose' as he has been called, who in the dialogue passages captures the easy conversational tone of educated men but elsewhere rises to heights where he consciously hovers between prose and poetry. As Eduard Norden has written: 'The *Symposium* is a drama, the δεύτερος λόγος of Socrates in the *Phaedrus* a lyrical poem, the beginning of the *Phaedrus* a prose idyll.' In oratory, too, there is a gamut of styles, the extremes of which are represented by the plain and severe expository style of Lysias and the elaborate epideictic style of Isocrates' *Panegyric*, in which he insists (11) on the difference between the plain manner (ἀφελῶς), appropriate in court pleadings, and the exhibition manner (ἐπιδεικτικῶς) appropriate to grander occasions.

With Isocrates, Greek artistic prose reached its technical perfection. Though he was a pupil of Gorgias, the consummate instrument that he elaborated owed no less to Thrasymachus. His general aim was to fashion a style for prose compositions which could rival that of poetry and even replace it in certain branches. In his *Panegyric* (8) he stresses the manifold power of words: ἐπειδὴ δ' οἱ λόγοι τοιαύτην ἔχουσι τὴν φύσιν ὥσθ' οἷόν τ' εἶναι περὶ τῶν αὐτῶν πολλαχῶς ἐξηγήσασθαι καὶ τά τε μεγάλα ταπεινὰ ποιῆσαι καὶ τοῖς μικροῖς μέγεθος περιθεῖναι, καὶ τά τε παλαιὰ καινῶς διελθεῖν καὶ περὶ τῶν νεωστὶ γεγενημένων ἀρχαίως εἰπεῖν... 'But since words have such a nature as to be able to dilate on the same subject in many different ways and to make the great humble and to give magnitude to what is trivial, to expound old things in a new way and to expound recent events in an antique way.' Elsewhere he insists on the notion of 'propriety' (τοῖς ἐνθυμήμασι πρεπόντως ὅλον τὸν λόγον καταποικῖλαι) 'to adorn the whole speech in a way which is appropriate to the thoughts'. In general, 'propriety' imposes restrictions on vocabulary: he avoided not only poetical words and expressions but also newly-coined words, which were so abundant in archaic prose. Apart from precision and purity of diction the supreme achievement of Isocrates was the elegance and logical transparency of his periods. Finally, attaching importance to the rhythmical and musical qualities of such formal speaking (εὐρύθμως καὶ μουσικῶς εἰπεῖν), he recommended the chief employment of iambic and trochaic rhythms, while among the 'musical' devices was the avoidance of hiatus which makes sentences limp (χωλός).

The *Panegyric* belongs to the genre of fictitious speeches which had become one of the instruments of political propaganda. Occasions for launching such compositions on the public were provided by the general religious assemblies of the Greeks (πανηγύρεις), such as the Olympic Games. Isocrates in his *Panegyric*, from which our example is taken, was following the example of his teacher who in 392 had published his *Olympic Oration* with much the same general theme—the appeal for unity among the Greeks and for a war of liberation against the Persians. It is possible that Isocrates first conceived the general

idea of his own work at this time for, although it was published
first in 380, there is a tradition that he worked on it for ten to
fifteen years. It was the most polished of all Isocrates's compositions and its literary influence was immense, for it became the
supreme model for later writers of exhibition oratory.

75–7

πλείστων μὲν οὖν ἀγαθῶν αἰτίους καὶ μεγίστων ἐπαίνων ἀξίους
ἡγοῦμαι γεγενῆσθαι τοὺς τοῖς σώμασιν ὑπὲρ τῆς Ἑλλάδος προκιν-
δυνεύσαντας· οὐ μὴν οὐδὲ τῶν πρὸ τοῦ πολέμου τούτου γενο-
μένων καὶ δυναστευσάντων ἐν ἑκατέρᾳ τοῖν πολέοιν δίκαιον
ἀμνημονεῖν. ἐκεῖνοι γὰρ ἦσαν οἱ προασκήσαντες τοὺς ἐπιγιγνο-
μένους καὶ τὰ πλήθη προτρέψαντες ἐπ' ἀρετὴν καὶ χαλεποὺς
ἀνταγωνιστὰς τοῖς βαρβάροις ποιήσαντες.

Οὐ γὰρ ὠλιγώρουν τῶν κοινῶν, οὐδ' ἀπέλαυον μὲν ὡς ἰδίων,
ἠμέλουν δ' ὡς ἀλλοτρίων, ἀλλ' ἐκήδοντο μὲν ὡς οἰκείων, ἀπεί-
χοντο δ' ὥσπερ χρὴ τῶν μηδὲν προσηκόντων. οὐδὲ πρὸς ἀργύριον
τὴν εὐδαιμονίαν ἔκρινον, ἀλλ' οὗτος ἐδόκει πλοῦτον ἀσφαλέστατον
κεκτῆσθαι καὶ κάλλιστον, ὅστις τοιαῦτα τυγχάνοι πράττων ἐξ
ὧν αὐτός τε μέλλοι μάλιστ' εὐδοκιμήσειν καὶ τοῖς παισὶν μεγίστην
δόξαν καταλείψειν.

'Those responsible for the greatest number of benefits and
worthy of the highest praise were, in my opinion, those who
risked their lives in defence of Greece. And yet it is not right to
forget those who lived before this war, and held power in each
of these two cities. For it was they who trained the rising
generation, impelling the masses to manliness and making them
into tough opponents for the barbarians. They were not heed-
less of public affairs, nor did they profit from public wealth as
though it were their own while disregarding it as though it
belonged to others, but caring for it as though it was their
personal possession, they abstained from it as though they had
no right to it. Nor did they measure happiness by money but
thought that the most secure and honourable wealth was
obtained by the sort of man who acted in such a way as would
bring him personally the highest repute and would leave to his
children the greatest glory.'

Modern scholars and critics who come to Isocrates from a
reading of Demosthenes's 'Ninth Symphony', the *De Corona* with

its force and vehemence, its passion and singleness of purpose, its infinitely varied and controlled stylistic virtuosity, find it difficult to understand the unique position which Isocrates occupied not only in Greek but also in Latin prose literature and, via Cicero, in Renaissance writers. Particularly puzzling is that Aristotle almost entirely neglects the Attic orators. Evidently we are viewing the problem from the wrong angle. The object of enquiry is form not content, manner not matter. While some scholars have saluted Isocrates as the father of humanistic education and also as a great political thinker, these are not questions of concern to the historian of the Greek language. The linguist will confine his attention to expression rather than content, and it would be presumptuous to dismiss what is an historical fact—the admiration of the generations who shared the language of Isocrates and strove to imitate him. However, the verdict of antiquity was not unanimous. One critic, Hermogenes, used an illuminating phrase when he described Isocrates's style as 'senile and schoolmasterly' (πρεσβυτικὸν καὶ διδασκαλικόν). Here he put his finger on the cancer to which Greek prose rapidly succumbed. If perfection of style is perfect adaptation of the linguistic means to its end and a writer's achievement is measured by his response to an occasion in the way that Demosthenes used all the resources of his eloquence to arouse the Athenians of his day to the danger of Macedonian imperialism, then it will be understandable why the loss of Athenian freedom and independence was fatal to prose. The reason was the drying-up of stimulus and occasion. Both Demosthenes and Isocrates had been writers of speeches for others to deliver on their own occasions. But whereas Demosthenes occupied the centre of public political debate, Isocrates never appeared even in court himself and for about forty years conducted a school of rhetoric at Athens before devoting the last dozen or so years of his long life to writing on themes of general interest. His 'schoolmasterliness' was a faithful reflection of his life.

One of Isocrates's latest works (346 B.C.) is the *Philippus*, addressed to Philip of Macedon, the new master of Greece, to whom he appeals as the 'benefactor' (εὐεργέτης) of the Hellenes. In the year in which Isocrates died (338 B.C.) Philip crushed the Athenians and Boeotians at Chaeronea. Thereafter the

story of Greek prose is one of decline and degeneration. In the
centuries that followed, as public life receded from the writers
and orators who might have found energy in serving the state,
they retired to the class-rooms and lecture halls of the rhetoricians
and played at being public men, writing compositions on set
themes invented for imaginary political and forensic occasions,
or others of an even more ridiculous triviality. Now the school
was master, and the further development of Greek prose was
like a retreat into second childhood.

In one form of such academic exercises the pupil, continuing
the practice of the early Sophists, conducted debates with an
imaginary opponent. This had two consequences: loose and
slovenly diction and the abandonment of the period in favour of
short, balanced clauses. Moreover, the moralizing character of
the set themes prompted a tone of theatrical pathos. This set of
circumstances favoured the revival of Gorgianism. Such was the
origin of one of the two styles which later came to be known as
'Asianism'. Despite its evident Sophistic origins, ancient critics
traced Asianism to Hegesias of Magnesia, whose floruit was the
middle of the third century B.C. His is a voluptuous and sensual
style, its vehicle being minute clauses with insistent rhythms
(often contrived by insertion of superfluous words), which critics
found 'lascivious'. His Gorgian devices of constant antithesis,
clause equalization, jingling word-play, highly poetical vocabulary and far-fetched metaphor combined to produce a style
which later critics found revolting.

We may also trace to the Sophists a second Asianic style
which has been described as a prose dithyramb, aspiring to
grandiloquence but suffocating through the sheer bulk of its
flabby corpulence, while its diction was archaic in being both
poetical and full of neologisms. The periods are tricked out with
every device of the rhetorical schools and natural word order is
distorted in the interest of rhythm. Such tumidity and bombast
were traced by Quintilian (XII 10. 17) to the 'passionate and
boastful character of the Asiatic race (*Asiana gens tumidior atque
iactantior*); it carried to absurd lengths the stylistic excesses which
Aristotle (*Rhet.* III 3, 1405 b) summed up as 'frigid' (ψυχρόν).
It is not surprising that such excess should have provoked a
reaction, though it was long in coming. In the Ciceronian age
Greek teachers of language and rhetoric at Rome preached the

gospel of Atticism and urged the imitation of the ancient Attic models of style and eloquence. Yet this reaction was in effect a counsel to keep company with the dead. The more successful such literary antiquarianism is, the less interest it holds for the historian of the Greek language.

VI

POST-CLASSICAL GREEK

1. The Common Dialect

In its most creative period, that is when the great works of literature were produced, Greece was politically and linguistically fragmented. The 'Greek language' was in fact a congeries of local dialects which were used by the separate city states in their public documents. The development of certain of these dialects into rich and subtle instruments of high literature with pan-Hellenic status has been traced in the previous chapters. The manifold variety of dialects in the archaic and classical periods contrasts strangely with the rigid uniformity of the documents of the Mycenaean world, but this, as we have argued, may be illusory. The language of the Linear B tablets was presumably the technical instrument of the Palace administrations, a governmental common language, based on a Peloponnesian dialect that screens from our view the doubtless greater variety of the real Mycenaean dialect world. The fact remains that on present evidence a common language was in exclusive use for the limited purposes attested by the Linear B archives, and such uniformity, matched as it is by the unity of culture observed by the archaeologists, implies a high degree of intercommunication, if not centralization. Whatever the place and date at which this Mycenaean Koine emerged, it appears everywhere in virtually the same form.

A general point may be made. Speech is acquired by imitation of those with whom we come into contact. Intense communication tends to produce uniformity of language within the limits of the social unit which uses it. On the other hand, differentiation of speech results from barriers to, and interruptions of, such intercommunication. So it was that after the twelfth century B.C., when the Mycenaean world was shattered, Greece broke up into restricted local communities, the isolation of which favoured the linguistic separateness mirrored in the dialect map of post-Mycenaean times. Yet this new Hellenic world was destined to grow together, culturally and politically, into larger units until it was forcibly unified by the Macedonian conquerors after the decisive battle of Chaeronea in 338 B.C. Once again a new Common Dialect was evolved for the purpose of government and administration. This was the Koine, which smothered and replaced the ancient local dialects. Its basis was historically determined: it was Attic.

The prestige enjoyed by Athens thanks to the leading role it had played in the resistance to the Persians hardened into political power. Athens became the metropolis of an empire, attracting thousands of foreigners on their various political, commercial, and legal occasions, to say nothing of the metics who settled there and the non-Athenians who served as rowers in the fleet. Command of the sea brought not only raw materials and commodities to the Piraeus; the language, too, was enriched (some would say 'adulterated') by alien borrowings. The 'Old Oligarch' wrote (II 8) that the Athenians speak a language that is a mixture of all the Hellenes and Barbarians. This process was reinforced by the practice of settling Athenians in colonies on imperial territory. Such a stirring-up of the population was bound to have linguistic effects. Mastery of so complex and sensitive an instrument as the Attic dialect with its many archaisms and irregularities required constant association and verbal communication within the native community for its preservation. How easy it was for a man separated from his fellows to lose his purity of speech emerges from a passage of Solon (36. 10) in which he claims to have brought back to Athens many Athenians who after long wanderings no longer spoke pure Attic (γλῶσσαν οὐκέτ' Ἀττικὴν ἱέντας, ὡς ἂν πολλαχῇ πλανωμένους).

In the fourth century we hear of one Euxitheos (Demosthenes 57, 18), who found his citizen status challenged because his father spoke in a foreign way (ἐξένιζεν). To explain this away he produced witnesses to prove that his father had been taken prisoner and had lived in slavery for many years before returning home. It was by such processes that Metropolitan Attic became Imperial Attic. The outstanding example in literature of such linguistic adulteration is Xenophon, who is rightly regarded as the precursor of the Koine. His life was largely lived abroad and, as an ancient grammarian (Helladius) observed, 'it is no wonder

that a man who spent much time on campaigns and in the
company of aliens should in some respects lapse from his native
speech'.

The challenge of empire was the stimulus which in a comparatively short time transformed Attic from a locally-restricted
dialect of somewhat archaic aspect into a linguistic instrument
of pan-Hellenic status. Historically decisive was the Phil-
hellenism of Philip II of Macedon. His court was Greek in its
way of life, and he employed Aristotle as tutor for his son
Alexander. More important was the adoption of Attic as his
official language and his use of it in diplomatic correspondence.
Once Alexander had destroyed the Persian empire, the whole
of the Eastern world as far as India was opened up to Greek
culture. In this way what we may now call the Macedonian
Koine became not only the language of government and
administration but the lingua franca of educated men throughout this huge expanse of territory. Rome in its turn could do no
other than use the same instrument of communication and
control once it had expanded into Greece, Macedonia and
Thrace, Asia Minor and Armenia, Mesopotamia, Syria,
Palestine and Egypt.

Profound linguistic consequences might have been expected
from the adoption of what was basically the Attic dialect by
users of not merely non-Attic, but non-Greek speech. In fact the
changes were remarkably slight. In phonology certain ten-
dencies already observable in the ancient dialects persisted. In
the morphology there was simplification and systematization
which ironed out a number of Attic idiosyncrasies. But the main
result of the immense extension of Macedonian power and the
use of the language for all the purposes and occasions of life in
a world empire—government, science, art and literature—was
a great enrichment of the lexicon.

2. Grammatical Developments

(a) Phonology

The traditional spelling concealed great changes which are
partially betrayed by orthographic lapses. The vowels were
affected by the process known as itacism: ι, ει, and η all eventually converged on the value [i]; the same was true of the

diphthong οι, which first developed to [y], thus coalescing with υ in its Attic pronunciation (see p. 205). The diphthong αι was monophthongized and coalesced with ε; the long diphthongs ᾱι (ᾳ) and ωι (ῳ) lost their second element. Important, too, was the change of the pitch to a stress accent and the loss of the phonemic distinction of quantity in the vowel system. On the development of the inherited diphthong *ei* to [ẹ:] in Attic by v B.C. see p. 205. The raising to [i:] occurs in other dialects at an early date (on Boeotian see p. 118); in Attic inscriptions the first examples occur as early as 300 B.C. and in the Egyptian papyri from iii B.C. onwards. The itacism of η (phonetically [ɛ:]) lagged behind that of [ẹ:]. In the papyri from the middle of A.D. ii it alternates with αι and ε, thus revealing its still open pronunciation, although there are also examples of confusion with ει and ι. As for αι and οι, while Boeotian had made early changes in these diphthongs, anticipating developments in the Koine (see p. 118), it was not until ii and iii A.D. that Attic offers examples of αι = [ε] and οι = [y], and the value [i] for the latter did not develop until towards the end of the first millennium A.D.

Fundamental changes took place in the prosodic system of the language. The elimination of the quantitative distinctions between the vowels went hand in hand with a change in the accent from pitch to stress, which eliminated the subtle oppositions between acute, grave and circumflex (see pp. 243 ff.). The beginnings of the blurring of vowel length distinctions can be detected as early as iii B.C. in orthographic alternations, such as ε × η (μεθενεί for μηδενί) and ο × ω (πρόσοπον for πρόσωπον). Later, in A.D. ii, there is metrical evidence that authors were uncertain of the old quantities, and by about A.D. 400 Nonnus wrote dactylic hexameters which take account of the stress accent, especially at the end of the verse. At a slightly earlier date Gregory of Nazianzus (A.D. 330–90), who was versed in the ancient measures and prosodies, also wrote some popular poems based on the accentual rhythms of the current speech of his day. In the structural presentation of these changes, however, the quantitative distinctions must be retained, for the long and short vowels had different developmental histories. The following diagram shows the Attic short-vowel system, which remained unaffected until ii B.C.

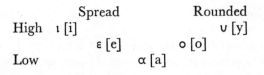

	Spread		Rounded
High	ι [i]		υ [y]
		ε [e]		ο [o]
Low		α [a]	

In the long vowels Attic had a system with four degrees of raising, for it made a distinction between mid-low and mid-high ($\bar{e̦} : \bar{ẹ}$ and $\bar{o̦} : \bar{ọ}$); $\bar{ẹ}$ and $\bar{ọ}$ are due to the contraction or compensatory lengthening of ε and ο and, from iv B.C., to the monophthongization of the inherited diphthongs ει and ου. But by ii B.C. the following changes had taken place: $\bar{ẹ} > \bar{i}, \bar{e̦} > \bar{i}$ and $\bar{ọ} > \bar{u}$. Moreover, certain diphthongs had also undergone changes which merged them into the long-vowel system: $ai > \bar{e̦}$ and $oi > \bar{y}$, while the long diphthongs ᾱι, ηι, and ωι had lost their second element. Finally, once the quantitative distinctions had been eliminated, the vowel system presented the following structure:

$$i \qquad\qquad y \qquad\qquad u$$
$$e \qquad\qquad o$$
$$a$$

Once the rounded front vowel [y], the product of ancient *u and *oi,[1] was eliminated (in the Early Middle Ages), Greek vocalism had attained the modern five-vowel system i, e, a, o, u.

The main change in the consonantal system, already noted, was the development of the ancient aspirated plosives to fricatives: φ = [pʰ] > [f], θ = [tʰ] > [θ], χ = [kʰ] > [χ]. Here, too, certain dialects had anticipated the general trend of the language: thus Laconian σ appears for θ as early as iv B.C., while Pamphylian offers φικατι for ϝικατι by ii or i B.C. However, in Latin transliterations f for φ is not encountered until A.D. i. Another symptom of the change in the corresponding voiced series is the occurrence of β to render Latin v (Φλαβιος, etc.), also about the beginning of our era. This development was anticipated in Corinthian ἀμοιϝαν for ἀμοιβαν (v B.C.) and Boeotian ἑυδομον for ἑβδομον (iii B.C.) and in the use of β for digamma as early as v B.C. in Laconia and Messenia. The dental and dorsal voiced plosives proved more resistant, though there

[1] This change, though complete in Boeotian by iii B.C., is rarely attested in the Koine and was not completed until Byzantine times.

are early examples of the disappearance of γ intervocalically (e.g. Attic ὀλίος for ὀλίγος).

Another phenomenon of Modern Greek, anticipated in the ancient dialects, was psilosis, that is loss of the initial aspirate, which was common to all Asiatic Greek dialects. In the Koine the first signs of this process appear in papyri of iii B.C.

Thus the phonological system of modern Greek developed at an early date. The main additional features that deserve mention are 1, the loss of pretonic initial vowels (aphaeresis) in the Early Middle Ages, 2, the loss of final ν before words beginning with a consonant in the same period and its complete disappearance in the following period, 3, the change of -σθ- > -στ- (this had been a regular feature of the North-west Greek dialects) and 4, the change typified in the development of ὀκτώ to ὀχτώ, the rule being that clusters of two plosives, whether voiceless or aspirated, develop to fricative plus plosive. Both 3 and 4 took place in the Later Middle Ages (1100–1453).

(b) Morphology

1. Nouns

The above sound developments were bound to affect the inflexional system of the noun and verb, which depended to a large extent on clear distinctions between vowels and diphthongs of different quantity and quality, e.g. μάχη, μάχῃ, μάχαι; λόγον, λόγῳ, λόγων, etc. With the disturbing factors must be reckoned also, at least in some regions and some levels of speech, the weak pronunciation or loss of final -n. In Modern Greek the rich variety of the ancient declensional classes has been simplified and transformed into a wholly different system. The beginnings of this process can be observed at an early date. Important was the removal of an anomaly in the accusative singular of the consonantal class, where -α was opposed to the -ν of all the vocalic stems (e.g. φύλακα v. μάχην, λόγον, πόλιν, πῆχυν) and was replaced by -αν. Although *ijatēran* occurs as early as v B.C. in a Cypriot inscription and κιονᾱν in a Thessalian inscription of ii B.C., such forms are not attested in the inscriptions and papyri until Roman times: γυναῖκαν, πόδαν, χεῖραν, μῆναν, etc. Of earlier date was the appearance of -ην for -η in masculine s-stems (e.g. Διογένην); in Attic the new form completely ousted the old from iv B.C. on.

7

Another important development was also anticipated in the dialects: this was the replacement of the accusative plural ending -ας by -ες, which was regular in north-west Greek (p. 60). Such forms do not appear in Attic until Roman times, but they are frequently attested in the papyri from ii B.C. on: χιτῶνες, γυναῖκες, πάντες, τέσσερες, etc. These two comparatively slight changes contained the germs of the new system which is presented in Modern Greek. Though the ancient system is still preserved in the written Koine, the more vulgar sources betray the confusions which herald its dissolution. In the ā-stems, the nominative occasionally appears with -ς: γραφής, καταπομπής. In the accusative singular forms like δεσποίνην and μελαίνην are due to analogical extension from δεσποίνης, μελαίνης, etc. Analogical are also ρη for ρᾱ in ἀρούρης, σπείρης, etc., and ιη for ιᾱ in ἱερείης, εἰδυίης, etc. On the other hand there are counter-examples like ἱερίσσᾳ, τελευτάν, ἀδελφᾷ and even ἀρτάβης μιᾶς ὅλας. In the masculines of this class the genitive τοῦ στρατιώτη (A.D. iv) anticipates the modern declension. The influence of the o-declension is shown in στρατιῶτοι (A.D. iv).

Noteworthy in the o-stems is the confusion of dative and genitive in ἐν τῇ Σοκνοπαίου νήσου and ἐν τῷ ἐποικίου, which can hardly be explained as a confusion of ου × ω, but heralds the disappearance of the dative case. Inflexional uncertainty is betrayed also by ὑπερωσι = ὑπερῴοις (A.D. ii), as though ὑπερῷον had become ὑπερών. The Attic second declension was confined to a few words (λεώς and νεώς gave way to λαός and ναός) and ultimately disappeared. Among the most persistent nouns was ἅλως 'threshing floor', but this was eventually replaced by ἅλων, the competition between the two stems producing the contaminated genitive τῆς ἁλώνω (ἅλω × ἅλωνος.

In the consonant class noteworthy forms are the genitives in -ου: μερίδου (A.D. i), γενημάτου (A.D. ii), τριπόδου (A.D. iv), which are matched by an accusative χθόνον, and a dative στομάτῳ. On the other hand the influence of the neuter s-stems shows itself in ὑδάτους (A.D. ii), but the tables are turned in μέρον (accusative), μέρου (genitive), and ἔτους (accusative plural, A.D. ii). Similar forms appear in the masculine proper names of this declension: Ἡρακλείου (genitive, A.D. ii), Σωκρατον (A.D. iv). The dative plural ἐσθήτεσι (A.D. ii) shows the same uncertainty as χοινίκεσι (A.D. i).

The *n*-stems also showed themselves susceptible to the influence of the second declension: accusative singular ποιμένον (A.D. vi), dative singular ῥινο (A.D. i), accusative plural χιθώνους (A.D. ii) and dative plural Ἀμάζοις (A.D. ii). Such confusions show the ancient system in the melting-pot.

In Modern Greek the noun declensions have been reorganized, but curiously enough in a way that is to some extent a return to the prehistoric state, in which the thematic *o*-stems were opposed to an athematic class, which also included the *ā*-stems. In historical times the last had been remodelled under the influence of the thematic class (p. 269).

Today the *o*-declension has remained unchanged (Class I), except for the loss of final -*n* in the accusative and the elimination of the dative; but the *ā*-nouns have been combined with the consonantal class (Class II). By a new principle of organization, this new class is split into two sub-classes according to gender: II A masculines, which show an opposition -*s*/zero in the nominative/genitive singular (πατέρας/πατέρα), ταμίας/ταμία, and II B feminines with a contrasting nominative–genitive opposition zero/-*s* (ὥρα/ ὥρας, ἐλπίδα/ἐλπίδας, μητέρα/μητέρας).

In the plural the absorption of the *ā*-stems into the consonantal class brought about the replacement in the nominative plural of -αι (which had >[ε]) by -ες, which does duty also for the accusative plural, whereas the *o*-declension still preserves the ancient distinction φίλοι [fili]/φίλους [filus].

What lies behind this bifurcation is the creation of new nominatives in -ς based on the extended accusatives like φύλακαν (earliest example ἀέρας A.D. iii). In the ensuing amalgamation the great predominance of feminines with the declensional oppositions nominative χώρᾱ/genitive χώρας, nominative νίκη/genitive νίκης proved decisive in determining the inflexional pattern of the feminines within the new superclass, which descriptively we may call 'non-*o*-class', though it is historically heir to the athematic class.

For the masculines the main problem is replacement of the ancient endings in II A 1 and 2, respectively -ου (πολίτου) and -ος (πατρός), by what is descriptively 'zero'. The *o*-declension does not provide a wholly satisfactory model to serve as an analogical base for these drastic changes. One proposed structural analysis interprets -*s*/-*u* as *s*/zero and finds here the 'dynamics of the system'; but this is purely a schematic device which smudges the given realities. If the same principle were applied to the singular/plural opposition in the accusative λόγο(ν)/λόγους, this would yield a structural opposition zero/-*s* for the singular/plural in this class. It is also difficult to find the impulse of the development in the forms of the definite article, masculine τοῦ [tu] *v*. feminine τῆς [tis], for there would have been mutual reinforcement in τοῦ ναύτου, yet we get τοῦ ναύτη. In purely descriptive terms, what mainly distinguishes the two major classes are the nominative plurals in -*i* and -*es* respectively, the latter serving also as accusative in one class, as opposed to -*us* in the other. In the singular of Class II one form with ending zero does duty for accusative and genitive, contrasting with -*o*/-*u* in Class I. In neither class can the loss of -*n* of the accusative singular be explained phonologically.

The influence of gender on the development of the declensional classes was by no means a new phenomenon in the history of Greek. In the prehistoric period the masculine *ā*-stems, which originally had the same nominative and genitive singular as the feminine nouns of this type (-*ā*/-*ās*), had received the distinctive endings -*ās*/-*āo* under the influence of the masculine *o*-stems, this being effective for a second time in Attic after the Attic-Ionic common period, when -εω was replaced by -*ou* (p. 62). What is striking is the reversal of this tendency in the post-Classical period. The earliest example known to me is τοῦ στρατιώτη (A.D. iv), but Latin loan-words also show the same pattern: ὁ σκρίβας, τὸν σκρίβα, τοῦ κολλήγα.

The following tabulation of the two major declensional classes of Modern Greek is arranged so as to show the historical components: I the *o*-stems and the opposed Class II with its sub-types A, masculines (1) of the *ā*-declension and (2) of the consonantal declension, B, (1) and (2), the corresponding feminines. We emphasize again the functional principle of gender that determines the declensional oppositions.

The neuters have remained a separate class with a declension virtually unchanged. The ancient type παιδίον appears as follows: singular nominative, vocative, accusative παιδί, geni-

		I		II		
			A		B	
			(1)	(2)	(1)	(2)
Sing.	Voc.	φίλε				
	Nom.	ὁ φίλος	ναύτης	πατέρας	νίκη	μητέρα
	Gen.	τοῦ φίλου	ναύτη	πατέρα	νίκης	μητέρας
	Acc.	τὸν φίλο	ναύτη	πατέρα	νίκη	μητέρα
Plur.	Nom.	οἱ φίλοι	ναύτες	πατέρες	νίκες	μητέρες
	Gen.	τῶν φίλων	ναυτῶν	πατέρων	νικῶν	μητέρων
	Acc.	τοὺς φίλους	ναύτες	πατέρες	νίκες	μητέρες

tive παιδιοῦ, plural nominative, vocative, accusative παιδιά, genitive παιδιῶν. The consonantal stems φῶς/φωτ-, κρέας/κρεατ-, κῦμα/κυματ-, ὄνομα/ὀνοματ-, πᾶν/παντ- still inflect in the old way, as do neuter s-stems like μέρος/μέρους/μέρη/μερῶν.

The most striking change in the above paradigms is the disappearance of the dative case in Modern Greek, its function having been taken over by the accusative and genitive or by prepositional phrases. The ancient Greek dative combined the functions of the dative proper, the instrumental, and the locative. In classical Greek the locative dative was constructed with a preposition, except for a few isolated phrases. Contributory to the loss of the dative was the loss of the distinction between motion towards (the directional dative) and rest (the locative dative). This is reflected in the confusion between adverbs like ἐκεῖ/ἐκεῖσε, ποῦ/ποῖ, etc., and also in the competition between εἰς with the accusative and ἐν with the dative, the final triumph of the former being preceded by a transitional phase in which each construction made gains at the expense of the other: e.g. κατέχων εἰς τὴν χεῖραν 'holding it in your hand', ἁλιεύειν εἰς ἄλλους τόπους 'to fish in other places', ἀνελθεῖν ἐν τῇ πόλει 'to come up to the city', κάθῃ ἐν Ἀλεξάνδριαν 'you sit in Alexandria', ἐπελθοῦσα ἐν τὴν οἰκία μου 'having come into my house'. The temporary vigour of ἐν is shown in its occasional use with the genitive where it replaces ἐπί, which in this period was synonymous with ἐν (ἐν κώμης). The instrumental dative was also reinforced by ἐν: γράφε ἐν ἥλῳ 'write with a nail' (A.D. iv).

2. Pronouns

The declension of the personal pronouns became the battlefield of conflicting analogical forces. In the accusative singular a final -ν was attached at an early date (A.D. i onwards): ἐμέν. This was then extended to ἐμένα, on the model of the consonantal declension, which it also followed in the further development to ἐμέναν (A.D. iv).

The second person assumed the initial ἐ- of the first: ἐσέν, ἐσοῦ (A.D. i), and this also developed in the corresponding possessive adjective ἐσός. The accusative forms σέν and ἐσέν are also attested in the papyri (A.D. ii), but not ἐσένα.

In the plural, owing to the convergence of η and υ, ἡμεῖς and ὑμεῖς were often confused (from A.D. i, in the papyri). This led to the creation of a new form σεῖς/ἐσεῖς for the second person (A.D. vi) while ἡμεῖς, ἡμᾶς, ἡμῶν were replaced by ἐμεῖς, ἐμᾶς, ἐμῶν. A set of enclitic forms was created with aphaeresis of the initial vowel. An early example is μῶν for ἡμῶν in a papyrus of A.D. vii.

Aphaeresis also affected αὐτός, αὐτή, αὐτό (e.g. τοῦ A.D. ii), and in this way a new demonstrative stem was created τόν, τήν, τό, etc. with an accidental resemblance to the definite article.

As in Attic after the beginning of iv B.C. the separate forms of the reflexive pronouns ἡμᾶς αὐτούς, ὑμᾶς αὐτούς, etc. dropped out of use, ἑαυτούς, etc. being employed for all persons. In the singular the third person ἑαυτός is also used for the second person.

3. Adjectives

In the comparison of the adjective the progress of the language towards regularity and simplification can be observed: -ίων and -ιστος tend to be replaced by -τερος, -τατος. Examples are καλλιότερον, ταχύτερος, ἀγαθώτατος, βραχύτατος, etc. Hypercharacterization, a widespread linguistic phenomenon in such formations, also makes its appearance: μειζότερος, πρεσβυτερώτερος, μεγιστότατος, πρώτιστα, and even μᾶλλον λεπτότερος.

4. VERBS

The same processes of simplification and regularization operated in the morphology of the verb. The athematic -μι verbs were progressively eliminated in continuation of a tendency which is observable in Ionic from the earliest texts (Homer, Hesiod, Herodotus). Contracted forms like ἐτίθει and ἐδίδου occur even in Attic. Thematic formations appear later and mostly in medio-passive forms, but active participial forms, such as ὑποτίθοντας (A.D. ii) also occur. For ἵστημι a present stem ἱσταν- was extracted from the infinitive ἱστάναι, but this occurs mainly in the infinitive (ἱστάνειν) and the participle (ἱστανό-μενος). At a later date this stem appears with aphaeresis of the initial vowel (στάνω, NT and papyrus A.D. iv). Another variant frequently encountered in Koine writers is the contracted form ἱστάω with later transfer to the -έω class (ἀφιστοῦμεν A.D. v). Yet another present stem is στήκω (LXX, NT, but papyri first in A.D. iii), which was made from ἕστηκα, a perfect with present meaning. This was the basis of modern Greek στέκω/στέκομαι.

The -νυ- verbs were particularly prone to thematization, δεικνύω occurring as early as Hesiod. The phenomenon was not confined to inflexion: new stems without -νυ- were coined from the non-present tenses. The three stages are illustrated in ἀνοίγνυμι, ἀνοιγνύω, ἀνοίγω (Pindar, Herodotus, but papyri first in i B.C.). The thematic forms of δίδωμι, though present at an early date in Ionic, do not appear in the papyri until post-Ptolemaic times, when from the imperfect ἐδίδουν a new present δίδω or διδέω (διδῶ) was created. Modern Greek has δίδω and δίνω. In the imperative the influence of θές (from τίθημι) produced a rich crop of analogical forms: e.g. ἀπόδες (A.D. i/ii), παράδετε (A.D. ii).

In Modern Greek the verb 'to be' appears as a deponent, a development which goes back to the beginnings of the Koine, for the imperfect ἤμην, ἤμεθα occurs in papyri of iii B.C. as well as in the LXX and the NT. However, the first papyrus example of the present indicative εἶμαι (spelt ἤμε) is dated to A.D. iv/v, while the second person εἶσαι occurs possibly in a text of A.D. v. In the third singular ἔνι occurs for ἐστί (chiefly in negative sentences); the paradigmatic pressure of εἶμαι, εἶσαι changed ἔνι first into ἔνε and then εἶναι, the modern form which also does duty for the plural, though there was a short-lived experiment ἔνουσι (A.D. iv).

In the imperfect second singular ἦσθα was replaced by ἦς. The third singular regularly appears as ἦν in the papyri, but this was replaced by the middle form ἦτο in the early Middle Ages. The third plural ἦσαν has remained in use until the present day, but the competing form ἦταν had also appeared by the Early Middle Ages.

In the paradigms ancient irregularities such as οἶδα, οἶσθα, οἶδε, ἴσμεν, ἴστε, ἴσασιν were levelled at an early date to οἶδα, οἶδας/οἶδες, οἶδε, οἴδαμεν, οἴδατε, οἶδαν.

In the tenses the aspectual distinction between aorist and perfect has been obliterated in Modern Greek. In the Koine there are numerous pathological symptoms heralding the coming fusion of the two tenses. The augment is substituted for the reduplication (e.g. ἐθύκαμεν (A.D. iv), ἐκαρπονήκαμεν (A.D. ii)), and the uncertainty is underlined by examples of the reverse influence as in the aorist πεπλήρωσα (A.D. iii), or even by combinations of both: ἐκέγραφα = ἐγέγραφα (A.D. ii), which occurs also in the infinitive ἐβεβλοφέναι (A.D. iv). The endings of the weak aorist penetrate into the perfect. The third plural -αν for -ασι came first (γέγοναν A.D. i, etc.). In fact in the papyri -ασι is seldom found later than the Ptolemaic period, and its occurrence in aorists like ἐπήλθασιν (A.D. iii) and εἴπασιν (A.D. vii) are erroneous applications of inflexions doubtless learned in school. Other aberrations are the first singular πέπρακον 'I sold' (A.D. ii), εἴληφον (A.D. iv), and third plural τεθελήκουσι (A.D. i). The substitution in the second singular of -ες for -ας came later, for this was possible only after this ending of the strong aorist had been introduced into the sigmatic type; but -ας did not survive later than A.D. iii.

In the aorist writers wavered between the endings of the two types. On the whole the endings of the sigmatic class prevailed, e.g. κατέφαγαν, ἦλθαν (A.D. i), ἐμάθαμεν (A.D. ii), ἔβαλα (A.D. iv); but in the second singular -ες is very frequent. Occasional examples of thematic inflexions are found elsewhere, especially in the middle, e.g. ἀπεγραψόμην (A.D. ii), ἐκομίσου (A.D. i), διαπέμψετο without augment (!) (A.D. iii). In the third plural the competition between the two types -ον and -σαν gave rise to transient 'contaminated' forms, such as the third plural in -οσαν, a phenomenon anticipated in Boeotian ἐλάβοσαν: εὔροσαν (A.D. i), ἐπήλθοσαν (A.D. ii), ἦροσαν (A.D. i). A similar form appears in the imperfect of contracted verbs in Modern Greek: ἀγαποῦσαν 'they were loving'. This seems to have been analysed as third plural ending -αν attached to a stem characterized by -ουσ-, and this has spread to the other persons, both singular and plural: ἀγαποῦσα, ἀγαποῦσες, ἀγαποῦσε, ἀγαπούσαμε, ἀγαπούσατε, ἀγαποῦσαν.

The strong aorists were also affected in their stems which progressively assumed sigmatic forms from ii B.C. onward: κατέλιψα (i B.C.), κατῆξαν (A.D. ii), ἔδρασα (A.D. iv), ἀπέγνωσα (iii B.C.), γνώσῃ (A.D. i). The extended suffix -ησ- occurs in ἀγαγῆσαι (i B.C.), λαβῆσαι (A.D. iii), and it appears in other types such as ἐγάμησα (A.D. iv). In the genesis of these new aorists the s-future played a part.

In Modern Greek the future tense has been replaced by periphrastic forms, especially θά, which goes back to θέλω ἵνα, followed by the subjunctive. The papyri offer examples of a periphrasis which is parallel to Latin *cantare habeo* > French *chanterai*.[1] This is ἔχω with the infinitive, the full meaning of which was 'have the means of doing', 'be in a position to do': e.g. ἐχόντων δαπανῆσαι (A.D. ii). But there are also examples which come close to a pure future: οὐκ ἔχεις ἀπ' ἐμοῦ ἀκοῦσαι 'you will not hear from me' (A.D. ii). Combinations of the infinitive with θέλω, βούλομαι, μέλλω, and ὀφείλω also occur. The close connection of the aorist subjunctive with the future indicative (pp. 310f.) continues to manifest its influence, for it occurs with the function of a plain future: ἀνενέγκω for -οίσω (A.D. ii), ἔλθω (A.D. iii–iv), καταγαγεῖται (A.D. iii), ἀφῶ (A.D. iv).

Of the moods, the optative had disappeared from the spoken language by the beginning of our era except in certain stereotyped phrases. The reappearance in letters of the fourth century A.D. is simply a reflection of Atticist teaching.

In the imperative the endings of the strong and weak aorists compete. Sigmatic aorists with the second singular in -ε are absent from the Ptolemaic papyri but are frequent later: πέμψε (A.D. ii), ἄσπασε (A.D. ii), κόμισε (A.D. ii), etc. In view of the frequency of the imperatival infinitive (see below) and the

---

[1] E. Benveniste has argued that *chanterai* < *cantari habeo*.

interchange of αι and ε, it is often difficult to distinguish between infinitives like πέμψαι and imperatives like πέμψε, etc. In the aorist middle the -σαι ending remains paramount. There is a tendency to eliminate the athematic type in -θι: διάβα (A.D. i) which anticipates Modern Greek. Other imperatives of this type like γράψα (A.D. iii/iv) have been extracted from the second plural γράψατε.

Of the numerous infinitive types in ancient Greek, that in -ειν (present, future, and strong aorist) has prevailed over -σαι (weak aorist) and -ῆναι (passive aorist). As usual there are temporary gains of the doomed forms: e.g. ἐφιδῆσαι (ii B.C.) and εἰδῆσαι later; ἀγαγῆσαι (ii B.C.). The new type in -εν in sigmatic stems, such as γράψεν (A.D. iv), πέμψεν (A.D. iv), ποιῆσεν (A.D. iv–v), are best taken as contaminations or recharacterizations of the -σαι type, for this could also be written -σε. But the same ending also occurs in the perfect: πέπρακεν (A.D. i), εἶδεν (A.D. ii).

The infinitives of the contracted o-stems show a type -οῖν for -οῦν. These are to be explained analogically on the pattern ποιεῖ: ποιεῖν: : δηλοῖ: δηλοῖν. The infinitives in their turn created imperatives like δήλοι, παραδήλοι for δήλου. Infinitives in -ειν show loss of final -ν, and this is the origin of expressions like θέλω γράψει in the modern literary language.

The participle in Modern Greek is invariable, forms like δένοντας serving for all genders, numbers and cases. In the papyri the participle still exhibits a variety of forms, but their employment is often irregular and uncertain. The masculine form is preferred to both feminine and neuter, and we see the germ of modern usage in expressions like τῶν δοθέν (A.D. i) and τὸ διαφέρον ἡμῖν οἰκίαν (A.D. vii).

Mutual influence of aorist and perfect has also been detected in the participles, but forms like φυγότα, εἰσελθότα, and the like are more plausibly explained by the loss of anteconsonantal -ν in φυγόντα, etc.

Another response of the language to its new cosmopolitan role as a 'language of civilization' serving a vast area was the enormous expansion of the lexicon. We have seen how much Ionic contributed to the formation of Attic literary prose. The process continued in the Koine, which evolved into a supple instrument adequate not only for the needs of government and administration, but also for the new developments in science and technology. If weight is given chiefly to vocabulary, then we could adopt Meillet's definition of the Koine as Atticized Ionic.

3. The Koine and the Ancient Dialects

This raises the question of the part played by the ancient dialects in the formation of the Koine. At first glance it is evident that the major contribution was made by Attic and Ionic for it exhibits the key features of this dialect-group (see pp. 62f.). 1, ᾱ > η but with the typically Attic 'reversion' in -ιᾱ and -ρᾱ; 2, the potential particle ἄν; 3, the pronouns ἡμεῖς, ὑμεῖς; 4, athematic infinitives in -ναι and 5, paragogic -ν. In the i-stems considerable weight attaches to the presence of the anomalous Attic πόλεως (instead of Ionic πόλιος) and genitives like πολίτου (instead of Ionic πολίτεω). The verb πράσσω is a compromise between Attic πράττω and Ionic πρήσσω.

Elements from other dialects are negligible in comparison and confined to isolated points. The expression 'no one' is of particular diagnostic interest. In the combinations οὐδ' εἷς, μηδ' εἷς Attic, of course, retained the aspirates, unlike the psilotic Ionic of Asia Minor. These words were probably always pronounced οὐθείς, μηθείς in Attic, and such is the regular spelling in Attic inscriptions after 330 B.C. These forms appear in the Koine, but that the psilotic pronunciation still persisted in the spoken language is suggested by the fact that as from A.D. i -θ- yields ground to -δ-. Modern Greek δέν is also testimony to the strength of another dialect tradition.

This leads to a consideration of the struggle between the official standard language and the local dialects. The political force brought to bear on the local dialects may be illustrated from a Thessalian inscription (Schwyzer, *Del.*[3], 590) of late iii B.C., recording resolutions passed by the city of Larisa in response to instructions given by Philip V. The record is in the local dialect, and includes the texts and translations of the king's letters, the originals of which are in the Koine. Again, in a Boeotian inscription of late iii B.C. (Schwyzer, *Del.*[3], 523) recording arrangements for the repayment of money lent to the city of Orchomenus by a woman Nicareta, though the resolutions are in pure Boeotian the original contract (σούγγραφος) and the agreement (ὁμολογά) are written in the Koine. The Thessalian example suggests an important motive in the preservation of the dialect: loss of political independence (the city is simply complying with Philip's instructions) stimulated municipal pride which finds expression in the use of its own dialect. Yet the presence of the Koine is persistent (as we see in the business documents in the possession of Nicareta), and increasingly penetrates the official inscriptions of the Boeotians from c. 200 B.C. on. Within a century the Koine is used almost exclusively, yet private inscriptions are still couched in the patois until A.D. i.

Boeotian also illustrates another pattern of resistance to the Koine—the persistence of restricted common languages. For a short time Boeotia became a member of the Aeolian league which had evolved a Koine of its own that exhibits two of the special features of North-west Greek (p. 60): ἐν for εἰς and -οις in the dative plural of consonant stems. Documents in the North-west Koine occur not only in the north-west of Greece but also in the Peloponnese and even in Crete.

Doric was the dialect which showed the greatest resistance to the Koine: on inscriptional evidence it survived longest in the Peloponnese and the Dorian islands like Crete and Rhodes. In the transition period between the time of the dialect proper and the triumph of the Koine, a watered-down form was evolved eliminating local peculiarities and incorporating elements from the Attic Koine. The name 'Doric Koine' is given to this official language, which prevails in the Doric inscriptions of the last three centuries B.C. There is ancient testimony (Strabo, Suetonius and Pausanias) to the survival of Doric speech in the Peloponnese and Rhodes until A.D. i and ii. That it persisted longer in isolated localities is shown by the existence of Tsakonian, which is still spoken in a small area on the south-east coast of the Peloponnese and exhibits some features of ancient Laconian, including initial v-.

Such 'resistance' is in fact to be explained by remoteness and isolation from the linguistic influence of the centres of power. This is why Doric contributed so little to the Koine. The material collected consists almost exclusively of loan-words which, as might be expected, belong largely to the military sphere. Some like λοχαγός 'company commander', ξεναγός 'commander of mercenaries', and ἄγημα '(army) corps' had already been incorporated in Attic. Nor need Doric be the direct source of two words which replaced their Attic equivalents that had the disadvantage of belonging to the anomalous 'Attic second declension'. One was λαός 'people', which was familiar to speakers of Attic and Ionic from Homeric and other poetry; the other was ναός 'temple', a central word of the Panhellenic religious vocabulary. A curious detail is that in the word for 'bird' the Doric stem form ὀρνιχ- 'bird' is used as well as ὀρνιθ-. The sole morphological feature is the masculine genitive in -ᾱ < -αο; but the ending is confined to non-Attic personal names, where it was also admissible in Attic.

4. Genesis of the Koine

At the beginning of this century two 'models' of the genesis of the Koine were advanced. Paul Kretschmer thought of it as a kind of pool fed by all the major dialect streams. This has recently been revived, and S. G. Kapsomenos (1958) regards the Greek linguistic world at the time of the formation of the Koine as a kind of melting pot. In this 'cosmogonic state', which contained all the features attested in the popular Koine and those which survive in the modern dialects, a kind of vortex developed distributing such dialect elements over areas of varying extent. However, such a 'model' hardly conforms to linguistic realities. As Meillet rightly says 'experience shows that a common language is generally based on a certain type of dialect' and, we may add, this tends to be one backed by political power, which is all the more effective if the dialect in question also enjoys cultural prestige. This is particularly true of what we have called 'imperial Attic'. It was both cultural prestige and administrative convenience that preserved Greek in the face of Roman political power. What is particularly interesting is the systematic way that the Roman heirs to the Macedonian Empire went to work. The existence of a well-organized translation office at Rome even in Republican times is indicated by the unvarying use of standard Greek equivalents for the necessary Latin technical terms, and the latinizing flavour of the Greek decrees of the Senate. Despite this, governmental and administrative pressure and doubtless also the personal inertia of Roman officials high and low forced Latin loan-words even into the vernacular (a number of them still survive in Modern Greek). Examples are (a) from the military sphere κεντυρίων, κουστωδία, λεγιών, πραιτώριον; (b) law and administration κῆνσος, κολωνία, σπεκουλάτωρ, φραγέλλιον (< Vulg. Lat. *fragellum* for *flagellum*); (c) trade and commerce λέντιον (= *linteum*), σουδάριον, μεμβράνα, μέμβρανον 'parchment'; (d) measures and coins μόδιος, μίλιον, δηνάριον, and κοδράντης (= *quadrans*). The last word illustrates the shifts to which the Greeks were put to represent a Latin sound which did not occur in Greek: Κουιρῖνος *Quīrīnus*, Κυίντιος *Quīntius*, 'Ακύλας *Aquila* exemplify the different ways of rendering *qu*.

Consonantal *v* first appears as ο ('Οαλέριος) and ου (Ούαλέριος), but β was used later when this sound had developed a fricative pronunciation (see p. 178). Latin *f* offered a similar difficulty until the aspirated plosives had become fricatives (A.D. i, see p. 178). For consonantal *i*, iota was used ('Ιούλιος).

For other Latin words Greek equivalents were devised by loan-translation, e.g. ἑκατόνταρχος (*centurio*), Σεβαστός (*Augustus*). Even whole phrases were rendered literally and unidiomatically: ἐργασίαν δοῦναι (*operam dare*), τὸ ἱκανὸν διδόναι (*satis facere*), and this occasionally would result in syntactical Latinisms like γεγραμμένῳ παρῆσαν (*scribendo adfuerunt*).

A new idiomatic and sophisticated procedure was to search for Greek analogues: *senatus* was rendered as σύγκλητος (βουλή), *praetor* as στρατηγός; *consul* was analysed as *praetor maximus*, hence the term ὕπατος (στρατηγός); ἔπαρχος was chosen as the equivalent of *praefectus*, whence ἡ ἐπάρχειος = *provincia*.

Some transplanted Latin suffixes struck root in Greek. One was the denominative -*ātu*- which has three functions in Modern Greek: 1, denoting physical abnormalities, e.g. γενᾶτος 'with a large beard'; 2, fruit preserves, e.g. μηλᾶτο 'apple jelly'; 3, adjectives with the meaning 'provided with', e.g. ἀφρᾶτος 'foamy'. A papyrus of A.D. vi has the word κυκλᾶτος 'shod'. The other suffix is -*ianu*- (originally used to form adjectives from names in -*ius*, but then extended to appellatives, e.g. στρατηλατιανός). The diminutive suffixes -ελλα and -ουλλα occur in the papyri only in Latin loan-words, but they were destined (along with Italian -*outsi*) to replace the ancient suffixes -αριον and

-ιδιον. On the other hand, verbs borrowed from Latin were naturalized by means of Greek suffixes, the chief being -ευω: βουλλεύω = *bullare*, δηληγατεύω, πραιδεύω, κουρατορεύω, etc.

The language, whose genesis and development have been examined in the previous pages, is known to us only in writing. Its unity over a vast territory of heterogeneous populations can hardly be symptomatic of everyday speech. This we should expect to betray itself in the 'errors' of the less-educated writers, and confidence in such an interpretation would be strengthened if such features recurred in the modern vernacular or could be plausibly regarded as intermediate stages between ancient and Modern Greek. The official papyri offer little such information, for they were largely the work of scribes trained in the use of stereotyped formulas. The private letters are of greater value to the linguist. A delightful example is the famous letter (A.D. ii/iii) from the little Theon to his father:

Θεων Θεωνι τω πατρι χαιρειν. καλως εποιησες. ουκ απενηχες με μετ εσου εις πολιν. η ου θελις απενεκκειν μετ εσου εις Αλεξανδριαν. ου μη γραψω σε επιστολην ουτε λαλω σε ουτε υιγενω σε ειτα. αν δε ελθης εις Αλεξανδριαν ου μη λαβω χειραν παρα σου ουτε παλι χαιρω σε λυπον. αμ μη θελης απενεκαι με ταυτα γεινετε. και η μητηρ μου ειπε Αρχελαω οτι αναστατοι με αρρον αυτον. καλως δε εποιησες. δωρα μοι επεμψες μεγαλα, αρακια. πεπλανηκαν ημως εκει τη ημερα ιβ̄ οτι επλευσες. λυπον πεμψον εις με παρα-καλω σε. αμ μη πεμψης ου μη φαγω ου μη πεινω. ταυτα.

'Theon to his father Theon greetings! A fine thing you have done. You did not take me to town with you. If you don't take me with you to Alexandria, I won't write you a letter, I won't talk to you and I won't take your hand and I won't greet you any more either. If you don't want to take me that's what will happen. And my mother wrote to Archelaus "that boy upsets me: take him away". A fine thing you have done. And the fine present you sent me: chickling! They fooled us here when you sailed on the twelfth. Anyway, do please send to me. If you don't send, I won't eat and I won't drink. All for now.'

The address on the back reads αποδος Θεωνι απο Θεωνατος υιω, Θεωνᾶς being a diminutive form of Θέων: 'Deliver to Theon from his son little Theon'.

5. Christian Greek

It was, of course, the language of everyday life and not the artificial literary language that the new religion used to reach the hearts of converts once it had spread beyond the frontiers of its native Palestine. The language of the New Testament was for long regarded by scholars as *sui generis*, a religious language that had evolved separately from the secular Koine, a view natural enough since, as a literary form, the Gospels were unique. However, study of the contemporary inscriptions, and in particular the papyri, showed that the language of the New Testament is, by and large, close to that of the popular language as reflected in the non-official papyri. This finding is not affected by the notable differences of style between the different authors, Luke, the Greek physician, being the most careful stylist. This was already remarked by Jerome (*Ep.* 19, 38), who noted that Luke 'was among all the Evangelists the one who was most learned in the Greek tongue'. This was demonstrated by Eduard Norden by comparison of corresponding passages in the three synoptic Gospels. His finding is that Luke almost invariably chooses the expression which from a purist point of view is 'better', a judgment confirmed by the witness of the Atticist lexicons. In matters of vocabulary Luke, who undoubtedly had enjoyed the contemporary literary education, tends to reject outlandish 'barbarous' words. Jerome explains thus the avoidance of *osianna*. Similarly he uses (12, 59) λεπτόν for the Latinism κοδράντης and substitutes (20, 22) φόρον for κῆνσον, and ἑκατοντάρχης for κεντυρίων. He even suppressed Γολγοθᾶν and used only the translation Κρανίον. In 22, 18 he uses ἀπὸ τοῦ νῦν for Matthew's ἀπ' ἄρτι, a usage condemned by the Atticists. Phrynichus' note 'Nowadays πτῶμα is applied to corpses, but this is not so in ancient authority' illuminates ὅπου τὸ σῶμα, ἐκεῖ καὶ συναχθήσονται οἱ ἀετοί 'where the corpse is there the vultures gather' in Luke (17, 37), whereas Matthew uses the expression ὅπου ἐὰν ᾖ τὸ πτῶμα, just as he does the verb τρώγω 'chew' in the vulgar sense 'eat' (cf. Lat. *manducare* > Fr. *manger*) for Luke's correct ἐσθίω. There are some expressions which Luke avoids not merely because they are vulgar but because they express notions or happenings which offended his sense of propriety. For instance, he not only forbears even from translating the Latinism φραγελλώσας 'after scourging him', but for 'handed him over to be crucified' he substitutes 'delivered him up to their will' (παρέδωκεν τῷ θελήματι αὐτῶν). Another expression of the same kind is the verb κολαφίζω. That κόλαφος 'clout on the head' belonged to the popular language is shown by Plautus' use of it and by Petronius' derived verb *percolopare*. This word, which was the ancestor of Italian *colpo*, French *coup*, curiously enough occurs in Greek texts almost exclusively in Christian literature. In the NT both Matthew and Mark used the coarse expression κολαφίζω 'slap', but Luke prefers the ancient colloquialism δέρω in the transferred sense it has in the proverb ὁ μὴ δαρεὶς ἄνθρωπος οὐ παιδεύεται 'spare the rod and spoil the child' (lit. 'the man who is not thrashed is not being educated'). Yet, despite his greater mastery of Greek, Luke also preferred to write his Gospel in language closer to the speech and to the hearts of the people. This evident fact is highlighted by the contrasting tone and style of the long and elaborate period which forms the Prologue addressed to Theophilus:

ἐπειδήπερ πολλοὶ ἐπεχείρησαν ἀνατάξασθαι διήγησιν περὶ τῶν πεπληροφορημένων ἐν ἡμῖν πραγμάτων, καθὼς παρέδοσαν ἡμῖν οἱ ἀπ' ἀρχῆς αὐτόπται καὶ ὑπηρέται γενόμενοι τοῦ λόγου, ἔδοξε κἀμοί, παρηκολουθηκότι ἄνωθεν πᾶσιν ἀκριβῶς, καθεξῆς σοι γράψαι, κράτιστε Θεόφιλε, ἵνα ἐπιγνῷς περὶ ὧν κατηχήθης λόγων τὴν ἀσφάλειαν.

'Seeing that many have undertaken to draw up an account of the events that were brought to fulfilment among us, as has been handed down to us by those who were eye-witnesses from the beginning and became servants of the Word, I too decided, having carefully gone over everything from the beginning, to write a connected account for you, most excellent Theophilus, in order that you may have exact knowledge of the reliability of the matters on which you have received instruction.'

While there is general agreement that the New Testament is written largely in the contemporary vernacular, there remains a persistent strangeness for the scholar steeped in the classical tradition. What the authors had to express was a new religious revelation that sprang from the world of the Jewish people, whose own language was Aramaic. As this new religious sect gained strength in the homeland, at first oral tradition was doubtless drawn on to instruct new adherents about the teachings of Jesus. At some stage this body of facts was given written form, and Biblical scholars have reconstructed a manual, presumably written in Aramaic, which was subsequently translated into Greek about the middle of the first century A.D. Other scholars have argued that the similarity of New Testament Greek to the contemporary vernacular has been greatly exaggerated. They stress the importance of the Septuagint, a Greek translation of the Old Testament produced for the needs of the Jews in the Diaspora, who now spoke Greek instead of Aramaic and could not understand Hebrew. The Septuagint abounds in non-Greek expressions, and this is due to the compulsion felt by the translator to follow closely the words of the original rather than to render its context idiomatically. Thus even if minute philological analysis of the New Testament established that the separate words as isolated units are Hellenistic, the pervading style is determined by Old Testament Greek. The inherent plausibility of some such developments in the given socio-linguistic situation would lead one to expect the distortions of natural language that commonly arise in translation, particularly of works regarded with great reverence (the Old Testament is a Holy Book both for Jews and Christians) and believed to have been divinely inspired even in their verbal expression. Such is the origin of the Semitisms which have long been debated by biblical scholars. The highly technical details lie outside the scope of an outline history of the Greek language.

6. The Establishment and the Popular Language

The popular language continued to be used in works of edification addressed to simple folk. They comprised writings which continued or supplemented what was contained in the New Testament, or they told the lives of the martyrs and saints. Vernacular elements were also admitted by Byzantine chroniclers like Malalas (A.D. vi). Precisely the vulgarisms of such modes of expression aroused the scorn and mockery of the cultured world and it was inevitable that, when the Church rose from its lowly origins and turned into the 'establishment', it could do no other than use the established language of polite society. Later the Eastern Empire, having adopted and developed the inherited Koine for governmental purposes, in the successive crises and revivals turned increasingly to its glorious past for cultural comfort and literary expression. Thus in the course of centuries the gap widened between the backward-looking official language and the living language of the people, which constantly grew and developed in response to the needs of life. In this way the State and Church establishment became the stronghold of linguistic reaction.

When the Greek state was re-established with the achievement of independence and Athens became its capital (1833), part of its inheritance was a deep linguistic division. On the one hand a traditional official language that could serve as a Pan-hellenic medium of communication but was dominated by a negative principle—the rejection of everything that was 'vulgar'. On the other hand, there was the living language which took the form of a congeries of local dialects, exhibiting an unmistakable Hellenic unity despite the differences, which, with one exception, had developed from the Common Dialect that had superseded the dialects of ancient Greece.

These are the roots of the 'language question' which is peculiar to the modern Greek State. The two poles are the 'purizing' official language, the *katharevousa* (καθαρεύουσα) and the popular language, *demotic* (δημοτική); but in fact usage covers a whole spectrum of varieties, ranging from the extreme traditionalism of the καθαρεύουσα to the radical demotic which has been called 'longhaired' (μαλλιάρη), with the 'mixed' language (μικτή or μέση γλῶττα), 'current' (καθομιλουμένη) speech and 'popular' (δημοτική) speech as intermediate stages.

Common to them all is phonology, for even the most die-hard traditionalist, though he writes his texts in the ancient orthography, in reading them aloud can do no other than accept the facts of the historical developments outlined above. The grammar, too, is much simplified in comparison with the Byzantine Koine. It is above all in vocabulary that the *katharevousa* stands apart: οἶκος 'house' *v.* σπίτι; οἶνος 'wine' *v.* κρασί; ἄρτος 'bread' *v.* ψωμί; ἵππος 'horse' *v.* ἄλογο; ὄνος 'ass' *v.* γαίδαρος; ἄνθος 'flower' *v.* λουλούδι, etc. Learned and archaizing, requiring much effort to acquire, it has remained the official language of the State, its organs and institutions, the Church, post-elementary education, the Universities and a great part of the Press.

Demotic is the standard spoken language of Greece today, in that it is the natural form of everyday expression used by all classes, regardless of differences of education. No less important is that since the beginning of the nineteenth century it has increasingly served the needs of creative literature. Here history has repeated itself in that poetry preceded prose: demotic was used at the beginning of the nineteenth century by Solomos and his school in the literary renaissance of the Ionian islands, whereas the first work of prose in demotic appeared in 1888. Political events likewise favoured the adoption of a national language based on the southern group of dialects because the Peloponnese was the gathering ground for the revolutionary fighters, and between 1821 and 1833, when Athens became the capital of the resurrected Greek state, there developed 'A new common language based on the dialects of the Peloponnese but with a good many Ionian features. Peloponnesian Greek was well fitted to be the basis of a national language. Without either the radical phonetic changes of northern Greek or the archaic features of Cretan or Cypriot, it was easily understood by all Greeks, and was sufficiently close to the language of late Byzantine and post-Byzantine vernacular literature to be acceptable to all as a common tongue.'[1] The triumph of demotic has recently been officially acknowledged. By a decision of the Greek Ministry of Education the 'katharevousa' has ceased by law to be the official language of the Greek state; 'demotic' has been taught from September 1976 in all Greek schools.

Yet for all the radical changes outlined in this chapter, the natural spoken language of Greece today is still recognizably the same as that of Homer. It remains a highly archaic language of unmistakably Indo-European structure in its nominal and verbal morphology.

[1] R. Browning, 105–6 (1969).

PART II

COMPARATIVE-HISTORICAL GRAMMAR

VII

WRITING AND PRONUNCIATION

The comparative method in linguistics rests on a simple fundamental fact: all speech consists of the use of vocal sounds to signal messages, and the connection between the vocable, the speech 'expression', and the meaning it conveys is *arbitrary*. Consequently, if we observe far-reaching resemblances between two languages, the fact of arbitrariness compels us to rule out the possibility of coincidence, that is independent invention, and to conclude that there must be some historical connection. This may, of course, be of the most superficial kind, for words may easily be borrowed from one language into another, like *potato* and *tomato*. Of greater importance for the comparatist are the resemblances of grammatical structure, about which a brief word may be said. In linguistic descriptions the speech corpus, taken as an adequate sample of the speech habits of a given community, is broken down into a finite number of minimal meaningful elements, S(ound)-M(eaning) units, the so-called 'monemes', the combination of which into more complex units at different levels by stated rules will generate all the conceivable utterances in the speech community in question. A small proportion of these monemes have structural functions within the utterances, and the part of the description which specifies these is called the grammar. Such structural devices are rarely borrowed, and it is on resemblances of this kind that the comparatist lays greatest stress in linguistic genetics.

Fundamental, then, for the comparatist is the establishment of the sound-meaning units in the languages to be compared. With contemporary speech the sound aspect is directly observed. But for the most part the historian of language must have recourse to written records. He cannot make a direct comparison, say, of the Greek alphabetic, or Linear-B syllabic word-forms with others written in the *devānagarī* of India. To make his comparison of S-M forms and so establish a basis for his deductions he must deduce the spoken expression from the written characters: he must seek to convert the graphemes into

phonemes. The first task of the historian of Greek must, therefore, be to present the problems that arise in determining the
pronunciation of the Greek alphabetic texts. The Linear B
script discussed in Chapter II, though historically earlier, is
scientifically secondary: the values of the syllabic characters are
arrived at by correlation with those of the later alphabetic script.

The whole series of Greek letters from *alpha* to *tau* was taken
over from a North Semitic alphabet.[1] From the tabulation
(Fig. 6) it emerges that the shapes of the characters are basically
the same, their names are virtually the same (with inevitable
adaptations), and the order is the same (with the exception of
the sibilants, see below). Another peculiarity is that at least the
first line in archaic inscriptions runs from right to left. In North
Semitic inscriptions the text was written in every line from
right to left, but in archaic Greek practice the even lines run
in the opposite direction to the odd lines. This method of
writing is known as *boustrophēdon* 'as the ox turns'. Such texts
may also begin from left to right with the even lines right to
left.

Boustrophēdon is common to all the early Greek local alphabets
and is one of the common divergencies from North Semitic
practice, a fact which indicates that the Greek alphabet
originated in a comparatively restricted area. Another change,
and this was a notable advance towards the goal of perfect
phonemic notation, was the use of certain characters denoting
Semitic consonants but superfluous for Greek, to render the
Greek vowels. '*Alep*, *hē*' and '*ayin* were used for *a*, *e* and *o*.
Yôd, which denoted the semivowel [j], a sound absent from
alphabetic Greek except as a glide sound for Mycenaean (see
p. 42), was used for the vowel [i], a value which it occasionally
also had in Semitic. *Wāw* was given two forms: one (*upsilon*),
taken over from a cursive Phoenician script, was used for the
vowel [ʋ]; the other (*digamma*) was preserved at its correct
alphabetic place in a number of Greek dialects (see pp. 226–8).

---

[1] The Greeks themselves described the letters of the alphabet as φοινικήϊα
'Phoenician'. Supporting evidence has been sought in the expression
φοινικάζεν (infinitive) 'to write' and the corresponding agent noun φοινι-
καστάς, which occur in an early fifth-century inscription from Crete of a
man proposed for the office as 'recorder' and scribe, but another suggestion
is that the verb and the derived noun refer to writing in red letters.

N. Sem. Alphabets	Greek Alphabets	Sem. Name	Greek Name	Greek Value
∢	A A ∧	ʾālep̱	ἄλφα	[a]
Ꝯ ᕒ	B Ᏼ Ꮧ ᑭ	bêṯ	βῆτα	[b]
ᐸ	ᒉ ᒋ ᒉ ⟩⟩	gīmel	γάμμα	[g]
Δ	Δ ᐯ ᐱ	dāleṯ	δέλτα	[d] '
ᖻ ᔕ	ᔕ E Ꝑ	hē'	εἶ¹	[e]
Ⴘ ᖻ ᒭ	ᒭ ᒣ Ꞙ ᖻ	wāw	' Ϝαῦ²	[w]
I	II ᛁ	zayin	ζῆτα³	[dz], [zd]
E ᗺ H	ᗺ ᗝ ᗺ H ᖻ	ḥêṯ	ῆτα	[h], [εː]
⊕ ⊗	⊗ ⊕ ⊙	ṭēṯ	θῆτα	[tʰ]
ᒿ ᒾ	ᕭ ᓵ ᒿ ᒾ ᒲ ᛁ	yôḏ	ἰῶτα	[i]
Ψ Ⴘ	Ꝅ Ꝅ	kap̱	κάππα	[k]
L ᒪ	ᒪ ᒣ ᐱ ᒪ ᒣ	lāmeḏ	λά(μ)βδα	[l]
ᕽ ᕟ ᗑ	ᗑ ᗑ ᗯ ᗰ	mēm	μῦ	[m]
ᒤ	ᒤ ᒫ ᖻ N	nûn	νῦ	[n]
ᖬ	ᖬ ᖬ ᖬ ᗗ ᘓ	sāmeḵ	ξεῖ⁴	[ks]
O	O	ʿayin	οῦ⁵	[o]
ᒆ	ᒆ ᒆ) ᑎ	pē'	πεῖ	[p]
Φ	Φ ᖰ	qôp̱	Ϙόππα⁶	[q]
ᖯ	ᖰ ᖰ ᖴ Ꝑ	rēš, rôš	ῥῶ	[r]
W	ᔕ ᒿ ᒿ Σ	šīn	σίγμα⁷	[s]
Ⴟ ᖻ	Ꞙ ᒣ	tāw	ταῦ	[t]
ᖻ ᖻ ᒭ	ᖻ ᐯ ᖻ		ῦ⁸	[u]

Fig. 6. The Greek Alphabet.

(1) Later ἒ ψιλόν   (6) The velar plosive used in
(2) Also ὒ ψιλόν   many local scripts before *o* and *u*
(3) Corresponds to *ṣāḏê*   (7) Perhaps from *sāmeḵ*
(4) Perhaps corresponds to *šin*   (8) Later ὒ ψιλόν
(5) Later ὄ μικρόν

This Greek proto-alphabet was further enriched by letters for the aspirated consonants Φ and X for p^h and k^h respectively, parallel to Θ for t^h. This alphabet, consisting of 22 letters, was used (with the omission of digamma which had no application in Attic-Ionic, see p. 226) by the Athenians down to the end of the fifth century B.C. It used E for all varieties of *e*, while O was used similarly for all varieties of *o*. H still stood for the aspirate but on occasion was used syllabically for *hē*. In 403 B.C., under the archonship of Eucleides, the more evolved East Ionic (Milesian) alphabet was adopted at the instigation of the reformer Archinos. This alphabet distinguished E (ε) from H (η) and O (o) from Ω (ω). It had also introduced the signs Ξ (ξ) and Ψ (ψ) for the clusters *ks* and *ps*,[1] possibly in parallel with Z (ʒ) in its original value *ds* (see below).

In determining the values of the characters of the Greek alphabet a variety of clues is used. First we have the modern use of its many descendants, notably the Roman alphabet and its derivatives. Pronunciation evolves, of course, while orthography remains unchanged. However, if the modern testimony is uniform, this gives a *prima facie* value for the earliest stage which can be tested. Thus there is little doubt that the ancient values π [p], τ [t] and κ [k] did not differ to any great extent from their present-day pronunciation. Then we have descriptions and comments by contemporary commentators on linguistic matters. Further, hints may be derived from onomatopoeia (as in the sheep's cry βῆ, βῆ or in the word μῦκάομαι cf. Lat. *mūgire*, English *mooing* for the lowing of cattle) and puns. Word borrowings from one language into another enable us to make cross-checks and to draw on other traditions. Such traditions may make specially valuable contributions when the alphabet is adopted or adapted for other dialects or languages. Finally, spelling variations give glimpses of phonological changes.

VOWELS

α in MnG has the value [a] and that this is true of OG is indicated by the history of the corresponding Latin *a* and by the

---

[1] The Western alphabets gave the value *ks* to X and *kh* to Ψ, while *ps* was rendered by the digraph ΦΣ (φσ).

Greek loan-words in other languages. There is no evidence that
the long vowel had a different quality (as it has in English
[ɑ:] *v.* [æ]).

ε was used in the archaic alphabets for all the mid-front vowels,
whether short or long. Many scholars hold that the short vowel
was a closed variety [ẹ], but this does not necessarily apply to
the corresponding long vowel (see below on η).

o in MnG is the mid-raised back vowel [ǫ] of a rather open
quality, which is higher than the vowel of English *got*. This was
probably also the value in OG, but as with ε many scholars hold
that the ancient value of the short vowel was of a closed
character [ọ]. For further discussion see below on ω.

υ is today pronounced [i] but it originally stood for the high
back rounded vowel [u]. In Attic-Ionic this sound was fronted
to [y] (see pp. 206f.). On the Boeotian use of ου to render [ʋ],
see p. 118.
     Among the long vowels the mid-raised front and mid-raised
back representatives require discussion. H (η) in early Attic
inscriptions (and in many local alphabets) stood for the glottal
fricative (the aspirate), but in Eastern Ionic, which had lost the
aspirate (*psilosis*), the letter was used for a long mid-low front
vowel [ɛ:]. This sound was distinct from the high mid-front long
vowel which came to be represented by ει. This digraph stood
in the earliest period for a diphthong, while ε denoted 1, the
short vowel, 2, its lengthened forms, e.g. ἔναι = [ẹ:nai] < *es-nai*
(see p. 264), the product of 'compensatory lengthening' and
the contraction (p. 239) of ε + ε, e.g. ἐφίλει < ἐφίλεε, 3, inherited
long *ē*, e.g. ἔθ̄εκεν and 4, the sound that developed in Attic-Ionic
from inherited *ā* (pp. 62f.), e.g. 'Aθ̄ενᾱ. That this uniform writing
concealed two varieties of long mid-raised front vowels is shown
by their different representations after the introduction of the
Ionic alphabet. H (η) was now used for inherited *ē* and the
product of *ā*, and this indicated that the sound was of an open
character [ɛ:] (see also above on the onomatopoeic βῆ, βῆ). This
is supported by the fact that some varieties of island Ionic use
H (η) for the product of long *ā* and keep it distinct from inherited *ē*, for which the notation is ε, e.g. ΚΑΣΙΓΝΕΤΗ < *kasi-
gnētā*. This suggests a very open pronunciation [æ:] for η. The

diphthong [ei], on the other hand, had become monophthongized by the fifth century with the value [ẹː]. The sequence
ει thus became a digraph with this monophthongal value and
it was used also for the products of the contraction of ε + ε.

The closed quality of ει appears also in its historical development: in the late fourth century B.C. there are occasional spelling
alternations between ει and ι, and these are the first pointers to
the later development of [ẹː] to [iː]. In this general 'itacistic'
tendency ει long preceded η. Transcriptions of Greek words in
Oriental languages and also in Latin indicate that η retained
its mid articulation until well into the Christian era. In Attic
the first spelling alternations between η and ι appear in the
middle of the second century A.D.

From the fact that lengthened ε is written ει with a closer
(mid-high) quality than η [ẹː] it has been deduced that ε, too,
had this closer articulation. This is open to doubt, for it is
common for long and short vowels to differ in quality.

The mid vowels of the back series closely parallel the history
of the o-series. Ω, a character invented by the Ionians about
600 B.C., had an open value [ɔː], as is indicated by the onomatopoeic βρωμᾶσθαι for the braying of the donkey and κρώζειν for
the cawing of the crow, and by the fact that the Ionic contraction of o + α is written ω. The contraction of o + o in the earliest
inscriptions is written o and ου was reserved for the diphthong
[ou]. During the fifth century ου came to be used also for the
products of the contraction and it would appear that by then
[ou] had become monophthongized to [ọː], paralleling [ei] >
[ẹː]. When the Boeotians adopted the Attic alphabet about
350 B.C., their use of ου to represent their u-vowels (υ in Attic
having the value [y]) indicates that by that date [ọː] had been
raised to [uː]. For structural reasons it has been argued that
this change may have occurred much earlier than the mid
fourth century. If the Attic change of [u] to [y] took place in the
period of the seventh to sixth centuries B.C., there would have
been an empty slot in the highest position of the back series,
and the tendency towards equality of acoustic distance would
have favoured the change of the series [āː], [ɔː], [ọː] to [āː],
[oː], [uː].

The diphthongs ι, αι, ει, and οι, 2, αυ, ευ, and ου were
originally pronounced in accordance with the spelling, i.e. there

was a glide from the vowel indicated by the first letter to the high position front or back respectively. For Attic the point must be made that the second element of the second series was not fronted to [y]. For the later development of the υ to a fricative [v] and other changes in the diphthongs, see p. 178.

Greek also inherited long diphthongs from IE and others were created within Greek itself by contraction: ᾱι, ηι, ωι. In the course of time these diphthongs were eliminated either by shortening (p. 215) or by the loss of the second element (p. 177). The modern practice of writing the iota 'subscript' ᾳ, ῃ, ῳ goes back to Byzantine times.

CONSONANTS

In the system of the plosive phonemes Greek used a triple opposition based on the two features of voice (V) and aspiration (A). Thus π, τ, κ were structurally $(-V-A)$, β, δ, γ $(+V-A)$ and φ, θ, χ $(-V+A)$. There was no series of voiced aspirates $(+V+A)$ like the Sanskrit *bh*, *dh*, *gh*. In MnG φ, θ, and χ represent the voiceless fricatives [f], [θ] and [χ], but in classical times they were still plosives. That this was still so at the time of their first contact with the Romans is shown by the transcriptions like *Pilipus* for Φίλιππος, *dracuma* for δραχμά and *tūs* from θύος.

Dionysius Thrax classifies the voiceless consonants (ἄφωνα) into three subclasses, 1, smooth (ψιλά)[1] κπτ, 2, shaggy (δασέα)[1] θφχ and 'media' (μέσα) βδγ. The pseudo-Aristotle *De Audibilibus* (*c.* 200 B.C.) applies the term δασεῖαι to sounds 'in which we expel the breath simultaneously with the sounds', an apt description of an aspirate. That the sounds were plosives is also indicated by the use of Π, Κ in early alphabets lacking the letters φ, χ. In Crete the feature of aspiration was simply ignored, but in Thera and Melos the digraphs π*h*, κ*h* were used, which led to the redundant spelling θ*h* for θ. Yet another clue is afforded by the dissimilation of the aspirates ('Grassmann's Law', pp. 230 ff.): τίθημι for *θι-θημι, cf. the alternation τάφος, θάπτω, and θρίξ, τριχός. Again, in instances of expressive gemination

---

[1] The opposing terms δασύς and ψιλός are used respectively of land covered with, or bare of, vegetation and of animals 'furry' or 'hairy' as contrasted with 'smooth' or 'hairless'.

a doubling of φ is written πφ, that of θ as τθ (τιτθή). Akin to this is the Greek loan σάκχαρ, σάκχαρις from the Prakrit *sakkhara*. In transliterations of demotic Egyptian words it is significant that the demotic letters are retained for the fricatives *f* and *h* and that φ and χ correspond to the digraphs *ph* and *kh*. In Coptic writing, too, φ, θ, and χ correspond to voiceless plosives, and in the Armenian alphabet they render the aspirates *pʿ*, *tʿ* and *kʿ*.

Finally, in syntagms like prepositions and nouns, if there is elision and the noun has an initial aspirate, the final consonant of the preposition is written φ (ἐφ' ἡμῖν) or θ (καθ' ἡμέραν). Similarly, the forms οὐκ and οὐχ alternate before words beginning with smooth and rough breathing respectively.

That the sounds classified by Dionysius Thrax as 'media' were voiced is clearly indicated first by their clustering: β, δ and γ may combine in clusters (ῥάβδος, σμάραγδος) and the same is true of π, τ, κ, φ, θ and χ (e.g. λείπω, λέλειφθαι, λέλειπται, λέγω, λέλεκται). This rule extends also to sandhi phenomena, as indicated by spellings like ἐγ βουλῆς. Thus there are two mutually exclusive cluster-classes, and the distinction is evidently one of voice. This is consistent with the above-quoted statement that the 'media' are intermediate between the voiceless stops and the aspirated stops in respect to aspiration. In English, too, *b*, *d* and *g* are followed by considerably less emission of breath than *p*, *t*, *k*, which are phonetically aspirated plosives. Further evidence in support of the feature of voicing comes from Greek loan-words and transcriptions in Latin (*barbarus*, *draco*) and the transcriptions of Greek names on Indian coins (*Arkhebiyasa* = 'Αρχεβίου, *Diyamedusa* for Διομήδου). For the later development of the voiced plosives to voiced fricatives (β, δ and γ in Modern Greek have the values [v], [δ] and [γ]) see p. 178.

The pronunciation of the nasals μ and ν and the liquids λ and ρ offers few difficulties. The articulation of labial and dental nasals is succinctly described by Dionysius of Halicarnassus. The velar nasal [ŋ] was a positional variant[1] found before velar stops and it was written in the standard orthography as γ (συγγίγνομαι, ἐγκαλῶ, τὸγ καλόν), though in earlier

---

[1] The few cases where there is a distinction between [gg] and [ŋg] hardly justify granting /ŋ/ phonemic status.

inscriptions ν is found (ἄνκυρα, ἐνγύς). According to the Roman grammarian Varro (on the authority of Ion) there was a twenty-fifth letter called *agma*, which was used for the velar nasal. The name implies a pronunciation [aŋma], and it follows that words like φθέγμα must have exhibited the cluster [ŋm], and this would explain a spelling like φθέγγματα. It is conceivable that γν was pronounced [ŋn], but the evidence for this is slight.

The articulation of λ is roughly described by Dionysius of Halicarnassus, but he merely indicates the tongue posture ('rising to the palate') and the concomitant sounding of the windpipe, but omits the characteristic lateral release. For all that, there is no doubt that this was a lateral consonant with dental rather than alveolar closure. A velar colouring before a consonant is suggested by the occasional substitution of υ in Cretan (ἀδευπιαί for ἀδελφιαί).

The descriptions of the ancients (e.g. Plato and Dionysius) indicate clearly that Ρ (ρ) was an apical trill. Plato refers to the 'vibration of the tongue', while Dionysius of Halicarnassus notes that the tongue is raised against the palate close to the teeth and 'beats back' (ἀπορραπιζούσης)[1] the breath. According to the grammarians, initial ρ was aspirated, as was the second ρ in the medial cluster ρρ: in all probability this 'aspirated ρ' was a voiceless [r̥].[2] This is supported by early spellings such as ρhοϝαισι (Corcyra) and hραφσα[ϝοιδοι] (Boeotian), and Latin transcriptions such as *rhetor* and *Tyrrheni*. Where ρ followed an aspirated plosive the whole cluster was aspirated, as is evidenced by Latin transcriptions such as *Crhestos*, *Prhygia* and *Trhacem*. Such an aspirated cluster appears in τέθριππον (< τετρα- + ἱππο-); here the ρ received its aspiration from the initial vowel of the second element ἵππος and communicated it to the preceding τ.

The sound represented by ϝ (digamma) was still preserved intact in Mycenaean (p. 44). Though lost at an early date in Attic-Ionic, it was maintained in certain positions in other Greek dialects (for details see Chapter VIII). Its articulatory closeness to the vowel Υ (υ) is shown not only by the origin of

[1] There is a variant reading ἀπορριζούσης 'fanning back'.

[2] The phonetic symbol subscript as in [r̥], etc. is used differently in Indo-European to designate the syllabic sounds m̥ n̥ r̥ l̥, see pp. 215f.

the two letters as variants of *waw*, but also by the substitution of Ⅎ for υ to indicate the second element of diphthongs, e.g. ἀℲτός, ΝαℲπακτίον, etc. It is also used to represent the glide after υ. A voiceless counterpart [w̥] (etymologically traceable to original *sw*, see p. 238) is indicated by spellings such as Ⅎhεκαδαμος (Boeotian) and Ⅎhε (Pamphylian).

Σ (σ) stands for the sole fricative of Attic Greek. It corresponds to *s* in many of the related IE languages and it is still a voiceless sibilant in MnG. This value also emerges from its description by Dionysius of Halicarnassus, and it is supported by transcriptions of Greek words on Indian coins and in Coptic, Armenian and Gothic. A voiced allophone [z] appeared before voiced consonants, and this was rendered by ζ when the cluster originally denoted by this letter had developed to [z] (see below). In certain dialects (Elean, late Laconian) [z] is rhotacized.

The rough breathing [h] is strictly speaking also a fricative consonant (a glottal fricative). This was represented by H, derived from the North Semitic *ḥêt*, which was a more vigorous and constrictive (pharyngeal) fricative than the aspirate. This was because the letter *hē'* had been used for the vowel *e* (see above). In the dialects of Asia Minor the aspirate had been lost (for this 'psilosis' see p. 179) before the time of our earliest records, so that when the East Ionic alphabet was adopted by the rest of Greece, the aspirate had no representative and it was ignored in writing. In some scripts (e.g. at Tarentum and in the colony Heraclea) Ⱶ, the left half of H, was used to denote the rough breathing. Later (third to second century B.C.) this was used as a suprascript above the initial vowel by Aristophanes of Byzantium with the counterpart ⱶ to mark the absence of the aspirate.

The inventors of the Greek alphabet appear to have regarded as units certain complex articulations, which we should analyse as consonant clusters. Z (ζ), for instance, must have had the value [zd] to judge by Ἀθήναζε < Ἀθήνας + δε, θύραζε < θύρας + δε. Further ὄζος 'branch' is etymologically derivable from *osdos* (cf. German *Ast*), and ἵζω is a reduplicated present tense (p. 262) < *si-sd-ō*, the root being *sed-* 'sit'. That the cluster began with [s] is shown further by the loss of a preceding *n* in compounds like σύζυξ < συν + ζυγ + ς, and the present stem πλάζω, with aorist infinitive πλάγξαι, passive πλαγχθῆναι.

The present stem must be reconstructed as *plangjō, with a further development to *πλανӡω. However, this and many other examples where ӡ is traceable to a palatalized *d or *g suggest that there was an intermediate stage in the shape of an affricated prepalatal or alveolar plosive [dž] which underwent metathesis to [zd]. Allen quotes as a parallel the Slavonic development of IE *medhjā- 'middle', OCS mežda, but Russian meža 'boundary'. He argues that when the Semitic letter zayin was borrowed, the affricate pronunciation still existed, for it would have been natural to represent a cluster zd as σδ. That the plosives were still palatalized and not affricated in Mycenaean has been argued above (pp. 31 f.). The assimilation of [zd] to [zz] took place in the early Koine. The voiceless counterpart of *gj is *kj and its Greek derivatives are represented by the digraphs ττ in Attic and Boeotian and σσ elsewhere; φυλάττω/ φυλάσσω < *φυλακ-j-ω. Here, too, phonetic considerations suggest an intermediate affricate stage [tʃ] or [ts]. In certain early Ionic inscriptions a special sign, the letter Ͳ, is used, and this resembles the Semitic tsade. The separate development in Attic and Ionic (p. 62) indicates that the affricate pronunciation (or the palatalized plosive) was still maintained in the Attic-Ionic period. In the initial position a single letter τ- or σ- is used for the products of this combination: e.g. τήμερον/ σήμερον, and it is likely that at least by classical times -ττ- and -σσ- (μέλιττα/μέλισσα) stood for true geminates [tt] and [ss], which had developed from the affricates.

That Ξ (ξ) and Ψ (ψ) had the values [ks] and [ps] is clear from their use in forms like ἔπεμψα (πέμπω), ἔτριψα (τρίβω), φύλαξ (*φυλακ-ς) and from grammarians' descriptions. The invention of letters for the clusters suggests that in the eyes (or rather ears) of the devisors of the alphabet they had an intuitive unity and a quasi-phonemic status. This was probably mainly due to the fact that these clusters could occur in the word-initial position. Another factor was possibly the occurrence of Ζ (originally Ι) with the suggested original affricate value, and the new letters were invented on this analogy.

On the prosodies of Greek and their notation see pp. 242 ff.

VIII

PHONOLOGY

1. Introductory

The sounds lying behind the letters of the Greek alphabet having been determined within fairly narrow limits, and the same preliminary work being assumed for the other languages such as Latin, Sanskrit, Hittite, etc., the work of comparison can begin. From the lexicons of these languages words of identical or similar meaning are picked out and their 'vocables' or 'expressions' compared. A stock example is the word for 'father':

Gk. πατήρ, Lat. pater, Skt. pitár-, Goth. fadar.

Each of these words consists of a string of phonemes in a given order and they are equated position by position:

$$p = p = p = f$$
$$a = a = i = a, \text{ etc.}$$

If we find the same set of 'correspondences' in a number of words, the conclusion is drawn that such phonemic parallelism of the expressions in words of identical or similar meaning cannot be accidental but is due to regular but divergent development from an ancestral language. By various methods the most likely phonetic features of the ancestral phonemes (to which the term 'diaphonemes' might be applied) are deduced. In the present instance the word reconstructed for IE is symbolized as *$p\vartheta tér$-. It should be stressed that the phonetic description of the postulated diaphoneme is not an essential part of its definition. The notation IE *p is simply shorthand for the set of correspondences $p = p = p = f$, etc. However, the determination of the phonetic features is essential for setting up the phonemic structure of Indo-European. In each of the observed languages, too, the phonemes form structures, and in the last resort our comparisons and historical deductions should deal with phonemes not as isolated units but as components of structures.

In writing the historical and comparative grammar of the individual IE languages, the ancestral reconstructed forms serve as triangulation points which facilitate the rather complex procedure of comparison and inter-linguistic cross-reference. The comparative phonology of Greek states the representation of the ancestral diaphonemes (e.g. $*p > π$) and illustrates this by adducing the correspondents in the related languages. The chapter falls into three main sections. The first two deal with the vowels and consonants; the third discusses the syntagmatic relations and especially the prosodies.

2. Vowels and Diphthongs

The vowel phonemes of late Indo-European are set forth in the following table:

i		u		ī		ū
e	o			ē	ō	
	a				ā	

The system comprises three degrees of opening (tongue height) along the two dimensions, front and back, plus the 'prosody' of length: all vowels may be short or long. The high vowels *i* and *u* have consonantal counterparts *j* and *w*. In other words, these sounds may, or may not, function as syllabic peaks and so may be classed along with the nasals *m*, *n* and the liquids *l*, *r* as 'sonants'. This grouping is in any case required for morphological or rather morpho-phonological reasons.

The late Indo-European vowel system was preserved virtually intact in proto-Greek (for the dialect changes see pp. 59 f.), as will emerge from the following representation:

a   *ag- 'drive' ἄγω, Lat. *agō*, Skt. *ájati*, O.Ice. *aka*.
     *aks- 'axle', ἄξων, Lat. *axis*, Skt. *ákṣas*, NE *ax-le*.
     *agros 'field' ἀγρός, Lat. *ager*, Skt. *ajrás*, NE *acre*.
e   *bher- 'carry', φέρω, Lat. *ferō*, Skt. *bhárati*, Goth. *baíran*.
     **dekm̥* 'ten', δέκα, Lat. *decem*, Skt. *daśa*, Goth. *taíhun*.
     **s(w)eks* 'six', (ϝ)έξ, Lat. *sex*, Skt. *ṣáṣ*, Goth. *saíhs*.
     *esti 'he is', ἐστί, Lat. *est*, Skt. *ásti*.
o   *domos 'house', δόμος, Lat. *domus*, Skt. *dámas*.
     *oktōu 'eight', ὀκτώ, Lat. *octō*, Skt. *áṣṭāu*, Goth. *ahtau*.
     *owis 'sheep', ὄ(ϝ)ις, Lat. *ovis*, Skt. *avis*.
ā   is presented in all dialects except Attic-Ionic.
     *māter- 'mother', μᾱ́τηρ (Doric, etc.), Lat. *māter*, Skt. *mātár*-.

*bhā- 'speak', φᾱμί (Doric, etc.), Lat. fā-rī, fāma.

*stā- 'stand', ἔ-στᾱ (Doric, etc.), Lat. stā-re, Skt. stha-.

In Ionic ā > η (φήμη φρήτηρ οἰκίη χώρη), but in Attic this
change was checked and reversed by an immediately preceding
ε, ι, or ρ: e.g. μήτηρ, but φρᾱ́τηρ, οἰκία, γενεᾱ́ (Ion. γενεή). On
the mechanism and chronology of these changes see pp. 62 f.

ē   *dhē- 'put', τίθημι, ἔθηκα, Lat. fēcī, Skt. dádhāmi.

     *plē- 'fill', πλήρης, Lat. plēnus, Skt. prātás.

     *mēns- 'moon', 'month', μήν, Lat. mēnsis, Skt. mā́s-, Goth.
      menoþs (< *mēn-ōt-).

ō   *dō- 'give', δίδωμι, δῶρον, Lat. dōnum, Skt. dádāti, dānám.

     *gnō- 'know', γιγνώσκω, Lat. (g)nōscō, Skt. jñātá-, OE
      cnāwan.

     *ōku 'quick', ὠκύς, Lat. ōcior, Skt. āśú.

i   *wid- 'know', ϝιδεῖν (aor.), Lat. videō, Skt. vidmá 'we know',
     Goth. witan.

     *qʷis 'who', τίς, Lat. quis, Hitt. kwis.

u   *jugom 'yoke', ζυγόν, Lat. iugum, Skt. yugám, Goth. juk.

     *rudhro- 'red', ἐρυθρός, Lat. ruber, Skt. rudhirás, O.Sl.
      rŭdrŭ.

     *medhu- 'honey', μέθυ, Skt. mádhu, O.Sl. medŭ, OE medu.

ī   *wīs 'strength', (ϝ)ῖς, Lat. vīs.

     *wīsos 'poison', (ϝ)ῑός, Lat. vīrus, Irish fī, Skt. víṣa- (with
      short i).

ū   *mūs 'mouse', μῦς, Lat. mūs, Skt. mū́ṣ-, OE mūs.

     *dhūmos 'smoke', θῡμός, Lat. fūmus, Skt. dhūmá-.

     *bhrū- 'brow', ὀφρῦς (on the prothetic vowel see pp. 221 ff.),
      Skt. bhrú-, OE brū́.

The vowels, both short and long, occur in diphthongal combination with the sonants i and u (for the morpho-phonological
parallelism with m, n, r, l, see below on Ablaut).

ai   *aidh- 'burn', αἴθω, Lat. aedēs, Skt.édhas- 'firewood'.

     *aiw- 'vital force', αἰ(ϝ)ών, Lat. aevum, Skt. ā́yu-, Goth. aiws.

     *daiwēr 'brother-in-law', δαήρ, Lat. lēvir (from dēvir), Skt.
      dēvár-, O.Sl. děverĭ.

ei   *ei-ti 'he goes', εἶσι, Lat. it, Skt. éti, Lith. eĩt(i).

     *deik- 'mark', 'show', δείκνυμι, Lat. dīcō, Goth. ga-teihan
      'proclaim'.

     *bheidh- 'trust', 'persuade', πείθω, Lat. fīdō.

oi   *woida 'I know', (ϝ)οῖδα, Skt. *véda*, O.Sl. *vědě*, Goth. *wait*.
     *oinos 'one', οἴνη 'one on the dice', Lat. *ūnus* (O.Lat. *oino*),
     Goth. *ains*.
     *woikos 'house, village', ϝοῖκος, Lat. *vīcus*, Skt. *véśa-*.

The diphthong *ui*, with two high components, is rare: an
example is υἱύς < *su-ju-s. Other instances are due to inner
Greek developments, e.g. μυῖα < *mus-jǝ. Preconsonantally υι
evolved to *ū*, e.g. the optatives like δαινῦτο (< *-νυ-ῑ-το) and the
diminutive ἰχθΰδιον for *ἰχθυ-ίδιον). A similar treatment of υι
antevocalically is exemplified in ὗῦς (vi B.C.) for υἱύς. On the
Mycenaean forms *i-ju*, *i-jo* see p. 276.

au   **aug-* 'increase', αὔξω, Lat. *augeō*, Skt. *ójas*, Goth. *aukan*,
     Lith. *áugti*.
     **tauro-* 'bull', ταῦρος, Lat. *taurus*, Lith. *taũras*, Welsh *tarw*.
     **aus-* 'draw (liquid, fire, etc.)', αὔω, Lat. *hauriō*, ON *ausa*.

eu   **jeug-* 'join', ζεῦγος, Lat. *iūgera* (nom. plur.), Skt. *yok-tár-*.
     **eus-* 'burn', εὔω, Lat. *ūrō*, Skt. *óṣati*.
     **leuk-* 'shine', λευκός, Lat. *lūx*, Skt. *rócate*, Goth. *liuhaþ*,
     'light'.

ou   Examples are rare in Greek except in Ablaut forms alter-
     nating with ευ (see below). σπεύδω/σπουδή. Ablaut alter-
     nation occurs in the word for 'udder' (see p. 278)
     **e/oudhr-*: οὖθαρ, Lat. *über* 'fruitful', Skt. *ū́dhar*, gen.
     ū́dhnas, OE *ūder*.

Long diphthongs *āi, *ēi*, etc. also occurred in Indo-European.
Greek shortened them before consonant (according to Osthoff's
Law a long vowel is shortened before sonant [*i, u, r, l, m, n*] +
consonant. Thus -ᾱι, -ηι and -ωι were only preserved in final
position. These forms will be discussed under Morphology.

3. Sonants

These are sounds (also called resonants, semivowels or semi-
consonants) which, according to their phonetic environment,
can function as consonants, as second elements of diphthongs
and as syllabic peaks. For Indo-European, on morphophonemic
grounds, we postulate (in addition to *i* and *u*) *m̥, n̥, l̥* and *r̥*.[1]

---

[1] On the sounds, see my *Descriptive and Comparative Linguistics*, 56–7. The
small subscript circle indicates the syllabic function of the sound. We may
compare the syllabic character of *l* and *n* in *little* [lɪtl̥] and *seven* [sɛvn̥].

For *ǝ and the 'laryngeals', see below. The morphophonemic
phenomenon in question is called Ablaut. By this is meant the
alternation of vowels observed in morphological systems such as
noun and verb formation, noun declension and verbal conjugation. English, *sing/sang/sung/song* and *drive, drove, driven, drift*
are good examples of this Indo-European phenomenon. The
system is seen at its simplest in roots with a short vowel:
λέγω/λόγος shows the alternation of *e/o*. πέτεσθαι 'fly' has the
aorist πτέσθαι and a derived noun πτε-ρόν 'feather'; πτ-, where
the vowel is lost altogether, exemplifies the 'zero grade'. We
tabulate some examples of the three grades, *e*, *o* and zero:

pet- 'fly'	πέτ-εσθαι	ποτ-ή	πτ-έσθαι
segh- 'hold'	ἔχ-ειν	ὄχ-οι	σχ-εῖν
bheidh- 'persuade', 'trust'	πείθ-ειν	πέ-ποιθ-α	πιθ-εῖν
leiqʷ - 'leave'	λείπ-ειν	λέ-λοιπ-α	λιπ-εῖν
bheug- 'flee'	φεύγ-ειν		φυγ-εῖν
ghew- 'pour'	χέ(ϝ)-ειν	χο(ϝ)-ή	κέ-χυ-ται

From these examples it emerges that in the zero grade the
simple short vowel disappears but the second element of the
diphthong is left as a residue: in the above examples *i* and *u*.
That the same rule holds good also for the diphthongs *em, en,
el*, and *er* is clear from the following table, which shows the
reflections of *m̥, n̥, l̥* and *r̥* in the zero grade.[1]

δέρκ-ομαι 'see clearly'	δέ-δορκ-α	δρακ-εῖν (aor. inf.)	< *dr̥k-
πέρθ-ω 'sack', 'destroy'	πέ-πορθ-α	πραθ-εῖν	< *pr̥dh-
τέμ-ω 'cut'	τόμ-ος	ταμ-εῖν	< *tm̥-
γέν-ος 'kin'	γόν-ος	γί-γν-ομαι	< *gn̥-
πένθ-ος 'grief'	πέ-πονθ-α	πάθ-ος	< *pn̥dh-
στέλλ-ω 'make ready', 'equip'	στόλ-ος	ἔ-σταλ-ται	< *stl̥-
πέλ-ομαι 'be', 'become'	πόλ-ος	πλ-έσθαι	< *qʷl̥-
εἷς (*sem-s) 'one'	ὅμ-ος	ἅ-(παξ) 'once'	< *sm̥-

It is important to note that these different Ablaut grades tend
to appear in different parts of the morphological system. Thus
the zero grade is particularly associated with the thematic root
aorist, the perfect middle, and the verbal adjectives in -*tó*-
(e.g. *tn̥-tó-s* < *ten-* 'stretch').

The Greek representation of the IE vocalic allophones

---

[1] Confusion may be caused by the different use of the subscript circle in IE
reconstructions and phonetic notations, where [l̥], etc. stand for the voiceless
sounds; e.g. Welsh *llan* 'church' is represented as [l̥an].

(written *ṃ, *ṇ, *ḷ, *ṛ) may be further exemplified from Attic
(for the dialect representations, see p. 68).

ṃ   *dekṃ 'ten': δέκα, Lat. *decem*, Skt. *dáśa*, Goth. *taíhun*.

    *(d)kṃtom 'hundred': ἑ-κατόν, Lat. *centum*, Skt. *śatám*,
      Goth. *hunda* (plur.).

    *septṃ 'seven': ἑπτά, Lat. *septem*, Skt. *saptá*, Goth. *sibun*.

ṇ   *newṇ 'nine': ἐν-νέ(ϝ)α, Lat. *novem*, *nōnus* (< *noven-os),
    Skt. *náva*, Goth. *niun*.

    *tṇtos 'stretched': τατός, Lat. *tentus*, Skt. *tatás*.

    *ṇ (negating prefix): ἀ-γνωτος, Lat. *īgnōtus*, Goth. *un-
      kunþs*.

ḷ   *mḷdu 'soft': ἀ-μαλδύ-νω, Lat. *mollis*, Skt. *mṛdú-*.

    *pḷt(H)u 'broad': πλατύς, Skt. *pṛthú-*.

ṛ   *ṛtko- 'bear': ἄρκτος, Lat. *ursus* (from *orcsos), Skt. *ṛkṣas*.

    *kṛd- 'heart': καρδία, Lat. *cord-*, Goth. *haírto*.

    *dhṛs- 'dare': θρασύς, θάρσος, Skt. *dhṛṣú-*, *dhṛṣ-ṇ-ōti*,
      Goth. *ga-daúrsan*.

A further sonant is postulated for IE, chiefly on the grounds
of morphological analysis. This is *ə, the so-called 'shwa', a
term taken over from Hebrew grammarians, who used it to
denote an indeterminate vowel, like the first sound of English
about [əbaωt]. The shwa is postulated as a diaphoneme to
account for equations like

Lat. *pater*, Skt. *pitár*.

The key to its place as a morphophoneme is given by the fact
that shwa also occurs in the zero slot of the ablaut alternations:

*stətós: Lat. *stătus*, Skt. *sthitás*.

Noteworthy is that the full grade is *stā-*, so that the alternation
is *ā/ə*. On the basis of alternations like Latin *dōnum*, *dătus* and
fē-cī/fă-ciō, which can be paralleled in the related languages, we
get alternations *ō/ə* and *ē/ə*. At first sight it is difficult to fit such
ablaut alternations into the simple and clear system of *e/o/zero*
outlined above. There, given the zero grade *CC*, it was possible
to reconstruct the full grades simply by inserting the vowel *e*
or *o*: *CeC*, *CoC*: e.g. *pt-*, *pet-*, *pot-*. If the same morphophonemic
notation is adopted for these skew examples, the notations would
be: *dhə/dheə; *stə/steə and *də/deə-. These postulated ancestral

forms yield Gr. θε-/θη-, στᾰ/στᾱ- and δο-/δω-. The transformation of the postulated diphthongs into the observed long vowels standing in the *e*-grade positions must be formulated by rules. Since it would be an offence against the sound-law principle to postulate three different treatments of one original diphthong, we have to posit three different shwas: $*e\partial_1 > \bar{e}$, $*e\partial_2 > \bar{a}$, and $*e\partial_3 > \bar{o}$. It was this structural morphophonemic analysis which prompted the postulation of three different sonants which appear as syllabic nuclei in the zero grade. They make possible a neat and tidy representation of IE Ablaut relations.

E grade	Zero grade
pet-	pt-
leiq^w-	liq^w-
bheudh-	bhudh-
nem-	nm-
gen-	gn-
derk-	drk-
q^{w}el-	q^{w}l-
dhe∂_1-	dh∂_1-
ste∂_2-	st∂_2-
de∂_3-	d∂_3-

These IE diaphonemes, quasi-algebraic notations representing morphophonemic relations, were gradually endowed with real phonetic features. It is a reasonable guess that they represent laryngeal consonants, and they have been given the notations H_1, H_2, and H_3. In 1927 the Polish scholar Kuryłowicz showed that with certain IE words beginning with $*a$- and $*o$- their Hittite correspondents began with an $ḫ$-phoneme.

> Lat. *ante* Gk. ἀντί Hitt. *ḫanti*
> Lat. *os* 'bone' Gk. ὀστέον Hitt. *ḫaštai*

The evidence indicated that while the postulated H_1 has left no trace ($ešzi < H_1esti$), H_2 and H_3 had real reflections for the first time in an IE language.

The morphophonemic ramifications of the laryngeals will be discussed in detail under Morphology. For the present it will suffice to state some basic rules.

In word-initial position (a) before consonants (the examples are most frequent before sonants) the laryngeals develop to 'prothetic' vowels, the timbre of which betrays the nature of the lost laryngeal: e.g. ἀμέλγ-ω < *H_2melg-, ὀρέγω < *H_3reg-. In a significant number of instances there are parallel examples in Armenian (p. 221). Hittite provides evidence for the laryngeal, for instance, in the word for 'wind' $h(u)want$-, Lat. *ventus*, Gk. ἄ[ϝ]ημι. (b) A laryngeal affects a following vowel with its inherent timbre before disappearing: *H_1e- > *e-, *H_2e- > *a-, and *H_3e- > *o-. Examples are: ἔδω < *H_1ed-, ἄγω < *H_2eg-, ὀδ-(ωδα) < *H_3ed-. It was this disappearance of the initial consonants that produced the apparent exceptions to the general rule that IE roots were normally of the pattern CVC, e.g. *pet- (see below, p. 220). There is some dispute about the action of H_2 on a following o: the noun ἀγός, for which we would expect an o-grade, suggests that the original form was $H_2ogós$. Other scholars would adduce ὄγμος and conclude that H_2 had no 'umlaut' effect on a following o. They would explain ἀγός as the result of analogy.

In the word-final position $VH > \overline{V}$ (see on the $\bar{a}$-stems on pp. 269 ff.). After a consonant the laryngeal was vocalized (see p. 299 on the first plural middle ending -μεθα). Internally the laryngeals disappeared between vowels. In sequences of the pattern VHC (where H stands for any laryngeal) the vowel was lengthened and took on the characteristic timbre (either e or a or o) of the laryngeal involved: examples have already been quoted: τί-θη-μι < *dhi-$dheH_1$-mi ἵ-στᾱ-μι < *si-$steH_2$-mi, δί-δω-μι < *di-deH_3-mi. Interconsonantally (CHC), the laryngeal is vocalized ($H̥$), and the vowel that appears in Greek reflects the inherent timbre of the laryngeal concerned. This is the explanation of the apparent lack of parallelism between Greek and Latin in θετός (Lat. *fă-c-*), στᾰτός (Lat. *stătus*) and δοτός (Lat. *dătus*). Another example is φατός < *$bhH_2tós$, with the zero grade of *$bheH$- 'speak' which yields φᾱμί. More complex is the treatment of interconsonantal sonant + laryngeal ($CSHC$):[1] there are two reflections, which may be exemplified by the extended root *$telH_2$- 'lift', 'bear', the zero grade of which would have been *tlH_2-. The participle with the expected form *$tlH_2tós$ appears as τλᾱτός, and this suggests that a 'prop-vowel' developed between sonant and laryngeal, *$tl°H_2to$-. This vowel derived its timbre

[1] Note the use of S for 'sonant'. Some authors prefer R (= 'resonant') and would write $CRHC$ = consonant + resonant + laryngeal + consonant.

from the particular laryngeal involved and subsequently underwent compensatory lengthening when the laryngeal disappeared: $*tl°H_2tos > *tlaH_2- > $ τλᾱτός.

The last example brings out the fact that the Ablaut is a morphophonemic phenomenon: it is concerned with the function of phonemes in the morphological system of a language. At this point it will be convenient to anticipate the next chapter and explain what is meant by a 'disyllabic base'. A root of the pattern *CVC* like *gen- 'knee' may be extended by a suffix *-w. This disyllabic base, *gen+w, exhibits Ablaut such that if the root has the full grade, the suffix is zero (*gen+w-, form I): if the root is zero, then the suffix may be full (*gn+ew-, form II); finally both elements may be zero (*gn+w-, form III). This theoretical system

I	II	III
*gen+w-	*gn+ew-	*gn+w-

is reflected in Lat. *genu*, Hitt. *genu* (both I); Goth. *kniu*, OE *cnēo*, E. *knee* (all from Gmc. *kne-w-am), IE *gn-ew-om (an extended form of II); and Gk. γνύ-πετος 'falling on the knee' and γνύξ 'kneeling' (both from *gn+w-, form III). The Ablaut relations are obscured if either the root or the suffix of the base contained a laryngeal. Thus the root *gen- 'beget' with ablaut grades *gen-/gon-/gn- may be extended by the suffix -H_I. This base may assume the three forms:

I	II	III
*gen+H_I-	*gn+eH_I-	*gn+H_I-

From form I come Greek words like γενε-τήρ; from II those like γνή-σιος 'genuine', 'legitimate'; from III those with γν- (γί-γν-ομαι 'I become', νεο-γν-ός 'newly born').

In such formations the rules relating to the representation of the laryngeals in Greek apply. Thus $*telH_2$- will appear as τελα- (e.g. τελαμών 'belt'); $*tleH_2$- as τλᾱ- (e.g. the athematic root aorist ἔ-τλᾱ-ν) and $*tl̥H_2$- as ταλα- (e.g. τάλας). Finally, a base $*terH_3$- is reflected in the following word-family. Form II $*treH_3$- 'bore', 'pierce', where $*eH_3 > ō$, appears clearly in τι-τρώ-σκω 'wound'; on the other hand, the form III $*trH_3$- accounts for the thematic root aorist ἔ-τορον 'I bored' (for these aorists, see p. 300).

Prothetic Vowels

In a number of words with clear IE etymological connections Greek presents an initial vowel absent from the other languages, with the exception of Armenian (and more dubiously Albanian).[1] An important basic observation is the differing timbre of the prothetic vowel in Greek. We first list examples which have clear Armenian congeners. The notes adduce other correspondences and indicate a 'laryngealist' reconstruction:

1. ἀνήρ 'man', *ayr*.
2. ἀστήρ 'star', *astł*.
3. ἔρεβος '(place of nether) darkness', *erek* 'evening'.
4. ἐρεύγομαι 'bellow', *orcam*.
5. ἐννέ(ϝ)α 'nine', *inn*.
6. ὀλίγος 'few', *alk'at*.
7. ὄνειδος 'rebuke', *anicanem*.
8. ὄνειρος 'dream', *anurǰ*.
9. ὄνυξ 'nail', *ełungn*.

1. Cf. Skt. *nar-*, Osc. *ner-* (cf. Lat. *nerō*), Welsh *ner* < *H_2ner-.
2. Goth. *staírno*, Skt. *stŕ-bhis* (instr. pl.), Lat. *stella* < *H_2ster-.
3. Skt. *rájas-*, Goth. *riqiz* < *$H_1regʷ-os$.
4. Lat. *rūgīre* < *H_1reug-.
5. Lat. *novem*, Skt. *náva*, Goth. *niun* < *$H_1newn̥$.
6. The connection with λοιγός 'ruin', 'havoc' and with Baltic, Albanian, and Irish is dubious.
7. Skt. *nid-*, Lett. *nidu*, Goth. *ga-naitjan* < *H_3neid-.
8. Also ὄναρ, nom./acc. (also as adverb 'in a dream') < H_3ner-/$H_3n̥$.
9. The *ł* of Armenian is due to the dissimilation of *n-n*; the other languages have either *ongh-*, *ṇgh-* (e.g. Lat. *unguis*) or *nogh-* (OHG *nagal*, OE *nagel*).

The prothetic vowel is regular before IE words beginning with *r-* (see below), and most of the other examples occur

[1] To be distinguished from these are the prothetic vowels which occur in words which may plausibly be assigned to the pre-Greek substratum: e.g. ἀσταφίς, ὀσταφίς, σταφίς 'dried grapes', 'raisins', cf. σταφυλή 'bunch of grapes'.

before the sonants *l*, *m*, *n*, and *w*. The correspondences with Armenian and the varying timbre of the Greek correspondences, however, make a strong *prima facie* case for the view that Greek and Armenian in their prothetic vowels reflect pre-consonantal sounds in initial position, and the laryngeal explanation in these instances commands considerable support.

The prothesis before **w* deserves separate treatment. In the root 'to blow' the word family represented by ἄ(ϝ)ημι, ἄ(ϝ)ελλα, αὔρα implies a base (see p. 220) I H_2ew-H_1-/II H_2w-eH_1-. From I come the words showing *awe-*, from II those with *(a)wē-* (Skt. *vāti*). The laryngeal appears in Hittite *ḫuwant-* 'wind', the participle of **ḫwa-*. Morphologically parallel is the family derived from the root 'increase': ἀ(ϝ)έξω/ αὔξω (Lat. *augeo*, Goth. *aukan*) < I H_2ew-g-/II H_2w-eg- (from which αὐξ-/ἀ(ϝ)εξ- are derived by the addition of the formative -*s*-). More difficult is the connection of ἀϝείδω 'sing' with αὐδή, which is universally admitted. The verb implies a base H_2w-ei-d-, the noun < *H_2w-d-. ἀ(ϝ)είρω could likewise reflect *H_2w-er 'lift', 'raise' with a corresponding I form *H_2ew-r-, but there are no obvious etymological connections.

A newly-emerged example (see p. 50 on Myc. *ewepeseso-mena*) supplies the *e*-grade of the root **webh-* 'weave' (OE *wefan*, OHG *weban*) corresponding to the zero grade **ubh-* (ὔφος, ὑφαίνω, etc.). There is nothing to support a laryngeal explanation for the prothesis in the future participle *ewepsĕsomena*, and prothetics appear sporadically in a number of other words beginning with *w-*: ἔ(ϝ)εδνα/ἔδνα, ἐείκοσι (Homer)/ϝικατι, ἐ(ϝ)έλ-δομαι/ἔλδομαι, ἐ(ϝ)έρση/ἔρση (Skt. *varṣá-*), ἔ(ϝ)ισος, ἴσος, ϝίσϝος.[1] The conclusion must be that there is no simple explanation of the prothetic vowels in Greek. It is legitimate to conduct morpho-phonemic explorations by means of the known relations of the Ablaut forms and the laryngeal hypothesis, but in the absence of confirmatory observations (such as the Hittite *ḫuwant-*) the majority of the laryngeal 'solutions' remain purely algebraic. The prothetic vowel in ὀφρῦς is not 'explained' by positing *$H_3bhrū$-.

---

[1] This may be derived from the root *weidh-/widh-*, detectable in ἠ(ϝ)ίθεος, Lat. *vidua*, *dī-vid-ō*, the basic notion being 'cut', 'separate'.

4. Sonants as Consonants

l   *leuk- 'bright', 'white': λευκός, Lat. *lūx*, Skt. *rocá*- 'radiant'.

    *plē- 'fill', 'full': πλή-ρης, Lat. *plēnus*, Skt. *prātá*-, Goth. *fulls*.

r   *reudh-/*rudh* 'red': ἐ-ρυθρός, Lat. *ruber*, Skt. *rudhirás*, Goth. *rauda*-.

    *dhwer-/*dhur* 'door': θύρα, Lat. *forēs*, Skt. *dvár*-, Goth. *daúr*.

The majority of IE words with initial *r*- develop a 'prothetic vowel' in Greek: to ἐρυθρός may be added ὀρέγω (Lat. *rego*), ἔρεβος (Skt. *rájas*, Goth. *riqis* < *reg^w-), etc. Similar vowels appear more sporadically before *l*-: ἐλαχύς (< *leg^w*h*-, see above), ἐλεύθερος (Lat. *līber* < *leudh-), ἐλαφρός (Skt. *raghú*- 'swift', 'light', OHG *lungar* < *leng^w*h*-/*l̥ng*^{w}*h*-). Such vowel prothesis occurs in Armenian, Greek and Luwian, but there is little parallelism. For a discussion see above on laryngeals (p. 221).

m   *mātēr 'mother': μᾱτηρ (μήτηρ), Lat. *māter*, Skt. *mātár*-, OE *mōdor*.

    *medhjos 'middle': μέσ(σ)ος, Lat. *medius*, Skt. *mádhya*-, Goth. *midjis*.

    *dem-/*dom*- 'build': δέμω, δόμος, Lat. *domus*, Skt. *dáma*-, Goth. *tim-rjan* 'build'.

    *wem- 'vomit': (ϝ)εμέω, Lat. *vomō*, Skt. *vámiti*, Lith. *vemiù*.

In word-final position -*m* > -*n*: e.g. *sem- 'one' (cf. ἅμα, Lat. *sem-el*, *semper*, Skt. *samá*- 'same') in the neuter form *sem > ἕν (for the other forms of this numeral, see p. 289); similarly *χιώμ > χιών.

n   *newos 'new': νέ(ϝ)ος, Lat. *novus*, Skt. *návas*.

    gnō- < *gneH₃- (p. 229) 'know': ἔ-γνω.

    *menos 'spiritual force': μένος, Skt. *mánas*-.

    *swepno-/*supno*- 'sleep': ὕπνος, Lat. *somnus*, Skt. *svápnas*.

Some words show a prothetic vowel (see p. 221): ἐν-νέ(ϝ)α < **newn̥*, ὄνομα (Lat. *nōmen*, Skt. *náman*-, Goth. *namo*), ἀνεψιός 'cousin', Skt. *nápāt* 'nephew', Lat. *nepōt*-), ἀνήρ (Skt. *nar*-, Umbrian *ner*-).

j   By the alphabetic period this IE phoneme[1] had been

---

[1] This is a voiced dorso-palatal fricative; it is often pronounced without friction as in the initial sound of English *yoke*. Other notations used by Indo-Europeanists are *y and **i̯*.

completely eliminated. For its sporadic appearance in
Mycenaean, see pp. 42 f. In the word-initial, antevocalic
position Greek presents two sets of equivalents, (a) the
aspirate *h*, (b) *z* (for the pronunciation, see pp. 210 f., 224).
There is no satisfactory explanation for this split, but the
sound-law principle would compel the postulation of two
different phonemes or different conditioning of one and the
same phoneme. The possibility that an original **j-* became
aspirated under certain conditions, at present undefinable,
is strengthened by a parallel split in the treatment of
initial **w-* (see below). For the representation in Mycenaean, see p. 44.

(a) **jos* 'who' (relative): ὅς, Skt. *yás*.

*jeq^wr̥ 'liver': ἧπαρ, Lat. *iecur*, Skt. *yakr̥t*, Lith. *(j)ẽknos*.

*jē- 'let go', 'throw': ἵημι (< **ji-jē-mi*), future ἥσω, Lat.
iacio, iēci.

*jōr- 'season': ὥρα, Lat. *hōrnus* (< **ho-jōr-(i)nos*), Avest.
yarə.

(b) **jugom* 'yoke': ζυγόν, Lat. *iugum*, Skt. *yugám*, Goth.
juk.

*jes- 'boil': ζέω, ζεστός, Skt. *yásati*, OHG *jesan*.

*jōs- 'gird': ζώννυμι, ζωστός, Avest. *yāsta-*, Lith. *júostas*.

*jewo- 'spelt': ζειαί, Skt. *yáva-*, Lith. *javaĩ*.

Intervocalically *-j-* had disappeared by the alphabetic
period: e.g. κεῖται 'he lies'/κέαται (< **kejn̥tai*) 'they lie';
τρέες, τρεῖς < **trejes* (cf. Skt. *tráyas*); δέος < **dwejos* (cf.
δεινός). The date of the loss of *-j-* depends on the assessment of the Mycenaean spelling fluctuations (see pp. 42 ff.).

In consonant clusters[1] *j* effected a wide variety of changes
comprised under the term 'yodization'.

*tj and **thj* > *s* initially and > *-ss-* intervocalically (simplified in certain dialects, e.g. Attic).

*tjeg^w- 'respect', 'revere': σέβομαι, σεμνός, Skt. *tyájati*.

*dhjā- '?': σῆμα 'sign', Skt. *dhyā-man* 'thought'.

*totjo- 'so many': τό(σ)σος (cf. Lat. *tot* < *toti*).

*pant-jə 'all' (nom. sing. fem.): πάνσα (for the development of this secondary *-ns-* see p. 236 f.).

*medhjo- 'mid': μέ(σ)σος, Lat. *medius*, Skt. *mádhya-*.

---

[1] Consonants are treated below, but it is convenient to discuss these
clusters here. For the labio-velars, see pp. 232 ff.

In certain morphological categories we have -*ss*- which is not simplified.

(i) present stems (p. 265) in -*t-jō* and -θ-*jō*: λίσσομαι (cf. λιτή), ἐρέσσω (cf. ἐρέτης), κορύσσω (cf. κορυθ-).

(ii) feminines in -*jə* (p. 270): μέλισσα (cf. μελιτ-), θῆσσα (cf. θητ-), βῆσσα (< *βᾱθ-*jə*, cf. βάθος).

(iii) comparatives in -*jos*- (pp. 279 ff.); κρέσσων, κρείσσων (cf. κράτος, etc.). On the Attic ττ for σσ in these categories see pp. 62 and 280. On the dialectal distribution of -σσ- and -σ- see above.

***pj** and ***phj** > πτ in all dialects: κλέπτω < *κλέπ-*jō* (cf. κλέπος, κλοπή), κόπτω (cf. κοπή), θάπτω < *θαφ-*jō* (cf. τάφος, see p. 231), βάπτω (cf. βαφή).

kj** and ***khj**, ***qw**j* and ***q***w**hj* > (a) σ- (Attic τ-) initially and (b) -σσ- (Attic -ττ-) intervocalically:

(a) σήμερον < *kj-āmeron, σῆτες < *kjā-wetes 'this year' (on Myc. *zawete*, see p. 43); σεύω < *kjew-, cf. Skt. *cyávate* (intervocalic -σσ- in Hom. ἐπι-σσεύεσθαι): σά (Megarian) < **q***w**jə* (see p. 287).

(b) φυλάσσω < φυλακ-*jō* (cf. φυλακ-); μάσσων < *mak-jon (cf. μακ-ρός); ἥσσων (cf. ἥκιστα); ταράσσω (cf. ταραχή); ὄσσα 'voice', 'rumour' < **woq***w**jə* (cf. Hom. acc. sing. ὄπα); ὄσσε 'two eyes' < **oq***w**je*, cf. ὄσσομαι (pres. stem in -*j*-), fut. ὄψομαι; πέσσω < **peq***w*-jō* (cf. Lat. *coquo*); ἐλάσσων < **elaq***w**h-jōn* (cf. ἐλαχύς).

dj**, *gj*, *gw**j* > 3

Ζεύς < *djēus: ἕ3-ομαι < *sed-jo-mai (cf. ἕδος); ὄ3ω < *ὀδjω (cf. Lat. *odor*); με(ί)3ων < μεγ-*jōn* (cf. μέγας); ἅ3ομαι (cf. ἅγιος); ῥέ3ω < *wregjō; 3ώω/3η- < **g***w**jō*-/ *g***w**jē*-; νί3ω < **nig***w**jō* (aor. ἔνιψα, giving rise to a new analogical present stem νίπτω).

The chronology of the changes in (3) and (4) depends on the interpretation of the Linear B signs transcribed as *za, ze, zo* (see pp. 31 ff.). In our view the changes are post-Mycenaean

Liquids and nasals +-*j*.

(a) In -*rj*- and -*nj*- the sonants are palatalized with the result that the preceding vowel develops a front off-glide: *χαρ-*jō* > χαίρω; *σμορ-*jə* > μοῖρα; *φαν-*jō* > φαίνω; *τεκτn̥-*jə* > τέκταινα. With vowels other than *a* and *o* the front glide results in a lengthening of the vowel: *κριν-

jō > κρίνω; *οἰκτιρ-*jō* > οἰκτίρω; *φθερ-*jō* > φθείρω; *τεν-*jō* > τείνω; *πλυν-*jō* > πλύνω; *ὀλοφυρ-*jō* > ὀλοφύρω. Note that the Attic-Ionic spelling ει in these examples represents [ẹ̄]. For the divergent dialect treatment of these clusters (consonant gemination instead of vocalic assimilation), see p. 61).

(b) There are no certain examples to illustrate the cluster -*mj*-: βαίνω is not necessarily < *$g^w m$-*jō* (see p. 241); nor does κοινός < *komjos* since Greek lacks the preposition *kom* (Lat. *cum*).

(c) *lj* > λλ, a geminated palatal lateral: *aljos* > ἄλλος (cf. Cypr. αἴλος); ἀγγελ-*jō* > ἀγγέλλω; *στελ-*jō* > στέλλω, *φυλ-*jo-m* > φύλλον.

For -*uj*-, -*wj*-, see below p. 227.

w This sound was still preserved in all positions in the Linear B inscriptions, but had been eliminated by the time of the earliest alphabetic inscriptions of Attic and Ionic (and East Doric). Elsewhere it was more resistant and has been preserved initially down to the present day in the Tsakonian dialect (see p. 190). For the digamma in Homer, see pp. 86f. Initially before a vowel there are three treatments, (a) with a prothetic vowel; (b) as ϝ; (c) as an aspirate.

(a) See p. 222 and for Myc. *ewepesesomena*, see p. 50.

(b) *weq^w-os* > ϝέπος; *wergom* > ϝέργον; *wetos* > ϝέτος; *woid-* > ϝοιδ-; *woikos* > ϝοῖκος; *wastu* (Skt. *vástu*) > ϝάστυ.

(c) ἕννῡμι, εἶμαι < *wes-* (Lat. *vestis*, Skt. *váste*, Goth. *wasjan*); ἕσπερος < *wesper-os* (Lat. *vesper*); ἑστία < *westiā* (?) (Lat. *Vesta*); ἑκών < *wek-/uk-* (Hitt. *wek-mi*), Skt. *váś-mi, uśánt-*. The conditioning factor for this treatment of initial *w*- may lie in the following *s* but no regular 'law' can be formulated.

The sole initial clusters beginning with *w*- are *wr*- and *wl*-. The dialect treatment is similar to that of initial antevocalic **w*: ῥέζω < *wregjō* (for ἔρδω < *ϝερζδω*, see p. 238); ῥίζα < *wrid-jə* (Myc. *wiriza*); ῥήτρᾱ < *werH₁-/ wreH₁-* (Lat. *verbum*, Hitt. *werija-*, Skt. *vratá-*, Goth. *waúrd*); ῥῦμα < *wrū-* (for Myc. *u-ru-to*, see p. 39); λῆνος 'wool' < *wlānos* (Lat. *lāna*, Avest. *varənā*, Lith. *vìlna*, Goth. *wulla*).

In initial clusters where *w* comes second only *dw-* still survived in the alphabetic period. In other clusters the *w* was eliminated:

(a) **dw-*: δέος < **dwejos* (Skt. *dvéṣṭi*); for the perfect δείδω < **de-dwoi-m̥*, see p. 95).

(b) **dhw-*: θαῖρος 'hinge', cf. θύρα < **dhw°r-jo-s*.

(c) **kw-*: πᾶμα, πάσασθαι < **kwā-/kū-* 'have power, possession' (Skt. *śvā-tr-á-* 'vigorous', 'strong'). The zero grade occurs in κύριος, ἄκῡρος.

(d) **ghw-*: θήρ (Aeol. φήρ) < **ghwēr-* (Lith. *žvėrìs*, O.Sl. *zvěrĭ*, Lat. *fĕrus*).

(e) **tw-*: σέ, σοί < **twe, *twoi* (see p. 288); σάκος < **twakos* (Skt. *tvác-* 'skin', Hitt. *twekkas* 'body'); σείω < **tweis-* (Skt. *tvéṣati*).

Internally *w* is less stable and it rarely occurs even in dialects which exhibit it in initial position. In Mycenaean, on the other hand, it survived in full vigour in all positions, including clusters with other sonants, *wj, wr, wl*: gen. sing. νᾱϝός > νᾱός, νηός, νεώς (see p. 277) < **nāw-os* (Lat. *nāvis*, Skt. *nāvás*); νέ(ϝ)ος < **newos* (Lat. *novus*, Skt. *návas*, Goth. *niujis*); κλέ(ϝ)ος < **klewos* (Skt. *śrávas-*, O.Sl. *slovo* 'word'); ῥέ(ϝ)ω, ῥόος < **srew-/srow-* (Skt. *srávati, srávas*); αἰών, αἰ(ϝ)εί, ἀεί < **aiw-* (Lat. *aevom*, Goth. *aiws*); ὄ(ϝ)ις < **owis* (Lat. *ovis*, Skt. *ávis*, Luw. *ḫawi-*).

-*wj*- καίω < **kaw-jō*, cf. καῦμα; φυίω (Lesb.) < **bhū-jō*, cf. ἔ-φῡ-ν, Lat. *fuī*, Skt. *bhávati*, etc.); δῖος < **diw-jos*; μείων (Myc. *meujo, mewijo*) < **meiw-jōn*.

-*Vwl*- and -*Vwr*- > -*ul*- and -*ur*-: ταλαύρινος < **tala-ϝρινος*; ἀπούρᾱς, Hom. aor. part. < **ἀπο-ϝρᾱς*. Analogical action preserved -*wr*- in the paradigms: e.g. Argive ϝεϝρēμενα, Attic εἰρημένα, cf. εἴλυμαι < **ϝε-ϝλῡ-μαι*.

There remain the clusters of consonants with *w*: -*dw*- is still preserved in Mycenaean, where the participle of **weid*- was *wid-ϝōs*, later (ϝ)ειδώς (Skt. *vid-ván*, Goth. *weit-wōþs*). For the Homeric evidence, see p. 95; -*tw*- > σσ/ττ: τέσσαρες, τέτταρες < **qʷetw°res*; -*kw*- > -*pp*-: ἵππος (Myc. *iqo*) < **ekwo*- (Lat. *equos*, Skt. *áśvas*). The sonant clusters -*nw*-, -*lw*- and -*rw*- were preserved in certain dialects until the alphabetic period. The divergent treatment in Attic and Ionic shows that the loss of -*w*- was later than proto-Attic-Ionic and later than the fronting of $\bar{a} > \eta$ (see pp. 62f.).

	Attic	Ionic	Doric
*ksenwos	ξένος	ξεῖνος	ξηνος/ξενϝος
*kalwos	καλός	κᾱλός	καλϝος
*solwos	ὅλος	οὖλος	
*korwā	κόρη	κούρη	κορϝᾱ
*φαρϝος	φάρος	φᾶρος	

For -ws- and -sw- see below.

5. Consonants

The consonantal phonemes attributed to IE comprised a rich variety of stops (plosives) with a structure of 'manner' and 'place' oppositions set forth in the following table. The only fricative was the sibilant *s* (with an allophone *z*). On the postulated laryngeal phonemes, see pp. 218f.

Place	Manner			
	Voiceless	Voiced	V° Aspirate	V Aspirate
Labial	p	b	(ph)	bh
Dental	t	d	(th)	dh
Palatal	k	g	(kh)	gh
Velar	(q)	(g)	(qh)	(gh)
Labio-velar[1]	q^w	g^w	$(q^w h)$	$g^w h$

The status of the parenthesized items (velars and voiceless aspirates) is disputed. They need no discussion here since both distinctions are irrelevant for Greek, where they have a single series of representations. Apart from the devoicing of the voiced aspirates (see pp. 5, 40) all the IE plosives were preserved faithfully until proto-Greek. There was, however, one striking phenomenon which may be taken as a constitutive feature of Greek: all plosives in word-final position were lost: μέλι < *melit*, γάλα < **galakt*, τό < **tod*, τί < **qʷid*, etc. The labio-velars, on the evidence of the Linear B tablets, still existed as distinct phonemes (except in the vicinity of a *u*-sound) until the end of the Mycenaean period. During the Dark Ages

---

[1] The labio-velars are velar plosives pronounced with simultaneous lip-rounding. They must be distinguished from clusters *k + w*, etc. The distinction may be illustrated by the contrasting phrases *free quarters* [friː kʷɔːtəz] and *freak waters* [frik wɔːtəz] (see *Descriptive and Comparative Linguistics*, 60–1).

preceding the alphabetic period they underwent a series of
complex changes, varying from dialect to dialect, which resulted
in their disappearance and absorption into the other phoneme
series, labial or dental according to their environment.

p   *pəter: πατήρ, Lat. pater, Skt. pitár-, etc.

    *ped-, pod- 'foot': ποδ-, Lat. ped-, Skt. pad-, Goth. fotus.

    *pro- 'forward': πρό, Lat. prŏ, Skt. pra, Goth. fra-.

    *serp- 'creep': ἕρπω, Lat. serpō, Skt. sarp-.

    *septm̥ 'seven': ἑπτά, Lat. septem, Skt. saptá.

b   βάκτρον, Lat. baculum.

               λείβω, Lat. lībāre.

    *bel- 'strong': βέλ-τερος 'better', Lat. dē-bilis 'weak', Skt.
       bála-.

t   *trejes 'three': τρεῖς, Lat. trēs, Skt. tráyas.

    *tod 'that': τό, Lat. (is)-tud, Skt. tád, Goth. þat-a.

    *pet- 'fly', 'fall': πέτομαι, Lat. petō, Skt. pat-.

    *anti 'before': ἀντί, Lat. ante, Skt. ánti.

d   *deH₃-/dH₃- 'give': δί-δω-μι, Lat. dōnum, dare, Skt. dá-dāti.

    *dekm̥ 'ten': δέκα, Lat. decem, Skt. dáśa, Goth. taíhun.

    *sed- 'sit': ἕδος, Lat. sedeō, Skt. sad-, Goth. sitan.

    *ed- 'eat': ἔδω, Lat. edō, Skt. ad-, Goth. itan.

k   *(d)km̥tom 'hundred': ἑκατόν, Lat. centum, Skt. śatám,
       Goth. hund.

    *klutós 'heard': κλυτός, Lat. in-clutus, Skt. śrutá-.

    *weik-, woik- 'house', 'village': (ϝ)οἶκος, Lat. vīcus, Skt.
       viś-, Goth. weihs.

    *deik- 'show': δείκ-νυ-μι, Lat. dīcō, Skt. diś-.

g   *gen-/gon- 'knee': γόνυ, Lat. genu, Skt. jắnu, Goth. kniu.

    *genos 'lineage': γένος, Lat. genus, Skt. jánas, Goth. kuni.

    *gneH₃- 'know': γι-γνώ-σκω, Lat. gnōscō, Skt. jñā-, OE
       cnāwan.

    *ag- 'drive': ἄγω, Lat. agō, Skt. aj-.

    *agros 'field': ἀγρός, Lat. ager, Skt. ajrá-, Goth. akrs.

bh *bher- 'bear': φέρω, Lat. ferō, Skt. bhar-, Goth. baíran.

    *bhrāter- 'brother': φράτηρ, Lat. frāter, Skt. bhrắtar-,
       Goth. brōþar.

    *nebh- 'cloud', 'mist': νέφος, Lat. nebula, Skt. nábhas, OHG
       nebul.

    *ambhi/m̥bhi 'on both sides': ἀμφί, Lat. ambi-, Skt. abhí,
       OHG umbi.

dh   **dhē-* 'put', 'make': τί-θη-μι, Lat. *fēcī*, Skt. *á-dhāt*, OE *dōn*.
      *dhūmos 'smoke': θῦμός, Lat. *fūmus*, Skt. *dhūmá-*.
      *widhewā 'widow': ἠ-ϝίθε(ϝ)ος, Lat. *vidua*, Skt. *vídhavā*,
        Goth. *widuwō*.
      **reudh-/rudh-* 'red': ἐρυθρός, Lat. *ruber*, Skt. *rudhirá-*,
        Goth. *rauþs*.
      *medhu 'mead': μέθυ, Skt. *mádhu*, OE *medu*, O.Sl. *medŭ*.

gh   **gheim-/gh(i)jem-* 'winter', 'snow': χεῖμα, Lat. *hiems*, Skt.
        himá-.
      **ghew-/ghu-* 'pour': χέ(ϝ)ω, Lat. *fundō*, Skt. *hutá-*.
      **wegh-/wogh-* 'cart': (ϝ)όχος, Lat. *vehō*, Skt. *vah-*, Goth.
        ga-wigan.
      **leigh-* 'lick': λείχω, Lat. *lingō*, Skt. *léhmi*, Goth. *bi-laigon*.

The aspirates were subject to a change formulated as 'Grassmann's Law'. This can be deduced by internal analysis of certain 'morphophonemic' alternations, exemplified in the following table:

θρίξ 'hair' (nom. sing.) : τριχός (gen. sing.)
θρέψω 'I shall rear' : τρέφω 'I rear'.

Here the aspirated stop alternates with the unaspirated counterpart, the latter appearing where the following syllable begins with an aspirate. The 'law' is thus an instance of dissimilation: in any word which contains two aspirated sounds not in direct contact the first suffers dissimilatory loss of the aspiration. This means that we can restore the stems of these two words as **dhrigh-* and **dhrebh-*, with the proto-Greek representatives *θριχ- and *θρεφ-. The verb 'to have' is even more instructive: ἔχω 'I have', ἕξω 'I shall have', ἔ-σχ-ον 'I had' (aorist). As will be shown later, the root in the aorist appears in the 'zero-grade' *skh-*, which implies the full grades **sekh-*, **sokh-* (see above). The form of the present stem will thus have been **sekh-* and initial antevocalic *s-* became an *h-* in Greek (e.g. *septṃ > ἑπτά; for details see pp. 216, 235). The resulting form *hex- thus presented two aspirated consonants, and the first suffered dissimilatory loss: hence the form ἔχω. In the future *sekh-s-*, however, the aspirate lost its aspiration and the cluster developed to -*ks-*. Thus the word-form contained only one aspirate so that the law did not apply, hence ἕξω. In the aorist stem *skh-* the *s* was not antevocalic so that there, too, the law was inoperative.

Certain examples enable us to establish the relative chronology. The law is operative in τάφος 'funeral rites', 'tomb' but not in the corresponding verb θάπτω. The latter is traceable to *dhṃbh-jō. In proto-Greek the cluster *bhj* developed to *pt* (see p. 225). It follows that Grassmann's Law operated after this characteristic Greek change, otherwise we should have the form *τάπτω. Another conclusion we must draw from this example is that the law operated after the proto-Greek devoicing of the aspirates: otherwise we should have *δαπτω. The example of ἔχω shows that the law was also later than the proto-Greek change of *s-* to *h-*. Thus, despite the fact that an analogous phenomenon is observable in Indo-Iranian, the law of the dissimilation of aspirates took place within the history of Greek. The fact that Grassmann's Law operated in all Greek dialects, in other words that the phenomenon is pan-Greek, suggests that the change should be assigned to the proto-Greek period. This has been the *communis opinio* among scholars until recently. Since the decipherment of the Linear B script, however, a much later date has been argued. The evidence offered is the word θεός 'god', the root of which also appears in compounds like θέσφατος 'spoken by god', 'prophetic', θεσπέσιος 'divinely uttered'. In proto-Greek *dhesós* would have become *thehós* and, by Grassmann's Law, *τεός. How then are we to explain the aberrant θεός? It looks as though the law could not have operated until after the elinination of the intervocalic -*h*-. Now on the evidence of the Linear B tablets we know that at least on the Mainland (for Knossos see p. 38) the -*h*- was preserved down to the time of the destruction of the palaces, so it has been concluded that Grassmann's Law must have taken place independently in all the Greek dialects including Dorian. The evidence offered seems too slight to justify so sweeping a conclusion. Moreover, there is no evidence that the law operated when the second aspirate was an *h*. In any case the preservation or restoration of the aspirated consonant in θεός might well have been due to the influence of compounds such as we have cited. Such analogical action has in any case to be assumed for instances like ἀφή 'act of touching', for which we should expect †ἀφή. The source of the initial aspirate is the verb ἅπτω < *ἅφjω. Another factor entering into the assessment is the double aspiration of ὗφος (*webh-/ubh-* 'weave'; on the Mycenaean future participle *ewepesesomena*, see p. 50). The first is due to the aspiration of initial *u-* (e.g. ὑπό). Now, this is also a pan-Greek phenomenon[1] which must have occurred after the operation of Grassmann's Law, for otherwise we should have had ὕφος.

Another stumbling-block, precisely from Linear B texts, is the Mycenaean word *anioko*, which is plausibly interpreted as ἀνιόχοι 'charioteers' (lit. 'rein-holders'). The elision of the final vowel of ἄνια- or ἄνιο- is difficult to understand if the second element of the compound still began with the aspirate, *-hokhos* (for the Linear B evidence, see pp. 41f.). The weight of the evidence would thus be in favour of assigning Grassmann's Law to the proto-Greek period.

The labio-velar stops were still preserved as a separate series of phonemes down to the time of the destruction of the Mycenaean palaces (see pp. 40f.). The exception to this statement is the loss of the labial feature in the neighbourhood of a *u*-sound: *gʷoukolos* 'cow-herd', but *aipolos* 'shepherd' < *gou-qʷolos*, *ai-qʷolos*. This change is pan-Greek and hence presumably proto-Greek. This root *qʷel-* 'go around', 'revolve', 'be busied about' illustrates the post-Mycenaean development of the labio-velars: they tended to become dentals before front vowels and labials before back vowels and consonants. Parallel is the development in: *gʷel-* 'thrust', 'throw' and *gʷhen-* 'strike'.

qʷel-: τέλομαι, πόλος, περι-πλόμενος
gʷel-: δέλλω (Arcadian), βάλλω, βόλος, ἐ-βλή-θην
gʷhen-: θείνω (*θέν-jō), φόνος, ἔ-πε-φν-ον

For the Aeolic treatment see below.

qʷ   1. Pan-Greek development in the neighbourhood of *u*: > κ. The root *qʷel-* also appears in the reduplicated form in the word for 'wheel': *qʷe-qʷl-os*/*qʷ°qʷl-os*, which yields Gk. κύκλος, Skt. *cakrá-*, OE *hwēol*, Tocharian *kukäl*.
neqʷ-t-/noqʷ-t-/n°kʷ-t 'night': νύξ, νυκτός, Hitt. *neku-z*, Lat. *noct-*, Skt. *nákt-am* 'by night', Goth. *nahts*.

---

[1] The dialect distribution seems adequate justification for this description of the phenomenon. We follow M. Lejeune (1972, 280–1), who also points out 'the phenomenon is thus later than Grassmann's Law'. Psilotic dialects like Lesbian do not, of course, enter into the assessment.

The -u- in Greek is the product of the reduced vowel (see p. 240) under the influence of the neighbouring labialized consonant.

g^w *$g^w en$-/$g^{wo}n$-: γυνή, Skt. gnā-, Goth. qino.

Here, too, the -u- has a similar origin to that of νυκτ-. The reduced vowel has a different development in Boeotian βανα, where the -a- occasioned a different treatment of the labio-velar. The anteconsonantal treatment is illustrated by μνάομαι 'I woo' < *βνᾱομαι < *$g^w n\bar{a}$-. The root $g^w ej$-ǝ- 'live' (see below) appears in the zero grade in the compound *su-$g^w ij$-es-, to which ὑγιής 'in good condition', 'healthy' is traced.

$g^w h$ *$leng^w h$-/$l\underset{.}{n}g^w h$- 'quick', 'light': ἐλαχύς, Lat. levis, Skt. laghú-. For the relation to ἐλαφρός, see p. 223.

*$eug^w h$- 'proclaim solemnly': εὔχομαι, Lat. voveo (< *$weg^w h$-), Skt. óhate. Under this heading, too, analogy has operated to preserve or restore the labio-velar. For Linear B qouqota 'cowherd', suqota 'swineherd' and ouqe 'neither', 'nor', see p. 41.

Dialect Changes

In the 'alphabetic' stage of Greek the labio-velars have been eliminated, being replaced by dentals or labials according to environment (see above).

q^w *$q^w i$-/$q^w o$- 'who', 'what', etc.: τίς, ποῦ, etc., Lat. quis, quod, etc., Skt. kás, cit, Hitt. kwis, Goth. hwa(s).

The form οὐκί 'not' is composed of the negative οὐ and the enclitic neuter *$q^w id$, with the regular treatment of the labio-velar after a -u-. In οὔτις the dental is due to the influence of τις. Similarly Mycenaean presents ouqe, with preserved or restored labio-velar, which develops to οὔτε even in the Aeolic dialects. The treatment of these sounds in enclitics offers a number of difficulties and they defy a general formulation (everywhere τε < *-$q^w e$), especially in the 'potential particle' (see pp. 67f. and 285).

*$q^w ei$-/$q^w oi$-/$q^w i$- 'pay': ἔ-τεισα, ποινή, τίσις, Skt. cáyate, Avest. kaēnā 'penalty', Lith. káina 'price'.

*$penq^w e$ 'five': πέντε (Aeolic πεμπε), Lat. quīnque, Skt. páñca, Goth. fimf (from *fimfi < *pempe).

*seq^w- 'follow': ἕπομαι, Lat. sequor, Skt. sácate, Lith. sekù.

*peqʷ- 'cook': πέψω (future; for the present πέσσω from *peqʷjō see p. 225), Lat. coquō (from *qʷeqʷō with assimilation of the initial labial to the following labio-velar), Skt. pácati, pácyate, O.Sl. pekǫ.

*qʷrij-ə- 'sell': Myc. qirijato, πρίασθαι, Skt. krīnā́ti, O.Ir. crenim.

*oqʷ- 'eye': ὄπωπα, ὄψομαι, Myc. aitijoqo = Aithioqʷs; the dual ὄσσε < *oqʷ-je or oqʷjHᵢ.

gʷ   Here we must distinguish, as regards the front vowels, between the treatment before e and i.

*gʷelbh- 'womb': ἀδελφός 'brother' (lit. 'of the same womb'), Skt. gárbhas.

Other examples with no extra-Greek congeners are implied by the alternation between dental and labial consonants. Among these is the verb (important for dialect relations) βούλομαι 'I am willing', which shows the following variations of the stem: δηλ- (Doric), βειλ- (Boeotian), βελλ- (Thessalian). It is possible that the Linear B qeromeno is to be interpreted as gʷēlomenoi or gʷellomenoi (see p. 69). Another example is the verb 'to thrust', 'throw', quoted above, which shows the variations βάλλω, δέλλω (Arcadian). If the Linear B word qeretirijo is to be interpreted as gʷlētriō for *gʷleHᵢ- (see p. 232), the labio-velar would be directly attested. The word for 'roasting spit' shows a similar alternation (ὀβελός/ὀδελός), and it may well belong to the same word family as βάλλω, βέλος.

Before i gʷ appears as a labial:

*gʷej-ə-/gʷojō-/gʷi-: βίος 'life', ἐβίων 'I lived' (aorist), Lat. vivus, Skt. jīvá- 'living', gáya- 'life', Goth. qiwa- (English quick is traceable to C.Gmc. *kwikwaz). An isolated example of the dental representation is the Heraclean ἐν-δεδιωκοτα = ἐμ-βεβιωκότα; βιός 'bow' is related to Skt. j(i)yā́, Avest. j́yā- 'bow-string'; βίᾱ 'violence' has its counterpart in Skt. j(i)yā́ 'power', 'domination'.

For a representation before a consonant:

neigʷ-/nigʷ 'wash': Myc. kherniqʷtēwes 'basins', χέρνιψ, νίψαι (aor.), νιπτήρ, Skt. ne-nik-té. On νίζω < nigʷ-jō, see p. 225.

gʷh   The dental representation before e is well attested.

*g*ʷhedh-/gʷhodh-* 'desire', 'demand': θέσσασθαι (aor.),
πολύθεστος 'much desired', etc. The noun πόθος shows
the action of Grassmann's Law (*g*ʷhodhos* > *q*ʷhothos* >
*q*ʷothos*). The Linear B word *qetea₂*, a term denoting a
transaction, may also be interpreted as *qʷhesteha*. Also
connected are O.Ir. -*gessam* (sigmatic subjunctive) and
guidiu 'I beg' and the Avestan *jaiδyemi* 'I ask'.

*g*ʷher-* 'hot': θέρος 'summer', θερμός 'hot', Lat. *formus*,
Skt. *gharmás*.

*g*ʷhen-/gʷhon-/gʷhn-* 'strike', 'kill': θείνω (< *θεν-*jō*),
φόνος 'slaughter', ἔ-πε-φνον (reduplicated aorist with
zero grade, see p. 301). The only example before *i* is
ὄφις 'snake' if this is to be connected with Skt. *áhi-*,
Avest. *aži-*, all from *og*ʷhi-*.

The chronological division between 1, the proto-Greek and
2, the post-Mycenaean changes is clear. Less certain is
whether, within the latter group, the development to
dentals preceded that to labials, so that there was an intermediate stage when, for instance, *t(h)e-* alternated with
qʷ(h)o- and *qʷ(h)C* (*C* = consonant): e.g. θένjō/qʷhόνος/
ἐqʷεqʷhνον. This chronological gradation has been postulated without cogent grounds. On the other hand, in
Attic-Ionic the early change of [aː] > [æ̈ː] > [ɛː] provides
a possible indication of relative chronology. Thus πῆ
'how?', 'in what way?' (< *q*ʷāi*) suggests that the change
of *qʷ* to *p* took place before the fronting of *ā*; otherwise we
should have *τῆ. However, it is quite feasible that such a
form would have in any case been changed to πῆ by the
analogical influence of ποῦ, πῶς, etc. We have a parallel in
Doric πεῖ 'where' instead of †τεῖ and πῦς 'whither'
instead of †κῦς (cf. Skt. *kû*).

The Sibilant

s was preserved before and after a voiceless stop and in word-
final position: στείχω < *steigh-/stigh-* (Skt. *stighnóti*, Goth.
steigan); ἐστί < *esti* (Lat. *est*, Skt. *ásti*); γένος < *genos* (Lat.
genus, Skt. *jánas*). Initially before a vowel *s* > *h*: εἷς, ἕν < *sems,
sem (Lat. *semel*, etc., see p. 289); ἕδος < *sedos* (see p. 210),
ἕπομαι < *seqʷ-* (Lat. *sequor*, etc., see p. 233), ἑπτά < *septm̥
(see p. 290). For augmentation and reduplication of verbs with

initial *s-*, see pp. 301, 304; for the loss of the aspirate (psilosis) in dialects see pp. 179, 205. Intervocalically the -*h*- was still preserved in Mycenaean (p. 42), but had disappeared by alphabetic times: ჳέω < *jes- (see p. 224), σείω < *tweis- (see p. 227), θεός < *dhesos (see p. 231). If the word begins with a vowel, the intervocalic aspirate is often transferred to it: εὕω < *ευhō < *eus- (Lat. *ūrō*, Skt. *óṣati*); ἱερός < *iheros < *iseros (Skt. *iṣirá*-). In the paradigms an -*s*- is often restored or preserved by analogy: e.g. ἔλυσα, λύσω, etc. (see p. 302). In verbal roots with initial vowel the expected initial aspirate sometimes does not appear: ἦα for †ἦα < *ēs-m̥* (see p. 295).

Clusters containing s

sm, sn, sr, sl. Initially the *s* is lost, an aspirate being presumably the intermediate stage: μέρος μοῖρα < **smer-/smor*-; μία < *smjH₂ (see p. 289); νυός < *snusós (Arm. *nu*); νέω 'spin' < *snē- (Lat. *neō*, Skt. *snāya-ti*); ῥέ(ϝ)ω, ῥόϝος < **srew-/srow*- (see p. 227); λήγω < *slēg- (cf. ἄλληκτος, see below); λάჳομαι, λαμβάνω, ἔ-λαβ-ον < *slagʷ- (OE *lǣccan*). That these initial sonants were aspirated is suggested by spellings in early inscriptions such as λhαβων, μhεγαλō, ῥhοϝαισι.[1]

Intervocalically the postulated -*hm*-, etc., show different treatments in the dialects; they lengthen either the preceding vowel or the following sonant:

	Attic-Ionic	Doric	Aeolic
*esmi >	εἰμί	ἠμι	ἐμμι
**wesmn̥* >	εἶμα	ϝημα	ϝεμμα
*selasnā >	σελήνη	σελᾱνᾱ	σελαννᾱ
*klewes-nos >	κλεινός	κληνος	κλε(ϝ)εννος
*gheslo- >	χείλιοι	χηλιοι	χελλιοι

Present stems of the type ἔννυμι, σβέννυμι show a divergent treatment of -*sn*-. They may well be comparatively recent creations, so that we have to do with secondary -*sn*-. With -*ms*- and -*ns*- we also have to distinguish between (a) original and (b) secondary clusters.

(a) -*ms*- and -*ns*- > -*mm*- and -*nn*- in Aeolic, but in the other dialects the sibilant disappears with compensatory lengthening of the preceding vowel. The aorist forms illustrate this.

[1] For the possibility that the *r*- was voiceless, see p. 209.

	Attic-Ionic	Doric	Aeolic
*e-men-sṃ >	ἔμεινα	ἐμηνα	ἐμεννα
*e-nem-sṃ >	ἔνειμα	ἐνημα	ἐνεμμα
(b)			
*pant-jH₂ >			
pansa >	πᾶσα	πα(ν)σα	παισα (Lesb.)
*bhanti >	φανσί >		φαισι (Lesb.)
	φᾱσί (Hom.)		
*montjH₂ >			
*monsa >	Μοῦσα	μωσα	μοισα (Lesb.)

Evidently (b) is later than (a).

The treatment of -ls- and -rs- in the aorist is similar:

| *e-stel-sṃ > | ἔστειλα | ἐστηλα | ἐστελλα |
| *a-wer-s- > | ἀεῖραι (infin.) | ἠραντας (Cret.) | ἀερρατε (Lesb.). |

This development is, however, exceptional. Homer presents a number of aorists in -rs- and -ls-, and there are quite a few ancient words which preserve the ancient clusters, e.g. Hom. ἄρσην (Avest. aršan-), κόρση etc., the Attic representatives of which have -ρρ-: ἄρρην, κόρρη, etc. (for the chronology see pp. 62 f.); ἄλσος, τέλσον (Homer).

For final -ms and -ns we distinguish likewise between (a) original and (b) secondary.

(a) μέλᾱς < *melan-s; μείς (Ionic), μής (Doric) < *mēns < *mēns (Osthoff's Law, see p. 215; Attic μήν is analogical); εἷς < *sem-s, κτείς < *kten-s.

The accusative plurals in -ns present a special problem. The articles (demonstratives) τονς, etc., if attached to a word beginning with a consonant, lost the sonant without compensation; τός, etc., cf. σύστασις < *συν-στασις, κεστός < κεν-στος < *kent-to-s), whereas before an initial vowel it was preserved. This gave rise to the doublets τους/τος (cf. εἰς/ἐς < ἐνς), which were subjected to different processes of selection in the dialects. Where -ns was preserved, it underwent the same changes as intervocalic -ns-: τούς/τως/τοις.

(b) Secondary -ns < *-nts. Relevant are the nominatives of participles in -ant-s: Attic ἀκούσας, Lesb. ἀκουσαις; Attic διδούς, Lesb. διδοις.

sj. The sole example in the initial position is ὑμήν < *sjūmēn (Skt. syū́man-). Intervocalically -sj- > -jj-, the first member

diphthongizing a previous vowel (a preceding *i* is lengthened):
ναίω (aorist νάσσαι) < *nas-jō; εἴην < *(e)sjēm (Skt. syām, see
p. 309); μυῖα < *mus-jH₂ (cf. Lat. mŭs-ca); τοῖο < *tosjo (Skt.
tásya, see p. 285).

sw. Initially the cluster > hw-, which is occasionally rendered as
Ϝh-: ἕξ, Ϝεξ < *sweks (on Myc., see p. 49); ἡδύς < *swādu-
(Lat. suāvis, Skt. svādús); ἑκυρός < *swekuro- (Skt. śváśuras);
ἔθος < *swedhos (Skt. svadhā́-, Lat. suēscō < *swēdh-skō), with
the aspirate of *hw- dissimilated according to Grassmann's
Law.

Intervocalically the postulated -hw- underwent divergent
treatments according to dialect: the *h* either lengthened a preceding vowel or it was assimilated to the sonant, -ww- then
producing a *u*-diphthong in the preceding vowel: *naswos >
nahwos > νᾱϜός (Doric) > νηός > νεώς (with quantitative
metathesis, see p. 62), but Aeolic ναῦος < *ναϜϜος; ἰός 'arrow'
(Hom.) < *iswos, cf. Skt. íṣu-. For secondary -sw- Attic ἴσος,
Ionic ἶσος, Doric, etc. ϜισϜος may be cited. It is derived from
the root *weidh-/widh- seen in Latin di-vidō. The postulated
adjectival form is *widh-s-wos > *wisswos > *wiswos. Cf.
possibly Mycenaean wisowopana.

There remain the clusters of the type CsC: -ksm- was still
preserved in Mycenaean aiksmā, later αἰχμή, where the -s- has
become an aspirate (cf. πλοχμός < *plok-s-mos). The loss of *s*
between a liquid and a voiced consonant is seen in ἔρδω <
*Ϝερσδω < *werg-jō and πτέρνη 'heel' < *persnā (Lat. perna,
Skt. pā́rṣṇi-, Hitt. paršina-, Goth. faírzna). Between a liquid and
a voiceless consonant there was divergent dialect treatment, but
usually there was loss of the liquid: παστάδες < *παρ-στάδες.
There was loss of the nasal in clusters NsC: δεσπότης < *dems-
potā- (see further above on tons + C, ens + C).

That IE also possessed plosives of more complex articulation
has been suggested by certain equations: κτίμενος (Myc.
κτιενσι, see p. 49), Skt. kṣéti, Avest. šaēiti; τέκτων, Skt. tákṣan,
Avest. tašan-; ἄρκτος, Skt. ŕkṣa-, Avest. arəsa-, Hitt. ḫartagga-;
κτείνω, Skt. kṣaṇóti; κτάομαι, Skt. kṣáyati; χθών, χαμαί, Skt.
kṣam-, Avest. zam-, Lat. humus, Hitt. tekan, HH takami,
Toch. A tkam; φθείρω, Skt. kṣar-, Avest. γžar-; φθίν(Ϝ)ω, Skt.
kṣiṇóti. It is arguable, however, that the correspondences Greek
κτ = Sanskrit. kṣ can be better (i.e. more plausibly from a

structural point of view) accounted for by postulating not a new series of unitary phonemes (e.g. *kp̌ or *kˢ), but initial clusters. The evidence suggests proto-Greek *tk-, *thkh-, and *thqʷh-, which were reversed in Greek (cf. τί-κτ-ω for *τι-τκ-ω); e.g. *dheghōm/dheghom-/dhghem-/dhghom- (for the Ablaut forms of the noun declension, see p. 267) 'earth' developed in Greek to *khthōn (with m > n in final position). Similarly ἄρκτος is traceable to *r̥tko-. The Sanskrit evidence is also open to explanation along these lines. The clusters also underwent simplification: χαμαί, Lat. humus, κτείνω/καίνω. A similar alternation of initial cluster and single consonant is observable in the doublets πτόλις/πόλις, πτόλεμος/πόλεμος.

6. Syntagmatic Phenomena

This section deals with the behaviour of sounds as links in the 'chain of speech'. The phenomena are those which contribute to economy of effort and ease of pronunciation—assimilation, dissimilation, simplification of clusters and the like.

VOWELS

The loss of intervocalic consonants such as -j-, -s- and -w- resulted in vowel clusters (hiatus) which were often (especially in Attic) simplified by 'contraction': e.g. *genes-os > γενεhος > γένεος > γένους; *genesa > γενεhα > γένεα > γένη (for the dialects, see pp. 59 ff.). Two vowels in hiatus may be pronounced as one syllable. In most examples the first vowel is e. Synizesis, as this phenomenon is called, is not reflected in writing, but appears from the scansion of the genitive endings -εος and -έων. On the supposed Mycenaean synizesis in ai-za, ka-za, su-za, see pp. 31 ff. In a three-vowel cluster the first may be removed (hyphaeresis). The vowels affected are ε and o: e.g. *ἀ-κλεϝεσ-ες > ἀκλεεες > ἀκλεές; *βοϝᾱθοϝεω > βοᾱθοεω > βο-ηθέω. Hyphaeresis also occurs in εο and οε when the second vowel is in a closed syllable: *δᾱμιο-ϝεργος > δᾱμιο-εργος > δᾱμιερ-γός or δᾱμιοργός/δημιοργός; a long vowel, most frequently e, is sometimes shortened in hiatus before a following vowel. *plējā > πληᾱ > πλέᾱ; *dhāwā > θᾱϝᾱ > θᾱᾱ > θεᾱ̈̆ > θεά (see pp. 62 f.); *āusōs > hāwōs > hǣōs > ἕως, cf. νεῶν 'of ships' < νηϝῶν < *nāwōm.

CONSONANTS

Consonantal clusters which begin a syllable (in the 'release' position) may be simplified by the insertion of a vowel. This phenomenon ('anaptyxis') is especially frequent in clusters containing a sonant as the second element (*j, w, m, n, l, r*). Latin examples are *dracuma* (δραχμά) and *mina* (μνᾶ). In the following reconstructions the postulated anaptyctic vowel is indicated by a raised °; its realization depends on its environment.

*$g^{w\circ}j\bar{o}$- 'live': βιῶναι, βίοτος (contrast 3ώω < *$g^w j\bar{o}$-).

*$q^w r^\circ j H_2$- 'acquire', 'buy': πρίασθαι. Here the vowel is assimilated to the following -*j*- and appears as -*i*-.

*$d^\circ w\check{o}$ 'two': δύο, δύω (Hom.), but Myc. *dwŏ*.

*$g^{w\circ}n\bar{a}$ 'woman': γυνή (Boeotian βανα).

*$q^{w\circ}q^w los$ 'wheel': κύκλος.

In these three examples the vowel is realized as *u* under the influence of its labialized neighbour. Before liquids and nasal the vowel is mostly realized as *a*.

*$q^w etw^\circ res$ 'four': τέτταρες.

*$dh^\circ nH_2$- 'death': θάνατος (contrast τέ-θνα-μεν).

*$t^\circ lH_2$- 'bear', 'lift': τάλας, ταλασίφρων (contrast τέ-τλα-μεν).

On the root *$telH_2$-/$tleH_2$-, see pp. 219f. For aorists like ἔβαλον, ἔμολον, etc., see pp. 300. Other realizations of the anaptyctic vowel show an *i*, but the conditions are difficult to formulate.

*$q^{w\circ}twr$-'four': πίσυρες (Homer); *sk°d*-'scatter': σκίδ-νη-μι; *$p^\circ t$-'spread': πίτ-νη-μι.

The clusters *NL* (nasal and liquid) develop glides *b* or *d*:

*$m\dot{r}t$- 'death': ἄμβροτος (< *ἄ-μροτος).

*$H_2 ner$- 'man': ἀνδρός (gen. sing. < *ἀνρ-ος).

*$melH_3$-/$mleH_3$- 'go': βλώσκω, μέ-μβλω-κα (< *$ml\bar{o}$-, contrast) ἔμολον (aor.) < *e-mlH_3-om.

Assimilations are of great frequency. They may be partial, e.g. the feature of voicing, as with *pd* > *bd* (ἐπίβδα), *gt* > *kt* (φεύγω, ἄφυκτος); *km* > *gm* (δέγ-μενος < *dek-$menos$); aspiration as in γθ > χθ (λέγω, ἐλέχθην); nasalization as in *bn* to *mn* (σεμνός < *σεβ-νός, cf. σέβομαι < *$tjeg^w$-; μνάομαι < *βνάο-μαι < *$g^w n\bar{a}$ 'woman'). Assimilation also affects place of articulation: e.g. *mt* > *nt* as in βροντή < *βρομ-τᾶ, cf. βρέμω; *np/nb* > *mp/mb*, *nk/ng* > *ŋk/ŋg* (e.g. forms compounded with σύν: συμπαθής, σύμβιος, συγκαλῶ, συγγενής). We may classify here the change of *kj > *tj (*kjāmeron* > σήμερον/τήμερον); *gj > *dj* (*bhugjH₂ > φύзα, cf. φυγή); *mj* > *nj (**gʷm̥jō* > βανjō > βαίνω; but see p. 223).

Total assimilation is widespread:

ts/ds/tʰs > *ss* (δάσσατο, δασμός < *dat-smos, cf. δατέομαι; ὀσμή < *od-smā, cf. ὄδωδα; κλῶσμα < *κλωθ-σμα, cf. κλώθω). *pm*, *bm*, *pʰm* > *mm* (*oqʷma > *opma > ὄμμα, λελειμμένος, cf. λείπω above; on *-ln-* > *-ll-* in Aeolic ὀφέλλω etc., see p. 96.

On *sr*, *sl*, *sm*, *sn* > *rr*, *ll*, *mm*, *nn*, see p. 236.

Some instances of *dissimilation* have already been dealt with, see for instance Grassmann's Law (pp. 230 ff.). Another characteristically Greek example is the change of *tt/dt* > *st*: e.g. *ϝιδ-θι > ἴσ-θι, *ϝοιδ-θα > οἶσθα, *πιθ-τις > πίστις. Further, *dl* > *gl* in γλεῦκος < *δλευκος (possibly Myc. *de-re-u-ko*). In an extreme form of dissimilation there is loss of one of the resemblant consonants: δίσκος < *δικ-σκος (cf. δικεῖν 'throw'), διδάσκω < *di-dH₂k-skō*, ἔκπαγλος < *ἔκ-πλαγ-λος. Occasionally there is loss of a whole syllable: ἄποινα < *ἀπο-ποινα, πότης < *ποτοτης.

The initial and final sounds of a word may undergo changes under the influence of neighbouring words in the sentence. The phenomenon is known as *sandhi*. Different sandhi forms (sentence doublets) may be generalized and so give rise to dialect differentiation. Thus ἐξ was simplified to ἐς before a consonant; some dialects preserve the distinction whereas others have opted for one or the other. Similarly ἐνς gave rise to εἰς and ἐς. The most frequent sandhi phenomenon is assimilation: τὸμ πόλεμον, τὸλ λόγον, τὸγ κήρυκα. The sandhi variety of vowel contraction results in *crasis*: ἁνήρ < ὁ ἀνήρ, οὑμός < ὁ ἐμός, ἐγῷδα < ἐγὼ οἶδα, προὔργου < πρὸ ἔργου, ὦνερ < ὦ ἄνερ, κἀγώ < καὶ ἐγώ. Most frequently, however, sandhi hiatus leads to *elision*, i.e. loss of the first vowel: γένοιτ' ἄν, ἀλλ' οὐκ, καθ' ἕκαστον, ἔλχ' ἕλκε, etc. Loss of the initial vowel of the second word (aphaeresis) is less frequent and it affects a short vowel preceded by a long vowel or diphthong: μὰ τὸν Ἀπόλλω 'γώ, μή 'μοιγε, μὴ 'κ < μὴ ἐκ, οὐκ ἀξιῶ 'γὼ 'μαυτόν.

7. Prosodies

In speaking, utterances do not simply consist of a series of sounds strung together with equal spacing and on a level pitch. Words cohere in groups (phrases) set off by pauses, the tempo varies and prominence may be given to certain segments by relative loudness and variations of length and pitch. These syntagmatic phenomena are collectively known as prosodies. Basic to their discussion is the notion of *syllable*. An utterance has as many syllables as there are peaks of prominence, prominence being defined in terms of sonority.[1] The sounds which are naturally endowed with a higher degree of sonority and so function as syllabic peaks or nuclei are the *vowels*, though in certain environments sounds of medium sonority (the sonants like *m, n, l, r*) may have this function. The valleys on either side of the peaks are constituted by the *consonants*.

The rhythm of the Greek word and sentence is *quantitative*, that is it depends on the alternation of short and long syllables. A syllable is short if it has a short vocalic nucleus and is 'open', that is if it does not end in a consonant. The number of consonants at the beginning of a syllable ('release', 'onset') is irrelevant. The pattern of a short syllable is thus $(C)CV$. All other syllables are long: they may be open but have a long vowel or diphthong $(C\bar{V}, C\breve{V}S)$ or have a short vowel followed by a consonant: $(C)\breve{V}C$. To determine the rhythm of a given stretch of Greek it is thus necessary to fix the syllabic boundaries (syllabification). If the vowels are separated by single consonants, the syllabic pattern is $CV|CV|CV$; that is, the syllables are open. A cluster of consonants separating two peaks (nuclei) is divided between the two: $CVC|CVC$. Thus *Iliad* A 3 is scanned

$$\overline{\pi o \lambda} \mid \overline{\lambda \alpha \varsigma} \mid \overline{\delta' \iota \phi} \mid \overline{\theta \iota} \mid \overline{\mu o \upsilon \varsigma} \mid \overline{\psi \upsilon} \mid \overline{\chi \alpha} \mid \varsigma' A \mid \breve{\ddot{\iota}} \mid \delta \iota \pi \mid \rho o \mid \breve{\ddot{\iota}} \mid \alpha \pi \mid \sigma \epsilon \nu.$$

All the closed syllables are long, as are the open ones with long vowel. Note that in this verse the first element of the initial cluster πρ forms the 'arrest' or 'coda' of the syllable διπ,[2] and

---

[1] See my *Descriptive and Comparative Linguistics*, 54–5. The syllable, though intuitively clear, as is shown by its basic importance in versification, is scientifically elusive. Phoneticians have not reached agreement on the acoustic and articulatory facts behind this intuitive unit of speech.

[2] In Attic, certain clusters (consisting of plosives and sonants) are treated as a unit. There is no lengthening of the preceding syllable.

that the penultimate syllable is απ, πσ being the necessary
resolution of the Greek affricate ψ. There are three short
syllables of the pattern V̆, with the vowel in hiatus; *h* does not
count as a factor in syllabification.

In discussing the rules of quantity the ancient writers described
both vowels and syllables as long and short. If the long syllable
(our closed syllable) contained a short vowel, it was said to be
long θέσει (by 'convention'). From this developed the unfortunate formulation that the *vowel* is 'long by position'.
W. S. Allen has proposed a terminology based on the Indian
grammarians: vowels are short or long, syllables are 'light' or
'heavy'.

One more notion requires elucidation before discussing the
prosodic phenomena of Greek. In practice there is a wide
variation in the actual phonetic length of syllables. As we saw,
the initial cluster is irrelevant: στρε- counts as the same length
as ἑ-. In Greek practice and theory, the basic quantitative unit
(the 'primary time', χρόνος πρῶτος) was the short vowel, and
this was applied also to the 'light' syllable. The long ('heavy')
syllable was taken as double the length of a short syllable. In
modern discussions the 'primary measure' is called a *mora*, and
a long vowel or diphthong is regarded as having two *morae*.

ACCENT

The prominence given to a syllable of a word is called *accent*
(*accentus* being a Latin translation of the Greek προσῳδία 'tune
played in accompaniment'). In Greek (as in IE) the accent was
essentially one of pitch, a musical accent as opposed to the
stress accent of English. The Greek terms τόνος and τάσις
(< *ten*- 'stretch'), with their reference to the string 'tension'
of musical instruments, implies this musical character, and this
is supported by the correlation of the melody with the tonal
pattern exhibited by the musical inscriptions from Delphi
(ii B.C.).

Short vowels were susceptible to only one kind of accent, the
ὀξύς 'sharp' (Lat. *acutus*); this raised the pitch up to an interval
of one fifth above the non-accented neighbours,[1] which were
said to be βαρύς 'heavy', 'low' (Lat. *gravis*) and in speech there

[1] W. S. Allen moots the possibility that the 'fifth' is the variation from
the mean.

was a falling glide from the high to the low tone. In long vowels
and diphthongs the acute accent could fall on either 1, the first
or 2, the second mora. In 1, there was a falling glide from the
high pitch on the first mora to the lower pitch on the second
mora; the accent was said to be δίτονος, 'two-toned', σύμ-
πλεκτος 'complex', or περισπώμενος (Lat. *circumflexus*). In 2,
the voice rose from low to reach its peak on the second mora:
there was a rising glide. The two accentuations may be seen in
Ζεύς (·.·), vocative Ζεῦ (·.·).

While Greek has preserved the IE pitch accent, it has modified
the placing. Whereas the IE accent was completely free and
could fall on any syllable (this being also true of Vedic Sanskrit),
in Attic Greek it cannot lie further back than the third syllable.
Even within the 'three-syllable rule' the accent is subject to
considerable limitation. In the final syllable 1, the short vowel
may bear the acute, but this becomes grave, unless the word has
sentence-final position: ἱερὸς βωμός; 2, a long vowel or diphthong may be either acute or circumflex (ἀλφή, ἀλφῆς). In the
penultimate syllable the accent is acute on a short vowel, but an
accented long vowel or diphthong is *perispōmenon* if the final vowel
is short, and acute if it is a long vowel or diphthong[1] (δῆμος,
δήμου). The antepenultimate syllable may be accented only
if the vowel of the final syllable is short. The sole permissible
accent is the acute. If in the declension of a word a long vowel
appears in the final syllable, the accent is brought forward to
conform to the three-syllable rule: e.g. ἄνθρωπος, ἀνθρώπου.
The accentual pattern may be represented as mora patterns in
1, final, 2, penultimate and 3, antepenultimate syllables.

1. ·́, ·.·́ (oxytones); ·.·. (perispomena).
2. ·.·|·., ·́|·., ·.·́|·. (paroxytones); ·.·.|·. (properispomena).
3. (.) ·́|·. (.) |·. (proparoxytones).

The general rule thus appears to be that the accent cannot go
further back than the last mora but two; the sole exceptions are
words of the pattern of ἄνθρωπος (·́|·.·|·.). To take account
of these R. Jakobson has reformulated the three-syllable rule as
follows: 'the span between the accented and the final mora

[1] Final -αι counts as a short syllable (except in the third singular aorist
optative), as does -οι except in the vocative singular of -ώ feminines (p. 277),
the locative singular in -οι (e.g. οἴκοι contrasting with nominative plural
οἶκοι), and the third singular optative in -οι.

cannot exceed a syllable.' W. S. Allen has proposed a still more concise form which introduces the concept of *contonation* (*In Memory of J. R. Firth* (1966), 8–14). As shown above, there is evidence from the musical texts that the Greeks used a post-tonic glide on the syllable following a high tone. This may have been what was designated by some writers, including Aristotle, as μέσος ('middle' tone) and Allen suggests that the term may have included the 'complex tone' as a whole, which from a phonetic point of view was probably similar to the glide on a long vowel or diphthong in the syllable following a high tone. Thus it is possible to regard the Greek accent as a complex phenomenon involving both the high tone and the subsequent fall. This is an instance of a 'contonation'. Allen's formulation of the three-syllable rule is 'not more than one mora may follow the contonation'. If we use the notation ˥ for the falling glide, the 'contonation' presented by ἄνθρωπος ˊ ˥˥ is possible only if the final vowel has a single mora, i.e. is short.

IX

MORPHOLOGY

1. Some Preliminary Notions

Word class, root, stem and inflexion

The form of a word may vary according to the part it plays in the function of a sentence. Thus ἀθάνατος 'immortal' shows a variety of endings (-ς, -ν, -ου, -ῳ, etc.), the so-called cases with functions briefly described as nominative, accusative, genitive, dative, etc. Such word-components having a syntactic function are called *inflexions*, and their complete tabulation is known as the *declension* of a noun or the *conjugation* of a verb. If the case inflexions are removed, the word-rump that remains is called the *stem*: ἀθανατο-. Comparison with other words with a negative meaning like ἄβατος 'untrodden', ἄγνωστος 'unknown', ἄγονος 'unborn', etc., reveals the existence of a prefix ἀ- with the meaning 'not'. θανατο-, when brought together with other words dealing with the notion of 'death' like the verb (ἀπο)-θνῄσκω, aorist (ἀπ)-έθανον, perfect infinitive τεθνᾶναι, is seen to contain one form of a nucleus θ-ν to which a suffix -το- has been added. The common element of this whole family of 'death' words is known as the *root*, and the varying vocalic guises in which it appears (θνᾱ-, θαν(α)-) are known as the Ablaut forms (see above). A whole variety of stems may be formed from a given root by different suffixes. From *dō-* 'give' we have the nominal forms δο-σι- (*do-ti-*), δο-σμο-, δο-τήρ, δώ-τωρ, δό-τειρα (< *do-ter-jH₂*), δώ-της, δω-τ-, δω-τῖν-η, δῶ-ρο-ν, δω-ρ-ύφιον, δω-ρ-εά, and further the verb δί-δω-μι.

The Greek word may thus contain three kinds of morphological units ('monemes'): the *root*, one or more *affixes* (suffixes and prefixes; on the 'infix', see below), which are attached to the root to form *stems* (there are also root-stems), and finally the *inflexion*, which transforms the stem into a complete word and indicates its syntactical function.

2. Stem formation

A. Nouns

Within the noun system the phenomenon of 'agreement' makes it necessary to make a distinction between substantive and adjective: the inflexions of the adjective are determined by the 'gender' of the substantive. The concept of 'gender' is required to account for this agreement of the adjective with the substantive which it qualifies, as in French *le beau garçon*, *la belle fille*, in German *ein schöner Garten* (masc.), *eine schöne Frau* (fem.), *ein schönes Buch* (neut.). The genders are named 1, masculine, 2, feminine and 3, neuter because of the preponderance of males, females and inanimate objects among the referents of the nouns that enter respectively into these different gender classes; but in principle grammatical gender has nothing to do with sex: cf. German *der Löffel* 'the spoon' (masc.), *die Gabel* 'the fork' (fem.), *das Messer* 'the knife' (neut.). The category of adjective is also required to account for the grammatical phenomenon of 'comparison', but this is a matter of stem formation and not inflexion.

I. SUBSTANTIVES

The chief productive suffixes of Greek will be listed in a functional classification.[1]

The suffix may be zero: these are *root nouns* belonging to the most ancient stock of words, like ἅλς, θήρ, ναῦς, πούς, χείρ, χθών, etc. Others have close connections with the verb: φλόξ/φλέγω, *ὄψ (ὄπα, ὀπός, ὀπί) < *weq^w- 'speak' (cf. εἰπεῖν), †ὤψ (acc. ὤπα) < *ὄq^w- 'see', κλώψ/κλέπτω, φώρ/φέρω, ῥώξ/ῥήγνυμι, σήψ/σήπομαι. These are in the main action nouns, designating objects, animals and abstract ideas, but rarely agents. When they figure as second members of compounds, however, they form agent nouns: πρόσ-φυξ (φεύγω), σύʒυξ (ʒεύγνυμι), χέρ-νιψ (< *neig^w- 'wash'), ἔπ-ηλυς (ἐλευ-). On the whole the root nouns are fossil formations and tend to be replaced by suffixed forms, especially those in -ᾱ (-η) and -ο-.

Ancient, too, are the formations characterized by the addition of the thematic vowel. These fall into two classes distinguished by the position of the accent. Those with oxytone are agent

[1] See *Latin Language*, 35 ff.

nouns: ἀγός, τροφός, ἀοιδός, νομός, τροχός, etc. The paroxy
tones are action nouns (but form agent nouns as second mem
bers of compounds): γόνος, τρόχος, βόλος, δρόμος, νόμος. Th
agent nouns are closely connected with a verbal root (e.g. ἄγω
τρέφω, τρέχω) and the sense is often passive: e.g. λοιπός, 'wha
is left', νομός 'pasture' (in the sense 'what is shared', 'share
land'), ὁλκός 'furrow' ('what is drawn').

A. Substantives from substantives

1. Diminutives are chiefly formed with the suffix -ιο-, but thi
often combines with the suffix of the noun to produce compoun(
forms, some of great productivity, e.g. -ιδ-ιο-, -αρ-ιο-.

(a) -ιο-: ἀρνίον, θηρίον, δωμάτιον, etc.

(b) -ιδ- was used to form diminutives, which often develope(
independent meanings, e.g. θυρίς 'window'. This formatior
provided the names for all sorts of technical objects and fo
birds, plants and parts of the body: ἀγκαλίς, 'bundle', σφραγί
'seal', περονίς 'pin', 'brooch', etc.

(c) -ιδιο-. This suffix enjoyed a great vogue in post-classica
Greek: ἀδελφίδιον, βιβλίδιον, ἀρτίδιον, κλειδίον, etc.

(d) -αριο-: δουλάριον, παιδάριον, κλινάριον, etc.

2. Other diminutives have the suffix -ίσκο- -ίσκη-: μηνίσκος
παιδίσκος.

One basic word may, at different dates, have a variety c
diminutives, sometimes with a great accumulation of suffixes
παιδίον, παιδίσκος, παιδάριον, παιδαρίδιον, παιδισκάριον.

3. Feminines.

(a) -ιδ- was also used to form feminines, at first in patro-
nymics of females: 'Ατλαντίς, Νηρηΐδες, etc. The suffix als(
figures in the feminine counterparts of certain masculin(
formations: δραπέτης/δραπέτις, δεσπότης/δεσπότις; ἀρτο
πώλης/ἀρτόπωλις. Agents in -τήρ have feminines in -τρί
(ἀλετρίς), and large number of such formations figure as name
for instruments. In Attic -τρίς was replaced by -τρια, whicl
remained productive in the Koine and survives in modern Greek

(b) In IE an important feminine suffix was *-jH₂[1] (for th

[1] On the alternation of -iH₂/-jH₂ yielding -ī/-ια, see above; an olde
notation is *-iə.

yodization of the final consonant of the underlying stem, see pp. 224 ff.): ἄνασσα (< *wanak(t)-), ἱέρεια, γραία (cf. γραῦς), etc. The suffix combined with -tĕr- to produce -τειρα and -τρια (δμήτειρα, καύστειρα, δότειρα, ἀλείπτρια, βάπτρια, etc.). Another compound suffix -n-jH₂/-n-iH₂ was inherited from IE: *potis 'master'/*pot-njH₂ 'mistress', Gk. πότνια (cf. Skt. pátnī). Other combinations which evidently arose from n-stems are seen in δέσποινα (δεσπότης) and θεράπαινα (θεράπων), τέκταινα (τέκτων); -αινα became productive and was used in nouns for female animals (δράκαινα), instruments (ἄκαινα) and repulsive diseases (γάγγραινα, φαγέδαινα).

-ισσα first arose in ethnic feminines. Its use in βασίλισσα 'queen' was the starting point of a great future. It spread to Latin and so to the Romance languages and eventually became productive in English, where -ess is added even to Germanic words like shepherd-ess.

(c) -ῑτιδ- was used to form feminine nouns and adjectives from agent nouns in -ίτης (see below). It was specially productive in the agricultural vocabulary in words denoting the nature of the soil: ἀμπελῖτις 'vine land'.

4. Agent nouns are formed

(a) with the suffix -της (< *-tās) (for the deverbatives, see below): ναύτης, κωμήτης, αἰχμητής, πολίτης. Extended forms of the suffix are:

-ώτης: δεσμώτης, θιασώτης, ἰδιώτης, etc.
-ιώτης: ἀγγελιώτης, στρατιώτης, πατριώτης, etc.
-ίτης: ὁπλίτης, τεχνίτης, ζευγίτης, Θερσίτης (a man's name < the neuter s-stem θέρσος), etc.
-έτης: οἰκέτης, φυλέτης, etc.
-ότης: δημότης, ἱππότης, τοξότης, etc.

(b) -εύς forms occupational names both of agents and instruments: ἁλιεύς, βαφεύς, γραμματεύς, ἱερεύς, ἱππεύς, etc. This suffix is abundantly attested in the Linear B texts, where it also forms adjectives, e.g. aigeus 'with goat protomes'. Originally the suffix had the general meaning 'one who has to do with the basic noun'. These nouns gave rise to the denominative verbs in -εύω, which became so independently productive that in later times the -εύς noun is often a back-formation from the verb.

5. Similar in function to -εύς are the suffixes which provide characterizations of persons, places and things.

(a) -ᾶς designates a man (i) in possession or concerned with a thing, e.g. γαλατᾶς 'milkman', ταριχᾶς, μαχαιρᾶς, ὀρνιθᾶς, etc.; (ii) with a personal characteristic, e.g. κεφαλᾶς 'with a big head'; locality names are formed in this way, e.g. καλαμᾶς. The suffix originally formed hypocoristics, abbreviated forms of proper names like Νικομᾶς, Μηνᾶς, etc., but it multiplied in the post-classical period and is now one of the most common suffixes in MnG.

(b) -ων also formed descriptive terms like στίγων 'tattooed', φείδων 'thrifty'. Some of these are derived from verbs, but the denominatives were especially productive: γάστρων, γνάθων, δρόμων, 'a fast ship', etc. This formation is of ancient origin: cf. Lat. *praedō* (*praeda*), *Catō* (*catus*) 'sharp', 'sly'.

(c) -(ε)ών was productive throughout the history of Greek to form locality names characterizing, in particular, places where plants grow and animals are kept. In MnG it survives in the form -ῶνας, -ιῶνας: ἀμπελών, ἀνδρών/ἀνδρεών, ἱππών, μυλών, etc.

(d) -ίας is also used to form masculine descriptions: ταμίας, καπνίας 'smoky', διφθερίας 'wearing a jerkin', etc. It occurs frequently in proper names: Νικίας, Ἀρχίας, Λοξίας, etc.

(e) We may classify here the tree-names in -έα formed from the name of the fruit, flower, etc. ἀμυγδαλέα, ἀκανθέα, συκαμινέα, etc.

6. Names of establishments and tools.

(a) -εῖον nouns are in the main derived from *s*- and *eu*-stems (*-esjo-, *-ēwjo- > -eio-). They denote establishments, tools, and payments connected with religious and technical activities: ἀρχεῖον, βαλανεῖον, γραφεῖον, ἰατρεῖον, ἀγγεῖον, etc.

(b) -τήριον is a compound suffix originating in the addition of -ιο- to agent nouns in -τηρ. It soon became independent and was added directly to verbal stems and provided the names of establishments, instruments and utensils: βουλευτήριον, δεσμωτήριον, ἐργαστήριον, καυτήριον 'kiln', σφαγιστήριον, etc.

7. Collectives in -ιά: πατριά, στρατιά, νεοσσιά, πρασιά, λαχανιά, σχοινιά, etc.

B. *Substantives from Adjectives*

1. Abstract nouns

(a) -ία was productive throughout the history of Greek to form abstracts from nouns, adjectives and verbs. It was especially prolific in connection with the denominative -έω verbs and will be discussed below.

(b) -σύνη was mainly productive in forming nouns denoting personal qualities. There was a rich development in the moral and philosophical vocabulary of Ionic prose: σωφροσύνη, ἀγνωμοσύνη, ἀπραγμοσύνη, δικαιοσύνη, etc.

(c) the feminines in -τητ- (*-*tāt-*) were principally formed from *o*-stems, and the component suffix -οτητ- was then attached to consonant stems: δεινότης, κοινότης, μετριότης, ὀξύτης, μελανότης, χαριεντότης, etc. The suffix remained vastly more productive than -σύνη until Byzantine times, the latter showing few new formations from the time of the Ptolemaic papyri onwards. In MnG there has been a surprising reversal of this situation, for -σύνη is frequent whereas -ότης is unproductive; -ία, however, is the most frequent formation in abstract nouns, being followed by those in -εια.

(d) -εια. The chief use of this suffix was to form abstracts from *s*-adjectives: ἀλήθεια, ἄδεια, ἀσέβεια, etc. Ionic presents corresponding forms in -είη. In the Koine -́εια continued its Attic function, but in the Byzantine chroniclers such formations are rare and in MnG they have been fused with the formations in -ία. In most of the oblique cases the forms in -́εια and -είᾱ were accentually indistinguishable and itacism brought about the fusion of ει and ι. Even in Attic there exist such doublets as ἀήδεια and ἀηδία, while from ἀτυχής and ἀμαθής there exist only ἀτυχία and ἀμαθία.

C. *Substantives from Verbs*

1. Abstract nouns. Such nouns name either the verbal action itself or its result.

(a) -ή. The suffix was inherited and remained productive even in post-classical times: ἀγορά, ἀγωγή, ἀκοή, κλοπή, πληγή, διαγραφή, etc. Throughout the history of Greek it suffered competition from the suffixes which are listed below, and in MnG it has become extinct.

(b) -ία. This was the most prolific suffix especially in connection with o-stem substantives and their denominative verbs in -έω. These verbs tended to be replaced by -ίζω formations with the consequence that we find -ία abstracts from this class, which however tended to favour formations in -σμός (see below). This process was already initiated in Attic, where we find ἀνδραγαθίζομαι/ἀνδραγαθία (ἀνδραγαθέω is late).

In Attic the verbal abstracts in -ία were found side by side with derivatives in -ιον, the latter denoting the fact or result of the action: μαρτυρία/μαρτύριον.

(c) -μός was an inherited suffix which has remained extremely productive down to the present day, especially in the form -ισμός: καθαρμός, ἀγμός, διωγμός, ἠθμός; αἰκισμός, ἀναλογισμός, ἀσπασμός, ἀγορασμός, etc. The suffix is also used to form nouns denoting the result or object of the action. An ancient example is the word δῆμος (δᾶμος < *dā(i)- 'distribute', 'share'); this was originally a land-tenure term which was also applied to the people occupying such land. Other ancient words with this more concrete meaning are θυμός, θωμός, βωμός, ὄγμος, etc.

(d) -μα is the Greek reflection of a zero grade n-stem *-mṇ. Such nouns commonly express the result of an action. The suffix was greatly productive in the language of tragedy and Ionic prose and it remained prolific in the post-classical period. Less frequently such formations are action nouns and so come into competition with -ή and particularly with -σις: e.g. ἐπίταγμα/ἐπιταγή, ἔνταλμα/ἐντολή, ἐπαύξημα/ἐπαυξή/ἔπαυξις. In MnG the suffix has become synonymous with -μός and only a few words have the original 'result' significance. Combination with the stem-vowel of the underlying verb produced the extended forms -ημα (-āμα), -ωμα, -ευμα, and -σμα: εἴλημα, ἄρωμα, βούλευμα, ἔδεσμα, etc.

(e) -σις, which is one of the most prolific Greek suffixes, goes back to an inherited suffix *-ti-, which formed action nouns, the root being normally in the zero grade, e.g. φάτις (φᾱ-/φᾰ-). In IE this suffix was mainly used in compounds, the corresponding suffix in simple words being -tu-. Greek has not preserved this distribution. The form -σι- shows the East Greek assibilation of -ti- (p. 60) and the proliferation of the suffix is due to the influence of Attic-Ionic. The original zero grade of the root is often replaced analogically by the full grade and this is particularly true of derivatives from denominative verbs. In the Byzantine chroniclers the suffix is not infrequent, especially in the form -ευσις. In MnG it has been replaced by the extended form -σία.

(f) -σία. In Attic it is frequently observed that a compound in -σία corresponds to the simplex in -σις. It is however likely that -σία is a composite suffix originating in the addition of -ία to *t*-stems: βοηλασία/βοηλάτης; -ασία was the normal form for derivatives from -άζω verbs, but the suffix developed independently later, especially in connection with -αίνω verbs. Examples are: ἐκκλησία, ἀταξία, εὐεργεσία, πλεονεξία; ἀγορασία, ἀθανασία, δοκιμασία, ὑπηρεσία, etc.

(g) -εία. These are action nouns which link up with adjectives in -ειος and with verbs in -εύω, a particularly prolific class in the Koine: ἀνδρεία, βουλεία, δουλεία, παιδεία, στρατεία, etc. The -εύω verbs were often derivatives of agent nouns in -της, and by a natural short-circuit -εία abstracts came to be derived directly from such nouns: ἀρχιπροφητεία, etc.

(h) -τῡ-. This suffix, with a widespread attestation in IE, appears in Greek with a lengthened vowel. The formation is still productive in Homer, forming action nouns like γραπτύς, ἐδητύς, ἐλεητύς, ὀαριστύς, ἀκοντιστύς, etc. In post-Homeric Greek a few nouns of this type appear in Ionic prose, but in general the suffix was ousted by its numerous competitors (note that Cretan offers both the ancient ἀμπαντυς, i.e. ἀμφαντύς 'adoption' and its new rival ἀμπανσις). Its archaism and Homeric flavour made it suitable as an ingredient of poetic diction, notably in Callimachus.

The various types of verbal stem show different preferences among the competing 'action' suffixes: -άω verbs have mainly -ησις nouns, with comparatively few formations in -σμός; from -έω verbs there is a great preponderance of -ία derivatives with -ησις a poor second and very few examples of -ησμός; -όω verbs have almost exclusively -ωσις; with -ζω verbs there is a great preponderance of -σμός over -σις, but, as noted above, -ασία frequently characterizes derivatives from -άζω verbs; -εύω verbs have a pronounced preference for -εία forms with comparatively few examples of -ευσις; while -νω verbs forms in -νσις were a productive type in technical and philosophic prose, but there was a tendency to form action nouns from -αίνω verbs with the suffix -ασία. In MnG, apart from fossils like θέλησι, the extremely prolific suffix -σις survives only in the extended form -σία.

2. Agent nouns

-τ-, -τήρ, -τωρ, -της. In the earliest texts these suffixes show a distribution inherited from IE: whereas the simple verbs form derivatives in -τήρ or -τωρ, compound nouns have the suffix -της: βοτήρ/συβώτης, ἡγήτωρ/κυνηγέτης. This picture was already blurred in the Homeric poems, which offer examples of -της from simple verbs and a few of -τήρ in compound nouns (e.g. μηλοβοτήρ). In Attic-Ionic, however, this distinction was largely effaced, and -τήρ agent nouns survived as words with an archaic flavour in the vocabulary of law and religion. The insertion of -τήρ for -της was a self-conscious device of high stylization. On the other hand, there are a large number of words for tools and instruments which preserve this suffix, the 'instrumental' function being closely allied to the 'agentive': κρατήρ, ἀρυστήρ, ξυστήρ, etc. It was in this branch of usage that the 'establishment' words in -τήριον arose.

The oxytones in -τήρ contrasted with paroxytones in -́τωρ. The latter were rarer and less productive than the former. As with -τήρ, -τωρ had an archaic and majestic flavour which made it suitable for the language of religion and poetry: ἀλάστωρ, δυνάστωρ, μελέτωρ, μιάστωρ, παντοκράτωρ, etc. This fossil suffix was brought to productive life by the introduction of Latin loan-words in the Greco-Roman period with the result that even such loan-words were transformed: e.g. κούστωρ (custōs), μαγίστωρ (magister).

The great productivity of the denominative -εύω verbs was mentioned above and this led to the replacement of the underlying -εύς agents by the deverbatives in -ευτής: βαλανευτής, γλυφευτής.

II. ADJECTIVES

From substantives and verbs

1. The most productive suffix is -ιο-, most of the examples being denominatives with a few examples of deverbatives, e.g. ἅγιος. When this suffix was added to consonant stems, the

phonetic changes discussed above took place: e.g. *-tios > -σιος, as in ἐνιαύσιος/ἐνιαυτός, δημόσιος/δημότης, ἑκούσιος/ἑκόντ-, etc.

The suffix -αιος originated in the attachment of -io- to ā-stems and it was particularly productive in Ionic: ἀγοραῖος, ἀναγκαῖος, βέβαιος, βίαιος, πεμπταῖος, νησαῖος, χερσαῖος, etc. It was later added to derivatives from adjectives in -ιος, such as nouns in -ια and -ιον, and the resulting compound suffix -ιαῖος became very popular: ἀρχιαῖος, ἐνιαυσιαῖος, τραυματιαῖος, δραχμιαῖος, ὀβολιαῖος, ἐκχυσιαῖος, etc. Another compound form productive in late Greek was -ιμαῖος (on -ιμο-, see below); ἀποβολιμαῖος, ἐντολιμαῖος, etc.

-ειο- has a dual origin: from the addition of -io- to 1, s-stems, (-*esjo-) and 2, to ew-stems (-ĕw-io-), e.g. Ionic βασιλήϊος. The use of -ειο- was then extended analogically: e.g. ἀνθρώπειος, ἀνδρεῖος, γυναικεῖος, etc.

Distinct from this is the suffix -ejo- of IE origin which formed material adjectives of the type of Latin aureus. Such derivatives in Greek vary between -εο- and -ειο- and this is already true in the Linear B texts (e.g. wrine(j)os). Examples are ἀργύρεος (Attic ἀργυροῦς), σιδήρεος/σιδήρειος, χάλκεος/χάλκειος, etc.; from names of animals, αἴγεος/αἴγειος, βόεος/βόειος, etc.

2. The suffix -ινο- was used to form adjectives denoting material, origin, etc.: ἀκάνθινος, ἀμπέλινος, ἀνθρώπινος, ἐλεφάντινος, etc. Distinct from this is the suffix -νό- forming temporal adjectives, which, on the Linear B evidence, goes back to -nwo-. This was added to a locative in -i: περυσινός < *per-uti-nwo-. Examples are: νυκτερινός, χειμερινός, ἡμερινός, ἐαρινός, θερινός, etc.

3. -ιμος is in origin a compound suffix resulting from the addition of the inherited -mo- to compositional forms in -i- (it is quite possible that adjectives like ἄλκιμος originated as hypocoristic shortenings of names like Ἀλκιμένης). The extended suffix became very productive, and these adjectives were formed chiefly from o-grade substantives: ἐπόχιμος, γόνιμος, νόμιμος, etc.

The suffix was also added to -σις abstracts, producing a compound form -σιμος: ἀπολύσιμος, ἀρόσιμος, βρώσιμος, ἐπιδόσιμος, etc. A substantivized form of this adjective later took the place of the infinitive: an early example (A.D. iv/v) is πότιμον καὶ βρώσιμον 'eating and drinking'.

4. -ής. This category consists almost entirely of compounds having an s-stem as the second member, e.g. εὐ-γενής (*-genos/ -genes). The system was productive throughout the history of Greek, and such formations are found even where no s-stem noun existed: βάπτω, βαφή, ἀβαφής, τύχη, ἀτυχέω, ἀτυχής. As a result of such systematic correspondences this suffix was used to form compound adjectives both from verbal and nominal stems characterized by -η-. The direct connection with a verb was established once the basic s-stem noun had been lost: θεοπρεπής < *πρέπος. On the analogy of such models a compound like νουνεχής could be formed even from the verbal phrase νοῦν ἔχειν.

5. A specially productive suffix belonging to this last category was -ώδης, which originated in compounds formed with the root *od- 'smell': ῥοδώδης. The semantic content of the second element had, however, become watered down even in the Homeric poems, and compounds of the type λυσσώδης 'raging' < λύσσα 'rage' appear. The suffix was productive in Attic-Ionic and in the earlier Koine, but by Byzantine times it was already sterile.

6. -κός. This is the most productive of the denominative adjectival suffixes, and it often replaces other adjectival suffixes as in the MnG νυχτικός for νύκτιος. The form -ιακός was probably due to dissimilation when -ικο- was added to nouns in -ιος and -ιον: *ἡλι-ικος > ἡλιακός, but the suffix was attached to other stems, e.g. σεληνιακός, μηνιακός, θεριακός, etc.

The compound suffix -(σ)τικός originated from the attachment of -ικός to agent nouns in -της and verbal adjectives in -τός. Such adjectives preserved the strong verbal force of these formations, the meaning varying between passive-intransitive (e.g. ἐνθουσιαστικός 'possessing enthusiasm' and active-causative 'inspiring enthusiasm'.) Once a relation with the basic verb was established, such adjectives could be formed even where no intermediaries in -της and -τός existed. -τικός was also added to ā-stems: κωμητικός, κεφαλητικός. In this way an extended form -ητικός arose, e.g. τροφητικός.

7. -τός. This suffix was used to form verbal adjectives and it is of widespread occurrence in the IE languages. Originally the formations were neutral as to voice, but the passive meaning became dominant. The suffix was originally added to the zero

grade of the root: κλυτός (*kleu-/klu-), βατός (*gʷem-/gʷm̥-), τατός (*ten-/tn̥-), but later there was much analogical levelling. The formation was most common in composition, ἄλυτος being opposed to λελυμένος, ἀκίνητος to κεκινημένος, a relationship which is also observable in the Mycenaean texts, where we have *khalkōi dedemena* 'bound with bronze' contrasting with *khalko-deta* 'bronze-bound'.

In later Greek -τός was progressively supplanted by -μένος, but in the Byzantine chroniclers it had lost little of its fertility, and even MnG has numerous examples of -τός in the function 1, of a perfect participle, 2, of a present participle and 3, in a purely adjectival function.

Besides these verbal adjectives there are a number of -τός adjectives derived from nouns: e.g. χολωτός with the same relationship to the noun χόλος as the Latin *barbātus* has to *barba*. In Greek (and in Latin) such adjectives are often attested earlier than the corresponding denominative verbs (χολόω), and even in IE it is likely that such denominative adjectives could be formed. In post-classical times -ωτός remained productive and in MnG it is productive in the substantivized form -ωτή.

8. -τέο-. This suffix was used to form gerundives, that is verbal adjectives with a meaning of obligation. They occur almost exclusively in predicative use, the first example of this kind being Pindar's γεγωνητέον. The explanations generally admitted bring this suffix into connection either with the Vedic infinitive (*ná...áttave* 'not for eating', 'not to be eaten'), or with the gerundive formant *-tavya*; *-tewo-* is regarded as a thematic derivative from the verbal noun suffix *-tu-*. The new Mycenaean evidence (see p. 51 on *qeteo, qetea₂*) has ruled out these explanations because of the absence of the postulated intervocalic *-w-*. It is more likely that we have a thematic derivative from the action suffix *-ti*: thus the earliest Greek example (used attributively not predicatively), Hesiod's οὔτι φατειός 'unspeakable', would be a derivative from φάτις.

9. -(ϝ)εντ-. This was another suffix inherited from IE. It was added to noun stems, the meaning of the resulting adjective being 'possessing...', like the corresponding Sanskrit suffix *-vant-*. The corresponding feminine form was based on the zero grade of the suffix *-wn̥tjH₂*, which would have yielded *-ϝασσα, but this was levelled to -ϝεσσα. Originally the suffix was added

directly to consonant stems, and this is still observable in the Mycenaean texts (p. 52). In the alphabetic texts the extended form -οϝεντ- has spread from the thematic nouns to the consonant stems. The suffix was still vigorous in Mycenaean times, but later it was productive only as a means of self-conscious poetic stylizing and to this end could be attached even to adjectives like ἀγριόεις, φαιδιμόεις, etc.

10. -ρό-. This inherited suffix appears in many adjectives belonging to the most ancient stock of words: ἐρυθρός, μικρός, πικρός, ὑγρός, etc. Such -ρό- adjectives often alternate with compositional forms in -ι and have substantival counterparts with s-stems: κυδρός, κυδιάνειρα, κῦδος. Various extended forms occur: -ερό- (κρατερός, κρυερός, στυγερός, etc.; -υρό- (γλαφυρός, λιγυρός, etc.); -ηρό-/-ᾱρό- (ἀνιαρός, ὀδυνηρός, τολμηρός, μοχθηρός, etc.); -ηρό- remained productive throughout the history of Greek, particularly in Ionic, but in the Koine it gave way to some extent to the suffix -ώδης. It was particularly active in providing adjectives from food-stuffs, materials, etc. In MnG such adjectives denote only qualities of things, whereas in ancient Greek they referred also to personal qualities.

11. -νό- survives in Greek in certain fossil formations derived from verbs: δεινός (*dwei- 'fear'), σεμνός (cf. σέβομαι, *twegʷ-), ἁγνός (cf. ἄζομαι). In the denominative formations the suffix shows a preference for s-stems: φαεινός (*φαϝεσ-νος, cf. φάος), ἀλγεινός (*ἄλγεσ-νος, cf. ἄλγος), etc. This compound suffix was then extended to other stems: e.g. φωτεινός, ἐρατεινός.

III. COMPOUND STEMS

Greek inherited from IE the capacity to form nominal stems by combining two (rarely more) stems, the inflexions being added to the second member of the compound. Functionally, the compounds fall into two main classes: 1, those in which the second element retains its substantival function (e.g. ἀκρό-πολι-ς) and 2, those in which the compound is adjectival, e.g. ῥοδο-δάκτυλο-ς, which does not mean 'rose-finger' but 'having rosy fingers'. Such a compound corresponds to a descriptive sentence predicated of the accompanying substantive. Such adjectives find their point of attachment outside themselves, and they are known as 'exocentric' compounds, as opposed to the 'endocentric' of type 1.

Compounds may also be classified according to the syntactical relation of their members. This criterion yields two classes: 1, those in which the two members are in apposition, e.g. νυχθ-ήμερο-ν 'a day and a night' (this type is rare in ancient Greek but is more common in modern Greek, e.g. ἀνδρό-γυνο-ν 'a married couple'); 2, the determinative compounds, in which normally the second member is determined by the first (the type ἱππο-πόταμο-ς 'river-horse' being late in Greek). There are three main sub-types:

(i) Adjective plus noun: ἀκρό-πολι-ς 'upper city'.

(ii) Noun plus noun: πατρ-άδελφος 'father's brother'. When the second member is an agent noun, the compound corresponds to a verb plus a direct object: πατρο-φόνο-ς 'father-slayer'.

(iii) The first member is a verbal stem governing the noun stem that forms the second member: ἀρχέ-κακος 'beginning evil', ταλα-εργός 'enduring work', φυγο-πτόλεμος 'fleeing war', φιλο-πτόλεμος 'loving war', φερέ-οικος 'carrying house' (i.e. a snail).

In some compounds of this type the first member is distinguished by the suffix -τι- which is used to form verbal nouns (see p. 252): ἀρτι-(ϝ)επής 'joining words', 'glib', βωτι-άνειρα 'feeding man', 'Ορτί-λοχο-ς 'rousing the army'. This suffix underwent assibilation in the East Greek dialects (p. 60), e.g. 'Ορσί-λοχος. However, not all the first members which have -σι- are traceable to this origin. In fact the greater number appear with verbs which have sigmatic features, desideratives or aorists, in their paradigms: πεισί-βροτο-ς 'persuading mortals' may serve as an instance, for the verbal noun is πίστι-ς < *bhid-ti-. Other examples are ἀερσι-ποδ- 'raising the feet', τερψι-μβροτο- 'delighting mortals', etc.

To turn now to the form of the compounds, we distinguish between the first and second members. The first may be (a) the pure nominal stem, e.g. βου-κόλο-ς. Ablauting stems tend to have the weak grade: e.g. γνυ-πετός 'falling on the knee', χειμά-ρρου-ς 'winter flowing', where the -α- < *-n̥-; (b) a case form: e.g. *Ποτει-δᾶς[1] 'Lord of the Earth' (vocative, cf. Lat. Jūpiter, *Djeu-pəter-), Διόσ-δοτο-ς, Διόσ-κουροι (genitive), ὁδοί-πορο-ς (locative), (ϝ)ιφί-νοο-ς, δουρί-κτητο-ς (instrumental); (c) one of a number of inherited elements, notably the negating

---

[1] This is the presumed basis of the name *Poteidā(h)ōn, Poseidōn*.

prefix ṇ̥- (e.g. ἄ-γνωτο-ς) and the so-called 'copulative' prefix, which in fact is the zero grade *sṃ- of the word for 'one' *sem-. This would regularly appear as ἁ- (ἁ-παξ, ἁ-πλοος, etc.), but lost its breathing according to Grassmann's Law (p. 230) when the second member contained an aspirate: ἄ-λοχο-ς, ἀ-δελφός (*sṃ-gʷelbho-s), ἀ-κόλουθο-ς, etc. The unaspirated form spread by analogy to compounds where no aspirate followed. There was, of course, no distinction in the dialects which lost the aspiration.

Other first elements are: ἀγα- (ἀγά-ννιφο-ς), ἀρι- (ἀρί-γνωτο-ς), ἐρι- (ἐρι-κυδής), δυσ- (δυσ-μενής), εὐ- (εὔ-μενής); (d) prepositions: ἔμ-πεδο-ς, ἐπί-σσωτρο-ν, ἀμφί-πολο-ς, ὑπό-κυκλο-ς, etc.; (e) adverbs (often fossilized noun cases (p. 283)): πᾶν- (παν-ῆμαρ, πάν-αιθο-ς), παλιν- (παλίν-ορσο-ς), παλαι- (παλαί-φατο-ς), χαμαι- (χαμαι-εύνη-ς); (f) cardinal numbers: δι-ποδ-, τρι-ποδ-, τετρα-ποδ-; τρυφάλεια 'having four φάλοι' appears to have a zero form of the word for 'four' *qʷtru-, but cf. τράπεζα and see p. 290.

A large proportion of first members were noun stems of the thematic declension whose stems ended in -ο-. As a consequence this vowel was regarded as a composition suffix *par excellence* and became attached to other stems: ψυχο-πομπό-ς, ἀνδρο-φόνο-ς, χειρό-νιπτρο-ν (earlier χέρ-νιψ).

Turning now to the form of the second members, we find in this position a certain number of stems which do not occur as separate words and also do not appear as first members. A number of these are ancient root nouns which have survived only in composition: σύ-ζυξ, βού-πληξ, χέρ-νιψ, βοῦ-κλεψ, etc. More usually such stems are extended by means of a compositional suffix: μεσό-δμ-ᾱ, δι-φρ-ό-ς, ὄ-ζ-ος (*ο-sd-ο-s, -sd- being the zero grade of sed- 'sit'). Another ancient compositional suffix is -t- (cf. Lat. sacer-dō-t), which appears in δαμ-αρ-τ-, προ-βλη-τ-, etc. In IE -ā also functions as a compositional suffix (cf. the Latin type agri-col-a) as in the ancient word δεσ-πότ-ᾱ-ς, the first member of which is traced to *dems-, perhaps a genitival form of the word for 'house'; -ā- may be added to -t-, -tā- being used to form compound agent nouns like πυλ-αρ-τᾱ-, περι-κτι-τᾱ-, ἀλφ-ησ-τᾱ- (-ησ- < *-ed- 'eat' + tā; for *dt > st, see p. 241).

B. Verbs

The Greek verbal conjugation comprises a number of different 'tense' stems, present, aorist, perfect and future. The first three were inherited from IE, but the future in all IE languages is a recent formation (see pp. 310 f.). These stems have distinctive Ablaut grades: e.g., present λειπ-, aorist λιπ-, perfect λε-λοιπ-. Although they are called 'tenses', the stems have no temporal references but relate to the type of action. The so-called present stem represents continuing action (the durative stem), the aorist refers to momentary action, while the perfect represents the state resulting from an event. Thus θνῄσκειν means 'to be in the process of dying', θανεῖν 'to expire' and τεθνάναι 'to be dead'. These different presentations of verbal events, durative, aoristic, and perfect, by distinctive stems are known as the 'aspects' of a verb. By different devices, which will be discussed below, the aspectual stems give rise to a variety of 'moods'— indicative, subjunctive, optative, imperative and infinitive. In the indicative, temporal distinctions can be made by means of the augment and inflexions: thus from one and the same durative stem, λεγε/ο-, we may form a present tense λέγ-ω and a preterite ἔ-λεγο-ν.

The description of the function of the 'present' stem as 'durative' does not cover all the facts. Thus when Socrates' friends visited him in prison they entered and 'found' him just relieved of his shackles. Nothing could be more momentary than this act of 'discovery'. Yet Plato uses the durative form κατελαμβάνομεν. This has greater directness and vividness: it represents the event as it unfolds as in a news-reel. We have called it the 'eye-witness aspect'. The aorist, by contrast, simply refers to the event as a unit of history (p. 293).

At this point only the formation of the 'present' stem will be under consideration. Although Greek inherited from IE a variety of present-stem formations, most of these survived as mere fossils. The productive types, which give the Greek verbal system its peculiar stamp, in the main owe their origin to a single inherited suffix *-je/o-, which could be added to both vowel and consonant stems. The exposition thus falls naturally into two sections (A) the fossils and (B) the -j- formations.

A.

1. Root stems. These are divided into two groups according to the presence or absence of the 'thematic vowel', a fundamental phenomenon in the Greek verbal conjugation, which may be illustrated from the contrast of φέρ-ο-μεν : ἴ-μεν, φέρ-ε-τε : ἴ-τε. In the first member of these pairs a stem-forming ('thematic') vowel e/o appears before the inflexion, but not in the second member. We have, then, (a) thematic root stems: ἄγω, φέρω, ἔχω (*segh-), λείπω, etc.; and (b) athematic: εἰμί (*esmi), εἶμι, κτεῖμι (Mycenaean, later replaced by κτίζω), φημί, etc.

2. With reduplication and zero grade: (a) thematic: γί-γν-ο-μαι (cf. γένος (Lat. gi-gn-ō)), ἴζω (*si-sd-ō, Lat. sīdō), ἴσχω (*si-skh-ō) (for loss of aspiration, see p. 230), πί-πτ-ω (cf. *pet-); (b) athematic: τί-θη-μι, ἵστημι (*si-stā-mi), δί-δω-μι, etc. A few verbs have a nasal consonant after the reduplication, e.g. πίμ-πλη-μι.

3. Nasal stems

(a) -νω (with zero grade of the root): δάκ-ν-ω (aor. ἔ-δακ-ον), τάμ-ν-ω (Doric; Attic τέμνω is an innovation), κάμ-ν-ω (aor. ἔ-καμ-ον). The last is based on a base *kemH₂-/kmeH₂/ k°mH₂-, the -n- being attached to form III of the base (see pp. 219 f.), cf. κάμα-το-ς.

(b) -νϝω. This suffix is postulated for certain verbs which have a short vowel in Attic and a long vowel in Ionic (Homer) and so fall into the phonological pattern exemplified by ξένος/ ξεῖνος (see pp. 227 f.): φθίνω (aor. ἔ-φθι-το), τίνω, φθάνω, ἱκάνω.

(c) -άνω appears in a number of verbs which have a long syllable, and this suggests that the suffix was *-°n-, with an epenthetic vowel: κευθάνω, ληθάνω, ἁμαρτάνω, αἰσθάνομαι, etc. This suffix was often added to stems with an infix nasal (of the type Lat. iu-n-g-ō, ru-m-p-ō, see below): μα-ν-θ-άν-ω (aor. ἔ-μαθ-ον), λα-ν-χ-άν-ω (aor. ἔ-λαχ-ον), πυ-ν-θ-άν-ω (aor. ἔ-πυθ-ον), λι-μ-π-άν-ω (Sappho, cf. Latin linquo, Skt. riṇakti).

(d) -νᾱ-(-νη-)/-νᾰ-. This type is traceable to a base consisting of a root with a laryngeal extension, a nasal being inserted between the root and the laryngeal. Thus for the root *dem- 'tame' a base *dem-H₂-/dm-eH₂-/dm-H₂- is postulated, the second and third forms with infix nasal, yielding Greek δαμ-

νᾱ-/δαμ-νᾰ-. Some verbs of this class, under conditions difficult
to determine, show an anaptyctic vowel -ι-: σκίδ-νη-μι (aor. ἐ-
σκέδα-σα), κίρ-νη-μι (ἐ-κέρα-σα), etc. On this vowel, see p. 240.

(e) -νῡ-/-νῠ-. This type had a similar origin to (d): a nasal
was infixed in roots extended by -u-. A clear example is Skt.
stṛ-nó-ti (3rd sing.)/stṛ-ṇu-(v)-ánti (3rd plur.) < *str-n-eu-/str-
n-u- (*ster- 'strew', 'cast down'). The expected Greek correspondents would have the suffix alternation -νευ-/-νυ- but this
appears as -νῡ-/-νῠ-, the change being due to the analogy of
-νᾱ-/-νᾰ-,: στόρ-νῡ-μι/στόρ-νῠ-μεν (the apparent o-grade of the
root has been explained as the reflection of the laryngeal H_3, see
p. 300). The expected zero grade of the root (characteristic of
the II form of the base) appears in ἄρ-νυ-μαι, τά-νυ-μαι
(*tṛ-n-u, *ten- 'stretch'), etc. Verbs with full grade such as
δείκνυμι, ζεύγνυμι, etc. are Greek innovations. Note in particular μείγνυμι, which replaced μίσγω (< *mig-sk-ō).

4. -σκω, -ίσκω. There is evidence that IE roots could be
extended by the suffix -s- (see below on the s-aorist, pp. 301 f.),
and this could be further extended by a -k-. A good example is
Hittite paḫs- 'protect', cf. Latin pās-tor with the corresponding
verb pāscō. Besides -s- a suffix -is- also occurs, as in Hittite
preterite dāiš 'put' < *dhē-is. This likewise occurs in the
extended form -isk-, especially in Greek and Armenian, where
it is often added to long-vowel roots. In Hittite -sk- was used to
form iteratives while in Latin the main function is inchoative,
and this appears in some Greek representatives (e.g. γηράσκω).
Homer preserves the archaic forms βάσκω (replaced in Attic by
βαίνω, a -j- formation < *gʷm̥-jō), which is equivalent to
Sanskrit gácchati (< *gʷm̥-sk-), and μίσγω (*mig-sk-ō). The zero
grade is also found in πάσχω (*pn̥th-sk-ō; cf. aor. ἔ-παθ-ον) with
full grade in πένθος. From bases with laryngeal extension we
have θρώσκω (*dhr-eH₃-sk-), βλώσκω (aor. ἔ-μολο-ν, *ml-eH₃-
sk-), etc. This type often has reduplication: γι-γνώ-σκω (*gn-
eH₃-), μι-μνή-σκω (*mn-eH₂- > mnā-).

A suffix -ισκ- appears in θνήσκω, κλήσκεται, and also in
εὑρίσκω and στερίσκω. A suffix -σκ-, not necessarily identical
with the above, also appears in certain Ionic (Homer and
Herodotus) preterites (imperfect and aorist) which have no
augment: ἐθέλεσκε, ἵστασκε, etc.

5. -θω. The function of the suffix is difficult to determine. Sometimes it seems to express a state arrived at by action, and perhaps we have here the origin of the aorist passive (see p. 302). Examples of present stems are: βρῖθω (cf. βριαρός), πλήθω, πρήθω, φλεγέθω, θαλέθω. A suffix -θ- also appears in some Homeric aorists: κίαθον, ἔσχεθον, ἦλθον, ἤλυθον (*el-/el-eu/el-u-). In φθινύθω and μινύθω the -θ- is added to a stem in -νυ-. On the other hand, *mi-n-u- is the infixed form of a base *mei-u-/mi-eu-/mi-u-, and this underlies the Linear B comparative forms me-u-jo/me-wi-jo 'smaller' (see p. 47).

B.

Stems in -je/o-. Here a distinction is made between a primary use (that is, direct addition to a root) and a secondary use (attachment to a suffixed root). The suffix was most productive in forming denominatives, especially those from vowel stems, where it gave rise to the so-called contracted verbs in -άω, -έω, and -όω. Because of Greek sound developments (loss of intervocalic -j- and 'yodization' of consonants (see p. 225)) this, the most productive of IE present-stem formants, is not directly attested in Greek. In view of the manifold phonetic changes the formations will be best classified according to the sound (consonant or vowel) immediately preceding -j-.

1. -αίνω < *-n̥-jō: ποιμαίνω (< *ποιμn̥-, zero grade of ποιμεν-), μελαίνω (cf. μελαν-), πημαίνω (cf. πῆμα), ὀνομαίνω, etc. This suffix then made itself independent of n-stems and was used to form factitives, particularly (a) the 'colour' verbs like λευκαίνω, (b) in the verbs 'make hot, cold, dry', etc., e.g. ξηραίνω. Other derivatives are intransitive, denoting physical and mental states, e.g. ἀφραίνω, μωραίνω, etc., such verbs often being appropriately in the middle voice. A few verbs are primary formations: μαίνομαι (cf. μένος, aor. ἐ-μάν-η, < *mn̥-j-).

2. -ύνω. This formation has close connection with u-adjectives and it appears to have originated in n-extensions like θάρσυνος: θαρσύνω, βαρύνω, αἰσχύνω, etc. It was later added to o-stems, and the proliferations took place mainly in three semantic fields: 1, dimensions (μεγαλύνω, βραχύνω, λεπτύνω); 2, physical consistency (ἀπαλύνω, σκληρύνω, τραχύνω), and 3, cosmetic expressions (this perhaps is an extension of 2): καλλύνω, ἀβ-

ρύνω, etc. It has been observed that such formations are foreign to pure Attic and are used in particular by Attic writers whose language is strongly tinged with Ionic.

3. *-rj-, *-lj-: ἐχθαίρω, ἱμείρω, οἰκτίρω, ἀγγέλλω, etc. (for the phonology, see p. 226).

4. -σσ- (Attic -ττ-). This formant results from the yodization of voiceless dentals and dorsals (pp. 225 f.): κορύσσω (κορυθ-), ἐρέσσω (ἐρετ-), φυλάσσω (φυλακ-), θωρήσσω (θωρᾱκ-), etc.

5. -άζω. This suffix originated perhaps in the attachment of *-jō to stems in -αδ- and -αγ-, but it was subsequently added to any type of stem, particularly to ā-stems: ἀγοράζω, αἰχμάζω, etc. This brought the -άζω verbs into competition with the type in -άω so that we find encroachments such as αἰτιάζω, ἀροτριάζω, ἀφορμάζω, etc.

6. -ίζω. The development of this suffix is parallel with that of -άζω, originating in the addition of -jō to -ιδ- (e.g. ἐλπίζω, ἐρίζω, φροντίζω, etc.). The compound suffix made itself independent and became attachable to noun-stems of all types. Its productivity had begun in prehistoric Greek, and it became one of the most prolific of all verbal suffixes. Such verbs have the meanings (a) to do something, or (b) to be something, connected with the basic noun, though the precise way in which the noun enters into the activity of the verb varies with each word: δειπνίζω 'entertain', κτεατίζω 'acquire', ἀκοντίζω 'throw a spear', 'hit with a spear', μακαρίζω 'congratulate', 'pronounce happy', etc.

7. -άω. The denominatives in -άω were originally -j- derivatives from ā-stems: βοάω, θεάομαι, νικάω, etc. This class remained relatively unproductive compared with the types in -έω and -όω. An important group among the analogical innovations in the classical period comprises the verbs denoting physical ailments (λεπράω, ποδαγράω, etc.) and abnormal mental states (κισσάω, φονάω, etc.). In the latter sense the compound suffix -ιάω was especially prolific: ναυτιάω, ὀφθαλμιάω, etc.

8. -έω. If we disregard the few primary verbs where -έω is due to the loss of a final root consonant (e.g. ζέω < *ζεσ-ω, πνέω < *πνεϝω) and those from disyllabic bases (e.g. καλέω, ἐμέω), this extremely productive type comprises (a) -j- denominatives from e/o- stems (e.g. φιλέω), (b) denominatives from -os/es-

stems (e.g. τελέω), and (c) deverbatives in -*ejo*- with iterative-causative meaning (e.g. τρομέω, φορέω). Although -έω verbs came to be made from any types of noun-stem, there is a surprisingly small number from simple nouns, this being the preserve of the suffix -*eu*- in forming verbs with the meaning 'to be such and such a person', 'to be active with such and such a thing' (see below).

9. -όω. These verbs are either factitive in meaning (δηλόω 'make clear', ἀλόω 'make blind', etc.) or instrumentative (θυρόω 'provide with a door', and by extension θανατόω 'put to death'). A weakened sense of the factitive is present in verbs meaning 'regard as', 'treat as' (δικαιόω 'regard as just', ʒηλόω 'regard with envy', etc.). Since the inherited denominatives from *o*-stems are represented by the -έω type, the -όω class is a Greek innovation, created in analogy of the -ἄω verbs. In the stated functions the -όω class competed with the verbs in -ίʒω and -αίνω. A number of them were used in the passive sense 'to be afflicted with a disease', this being also a function of the verbs in -ιάω. Consequently we find competing formations: γαυρόομαι/γαυριάω, κοπόομαι/κοπιάω. The suffix remained productive in Byzantine Greek and today it is represented by the verbs in -ώνω.

10. -εύω. These verbs derive from -εύς nouns (pp. 249 f.). The expected form of the suffix -είω < *-*ēw-jo*- is attested dialectically (Elean φυγαδειην), but in general -ευ- has been restored from the non-present stems and the underlying nouns. The function of the suffix resembles that of the -έω class, the sense being 'to be such and such' (ἀριστεύω, δαιτρεύω) or 'to be active with regard to such and such' (ἀγορεύω, θηρεύω, παιδεύω). In the main, simple nouns form -εύω denominatives, whereas compound nouns favour the -έω type. In Byzantine Greek -εύω was much used in naturalizing Latin loan-words: ἀννωνεύομαι, κουρατορεύω, ῥογεύω (= *erogo*), etc.

3. Inflexion

A. The Declensional Classes and the Case Inflexions

Greek is an inflexional language in which different monemes are added to the noun stem according to its syntactic function within the sentence (see above). There may be different sets of such case inflexions with identical functions, as in the Latin *senatus/populus*, *senatum/populum*, *senatūs/populī*, *senatuī/populō*, *senatū/populō*. The noun stems which exhibit a given set of case monemes form a noun declension.

Even in IE there are separate forms for all eight cases only in the singular of the *o*-stems (the thematic declension) and it is a characteristic of all neuters that they do not distinguish nominative and accusative. In all the other declensions the ablative and genitive singular are identical. In the plural IE had only six case distinctions: the dative and ablative are identical and there is no vocative form. In the separate languages there were further simplifications. Certain fossil survivals apart, Greek combined the genitive and ablative, and the dative with the locative and perhaps the instrumental. This phenomenon is known as the 'syncretism' of the cases. The following table sets forth the case endings postulated by comparatists for IE:

	Singular	Dual	Plural
Nominative	-s, -ø	-e, -ĭ̄	-es
Vocative	-ø	-e, -ĭ̆	-es
Accusative	-m/-m̥	-e, -ĭ̄	-ns/-n̥s
Genitive	-es/-os/-s	-ous	-om/-ōm
Ablative	-es/-os/-s, -ed/-od	-bh(y)ō, -mō	-bh(y)os, -mos
Dative	-ei	-bh(y)ō, -mō	-bh(y)os, -mos
Instrumental	-e/-o, -bhmi/-mi	-bh(y)ō, -mō	-bhmis/-mis, -ōis
Locative	-i	-ou	-su

-ø stands for zero inflexion, which in certain declensions of the animate gender is accompanied by extension (*vr̥ddhi*) of the suffix. On the distribution of the alternative forms (e.g. the *m*-cases) in the IE dialects, see p. 6.

The case monemes show Ablaut alternation: e.g. genitive *-es/-os/-s*, ablative *-ēd/-ōd*,[1] instrumental *-e/-o*. The same is true of the stem, the general rule being that the full grade appears in the nominative, vocative and locative of the singular and the nominative, vocative and accusative of the plural, these being the 'strong' cases. In the nominative singular of certain classes an extended grade of the Ablaut appears. The other cases have the zero grade of the stem. This ideal picture was, of course, obscured by frequent analogical phenomena.

[1] The long vowels result from the contraction of *-ed* and *-od* with the preceding thematic vowel.

Even in IE contraction took place when a case beginning
with a vowel was added to a vowel stem and this was the
beginning of the process which diversified a single original IE
declension into the different declensional classes presented by
the descendant languages. These are best organized and
analysed according to the final sounds of the stems. The
thematic declension (*o*-stems) stands apart from the athematic
group, comprising stems in -*ā*, plosives, liquids and nasals,
s-stems, and stems in -*i*, -*u* and diphthongs.

1. *O-stems*

Singular

> Nom. **-s*: δοῦλο-ς. Neuters do not distinguish nom. and
> acc., both of which have the ending -*om*.
> Voc. bare stem with *e*-grade: δοῦλε.
> Acc. **-m*, which regularly > -*n* in Greek: δοῦλον.
> Gen. **-osjo*: δούλοιο.
> Dat. **-ōi* (< **-o-* + **-ei*): δούλωι.

Dual Nom., Voc., Acc. **-ō* (< **-o* + **-e* since -*e* is the ending in
> the consonant stems.

> Gen., Dat. **-ous*.

The Greek -οιιν, -οιν has no parallel elsewhere, but Arcadian
has the form -οιυν. The Sanskrit -*ayos* is thought to be an
extension (the -*ay*- originating in the pronouns and in the word
'two', *dvayos*) of the original ending **-ous*, to which the O.Sl.
ending is traceable. In view of the Mycenaean locative form
duwoupi 'in two (land portions)' it is possible that the Greek
forms in -οιυν also owe their genesis to the influence of the word
for 'two', though the spelling rules make it impossible to decide
whether the Linear B word stands for *dwounphi* or *dwouphi*. It is
just conceivable that the Gree. ending went through the stages
-οιυν, -οιιν, -οιν, Attic having further the dissimilated form
δυεῖν for δυοῖν.

Plural

Nominative **-ōs* < **-o-* + **-es*. This was replaced in Greek as
early as the Mycenaean period by -*oi* taken from the pronominal
declension (see below). The neuters utilized as their plural an
old collective formation (still taking the singular verb in Attic

Greek) in *-ā, which may come from *-oH, which > -ā before
a consonant and -ă before a vowel. Greek generalized the short
form (but cf. Skt. *yugā*).

Accusative *-ns. -ονς still survives in a number of Greek
dialects (e.g. Cret. ἐλευθερονς), but it developed variously to
-ως, -ους, or -οις in others (see below).

Genitive *-ōm/-om. Greek -ων (δούλων) corresponds to
Sanskrit -ām. The disyllabic scansion in Vedic suggests that
-ōm arose in the o-declension from *-o-om, whence it spread to
the other declensions. The archaic Latin forms like *deum* may
derive from either -ōm or -om.

Dative. The Greek datives descend from either locatives in
*-oisu or instrumentals in *-ōis. Mycenaean still distinguishes
datives in -o-i (most probably representing -oihi) and instrumentals in -o standing for -ois, the vowel having been shortened
by Osthoff's Law (p. 215). The change of *-oisu to *-oisi may
have been due to the influence of the singular *-oi, the further
change to -oihi being regular. The intervocalic -s- in -οισι is
presumably due to the influence of the consonant stems. On the
selection between -οισι and -οις in the Greek dialects see p. 124.

The IE locative singular *-oi survives in forms like οἴκοι,
πέδοι, etc., and the alternative Ablaut form *-ei in adverbs like
ἐκεῖ (on Doric τειδε, ἀλλει, etc., see p. 286). On the Attic
peculiarities occasioned by quantitative metathesis (νᾱϝός >
νεώς) and by contraction (πλόϝος > πλοῦς) see pp. 62 f. On the
-φι case see below. On other case relics see under Adverbs
(pp. 283 f.).

2. *Ā*-stems

This declension occupies an intermediate position between the
thematic and the athematic types. Thus it has the genitive in -s
and not that in *-osjo. On the other hand, like the o-stems, it has
replaced the inherited nominative plural *-ās (< *-ā + *-es) by
-ai on the analogy of -oi, taken by the o-stems from the pronominal declension. This interaction of the -o- and -ā-stems was
occasioned by the fact that -ā was used to form feminines corresponding to the masculines of the o-class. This is thought to have
been a specialization of a wider function of the -ā-suffix. Since
*-ī- and *-ū- feminines correspond to i- and u-stems, it is likely
that all three feminine formations go back to a laryngeal, so

that -ā < *-o + H_2. To this declension also belong feminines with the suffix *-jH_2 (Skt. -ī, see pp. 248 f.): μέλαινα, λύουσα (< *λυοντ-jH_2), etc., which show Ablaut alternation -ἄ/-ᾱ.

The other case forms call for little comment. In the singular, the vocative originally ended in -ἄ (e.g. νύμφα), accusative -ἄν < *-ἄ+m, dative -ᾱι < *-ā+-ei, this form converging with the locative < *-ā+i. In the plural accusative *-āns > -ανς, which developed alternative sandhi forms -ανς/-ἄς before vowels and consonants respectively. On the dialect selections and the developments of -ανς to -ανς/-ᾱς/-αις, see above. In the genitive, Greek, like Italic, replaced *-ōm by *-sōm, drawn from the demonstrative pronoun (Skt. tāsām, Lat. (is)tārum, Gk. τἄ(h)ων). In Attic-Ionic -ᾱων > -ηων > -εων > -ῶν. The dative presents alternative forms traceable to 1, -āis, an instrumental analogous to *-ōis, which regularly > -ἄις, and 2, -āsi, a locative still preserved in 'Αθήνησι, θύρᾱσι, etc. The endings -ησι and -αισι are blends. For the dialect distribution, see above. In the dual, *-ai (cf. Skt. -e) was replaced by -ā on the analogy of the -ō of the o-stems. For the Mycenaean nominative torpezo and dative wanasoi, see p. 46.

The genitive and dative dual have -αιν/-αιυν, parallel with -οι(ι)ν/-οιυν. The masculines of this declension show features ascribable to the influence of the o-stems: 1, -s is added to the nominatives (πολίτᾱ-ς, etc.), and 2, the genitive ends in -ᾱο (πολίτᾱ-ο; for the dialects, see above), which Attic replaced by -ου. For the vocative there are numerous archaic forms with -ἄ: συβῶτα, etc. For the Mycenaean duals in -ae see p. 46.

3. The Athematic Declension

In this class an archaic feature of basic importance is the shifting of the accent from the stem to the inflexion with the concomitant Ablaut alternations; this gave rise to the distinction between the strong and the weak cases, the accent falling on the terminations of the latter. Lengthening (vṛddhi) is often observed in the nominative singular of animate nouns. In the ideal example the strong cases are singular: nominative, vocative, accusative and locative; dual: nominative and accusative; and plural: nominative, vocative and accusative; but the system was already in dissolution even in IE times. Sanskrit pitár- 'father' serves as an example of stem alternations: vṛddhi in singular nominative *pitā́*; normal grade in singular accusative *pitár-am*, vocative *pítar*, locative *pitár-i*, dual nominative accusative *pitár-ā(u)*, plural nominative *pitár-as*, vocative *pítar-as*; zero grade elsewhere, e.g. singular instrumental *pitr-ā́*, dative *pitr-é*, plural locative *pitṛ́-ṣu*.

Singular

Nominative. **-s* in most classes, but some have lengthening (vṛddhi) of the stem: e.g. *n*-stems (ποιμήν), *r*-stems (πατήρ), and *s*-stems (εὐγενής/*εὐγενεσ-). Neuters have a zero ending and lose the final plosive(s) of the stem (p. 5): μέλι(τ-), γάλα(κτ-).

Accusative. After consonants **-m̥* > -α (φύλακ-α). After vowels **-m* > -ν (πόλι-ν).

Genitive. **-os* > -ος (φύλακος, ποδός).

Dative. *-ei* is still largely preserved in Mycenaean (p. 46), but later survives only sporadically (e.g. Διϝεί-φιλος). This termination was replaced by *-i*, a locative formation (ποδί), the process having begun already in Mycenaean, particularly in the *s*-stems.

Plural

Nominative. **-es* is preserved (πόδες). The neuters have -α < **-H₂* (ὀνόματ-α).

Accusative. **-m̥s* (after consonants) > -ας (πόδ-ας). For the dialect developments of **-ns* after vowels, see p. 237.

Genitive. **-ōm* > -ων (ποδ-ῶν).

Dative. **-su* > -σι, under the influence of singular *-i* (φύλαξι). For the phonetic developments in various stems, see below. For the analogical extension in Aeolic of -εσ-σι (originating in *s*-stems) see pp. 55 f., 96.

The dual endings -ε and -οιν need no further discussion.

Post-Mycenaean Greek presents a case-ending -φι in a variety of functions—locative (ὄρεσφι), instrumental (ἶφι) and ablative ('Ιλιόφι), both in the singular and the plural. But this was largely an artificial development of the original usage still evident in Mycenaean, where it is used almost exclusively (a) in the plural, (b) of athematic stems, and is added directly to the stem (see p. 45). Thus Greek maintained the IE distinction between the instrumental plural endings *-ois* and *-bhi(s)* which is also reflected in the Sanskrit declensions (-*āis*/-*bhis*). The formant -*bhi*- also appears in the IE (on the dialect distribution see p. 6) dative–ablative dual (*-*bhyō*) and plural (*-*bhyos*). Meillet pointed out that labial plosives figure neither in the suffixes nor terminations of IE. It is conjectured that these case forms originated in a 'postposition' *-*bhi*.

Plosive Stems

The different stem-classes require further comment. Among those ending in a plosive, the vocative ἄνα shows the bare stem ϝανακτ with loss of the final plosives. The same may be true of γύναι < *γυναικ, although it has been suggested that γύναι is an ancient vocative form. The word for 'foot' has *o*-grade ποδ- (possibly originating in compounds) contrasting with the Latin *ped*-. A lengthened vowel πώς appears in the nominative (cf. Sanskrit *pád*). The Attic πούς cannot be original and is presumably due to some analogical influence difficult to determine. In the dative plural the -*s*- occasioned a variety of phonetic changes. With dental stems -*ts*- and -*ds*- > -σσ-, which was simplified: ποσί < *ποδ-σι. In stems like ὀδοντ-, ὀδόντ-σι > *ὀδον(σ)ι > ὀδοῦσι. This stem originally showed Ablaut alternation: *dont*-/*dṇt*- (Skt. accusative *dánt-am*, genitive *dat-ás*). The full grade has been generalized in the Greek declension (as opposed to Latin *dent*- < *dṇt-) but the zero grade survives in the Mycenaean derived adjective *odatwent*- < *odṇt-went- (p. 52). In the dative plural -*ont*- stems converged with -ŏ*n*-stems, with the consequence that a number of stems form nominatives in -ων, notably the participles like λύων/λυοντ- (see pp. 312 f.). Conversely -ων stems were declined like -*ont*- stems: e.g. λέων (feminine λέαινα < *lewṇ-jH₂, cf. Lat. *leō*, *leōnis*), λεοντ-. In these nouns the vocative was formed with the bare stem, with regular loss of the final plosive: γέρον.

Liquid Stems

Liquid stems have vṛddhi in the nominative singular, zero grade in the genitive and dative singular and dative plural, with normal grade elsewhere (singular πατήρ, πάτερ, πατέρα, πατρός, πατρί; dual πατέρε, πατέροιν; plural πατέρες, πατέρας, πατέρων, πατράσι (< *pətṛ-su). This departs from the IE pattern in which the zero grade appeared also in the accusative and genitive plural (see above on Skt. *pitar-*). On the other hand there was analogical extension of the zero grade in forms like θύγατρα, θύγατρες, θύγατρας. Similarly ἀνήρ has variously ἀνέρα/ἄνδρα, ἀνέρος/ἀνδρός, etc. (for *ἀνρ- > ἀνδρ- see p. 240). Χείρ derives from a stem *χεσρ- < IE *ghesr- (cf. Aeolic χερρ-, Doric χηρ). The nominative *χερς developed regularly to χείρ in Attic, and this form of the stem was carried throughout the declension except for the dative plural χερσί (< *χερσ-σι).

Nasal Stems

Nasal stems in IE had *-ōn, with lengthened *o*-grade, in the nominative singular, *-en- with normal *e*-grade in the accusative and locative singular and in the nominative plural, but zero grade -n- elsewhere. By different analogical processes Greek evolved types in -ων/-ον- (δαίμων/δαίμονος), -ην/-εν- (φρήν/φρενός), -ην/-ην- (σφήν/σφηνός). The zero grade appears in φρασί (< *bhrṇsi); in Attic φρεσί the vowel of φρένες, etc. has been generalized, just as δαίμοσι has been substituted for *δαίμασι. The vocative has the bare stem in the normal grade: δαῖμον, Ἄπολλον, etc.

There is a trace of the ancient alternation *-ōn/-en- in the adverb αἰϝέν, cf. αἰ(ϝ)ών. For αἰές and αἰεί see Adverbs, p. 284. Ancient, too, is the declension of κύων, which may contain the zero grade of *kew- 'watch' (κοέω, Lat. *caveō*) and so meant originally 'the watcher'. The oblique cases have the zero grade κυν-, this declension being paralleled in Skt. *ś(u)vā̆/śúnas*, and Lith. *šuõ/šuñs*. Neuters in -mṇ are an inherited class: ὄνομα (cf. Skt. *nāma*, Lat. *nōmen*). In Greek this stem shows an extension -*t*- (ὀνόματος), which does not appear in the denominative ὀνομαίνω (*onomṇ-jō).

S-stems

The declension of the *s*-stems is complicated in Greek by the aspiration and subsequent loss of intervocalic -*s*-. Thus the neuter type *genos/genes*- produced γένε(h)ος/γένους, γένε(h)ι/ γένει, γένε(h)α/γένη, γενέ(h)ων/γενῶν, γένεσσι/γένεσι. The corresponding animate declension has vṛddhi in the nominative εὐγενής, but elsewhere the normal grade (e.g. nominative plural εὐγενέ(h)ες/εὐγενεῖς). On the phonetic complexities of the compounds in *-klewēs (*klewos 'fame') see p. 239.

Another inherited type comprised the animate nouns in *-ōs-/-ŏs- (cf. Latin honōs, with e-grade in hones-tus): αἰδώς *αἰδό(h)α/αἰδῶ, *αἰδό(h)ος/αἰδοῦς, *αἰδό(h)ι/αἰδοῖ. *ausōs 'dawn' (Lat. aurōra) originally followed the same declension: ἀ(ϝ)ώς, *ἄϝο(h)α, *ἄϝο(h)ος, *ἄϝο(h)ι, are reflected in the Homeric ἠώ, ἠοῦς, ἠοῖ. In Attic the regular phonetic development produced ἕως (with retraction of the accent), and this was absorbed into the 'Attic second declension' (p. 191). Certain nouns of this inflexion acquired the t-extension of the stem, e.g. Attic χρώς, χρωτός as against Homeric χρώς, χροός.

The class of neuters in -ας represents another IE heirloom in Greek although it has been argued that some of them are transformations of stems in -αρ (e.g. γέρας, but adjective γεραρ-ός, denominative γεραίρω). The declension is as follows: singular κρέ(ϝ)ας, *κρε(ϝ)αhος > κρέως, *κρε(ϝ)α(h)ι > κρέαι; dual *κρε(ϝ)α(h)ε (cf. Myc. dipae) > κρέᾱ, *κρε(ϝ)α(h)οιν > κρεῶν; plural *κρε(ϝ)α(h)α > κρέᾱ (see below), *κρε(ϝ)α(h)ων > κρεῶν, *κρε(ϝ)ασσι > κρέασι. The nominative–accusative plural is often κρέᾱ. This may be due to the influence of other declensions like ὀνόματα, but it has been suggested that it goes back to an old collective *krewH₂. The -os-/-es- neuters also exert a pull on this declension: e.g. οὖδας has the genitive οὔδεος, dative οὔδει. Some of the -as- neuters also have the t-stem in oblique cases, and this has been regarded as another indication that they were once -αρ stems with the heteroclite oblique stem -n̥t- (see below). An example is τέρας, τέρατος, etc.; in the plural we have the alternative forms τέρατα/τέρᾱ (< *tera(h)a), τεράτων/τερῶν (< *tera(h)ōm).

The word for 'month' in Greek originates in *mēns-, an old s-stem. In Aeolic the genitive *mēns-os > μηννος (for the stem cf. Lat. mensis), but in other dialects > μηνός, which gave rise to the analogical nominative μήν. The nominative *mens-s > *měns > μείς (Attic) or μής (Doric). Elean μεύς was created on the model Ζηνός : Ζεύς (see below).

Another s-stem with heteroclite declension is the word for 'ear': nominative singular Attic οὖς (not a diphthong on the evidence of the early spelling ΟΣ), Doric ὦς; genitive, etc. ὠτ- points to *owos/*own̥t-, the latter > *ὀ(ϝ)ατ- > ὠτ-. The stem *owes- appears in ἀμφῶες 'with two handles', cf. Myc. *anowe* = *anōwĕs* 'without handles'. Other languages, however, show a stem *aus-, e.g. Lat. *auris* (the *i*-stem perhaps from a dual form *ausī*), *aus-culto*, and this forms the basis of παρειαί, παρήϊον, Myc. *parăw(w)aiō* < *par-āus-io-/-iā*. Homer, again (also later poets and inscriptions) had οὐατ-. To accommodate all these forms some scholars posit *ōus-, with zero grade *aus-; others again *ousos/*ouses-/*ousn̥t-. A more recent view postulates *aus-/*us- with an *s*-stem *ausos/*auses-, *ausos changing to Greek *ουσος under the influence of *oqʷ- 'eye'. The declension became heteroclite on the lines of other anatomical words. The Homeric οὐατ- is explained as metrical lengthening, and the similar inscriptional forms are dismissed as Homericisms.

Stems in -i, -u, *and* -eu

Here two types are distinguished: 1, those in which the suffix remains invariably -i or -u, and 2, those in which it ablauts *-i/-ei, *-u/-eu, with a lengthened form (vr̥ddhi) *-ēi and -ēu in certain positions, the Ablaut alternations being occasioned originally by accentual shift. An example of 1 is the word for sheep *owis > ὄ(ϝ)ις > οἶς, *owim > ὄ(ϝ)ιν > οἶν, *owjos > ὀ(ϝ)ιός > οἰός, *owjei > ὀ(ϝ)ιί > οἰί (also ὀΐ), *owjes > ὄ(ϝ)ιες > οἶες, *owins > ὄ(ϝ)ινς > οἶς, *owjōm > ὀ(ϝ)ίων > οἰῶν, *owisu > ὀ(ϝ)ισί > οἰσί. More frequent was type 2 with -e-grade of the suffix originally in the vocative, genitive, and dative singular and the nominative plural: *-is, *-ei, *-im, *-eis, *-ejei, *-ejes. Particularly characteristic is the replacement of the genitive singular *-eis in Greek by -i-os.

In Attic Greek there was considerable rearrangement, with the consequence that the zero grade appears only in the nominative and accusative singular: πόλις, πόλιν. The IE vocative had the full grade of the suffix -ei, and this survived in the divine name Ποσει(-δᾶ-ων) 'O Lord of the Earth'. In the declension it has been replaced by the zero grade. In the nominative plural *polej-es regularly > πόλεις, and the -e- has been extended to the accusative plural πόλεις < *polens (for original *πολινς > πόλῑς), the genitive πόλεων, and the dative πόλεσι. In the singular there is evidence for a dative (an ancient locative) with vr̥ddhied stem πόληι, and this stem-form was transferred also to the genitive, thus replacing *πολεις by *πόληος, which > πόλεως by quantitative metathesis, the position of the accent betraying the originally short final vowel. An alternative explanation, which starts with a declensional pattern *polēi-s/ polj-os, etc., with a levelling to *polēj-os etc., hardly seems preferable, for this analogical generalization would have to be dated before the proto-Greek change *poleis to polĕis (Osthoff's Law), while the insertion of polis, polin in this levelled declension would remain without explanation. In all dialects except Attic the stem form -i was extended throughout the declension: πόλις, πόλιν, πόλιος, πόλῑ, etc. The accusative form πόλιας owes its ending to the consonant stems.

In the u-stems type 1 is represented by *doru > δόρυ, *dorwos > δουρός, *dorwei > δουρί, *dorwH₂ > δοῦρα, *dorwōn > δούρων. In the type 2 the original inflexions were: singular, *-us, *-ou, *-um, *-eus, *-ewei, *-ēu; plural *-ewes, *-uns, *-uwom, *-usu. In Greek the e-grade, as with -i/-ei stems, was extended to all cases except the nominative, vocative and accusative singular: e.g. πῆχυς, πῆχυ, πῆχυν, with the plural πήχεις < *πᾱχεϝες, πήχεις (< *πᾱχενς), πήχεων, πήχεσι. In Attic the genitive is πήχεως, where the accent indicates an earlier *πήχηϝος, with a grade which might be traced to the vṛddhied locative form in *-ēu. It is conceivable, however, that a word like ἄστυ might have been influenced by the declension of πόλις so that ἄστεως parallels πόλεως. In non-Attic dialects the genitive singular has -εος (πήχεος), and this is found even in Attic in the u-adjectives, e.g. ἡδέος < *swādewos, this being a refashioning of the expected *ἡδευ-ς. *suju- 'son' shows forms belonging to both declensional types: υιυς (Cretan), ὑύς (Attic), υιυν (Cretan), υἱός (Homer) < *suwjos, υἷι (Homer) < *sujwi, υἷες (Homer) < *sujwes, υιυνς (Cretan) < *sujuns. The full-grade suffix -ew- also appears in υἱέ(ϝ)ος, υἱέ(ϝ)ι, υἱέ(ϝ)ες > υἱεῖς, υἱεῖς, υἱέσι.

Mycenaean presents the dative form ijewe, plausibly interpreted as hijewei, with nominative iju = hijus, both with dissimilatory loss of the first u. Dissimilation was also presumably responsible for the passage to the thematic class υἱός, etc. (Homer, etc.). To the u- stems also belong the diphthongal stems of the type Ζεύς, βοῦς, and ναῦς. The root *dei- 'shine' with u-suffixation gave rise to the base forms I *dei-w- (Latin deivos/dīvus) and II *dj-ew-. From the latter comes the vṛddhied nominative *dj-ēu-s. In the accusative the IE form *djē-m, with loss of the second element, is postulated (cf. βοῦς, βῶν < *g^wōus, *g^wōm). The III form of the base di-w- appears in the genitive *diwós and the dative *diwei. This series of forms by regular development produced the paradigm nominative Ζεύς (with shortening according to Osthoff's Law), accusative Ζῆν, genitive Δι(Ϝ)ός, dative Δι(Ϝ)εί. The accusative suffered two kinds of transformation. In Δία the stem form of the genitive and dative has been introduced, while Ζῆνα has received the characteristic case-ending of the consonantal stems. The stem Ζην- extracted from this form gave rise to the levelled declension Ζηνός, Ζηνί (already Homer, but Mycenaean has diwo, diwe) and even a nominative Ζήν.

Similar is the origin of βοῦς, βῶν (Doric; Attic βοῦν is analogical), βο(Ϝ)ός, βο(Ϝ)ί, βόϜες, βο(Ϝ)ῶν, βουσί, which go back to *g^wōus, *g^wō(u)m, *g^wowos, *g^wowei, *g^wowes, *g^wowōm, *g^wousu. In the accusative plural Doric βῶς (Attic βοῦς parallels the singular βοῦν) resembles Skt. gās, but we should expect *g^wown̥s, which has its regular reflection in βόας (Homer). Ναῦς (*nāus, or perhaps < *naʜ-u-s) shows no Ablaut alternations, for ναῦς and ναυσί have regular shortening (Osthoff); the other cases have the inherited long vowel (cf. Latin nāvis) with ā > η in Attic-Ionic; νῆ(Ϝ)α, νη(Ϝ)ός, νη(Ϝ)ί, νῆ(Ϝ)ες, νῆ(Ϝ)ας, νη(Ϝ)ῶν. The long vowel has spread analogically to νηῦς and νηυσί. Shortening of η in hiatus produced the Ionic forms νέα, νεός, νέες, νέας, νεῶν. In Attic the accusative plural is ναῦς, parallel with the singular ναῦν.

A vṛddhied suffix -ēu- also appears in the Greek nouns of the type βασιλεύς with a declension βασιλῆ(Ϝ)α, βασιλῆ(Ϝ)ος, etc. Quantitative metathesis produced the Attic forms βασιλέᾱ, βασιλέως, βασιλέᾱς, and the ε was introduced also into the dative βασιλεῖ. The early Attic nominative plural βασιλῆς is the regular development < -ηϜες, but the generalization of the stem-form βασιλε- gave rise to the later form βασιλεῖς, which was also substituted for the earlier accusative plural.

The suffix in the feminine diphthongal stems of the type πειθοι- may be regarded as an ablaut alternation of *-ei- with vṛddhi in the nominative singular πειθώ (cf. the Sanskrit type sakhā, accusative sakhayam, dative sakhye) but -οι- in the other cases: vocative πειθοῖ, accusative πειθώ < *πειθο(j)α (< *bheidhoj-m̥), genitive πειθοῦς < *πειθο(j)ος, dative πειθοῖ < *πειθοj-ι.

Heteroclitic Nouns

IE possessed in abundance a type of neuter nouns in which the nominative–accusative had the stem in -*r*-, but the oblique cases in -*n*-. This type survived as sparse fossil remains in most IE languages but was still vigorous in the Hittite declension, both in the simple forms -*ar*/-*na*- as well as in the compound forms -*mar*, -*sar*, -*tar* and -*war*. Hittite *ešḫar*/*ešnaš* 'blood' is paralleled by Skt. *ásṛk*/*asnás*; but in Greek ἔαρ 'blood' the *r*-stem has been generalized. Skt. *údhar*/*ūdhnás* is reflected in οὖθαρ/οὖθατος < *oudhṛ/*oudhṇ-. The -*t*- is a stem extension which figures in the Skt. nominative *yákṛt*, genitive *yaknás* 'liver', cf. ἧπαρ/ἥπατος (< **jēqʷṛ̥*/*jēqʷ*-*ṇ*-*t*-*os*). Some nouns have a vṛddhied form of the suffix. An example is ὕδωρ, with which the Hittite plural *widār* (singular *watar*) may be compared, though the latter has full grade stem *wed*- (cf. dative–locative *wedeni*). The -*r*/-*n* alternation recurs in Gothic nominative *watō* (*wodōr), genitive *watins* (< *woden(*o*)*s*), and it is still reflected in the opposition of English *water* versus Swedish *vatn*.

There are a few traces of a heteroclite declension -*on*-/-*os*-: κυκεών has the Homeric accusative κυκε(ι)ῶ (< *-*o*(*h*)*a* < *-*osṃ*); εἰκών has accusative singular εἰκώ, genitive singular εἰκοῦς and accusative plural εἰκούς. Add to these the accusative Ἀπόλλω and Ποσειδῶ. Finally, the accusative αἰῶ < *aiwos-ṃ may be compared with the adverbs αἰές and αἰέν, both locatives with zero inflexion (p. 284).

The complex morphology of the word for 'head' centres round the root καρ- < *kṛ-, the zero grade of *ker-, which provides κέρας 'horn' (< *ker-H₂-s). A stem form *kṛ-s- would satisfactorily account for the fossil κάρ in the phrase ἐπὶ κάρ 'headlong'. The *s*-stem may receive an *n*-extension (e.g. Skt. *śíras* 'head', genitive singular *śírṣnás*); so that **k°rH₂sṇ*-, with -*ṇ* in the nominative as in *onom-ṇ, would satisfactorily account for the Attic κάρα via *kara(*h*)α, where the three vowels *a* all have different origins. A thematized version of this stem **k°rH₂s-no*- would develop to the Ionic (Homer) κάρηνα via *karasna. The heteroclite stem *-*ṇ-t* (with -*t*- extension) appears in κράατος, κράατι, κράατα, contracted to κρατός, κρατί, etc., with κρᾱ- presumably from the II base form *kreH₂-s-n- (cf. κρᾱνίον < *kreH₂-s-n-). In other Homeric forms the nominative stem καρη- has been introduced: καρήατος, καρήατι, καρήατα, etc. An r-stem appears in the compounds ὀρθόκραιρα, εὔκραίρη, ἡμίκραιρα, and in the gloss καράρα· κεφαλή (< *$k^°rH_2srā$). Mycenaean, too, presents compounds with r-stem: the instrumental singular -karaore, instrumental plural -karaapi, which reflect *$k(a)rǎ̆ŏr$-ei/*$k(a)rǎ$-ṇt-phi. The Linear B spelling tells against the assumption of *$k^°rH_2$-s- since we should expect ka-ra-a₂-pi. The underlying base must therefore be *$kreH_2$- or *$k^°rH_2$-. This would give rise to a declension κρᾱ-/καρα-, and this opens the possibility that the nominative κάρᾱ is due to a levelling within this declension. As the second element of the compound we thus have the stem *$kreH_2$-ŏr-/ *$kreH_2$-ṇt-, with feminine formations *$kreH_2$-r-jH_2, or *$kreH_2$-er-jH_2.

Adjectives

The adjectives do not differ declensionally from the substantives. The category is required primarily to account for a syntactical phenomenon: the adjective agrees with the noun it qualifies in number, case and gender. Thus the gender distinctions are the main morphological characteristics of the adjectives. The category is also set up because the adjectival stems have the peculiarity of combining with certain suffixes which express the 'degrees of comparison'.

Comparative and Superlative

The Greek comparative stems are formed with suffixes inherited from IE. One is *-jes-/-jos- with a zero grade *-is-, the suffix being attached directly to roots. Such formations convey the idea that the quality denoted by the underlying stem is present to an abnormal degree, rather like the English -ish in 'biggish', i.e. rather big, 'too big'. When the standard of assessment is explicitly mentioned (in Greek with the ablatival genitive; in Latin with the ablative) the 'comparative' sense 'more than' emerges. In IE the Ablaut alternations of the suffix had the following distribution within the declension: singular nominative masculine and feminine *-jōs, accusative *-jos-ṃ (nominative and accusative neuter *-jŏs), genitive *-jes-os, dative (locative) *-jes-i; plural nominative masculine and feminine *-jos-es, accusative *-jos-ṇs (nominative and accusative neuter

*-josH₂), but at the earlier stage the weak cases would have had
the weak grade *-is- of the suffix, which has survived in the
Latin adverb *magis* as against neuter *maius* < *mag-jos. Forms
traceable to *-jos-ṃ, *-jos-es and *jos-H₂ survive as irregularities
within the Greek declension: e.g. με(í)ʒω < *meg-jos-ṃ,
με(í)ʒους < *meg-jos-es, με(í)ʒω < *meg-jos-H₂. Mycenaean confirms the *-s- by the spelling with a_2 = *ha*: e.g. *mezoa₂* = μεγjoha
(p. 47), but that is its only contribution to our knowledge,
since the only forms attested are singular nominative masculine,
feminine, neuter, dual nominative masculine and neuter,
plural nominative masculine, feminine, neuter. In particular
the singular nominative form *mezo* leaves us in the dark about
the nature of the final consonant. We have no means of determining whether the spelling stands for *megjōs* or *megjōn*, and there
is no certain evidence for the oblique cases. The Mycenaean
evidence, therefore, provides no basis for the assertion that the
declension presented in alphabetical Greek texts is a post-
Mycenaean development.

*-jos- was a primary suffix added directly to the root (the
e-grade) and not to the stem of the positive: e.g. Lat. *senior*, Skt.
sányas- < **sen-jŏs-*. For the phonetic changes caused by 'yodization' of the final consonant of the root, see p. 225. Examples
are: ἥττω (cf. ἥκ-ιστα), ἐλάσσω (cf. ἐλαχύς), θᾶττον (cf.
ταχύς), κρε(í)σσω (< *κρετ- cf. κρατύς), etc. It was because of
these changes that Greek tended to favour the alternative
suffix *-tero- discussed below. In post-Mycenaean Greek the
comparative stem appears in an extended form, nominative
-iōn-, oblique cases *-ion-* (ἡδίων, ἡδίονος, etc.), which is traced
to *-ison-, the first component of this being the zero grade of
*-jos-/-jes- quoted above. The Germanic comparative (Gothic
manag-iza, genitive *manag-izins*, the comparative of *manags*
'many') < *-isōn/*-isen- offers a parallel which justifies the
ascription of the extended suffix to IE.

The form of the suffix varies between *-jōn* and *-i(j)ōn*. The
alternation reflects a rule of IE syllabification (Sievers's Law):
-íων appears mainly after a heavy syllable, e.g. αἰσχίων,
ἀλγίων, κερδίων, ἡδίων, etc. In Attic, for obscure reasons *ī*
appears (e.g. ἥδῑον), and there is also lengthening of the root
vowel, e.g. μείʒων, κρείττων. Lengthening is general in some
forms with the root vowel *a*: θάσσων, μᾶλλον. In ἆσσον (cf.

ἄγχι) the lengthening is due to the loss of *n* before *s*: < *ansson < *ankhjon. In a number of adjectives comparative and superlative stems are 'suppletive', i.e. they are based on a root different from that of the positive. For instance, ἀγαθός 'good' has a number of comparatives: βελτίων (also βέλ-τερος), ἀμείνων, λωΐων, and ἀρείων. For the last, Mycenaean has *aro₂a* = *arjo(h)a*, and this supports the suggestion that ἀρείων has been adapted from the positive ἄρειος, this being a derivative from the *s*-stem ἄρος 'benefit'.

The adjective κακός has not only κακίων (cf. Myc. *kazoe* = *kakjo(h)es*), but also χείρων (Hom. χερείων, which may be a refashioned positive χέρειος). Ὀλίγος and μικρός, besides ὀλείζων, have μείων, which links up with Myc. *meujo, mewijo* = *meujo(n)*. Since the root is **mei-*/**mi-*, the base must have a *u*-extension: **mei+u-*/**mi-eu-*/**mi-u-* (the latter with infix nasal yields **minu-*, see p. 264); **mj-ew-jos-* will, therefore, account for the Mycenaean forms, *u/wi* being alternative spellings for the cluster *-uj-*. Less plausible is the proposal which derives μείων from **mei-jos-* and ascribes the Mycenaean intrusive *-w-* to the influence of πλείων. This form, like the superlative πλεῖσ-τος, connects with the base < **pelH₁-*/*pleH₁-*/*plH₁-*. The comparative is formed from the II form **pl-eH₁-jŏs-* (cf. *mj-ew-jos-*), as is confirmed by the Indo-Iranian evidence (Skt. *prắyas* 'mostly'). This **plē-jŏs-* > πληως/πληοσ-, both forms yielding Attic πλέως (the first by shortening of η in hiatus and the second by quantitative metathesis). Other dialects would show πλέως/πλέος with declension **πλεο(h)α, **πλεο(h)ος, etc. On the other hand *pleH₁-is-ŏn would yield πλείων. Complex phonetic (e.g. hyphaeresis in a succession of three vowels, or contraction) and analogical processes yielded the manifold Greek forms which include πλέες, πλέας (Homer), with πλε- generalized from genitive plural πλέων (< **πλεο-(h)ōν) and Attic with πλεῖν, which, however, may be no more than a colloquial allegro reduction of πλεῖον.

The superlatives are formed by adding *-to-* to **-is-*, the zero grade of **-jos-*, and the root normally has the zero grade, e.g. κράτιστος, ἄριστος, χείριστος, etc.

**-tero-*, **-tm̥-to-* (-τατο-). IE possessed a suffix *-tero-* which perhaps originated in the addition of the accented thematic vowel to form adjectives from neuters in *-ter*. This was a secondary

suffix attached in the first instance to pronominal and adverbial
stems, and this limitation persisted in Italic and Celtic. Only in
Greek and Indo-Iranian did it develop to a regular formant of
the comparative. Some of these formations connect with prepositions, e.g. Skt. *ántara* (cf. Lat. *inter*), Greek πρότερος (cf.
Skt. *pratará-*), ὑπέρτερος, etc. Perhaps from pairs like *laevus/
dexter* (cf. δεξιτερός) *-tero-* came to mark the second member of
contrasting pairs (e.g. Lat. *alter* 'other of two' as against *alius*),
and thence it was specialized as a comparative suffix. The
corresponding superlative also exhibits the *-to-* of *-ιστο-*. The
original function of this suffix was to mark the final stage in a
numeration, as in the so-called ordinal numbers (p. 291):
e.g. τρί-τος.[1] The extended form -ατος originated in *$dekm̥t$-o-
'tenth' > δέκατος and this is found in certain adjectives
denoting special extremities, e.g. ὕπατος. The corresponding
Latin suffix is *-mo-* (*summus*, *īmus*, etc.), an extended form *-$tm̥o$-
being attested in Indo-Iranian (*-tama*, cf. Lat. *-timus*). The
suffix -ατο- also recurs with a further extension as -τατο-, which
may be an instance of hypercharacterization, -ατο- being added
to a form in *-to-*.

The suffixes -τερο- and -τατο- are regularly added to *e/o*-
stems with a prosodic peculiarity: if a light syllable precedes the
thematic vowel of the stem of the positive, the *-o-* is lengthened
to avoid a succession of three light syllables: πικρότερος,
ὑψηλότερος *v.* νεώτερος, σοφώτερος. Certain adjectives in -αιος
drop the thematic vowel, e.g. παλαιός/παλαίτερος, this originating perhaps in a direct derivation from the adverb πάλαι.
The compound suffix -αιτερο- has spread to certain semantic-
ally-related words like πρωιαίτερον. Stems in -ησ-/-εσ- regularly
have -εστερο-, e.g. εὐγενέστερος. When -τερο- is added to the
suffix of adjectives in -ϝεντ- (p. 257), the regular development
was *-ϝεντ-τερο- > -(ϝ)ε(ν)σ-τερο- (p. 241): hence χαρίεις/
χαριέστερος. The extended suffix -εστερο- spread to -ων/-ον-
stems: εὐδαίμων/εὐδαιμονέστερος and it is found with other
stems in non-Attic dialects.

---

[1] So E. Benveniste. This has been challenged by W. Cowgill. In purely
descriptive terms, the *-to-* adjectives pick out individuals as ordered members
of a group: 1, as 'first' and 'last' and 2, within these extremities (which
may have been spatially conceived) as counted members, e.g. 'number
three' (see p. 291 on the ordinal numbers).

Comparatives and superlatives are much prone to the phenomenon of hypercharacterization. Hence the addition of suffixes
to forms already characterized: e.g. προτεραίτερος, ἀσσότερος,
ἀμεινότερος, μειζότερος, πρώτιστος, etc. The suffix -tero- (in its
original contrastive functions) is also attached to pronominal
stems: e.g. ἡμέ-τερο-ς and ὑμέ-τερο-ς, < *n̥sme, *usme. Similar is
σφέ-τερο-ς (on the stem see p. 288). Finally, ἅ-τερο-ς (< *sm̥-
tero-s) is based on the zero grade of *sem- 'one' (p. 289). The
earliest example is Myc. a₂tero (weto) = hateron (wetos) 'next
year'; cf. also Attic θάτερον < τὸ ἅτερον.

B. INDECLINABLES: ADVERBS AND PARTICLES

Most of the noun cases are, from a syntactical point of view,
'adverbial', and a number of Greek adverbs are case forms
which preserve inflexions no longer in declensional use, and
sometimes also stems which have otherwise vanished from the
inherited stock.

The *nominative* (either qualifying the subject or with predicative function) appears in ἰθύς (cf. Skt. *sādhú* 'leading to the
goal', 'straight', 'unerring' < *sādh-/sidh- 'reach one's goal',
< *siH-dh- > *ῑθ- > ἰθ-), εὐθύς (of obscure etymology), and
ἐγγύς, which is possibly a compound of ἐν + γυ-, the old word
for 'hand'.

Accusative. δήν 'long' (cf. δηρός, δηρόν, δῆθα) < *δϝᾱ-, cf.
Skt. *dūré* (locative) 'afar', Hitt. *tuwaz* 'from afar', Lat. *dū-dum*;
πλήν < πλᾱ- (cf. πέλας, πλησίον < *pelH₂-/pleH₂-); εὖ (neuter
singular) < *esu 'good'; δίκην 'in the manner of' (preserving
the earlier meaning 'limit' of δίκη; for the semantics cf. Lat.
modo); τήμερον/σάμερον 'today' < *kj-āmero-, the first element
being the demonstrative stem *ki- (cf. Lat. *cis*). The extracted
element *kjā-* (by false division) appears in Myc. *zawete* = *kjā-
wetes* 'this year' > τῆτες/σᾶτες.

Genitive. δεξιᾶς, ὑψοῦ, προικός 'gratis' (< προίξ < *pro-
ik-s); ποῦ 'where' is often listed as a genitive, but there are no
uncontracted forms and a case inflexion or particle -u must be
postulated (see below).

Dative: κύκλῳ, σπουδῇ, ἰδίᾳ, κοινῇ, etc.

Ablative: ϝοίκω (< *-ōd), ἔξω.

Instrumental: (οὔ)πω, ὧ-δε, λάθρᾱ, κρυφῇ (for examples with
-φι see p. 269). Greek -ω may go back either to ablative *-ōd or

the instrumental *-ō. It may be extended by -s (possibly genitival). Originating in the pronominal declension (ὥς, οὕτω(ς), τῷ, τῶς, etc.), it became the regular suffix for the formation of adverbs from adjectives: ἄλλως, μεγάλως, ἐπιστα-μένως, etc. Doric are the old instrumentals in -ē like ᾗ 'where'; for ὅπει, ὅπη, and Myc. *oqe*, see p. 51.

Locative: οἴκοι, οἴκει, ἄρτι, θύρᾶσι, πέρυσι (< *per+ut-, the zero grade of *wet- 'year'), ἐκεῖ. The root *aiw- 'life', 'dura-tion', 'permanence' yields αἰέν, a locative with zero inflexion of the *n*-stem; αἰές is a similar locative of the *s*-stem, while αἰεί < *aiwes-i.

The adverbs are sometimes fused prepositional phrases: ἐκποδών (ἐμποδών by analogy), ἐνῶπα, ἐνάντα (ἀντ- 'face'), ἐξαίφνης, κατόπιν, ἔνδον (*en+*dom 'house'), etc. Other adverbs have the case strengthened with a variety of particles: e.g. the 'emphatic' particles *-ghi (ἦχι, cf. οὐχί, and Sanskrit *hí*), *-u (πάν-υ, cf. Skt. *ú*); -χυ as in πάγχυ appears to be a fusion of χι + υ; -δε strengthens the 'whither' accusative: οἴκαδε, θύραζε (= θύρας-δε), ἀγρόνδε; for Mycenaean examples, see p. 45.

There are a number of adverbial suffixes which may be survivals of old case-endings. Notable is the group with *-dh-: -θι is evidently locatival (πόθι, ἄλλοθι, αὐτόθι, ἠῶθι), as is -θα (ἰθα- surviving in ἰθα(ι)γενής < *idha, cf. Skt. *ihá*); ἔνθα possibly preserves a pronoun *em- or *en-; -θεν with ablative function (ἔνθεν, ἐγγύθεν, ὄπιθεν) also figures in the nominal and pronominal declension (ἐμέθεν, οὐρανόθεν, πατρόθεν): -θε (some-times alternating with -θεν) is often locatival (πρόσθε, ὕπερθε, ὄπισθε).

Another group has the consonant *-d-: -δόν (σχεδόν 'close at hand', παρακλιδόν); -δα (κρύβδα, μίγδα, φύγδα); -δᾱν/-δην (χύδην, ἅδην, βάδην). The last group may be accusatives of stems in -dā-, with zero grade of the root; ἀδήν < *H₂es-H₂-/H₂s-eH₂-/H₂sH₂- 'sate with drink'. A compounded form -ίνδην is used to form adverbs from nouns denoting distinctions of social class (ἀριστίνδην, πλουτίνδην).

Yet another group of suffixes has the consonant *-t-: -τε with the function temporal locative (τότε, πότε); -τός with ablatival function (ἐκτός, ἐντός, cf. Skt. -*tas* in *itás* 'from here', *tátas* 'from there'); -σε, with the 'whither' function, may be due to the assibilation of *-te (πόσε, ἄλλοσε, ὑψόσε).

There remain a few particles of importance for Greek syntax. Thus εἰ 'if' is variously explained as an interjection, or as the locative of a demonstrative *e-/o- which appears in εἶτα. Doric and Aeolic have αἰ, which is also interpreted as an interjection. The 'potential' particle expressing contingency varies according to dialect: Attic-Ionic ἄν, Aeolic κε(ν), Doric κᾱ, and Arcado-Cypriot (κ)αν, κε. These are possibly all adverbial forms of the demonstrative stem k- (p. 286) with the meaning 'in this case': *ken/kn̥ would yield κεν/κα(ν). The latter might be the source of ἄν by false division of οὐ καν. Doric κᾱ might go back to an adverbial form *kā. For Mycenaean qe in a 'prospective' sense, and the possibility that the proto-Greek form was *qʷen/*qʷn̥, see pp. 67 f.

C. Pronouns

Four groups are distinguished: 1, the demonstratives, 2, the interrogative-indefinite, 3, the relatives and 4, the personal pronouns. In the pronominal declensions some of the case inflexions differ from those of the noun. Within the declension there is also stem suppletion, e.g. in the demonstrative *so-/ *sā/*to- and in the personal pronouns *egō/*me. The demonstratives are prone to hypercharacterization, two or more stems often being combined and deictic particles attached (the 'that there', 'this here' phenomenon). The demonstratives form a deictic system with three or four oppositions: (a) 'this (near me)', (b) 'that (near you)', (c) 'that (near him)' and (d) 'yon'. In the Latin system hic/iste/ille, the last combines oppositions (c) and (d).

1. Demonstratives

The so-called article is a post-Homeric development of an old demonstrative nominative *so, *sā, *tod (Skt. sá, sā́, tád) > ὁ, ἡ, τό (with loss of -d, an ending which is peculiar to the pronominal neuter singular, cf. Lat. is-tud, quod). The masculine shows the bare stem *so-, but *sos occurs in certain expressions like ἦ δ' ὅς 'said he'. The other cases in all genders are formed from to-/tā-, and the declension is that of the o- and ā-stems, with elimination of the IE inflexions such as dative *tosmei/ *tosjāi/locative *tosmi(u). In the plural nominative *toi/*tās have been levelled to τοί, ταί, but Attic-Ionic (and certain

other dialects) have changed these to οἱ, αἱ on the analogy of
the singular. In the dual, τώ serves for masculines and feminines. The genitive plural feminine *tāsōm (Skt. tāsām, cf. Lat.
is-tārum) > τᾱ́ων > τῶν.

The other demonstrative stems are of a complex character.
We appear to have simple reduplication in the Mycenaean toto
(weto) 'this year', and this form possibly occurs on an early
Attic inscription, but both reading and interpretation are uncertain. The deictic (or emphatic) element u (cf. above on
πάνυ) is inserted in ὁ-ῦ-το-/ἁ-ύ-τη/το-ῦ-το. In the nominative
plural Attic-Ionic and Lesbian have the analogical forms οὗτοι
and αὗται. In all dialects τούτων is the form for all genders.
Ὅδε, ἥδε, τόδε have the particle -δε, which is perhaps identical
with the directional particle discussed above. This pronoun is
'ego-deictic', i.e. it denotes proximity to the speaker. Another
demonstrative stem -n-, with added deictic elements -ε, -ι, -υ,
appears in the dialect forms ονε (Thess.), ὁνι (Arc.), ονυ
(Cypr.); the particles -i and -u may possibly once have been in
contrast, with the functions of proximal and distal deixis (for a
Skt. particle -au/-u, denoting distance, see Burrow, p. 277).

A particularly complex stem is (ἐ)κεῖνος 'that' in which we
detect the stems *ke- (cf. locative (ἐ)κεῖ, instrumental Aeol. κῆ;
cf. Lat. cedo and cis) and eno- (Hitt. eni-), with a prefix e- (Lat.
e-quidem, Osc. e-tanto, and possibly Skt. a-saú). The Doric
τῆνος similarly resolves into *τε-ενο-ς (cf. Dor., Thess. τεῖ-δε
'here').

In αὐτός 'self', which also serves in the oblique cases as the
third personal pronoun, the stem το- is prefixed with an element
αὐ-, which is perhaps identical with that of αὖ, αὖτε, etc.
Mycenaean has the anaphoric accusative mi = μιν, which is
also found in Homer and Herodotus, while Doric has a corresponding νιν. In both stems the IE *i- (Lat. is, id, Cypr. ἰν < *im)
has been detected, compounded respectively with a demonstrative stem m- or n-.

2. INTERROGATIVE INDEFINITE

The interrogative pronoun serves also as the indefinite when it
is enclitic. *q^wis/*q^wid > τίς/τί (Lat. quis, quid). The accusative
*q^wim > *τιν was recharacterized by adding -α of the con-
sonantal stems, and the resulting stem τιν- was generalized

(τίνα, τίνος, τίνι, etc.), except for the dative plural τί-σι. In certain cases an *e/o*-stem appears, e.g. genitive *q^we-sjo*, which is reflected in Hom. τέο, Att. τοῦ, and the stem τε- was extended to dative τέῳ/τῷ and the genitive plural τέων. The neuter nominative–accusative plural was *q^wjH_2* (cf. Lat. *quia*), which > ττα/σσα, as reflected in Boeot. τά, Meg. σά. Attic-Ionic ἄττα/ἄσσα owe their initial vowel to false division ὁποῖά ττα/ ὁποῖά σσα. The aspirated forms ἅττα/ἅσσα are based on the relative stem *i- (see below): < *jH_2-q^wjH_2 (in the older notation *$jə$-$q^wjə$).

3. RELATIVE PRONOUNS

IE possessed thematized forms of the demonstrative *i-: *jos/*$jā$/*jod*, with an originally demonstrative function. This developed regularly to ὅς, ἥ, ὅ and was used as a relative pronoun, like Skt. *yás, yā́, yád*. A form ὅτερος (Cretan) is also attested, as well as numerous combinations and derivatives, such as ὅστις, ὅτε, ὅσπερ, οἷος, ὅσος. On Mycenaean *jo-*, see p. 42.

4. PERSONAL PRONOUNS

The first and second personal pronouns are in essence deictic; they refer to the person speaking and the person addressed. There are no gender distinctions, and this is true of IE. The pronoun of the third person is in effect anaphoric: it stands for a noun previously used in the context and this entails gender distinctions. In the personal pronouns distinct stems appear in the singular, plural and dual, and in the first person the nominative stem is different from that of the oblique cases.

First person singular nominative ἐγώ (Lat. *ego*) < *$egō$ < *$egoH$. Strengthening particles may be attached, e.g. ἔγωγε, etc. The oblique cases have the stem *$(e)me$: acc. με/ἐμέ (Skt. *mā́m/mā*, O.Lat. *mēd*) < *$(e)me$; gen. μου/ἐμεῖο/ἐμέο/ ἐμοῦ, with an inflexion based on that of the *o*-stems instead of *$mene$ (cf. Skt. *máma*, Avest. *mana*; for ἐμέθεν see p. 284); dat. μοι/ἐμοί is based on an enclitic form *mei/*moi (cf. Skt. *me*), which also had genitival functions. In Greek it gave rise to the tonic form ἐμοί; elsewhere there are strengthening particles, e.g. Lat. *mihi* < *me-$ghei$/-ghi; cf. also Skt. *mahya(m)*.

First person plural. There is stem suppletion; *wei- (Skt.

vayám, Goth. *weis*, Hitt. *weš*)/**n̥s* (Goth. *uns*). The latter stem, which appears in the Skt. *asma-*, accounts for Aeolic ἄμμε, Doric ἅμε, but Attic-Ionic has re-characterized it by the addition of the inflexion -ας: ἡμέας, ἡμᾶς. Greek has generalized **n̥s* (the full grade appears in Skt. enclitic *nas*, while Lat. has the lengthened form *nōs*): nominative Aeol. ἄμμες, Dor. ἅμες, Attic-Ionic ἡμέ-ες > ἡμεῖς, genitive ἀμμεων/ἀμεων/ἡμῶν. The dative is ἀμμῖν/ἄμιν/ἡμῖν, the 'synchronic' inflexion being thus -ῐν and not -μι(ν). IE **n̥smei* is posited on the evidence of Vedic *asmé*, a locative also used as dative and genitive, this being 'an archaic characteristic' (Burrow, p. 267).

Second person singular. Nominative **tŭ* > τῠ́ (Dor.), with strengthening particle in Homer τῠ́-νη. In σύ the assibilation is proper to the oblique stem **tw-*: accusative **twe/te* > σε/τε (the latter in Doric as an enclitic), which forms the basis of genitive σου/σεῖο (Hom.), σέο, σοῦ (for σέθεν see p. 284). The IE genitive *tewe/tewo* may be reflected in τεῖο/τεοῦ. There existed an enclitic genitive **t(w)ei/t(w)oi* (used also as a dative) >σοι, τοι (Skt. *te*), the form τοι surviving as a particle ('mark you') in Attic.

Second person plural. There is no trace of the ancient stem suppletion **jus/wes/wos/us*, for Greek has generalized **us*: accusative **us-me* regularly > Aeol. ὕμμε, Dor. ὕμε, while Attic-Ionic recharacterizes ὕμε-ας > ὑμᾶς. Hence nominative ὕμμες/ὕμες/ὑμεῖς, genitive ὑμμεων/ὕμεων/ὑμῶν, dative ὑμμι(ν)/ὑμῖν.

The sole pronominal dual stem surviving in Greek is νώ (cf. the enclitic Skt. *nau*, serving as accusative, genitive and dative, Avest. *nā* and O.Sl. *na*), with recharacterized forms νῶϊ (Hom.), νῶε (Corinna) and genitive–dative νῶϊν/νῷν.

5. THE REFLEXIVE PRONOUN

The reflexive pronoun of IE had stem alternations **sewe-/swe-/se*. The Greek accusative (ϝ)ἕ, dative (ϝ)οῖ (the accented forms being reflexive, and the enclitic anaphoric), < **swe*, **swoi*, from which a genitive (ϝ)εῖο > (ϝ)έο > οὗ was formed. The accusative ἕέ (Hom.) < **sewe*. The plural has a stem σφε-/σφι- (σφεῖς, σφᾶς, σφῶν, σφίσι), which also appears in σφέτερος, and possibly Myc. *pei* = *sphe(h)i* (also interpreted as *spheis*, cf. Arc. σφεις). It is conceivable that this originated in the dative form *s-bhi/*s-bhei (cf. Lat. sibi). A corresponding dual accusative σφωε genitive–dative σφωϊν appears in Homer.

The phonetically-weak reflexive forms were strengthened by the addition of αὐτός (p. 286), which also took on the anaphoric functions of *swe: ἓ αὐτόν, οἳ αὐτῷ, etc., and were contracted in Attic to ἑαυτόν, etc. In the plural early Attic has the expected combinations σφᾶς αὐτούς, etc. The pronominal stems were used to form possessive adjectives by the addition of the accented thematic vowels: ἐμός, σός < *tw-os (cf. Skt. tva-), but also τεός (Hom. etc.) < *tew-os (cf. Lat. tu-us). In the plural Aeol. ὕμμος, Doric ὗμος show adjectival thematization, but elsewhere the 'contrastive' suffix -*tero- (p. 282) was used: ἡμέτερος, ὑμέτερος. In the third person ῾(ϝ)ός < *sw-os (cf. Skt. sva-) and ἑ(ϝ)ός < *sew-os (cf. Lat. suus). The corresponding plural forms are σφός and σφέτερος, but they were superseded in Attic by the genitive of ἑαυτός.

D. Numerals

Among the IE numerals only 1–4 and 100 were declined.

1(a). *sem-s/*sm-jH₂/*sem (cf. Lat., sem-el, etc.) > εἷς, μία, ἕν. The -ν of the neuter (< *-m) was generalized in the declension (ἕνα, etc.), but Myc. still presents eme = hemei (dative singular).

1(b). IE possessed another root *oi- with the meaning 'alone' and this appears in οἴνη 'the one on the dice' (an n-suffix, seen also in O.Lat. oino = unum, Ir. óin, Goth. ains) and οἶ(ϝ)ος 'alone' (cf. Avest. aēva).

2. *duwō (*dwō), masculine, *duwoi (*dwoi), feminine, neuter (cf. Skt. duvā, dvē). In Greek the distinction of gender is lost: Myc. dwo, d(u)wouphi (p. 48); long ō still in δύω (Hom. etc.), but later δύο (Lat. duo, Goth. twai, etc.). The Attic genitive–dative δυεῖν is dissimilated from δυοῖν. The apparently plural inflexion of Elean δυοιοις may in fact be an old dual parallel with Skt. genitive–locative dváyas (cf. O.Sl. dvoju), but other plural forms are Ionic δυῶν, δυοῖσι, late Attic δυσί, etc.

3. *trejes, masculine/*t(r)isres, feminine/*trī (< *triH₂) neuter; cf. Skt. tráyas, tisrás, trí. Greek has lost the feminine form: τρεῖς (< τρεες < *trejes), τρία (cf. Lat. trēs, tria). The oblique cases had the zero grade *tri-: accusative *trins > τρῖς (Cyrene, Cret. τριινς), replaced in Attic by nominative τρεῖς,

genitive τριῶν, dative τρισί, and this also appears in compounds, e.g. τρί-πους.

4. *$q^wetwores$ masculine/$q^wetesres$ feminine/$q^wetwōr$ neuter (cf. Skt. *čatvā́ras, čatásras, čatvā́ri*), with oblique cases *$q^wetur-n̥s$, *$q^wetur-ōm$, *$q^wetwr̥-su$.

Greek eliminated the feminine, and no Greek dialect preserves the original stem alternations. Doric τέτορες < *$q^wet(w)$-ores, with w lost by dissimilation. Lesbian πέσυρες has the zero grade < *-twr- of the oblique cases (for q^we- > πε- in Aeolic, see p. 60; the vowel of Homeric πίσυρες is unexplained); Homeric τέσσαρες (Attic τέτταρες) < *-twr̥-, the stem form of the locative. Ionic τέσσερες is not ancient but due to assimilation. In composition τετρα- (τετράπους) < *$q^wetr̥$- which appears in Myc. *qet(o)ro-*.

5. *$penq^we$ (Skt. *páñca*, Lat. *quīnque*) > πέντε (Aeol. πεμπε).
6. *$s(w)eks$ (Skt. *ṣaṣ-*, Lat. *sex*) > (ϝ)έξ.
7. *$septm̥$ (Skt. *saptá*, Lat. *septem*) > ἑπτά.
8. *$oktō$ (Skt. *aṣṭā́(u)*, Lat. *octō*) > ὀκτώ.
9. *$newn̥$ (Skt. *náva*, Lat. *novem*) > (ἐν-)νέ(ϝ)α, with the same unexplained prothesis as Armenian *inn*.
10. *$dekm̥(t)$ (Skt. *dáśa*, Lat. *decem*) > δέκα.

For 11–19 Greek uses a combination of 1–9 with δέκα: note δώδεκα < δϝω- (but also δυώδεκα). In the numerals 20–90 the basic stem is a noun *$dkomt$-, an Ablaut variation of *$dekm̥t$-.

20–90. *$wī-dkm̥tī$ (*wī* 'two' and the dual ending of the noun) > ϝῑκατι (Doric, with shortened ĭ). Attic etc. εἴκοσι is due to (a) a vowel prothesis (Hom. ἐείκοσι < *ἐ-ϝῑκοσι), (b) the assibilation of -τι to -σι, and (c) the introduction of -ο- from the numerals 30–90, which have the neuter plural -κοντα < *(d)-komt-H_2. In the consonant cluster of *$dkomt$-H_2 the d- disappeared with consequent lengthening of the final vowel of *$penq^we$*; hence πεντήκοντα, which provided the model for ἑξήκοντα, ἑβδομήκοντα, ὀγδοήκοντα (these two with the ordinal numeral as the first element) and ἐνενήκοντα with a reduplication (the forms ἐννήκοντα and ἐνήκοντα are also attested). For 40 an IE neuter form *$q^wetwr̥$-dkomtH_2 has been constructed, $r̥$ being lengthened when d was lost. This is the source of Latin *quadrāgintā*. The proto-Greek form would have been *$q^wetwrā-konta$, which caused the change in the word for 30 from *trī-konta (cf. Latin trīgintā) to triākonta before itself being altered to *qʷetwarakonta > τεττᾰρᾰκοντα.

100. (d)kṃtóm (Skt. śatám, Lat. centum) > (ἑ)-κατόν, with a prothesis which is traced to *sem-/*sṃ- 'one' (but elsewhere this appears as ᾰ-, p. 260). The hundreds are based on an adjectival derivative -κᾰτιοι/-κᾰσιοι of *kṃto-, which Attic-Ionic changed to -κοσιοι under the influence of -κοντα. Analogy of τριᾱκόσιοι is seen in διᾱκόσιοι, while the ᾰ of τετρακόσιοι, ἑπτακόσιοι has been taken over by πεντακόσιοι, ἑξακόσιοι, ὀκτακόσιοι and ἑνακόσιοι.

1000. There is no general IE word, but Skt. sa-hásra-m is a compound of *sṃ 'one' and a stem equatable with χέλλιοι (Lesb.), χείλιοι (Ion.) < *gheslo-. Attic χῑλιοι is due to assimilation.

The ordinals were originally adjectives formed by adding the thematic vowel to the cardinal: e.g. Skt. saptam-á-, daśam-á-; Lat. septimus, nōnus < *novenos, decimus < *dekṃos. In ἕβδομος and ὄγδο(ϝ)ος, -πτ- and -κτ- have been voiced. The other ordinals are formed with the suffix -το- (p. 282): τρίτος (hyper-characterized in Hom. τρίτατος), τέταρτος/τέτρατος, πέμπτος, (ϝ)ἕκτος, ἕνατος, δέκατος. Πρῶτος (Dor. πρᾶτος) has the suffix attached to a stem *pr̥̄ (*pr̥H₂), which may link up with πέρας 'limit' (*perH₂-/*preH₂-/*pr̥H₂-):[1] δεύτερος has the 'contrastive' -τερο- (p. 282) attached to a root δευ- meaning 'inferiority', 'deficiency' (δέ(ϝ)ος 'need', δέω/δεύω 'lack', 'be inferior'), which links up with Skt. doṣā́ 'lack' < IE *deus-. The ordinals 20–90 undergo the regular phonetic transformations: *-κοντ-το- > *-κονσ-το- > -κοστο- (p. 241): τριακοστός, etc. (Boeotian ϝικαστος < *wī-kṇt-to-). The suffix -οστο- was carried over to the hundreds (διακοσιοστός) and the thousand (χιλιοστός).

---

[1] Another possibility is that πρῶτος/πρᾶτος replaced an original *pro-mo-s after this was specialized in the sense 'headman', 'chief', 'prince'. The dialect forms < *pro-ato-s (for the suffix see p. 282). If this form was due to the dissimilation of *pro-tato-s, the counterpart of pro-tero-s, then the 'common Greek' *pro-ato-s must considerably post-date 'proto-Greek' *pro-mo-s.

E. The Verb

I. INTRODUCTORY

Whereas in noun inflexion the major concept is 'case' with 'number' as minor, verbal inflexion is dominated by 'person', which is modified not only by number, but also by 'voice' and 'tense'. In considering verbal stem formation the predominant category is 'aspect', to which 'mood' must be added. These categories and concepts will now be defined.

The '*persons*' are those discussed under pronouns; in fact there is plausibility in the speculation that the verbal inflexions originated in the attachment of pronominal elements to the verbal stem, although there is only slight confirmatory evidence. To abbreviate reference, the nine theoretically possible endings (three persons × three numbers) are numbered: singular 1, 2, 3; plural 4, 5, 6; dual 7, 8, 9. Tense in IE comprises a binary opposition present:past, for there was no grammatical device to express 'future'. It is plausibly argued that at an earlier stage of IE there was a single 'primitive' set of terminations for both present and preterite; e.g. *-m for first singular active. At a later stage a deictic particle -*i* 'here and now' was added to emphasize the 'present' reference, and the opposed unmarked *-m was then confined to the 'past'; *-*mi*/*-m then formed an opposition known as 'primary'/'secondary' (hereafter P/S). Not all persons developed this opposition. The reference to the past, signalled by the secondary endings, was emphasized in Greek (as in a few other IE languages, see p. 7) by the use of a prefix, the augment, which plausibly originated in an accented adverb of time to which the verb was attached as an enclitic: e.g. ἔ-φερο-ν < *é-bhero-m. The augment appears only in the indicative.

For 'voice', too, there was in IE a binary opposition active/middle. The active verb was used to present an activity proceeding from a subject outwards: when the event took place within the subject or was reflected on the subject, then the middle voice was used. The stock example is λούει 'he washes' (an external subject), v. λούεται 'he washes himself'. The Sanskrit grammarians expressed the opposition between active and middle as *parasmai-padam* 'word for another' v. *ātmane-padam* 'word for oneself'. Inherent in the middle is the notion of the 'passive', formal grammatical distinction of which developed gradually within Greek.

Mood conveys the attitude of the speaker towards the event (in the broadest sense) referred to by the verb. 1. The indicative is the unmarked member, and its function may be defined as neutral attitude: it states the verbal event as a fact. 2. The subjunctive projects the event into the future and may be semantically divided into (a) expectation ('prospective' or 'eventual') and (b) will (the 'voluntative'). 3. The optative similarly divides into (a) wish (the 'optative' proper) and (b) contingency (the 'potential'). 4. The imperative is used for giving commands.

Aspect

In IE the verb had three main stem forms which are called 'tense' stems although their functions are not concerned with distinctions of 'time', but with 'aspect'. 1. The verbal event may be presented as a global unit, an item of history, without further embellishment or 'definition'. The corresponding stem is known as the 'aorist' (ἀόριστος 'undefined'). 2. The event may be presented in all its immediacy as a process, a kind of 'eye-witness' aspect; the corresponding stem is known most inappropriately as the 'present' stem, although a preterite is formed from it (see below on the imperfect). On the manifold ways of forming 'present' stems, see pp. 262 ff. 3. The speaker may refer to a state of affairs which has come about as a result of an event. The 'perfect' stem is then used.

These three oppositions are known as the 'aspects' of the verb. This term is a mistranslation of the word used by Slavonic philologists, who for each verb distinguish two *vidy*, stems denoting 1, action in progress and 2, completed action. These were regarded as the two 'species' of the verb. It has been suggested that the three 'tense' stems of IE were not concerned with 'aspect', but the analogies of Greek and Sanskrit usage leave no alternative to the above exposition. The temporal references of the verbal forms are made by augment and secondary inflexion and are in any case confined to the indicative: φέρω 'I am carrying'/ἔ-φερ-ο-ν < *e-bher-o-m 'I was carrying', whereas the modal forms (including the infinitive) based on the same stem have no temporal reference.

Thematic and Athematic

The terminations in the example just quoted require a fundamental morphological distinction which divides the Greek verbs into two opposed systems: the stem immediately preceding the inflexion shows a vowel -o- (added to the root *bher-), which alternates with -e- in the conjugation: e.g. φέρ-ο-μεν, φέρ-ε-τε. Other verbs show no such vowel: τί-θη-μι, τί-θη-ς, τί-θη-τι/ τί-θη-σι, τί-θε-ντι. The two conjugational types differ not only in the personal endings (in 1, 2, 3, and 6), cf. φέρω, φέρεις, φέρει, φέροντι > (φέρουσι), but also in the formation of the moods and the infinitive (see below).

Augment

The augment appears as an optional feature (on Mycenaean see p. 49) in early Greek (e.g. Homer) as it is in the earliest Sanskrit.

Before consonants the normal form of the augment is *e-. In verbs beginning with a vowel, this was lengthened already in late IE by contraction with the augment: ἄγε (ἦγε), Skt. ájat, ἦς (Dor.) 'he was', Skt. ás 'was' (*e-es-t > *ēst). This was the so-called 'temporal' augment contrasting with the 'syllabic' augment. From a synchronic point of view, in Greek vowel lengthening constituted augmentization in the case of verbs with initial vowel, and this was applied to words which originally began with an s: ἵζω/ἵζον (*si-sd-ō/*e-si-sd-o-m), ἅλλομαι/ ἡλλόμην (*saljo-/*e-salj-o-mān).

In some Greek verbs beginning with w- the augment appears in a lengthened form: ἡ(ϝ)είδη. The root wra-, which appears in the Homeric aorist participle ἀπο-ύρας, has the indicative ἀπηύρα. In Vedic the long augment may be used not only before v-, but also before j, n and r, so that the phenomenon may be IE (in the limited area discussed p. 7). In Attic the long augment is disguised by quantitative metathesis: ἑώρων < *ἠ-ϝορ-αον, ἑάλων < ἠ-ϝαλ- (cf. ἁλίσκομαι, ἁλῶναι). Sometimes ἐ- is used (ἔ-ειπ-ον, see below) and the alternation η/ε may be due to lost laryngeal consonants.

11 The Personal Endings

The personal endings may now be tabulated, those of the perfect being reserved for treatment below. First the active:

	Primary	Secondary
1.	*-mi/-ō > -μι, -ω	*-m > -ν/-α
2.	*-si > -σι/-hι	*-s > -s
3.	*-ti > -τι/-σι	*-t > -∅
4.	*-mes > -μες (-μεν)	*-me- > (-μες/-μεν)
5.	*-te(s) > -τε	*-te > -τε
6.	*-nti > -ντι/-(ν)σι/-ατι	*-nt > -ν
7.	*-wes/-wos	*-we/-wē
8.	?	?
9.	?	?

1. The thematic inflexion -ω (φέρω, Lat. ferō, etc.) may possibly owe its length to a lost laryngeal (see below); *-m regularly > -ν, while Cm̥ > Cα:*ēs-m̥ 'I was' > ἦα, *e-dēiks-m̥ > ἔδειξα, etc. On the optative form ἐξελαυνοια < *-oi-m̥, see p. 310.

2 and 3. The Greek representation of the IE endings has been much discussed, and no general agreement has been reached. A synchronic structural analysis will bring out the facts which have to be explained, and this shows a clear difference between the athematic and the thematic conjugations. It seems a priori unlikely that phonetic and analogical processes operating on a single set of IE endings can have produced this distinction between the two classes.

The athematic verbs show regularly 2, -ς: τίθη-ς, etc. If this were a recharacterization of *τιθη-(h)ι < *-si one would expect *τιθηις, etc. Another difficulty is offered by the forms for 'thou art'. Given the general system represented by *τιθη-μι : τίθη-ς, etc., we should expect Greek *ἐσ-ς, and this form may account for Homeric εἶς, which would be purely graphic for the long syllable (cf. Plautine ess in Latin). Within a synchronic system *esmi, *ess, *esti, *ess would be levelled to essi, and this form is actually found in Aeolic and Doric. The Attic εἶ falls out of the system. Yet it is taken as the representative Greek form, equated with Skt. asi and an IE *esi is constructed. This strange form, however, requires the postulation of an ad *hoc* IE 'sound law', simplifying the *-ss-* of the *es-si, required by the system. Thus *essi cannot be assigned to the late IE constructed on the basis of Greek and Indo-Iranian; it is a postulated early IE form arrived at by internal reconstruction and so should be written **essi. Given the succession early IE **essi > late IE *esi, it would be a contradiction to say that Greek preserves the ancient **essi. On the contrary, within the synchronic system it appears as a levelling of *ess, rather like 2, συντιθησι (Epidaurus) for συντιθης. If we start with *-*mi*, *-*si*, *-*ti*, what requires explanation is the disturbance of the system by the introduction of the anomalous 2, -*s*. It is no explanation to say that the athematic class 'borrowed' the secondary ending ἐ-τίθη-ς. Starting with the Greek facts, we should say that the anomaly is probably what has been inherited. Thus Attic εἶ is not to be equated with Skt. *asi*. The equation is made more difficult by the accentuation of the Greek word, for the other persons are enclitic (as is εἶς), and the difficulty is merely underlined by the necessity to postulate additionally an analogical influence of εἶ 'you will go'.

Nor is there any direct evidence within Greek for 2, -*si* in the thematic conjugation. Here 2, λέγ-εις contrasts with 3, λέγ-ει. Purely synchronic analysis suggests that in both persons an -*i*- has been added to the stem λεγε-. In 3, there is zero inflexion (the bare stem suffices) with addition of the primary (deictic) -*i*-. In 2, the normal inflexion -*s* has been added. That the second person was formed from 3 has the greater statistical probability.

Methodologically it is preferable to treat the problem structurally; we have two contrasting sub-systems in the singular active of the athematic and thematic verbs. The desirability of making the structural contrast the basis of comparative treatment is given further point by the contrast of these two verbal classes in the formation of subjunctive, optative, imperative and infinitive. We start with an agreed point: in the contrast -*mi*/-*ō*, the lengthened thematic vowel of the latter suggests, as we saw, an original *-*oH*. This guides the search of the comparatist. He will look for evidence of structurally opposed -*mi* and -*H* verbal systems. This is a feature of Hittite, and it is in the -*ḫi* conjugation that a third singular -*i* is found. It has been plausibly suggested that paradigms like that of *šak*- 'know' 1, šaggaḫḫi (šākhi), 3, šakki may provide a parallel for the Greek thematic endings -ω/-ι.

Recent contributions have veered round to the derivation of all the Greek 2 and 3 endings from *-si and *-ti. They all require, however, the postulation of phonological and analogical processes, the complexity of which reduces plausibility. The latter are essentially levelling processes resulting in uniformity and regularity; yet in the end we are left with the anomalous τίθη-ς, etc. and the necessity to suspect 'borrowing' of the secondary ending. Moreover, the Mycenaean evidence has been overlooked. If *bhere-si > *phere-hi > phere-hi-s, the last form would have remained trisyllabic until the loss of -h-, and the same would have been true of 3, *phere-hi modelled on the 2 form. According to the Linear B spelling rules a form like ekhehi would be written e-ke-i, just as e-ke-e stands for the infinitive ekhehen. What we have, however, is e-ke, that is a disyllabic form with a final diphthong -ei. This evidence is thus decisive against the derivation of φέρε-ι-ς < *bhere-si-s.

In 3, the primary *-ti > *-si in Mycenaean, Arcado-Cypriot, Attic-Ionic and Lesbian. There are a few forms with zero ending which have been extracted from 2: τιθη, διδω, δεικνυ, on the analogy of ἱστη-ς/ἱστη, etc. The secondary -t being lost in Greek, the sigmatic aorist *ἐδειξ-τ repaired the loss by taking over -ε from the perfect.

4. *-mes survives in West Greek, but the other dialects have an unexplained -μεν. A similar form occurs in Hittite -weni/-wen, and this resembles the Sanskrit dual ending -vas/-va. On the possible P/S opposition *-mes/-me, see below.

5. All Greek dialects present -τε and, as with 4, there is no distinction between primary and secondary.

6. -ντι survives in West Greek; in the other dialects > -(ν)σι with compensatory lengthening for loss of -ν. The athematic ending was -εντι, e.g. *s-enti (as in Osco-Umbrian sent), whence Doric ἐντι for *ἑντι. Mycenaean offers kitijesi = ktiensi, with the zero grade of the root *ktei-. With roots ending in a long vowel (e.g. ἀφη- 'blow') there would have been 1, contraction with the vowel of -εντι, 2, shortening of the long vowel (Osthoff's Law) *-ηντι > -εντι > -ενσι > -εισι. Reduplicated verbs show the inflexion *-nti: δι-δο-ντι > διδονσι > δίδουσι (also

τίθεισι, ἱστᾶσι), and these forms were influenced by the contracted verbs (-άω, -έω, -όω) and in Ionic received pro-perispomenon accentuation διδοῦσι, τιθεῖσι, ἱστᾶσι.

After consonant *-ṇti > -ατι, which appears in West Greek inscriptions (ἱερητευκατι), while Ionian has a few corresponding forms in -ᾱσι, e.g. πεφύκασι (Homer). The ending -ατι was mostly recharacterized to -αντι > -ανσι > -ᾱσι, the last being the regular Attic-Ionic ending in the perfect: λελύκᾱσι. In Attic-Ionic this inflexion has spread elsewhere: ἔᾱσι (Homer), ἴᾱσι 'they go' (Homer and Attic), the reduplicated presents (τιθέᾱσι, διδόᾱσι) and the -νυ- verbs (δεικνύᾱσι, etc.).

The secondary ending -(e/o)nt lost the final plosive: hence ἔφερον, etc. In the athematic type *-ent appears in ἦεν 'they were' and in the optative (p. 309) εἶεν, etc.; *-ont is rare (Hom. ἤϊον 'they went' and in the -νυ- verbs); *-nt in ἔθεν, ἔγνον, ἔβαν, ἔφαν, etc. (on the Attic-Ionic substitution of -σαν from the s- aorists, see p. 62).

7, 8, 9. Traces of the dual survive: 8. -τον (both primary and secondary) is in origin secondary (ἐφέρετον = Skt. *ábharatam*), and 9, with primary -τον and secondary -τᾱν/-την, cf. Skt. *-tām* (ἐφερέτην = Skt. *ábharatām*).

Middle

Primary	Secondary
*-(m)ai > -μαι	*-(m)ā(?) > -μᾱν
*-soi > -σοι/hοι	*-so > -σο/-hο
*-toi > -τοι	*-to > -το
*-me(s)dhǎ > -με(σ)θα	
*-dhwe > -(σ)θε	
*-ntoi > -ντοι	*-nto > -ντο

The majority of the Greek dialects have 1, -μαι, 2, -σαι, 3, -ται, 6, -νται as the primary endings. However, the secondary endings are 2, -σο, 3, -το and 6, -ντο, and it is plausible to assume that the primary endings, as in the active, were made by the addition of -i. In fact Arcado-Cypriot (and Mycenaean) show in 3 and 6 -τοι and -ντοι. In 1, if it is plausible to suppose that -μᾱν is a recharacterization of *-μᾱ, then the opposition -μαι/*-μᾱ could be accounted for by assuming *-(m)aHi/ *-(m)aH, (to posit *-(m)oH₂i/*-(m)oH₂ would raise phonological problems concerning the laryngeal). At all events it is arguable

that -μαι was the source of the change which in all dialects
except Arcado-Cypriot changed -σοι, etc., into -σαι, etc. In the
thematic verbs *φέρεσαι, (ἐ)φέρεσο, etc., > φέρε(h)αι, (ἐ)φέρε(h)ο,
and these > Attic φέρῃ, ἐφέρου.

In the athematic class -σο(ι)/-σαι was preserved after a consonant; it should develop to -(h)ο(ι)/-(h)αι between vowels
(Homer δίζηαι, κατάκειαι, etc.), but the -σ- was restored on the
analogy of the consonant stems: ἧσαι, κεῖσαι, δύνασαι, etc.
Similarly in the secondary tenses, but in Homer the -σ- is
rarely restored: κεῖσο.

Greek -μαι corresponds to Indo-Iranian -ē < *-ai, and it is
conceivable that the Greek inflexion has been remodelled
under the influence of the active in -m(i).

In 4, -μεθα obviously belongs with Indo-Iranian *-madhai (Skt.
-mahe, Avest. -madē), and this implies IE *-medha (or perhaps
*-medhā), to which the primary -i was attached. The Homeric
-μεσθα (cf. Hittite -wasta) analyses as -μεσ-θα, and it is conceivable that this was a primary ending contrasting with secondary
-με-θα.

In 5, -(σ)θε is equatable with Indo-Iranian *-dhva(m) (Skt.
-dhve/-dhvam, Avest. -dve/δwəm), implying IE *-dhwe. The -σ-
perhaps originated in athematic verbs ending in -s, or a dental
plosive where -τθε regularly > -σθε: e.g. πέπυσθε < *πε-πυθ-θε.

In 6, Greek has reflexes of (a) *-onto(i), (b) *-nto(i) and
(c) *-n̥to(i): (a) τανύοντο, κέονται, (b) τίθενται, ἐτίθεντο,
δίδονται, ἐδίδοντο, (c) βεβλήαται, εἰρύαται, ἥαται (< *ēs-
n̥tai), τετεύχαται.

In 7, περιδώμεθον (Hom.) is a Greek innovation, the analogical model being λύεσθε:λύεσθον::λυόμεθα::x.

In 8 and 9, -σθον/-σθην have been coined from -σθε on the
analogy of -τε, -τον, -την.

III THE TENSES

The formation of the present stem was discussed above.

Aorist. As stated above, the aorist is the kernel of the Greek
verbal system in the sense that in this 'tense' the verbal root,
consistently with the 'undefined' function, may appear with no
added formatives. The Greek system reflects faithfully the IE
distinction between root aorists and the sigmatic aorist, to which
the intransitive (developing to 'passive') types in -η- and -θη-

must be added. Root aorists divide into (a) athematic and (b) thematic.

In (a) the full grade originally appeared in the singular active and the zero grade in the plural active, dual active and everywhere in the middle voice; but the system has throughout been affected by analogical developments. The alternation is still preserved in ἔ-θη-κα/ἔ-θε-μεν/ἐ-θέ-μην, ἔ-δω-κα/ἔ-δο-μεν/ἐ-δό-μην, ἧ-κα/εἷ-μεν/εἷ-μην. Certain ancient monosyllabic roots, e.g. ἔστη (Skt. *ásthāt* < **e-stā-t*, middle third singular *ásthita* < **e-stH₂-to*), ἔβη (Skt. *ágāt* < **e-gʷā-t*), have levelled the long vowel, but a few Ablaut traces remain, e.g. βάτην (Homer), φάτο, ἔφθην/φθάμενος (Homer). The zero grade also survives in certain diphthongal roots: ἔ-κτα-μεν, ἀπ-έ-κτα-το, κτάμενος (< **kten-/ktn̥-* 'kill'), σεύω, ἔ-σσυ-το (< **qjew-/qju-* 'set in motion', 'speed'), and ἀ-πέ-φα-το 'he was slain' (< **gʷhen-/gʷhn̥-*, see below on ἔπεφνον).

Bases with laryngeal root suffixation lie behind ἔπτην/ἔπτατο (< **pteH₂-/ptH₂-* 'fly'), -θνῄσκω/ἔθανον (< **dhneH₂-/dh°nH₂-*), βλητός/ἔβαλον (< **gʷleH₁-/gʷ°lH₁-*, see p. 220), μέλλω/βλώσκω (**μλωσκω*)/ἔμολον < **melH₃-/mleH₃-/mlH₃-*).

Myc. *qirijato* = *qʷriato*, cf. πριάμενος. Ἀ-πρίατος has the zero grade which is reflected in Skt. *krītá* (on the laryngeal and the phonology, see p. 240). An instructive contrast is provided by another root with laryngeal extension which has the active root aorist based on the II form, that is a form of the full grade of the base: ἐβίων < **gʷ°j-eH₃-*, cf. form III βίοτος < **gʷ°j-H₃-* (see p. 240 on the root *gʷei-* 'live').

In certain roots, where the accumulation of consonants would cause difficulty, the zero grade also has the form *CeC*: γέντο 'he seized' (< **gem-*), λέκτο 'he lay down', δέκτο 'he received', cf. ἔμικτο and ἆλτο, (ἐπ-)άλμενος.

In the thematic aorist the zero grade was regular in IE with the accent on the thematic vowel, which still persists in the infinitive λιπεῖν and the participle λιπών. Examples are εἶδον < **ἐϝιδον* (cf. Skt. *ávidat*), ἔφυγον (φεύγω), ἔδρακον (δέρκομαι, cf. Skt. *dṛśán*),[1] ἔλιπον (Skt. *áricat*), ἔδραμον, ἐσπό-μην, σπόμενος (< **seqʷ-/sqʷ-*), κύθε (cf. κεύθω), ἔπλετο, (περι-)

---

[1] The Skt. form is an athematic root aorist. It is plausibly argued that the thematic root aorist had already developed from the athematic type in late IE.

πλόμενος (< *qʷel-/qʷl-), ἔπραθε (cf. πέρθω), ἤλυθε (cf. ἐλεύσομαι), ἐπύθοντο (Skt. bhúdhanta).

More concealed examples are δ(ϝ)ίε 'he feared' (< *dwei-/*dwi-, see below on δείδω), the Homeric (Aeolic) εὔαδε = ἐϝϝαδε (< *swad-, see p. 238) and ἤμβροτον = ἥμαρτον (aorist of ἁμαρτάνω, but the etymology is unknown) < *amṛt-.

On the root aorists from bases with laryngeal suffixation, ἔθανον, ἔβαλον, ἔμολον, etc., see above.

A sub-type of this class shows reduplication with zero grade of the root: in ἔ-πε-φν-ο-ν 'I slew' the constituent parts are transparent: < *gʷhen-/*gʷhn- 'slay', cf. θείνω < *gʷhen-jō and (ἀπ-έ-)φατο above. Others are ἐκέκλετο (κέλομαι), ἔτετμον (etymology unknown), λέλαθον, πεπιθών, and possibly ἐσπόμην < *se-sqʷo-mān, but this may be < *e-sqʷ-o-, with aspiration on the analogy of ἕπομαι. The form εἰπεῖν is traced to *we-wqʷ- (with zero grade of the root weqʷ- seen in ϝέπος), with dissimilation of the second w. For the reduplication cf. Skt. ávocat < *a-va-vc-a-t < *e-we-wqʷ-e-t.

The most productive type of aorist (as in IE) was an athematic type formed by the suffix -s-, the sigmatic aorist, which progressively replaced the strong aorists (ἔδεισα, ἔπεισα, ἔζησα, etc.). In Sanskrit the root is lengthened (vṛddhied) in all numbers of the active, but in the middle the zero grade appears in roots of the structure CVSC, where S = i, u or ṛ (and more restrictedly elsewhere). In Greek Osthoff's Law would obliterate the distinction, e.g. between *dēiks- and deiks-. However, certain traces tilt the balance in favour of the vṛddhied stem also in proto-Greek: the aorist passive ῥαγῆναι implies a root *wreg- (not *wrēg-), to which the aorist ἔρρηξα was formed. Again, the vṛddhi in the present γηράσκω (as against the normal grade in γέρας, γέροντ-, Skt. járant-) has been ascribed to an aorist ἔγηρα < *e-gērs-ṃ. Such an analogical action must have taken place before the shortening of *egērsa to egĕrsa (Osthoff's Law). An alternative explanation would find the source of the lengthening in an old athematic aorist ἐγήρα. In Greek there is no trace of the Ablaut alternation in this class, and the -α of the first singular (< *-ṃ) has been generalized as a kind of false thematic vowel, except in third singular, where ἔ-δειξ-ε, etc. has the same ending as the thematic imperfect and the perfect.

The Epic language presents some sigmatic aorists with

thematic endings, e.g. δύσετο. They appear to be purely literary forms, originating perhaps in the imperatival use of future forms; thus ἄξεσθε gave rise to ἄξοντο, ἀξέμεν, and οἴσετε to οἰσέμεν.

In intervocalic positions -s- would regularly be lost, but it has been preserved (or restored) by analogy: ἐτίμησα, ἐφίλησα, etc.

The phonetic development of the sonants plus s, with disappearance of s and compensatory lengthening of the sonant or the preceding vowel, has been discussed on pp. 236 f.: hence the dialect varieties ἔφηνα/ἔφᾱνα, ἔμεινα/ἔμεννα, ἤγγειλα/ἄγγελλα, etc. For the West Greek use of -ξα not only in -σσω and -3ω verbs from *-kj-/*-gj-, but also in dental stems like ἐλπίζω < *ἐλπιδ-jω, see pp. 50, 60.

Intransitive Aorists.

In the IE verb we find a class of formations with the suffix *-ē-/-ō- which expressed a state. Examples are Lat. habēre (Goth. haban), tacēre (Goth. þahan), silēre (Goth. ana-silan), iacēre, latēre. It is likely that such formations originally existed only as present stems, with an athematic inflexion and ablauting suffix -ē-/-H-. Greek has incorporated the forms in the aorist: ἐμάνη 'he flew into a rage' (present μαίνομαι), ἐχάρη 'he rejoiced' (present χαίρω), ἐφάνη 'he made an appearance' (φαίνω). The accent was on the suffix with zero grade of the root (μανείς, μανῆναι), but Greek has generalized the full grade of the suffix. Other examples are: ῥύη 'flowed', ἐδάη 'got to know', ἐτράφη 'was raised', ἐκάη 'burned', ἐτύπη 'was struck'. The sole aorist with -ō- is ἁλῶναι.

IE had no separate forms for the passive, as distinct from the middle, and in Homer the -η- formations are, in general, intransitive. In the Epic, however, about a quarter of the -θη-aorists are purely passive. This was a composite suffix which was perhaps made by combining the suffix -θ-, which also expressed a state (e.g. τελέθω), with -η-. That the formation was of comparatively recent date is shown by the fact that it often takes the place of athematic middle aorists (e.g. πλήσθη for πλῆτο) and that many of the examples are found only in the Odyssey and the later parts of the Iliad. Examples are ἐμίχθη (cf. ἐμίγη), χύθη (also χύτο), λύθη (also λύτο), πῆχθεν (cf. ἐπάγην).

Perfect

This IE 'tense' possessed a special set of endings which emerge clearly from the paradigm of (ϝ)οῖδ- 1, ϝοῖδ-α, Skt. *véda*; 2, (ϝ)οῖσ-θα < *(ϝ)οιδ-θα, Skt. *vét-tha*; 3, (ϝ)οῖδ-ε, Skt. *véd-a*; 4, (ϝ)ίδ-μεν, Skt. *vidmá*; 5, (ϝ)ίσ-τε < *ϝιδ-τε, Skt. *vid-á*; 6, (ϝ)ίσ-ᾶσι < *ϝιδ-n̥ti, Skt. *vid-úr*.

From this and other comparative evidence it is clear that the IE endings were 1, *-*a*, 2, *-tha*, 3, *-e*, 4, *-me*. In 6, Latin *-ēre* < *-ēro*, Hittite *-ir*, Toch. B *-āre/-are* show that the *-r-* of Skt. *-ur* is original and that the *-ᾶσι* of Greek comes from the non-perfect tenses (p. 298). In 2, *-θα* is preserved in the perfect only in ϝοῖσθα, the normal ending *-ας* being elsewhere introduced from the *s*-aorist.

Since the perfect is essentially intransitive and expresses a state of the subject, there was no occasion for a separate set of middle endings: πέποιθα means 'I believe' (as a result of persuasion). Nevertheless, since it was the function of the middle to express a subject-bound action, it is understandable that the perfect should develop middle inflexions, particularly with the development of the 'resultative' perfect, in which the result of the action persists in the object. However, in Homer few verbs have both an active and a middle perfect (exceptional is the opposition βεβλήκει/βέβλητο), which are active/passive, but more often the active and the middle form are intransitive: ἔμμορε is Aeolic corresponding to Ionic εἵμαρται. Of particular interest is the Homeric participle τετευχώς 'made of', which stands for τετυχϝώς, as is shown by the corresponding Myc. *tetukwo(h)a*; elsewhere the Epic has τετυγμένος, τέτυκται, τέτυκ-το. We add that such middle perfects already existed in Mycenaean: *epidedato* = *epidedastoi*.[1] The perfect middle has the primary inflexions discussed above. In third plural *-n̥tai* is used after consonants (εἵαται stands for ἥαται < *ēs-n̥tai*), and it is also usual in Homer after *i* and *i*-diphthongs: κεκλίαται, κέ(ι)αται. Later Attic generalized *-νται* (κέκλινται, κάθηνται) whereas Ionic extended the range of *-αται* < *-n̥tai*. In the case of third plural endings in *-φαται*, *-χαται* (and *-δαται*) and in the stems ending in *-λ*, *-ν* and *-ρ* Attic substituted periphrastic forms consisting of the perfect participle middle and εἰσί 'they

[1] With passive meaning 'has been assigned in addition'.

are'. Stems ending in a dental changed this consonant regularly (p. 241) to -σ- (*πεπυθ-ται > πέπυσται) and -σ- was thence extended to the other forms: πέπυσμαι, πεπυσμένος, etc.

The perfect is an athematic type, i.e. the endings were added directly to the stem. The stem is formed 1, by reduplication (in the vast majority of examples) and 2, with o-grade of the ablaut (λέ-λοιπ-α, γέγον-ε) in the singular and zero grade elsewhere (ϝίδ-μεν, -γε-γά-την, with γα- < *gn̥-). In the reduplication the vowel is invariably ε and the preceding consonant is the initial consonant of the root or the first consonant if the root begins with a cluster of plosive and liquid: γέγραφα, κέκλοφα, κέκρᾱγα, πέπληγα. Certain sound developments have obscured the reduplication: εἴληφα < *se-slābh-, εἴωθα < *se-swōdh-, εἵμαρται < *se-smr̥-; ἔοργα < *we-worg-, ἔοικα < *we-woik-, εἴρημαι < *we-wrē- (p. 227).

A different form of reduplication appears with roots of the structure VS, where S = l, m, n, r: the first syllable is repeated with lengthening of the vowel of the root: ἄρ-ηρ-α, ἐλ-ήλυθ-α, ὄλ-ωλ-α. This type spread to other roots with vocalic first element (e.g. ὄδωδα, ὄπωπα, etc.), and it is particularly frequent in Attic; hence the term 'Attic reduplication'. The origin of this reduplication is disputed. In essence it resembles the intensive reduplication of the whole initial syllable (γαργαίρω, μαρμαίρω, παμφαίνω, etc.). If reduplication was felt to be a necessary feature of the perfect, then in the absence of an initial consonant the intensive type was the obvious alternative. This, however, leaves the lengthening of the root vowel unexplained. Some scholars trace this to IE lengthened perfects like Lat. ēdī, ōdī, a formation resembling that of Sanskrit roots beginning with a, which have ā (< a+a) in the perfect, e.g. āda < ad- 'eat', āsa < as- 'be'. These have been traced to forms reduplicated with an initial laryngeal consonant: *H_1e-H_1d- > *ēd-, *H_3eH_3d- > ōd-. This construction assumes, of course, generalization of the zero grade from the plural and dual to the active, and it does not explain ēgi, etc. Besides (ϝ)οἶδα, Greek offers a few examples of perfect without reduplication: ἄν-ωγα (imp. ἄνωχ-θι), cf. ἦ 'he said' < *ēg-/ōg- (with *Hg- in Lat. aiō from *Hgjō), ἦγμαι (on ἦχα, see below), ὦμμαι (cf. ὄπωπα).

It remains to explain how such a long-vowel perfect came to be recharacterized by the reduplication. It has been pointed out that, as a consequence of phonetic changes, certain forms of some verbs would have lost their connection with the system, e.g. *ed-tós > *ἐστός; reconnection was established by re-characterization to ἐδεστός. However, this is hardly satisfactory as a basis since the -to- verbal adjective is not characterized by reduplication. It would appear then that Greek inherited from IE a form of intensive reduplication limited to roots of the above structure and that this type was the model for further extension in Attic: ἀκήκοα, ἐγήγερκα, etc. An anomalous form is ἐγρή-γορα from ἐγείρω. The root is *ger- with a prothetic vowel, so that a perfect *ge-gor-a might be expected, or (on the evidence of Skt. jāgāra) *gē-gor-a: *γηγορα must then have been trans-formed to ἐγρήγορα under the influence of the aorist stem ἐγρέσθαι.

Some roots beginning with two consonants other than plosive and liquid have the augment instead of reduplication. This is particularly so if the first consonant is s: ἔσκαφα, ἔσταλμαι, ἔζευγμαι, ἔψευσμαι, ἔγνωκα, ἔφθορα, ἔφθιτο. The verb κτάομαι shows both formations: κέκτημαι (Attic) and ἔκτημαι (Homer and Ionic). In certain verbs the initial ῥ- disguises a cluster < *wr- or *sr- (pp. 227, 236), so that ἐρρ- may represent either *we-wr- (e.g. ἔρρωγα, ἔρριμμαι) or *se-sr- (ἔρρῑγα, ἐρρύηκα).

The Perfect Stem

The Ablaut alternations within the perfect system were as follows: o in the active singular and zero in the active plural and throughout the middle. In the Attic conjugation of οἶδα the e-grade appears in the subjunctive, optative, the infinitive and the participle (on all these, see below). Within the finite verb Homer offers numerous examples of the zero grade: μέμονα/μέμαμεν (*men-/mn̥-), πέποιθα/ἐπέπιθμεν, πέπονθα/πέπασθε (< *πεπαθ-τε < *pn̥th-), (ϝ)έ(ϝ)οικα/(ϝ)έ(ϝ)ικτον, γέγονα/-γε-γάτην. A concealed example is δείδω/δείδιμεν (< *de-dwoi-a/de-dwi-men, < *dwei- 'fear'). Even at this early date, however, there are a good many perfects with o-grade throughout the active, and in Attic the Ablaut alternation has been lost (except for ἴσμεν, etc.). In the middle the zero grade is better preserved, ἔμμορε (see above)/εἵμαρται (*se-sm-r̥-), τέταμαι (*te-tn̥-), εἷμαι (*je-jH₁-mai) to ἵημι (*ji-jē-mi), πέφαται (*gʷhe-gʷhn̥-, cf. θείνω, φόνος, *gʷhen-/gʷhon-).

Roots with nuclear vowel $\bar{a}$ show the alternation $\bar{a}/\breve{a}$: βέβηκα/βέβαμεν. Roots with laryngeal suffixation have the II form of the base: ἔγνωκα (< *gneH₃-), μέμβλωκα (< *mleH₃-), βέβλητο (< *gʷleH₁-), τέτληκα (< *tleH₂-), etc.

The difficulty of attaching inflexions with initial vowel (or consisting of a vowel like -α and -ε) to stems terminating in a vowel was overcome by the insertion of a -κ-, which is also observed in the singular of the aorists ἔθηκα, ἧκα, ἔδωκα. In Homer, too, this suffix appears predominantly in the singular of stems ending in a long vowel or diphthong, with a few examples in the third plural (e.g. ἑστήκᾱσι). Attic, too, still has relics of this older system (e.g. τέθνᾰμεν, ἕσταμεν), but after Homer -κ- became the suffix *par excellence* of the perfect, the root being increasingly in the zero grade, thus showing the influence of the middle: τέθεικα, λέλυκα, ἔσταλκα, δέδεκα, κέκλικα, ἔφθαρκα, etc. In due course even stems ending in a plosive were brought into the system by means of the composite suffix -ηκ-: e.g. λελάβηκα (for εἴληφα), γεγράφηκα (for γέγραφα).

The last two examples, in which the root ends in an aspirated plosive, lead on to the aspirated perfect, which was a development of Attic. In the middle, the plosive underwent assimilation: εἴληφα/εἴλημμαι, and this was also the case with roots ending in -π- and -β-: λείπω/λέλειμμαι, τρίβω/τέτριμμαι. The identical middle forms (especially λέλειφθε and λέλειφθαι) were the switch-point for analogical active perfects in -φα, and by a similar process also in -χα. These appear only in Attic and Ionic from the fifth century on, and they are invariably resultative in meaning. The process started in the third plural middle, where the beginnings appear in Homer: τετράφαται (τρέπω), ἔρχαται (εἴργω). Attic examples are: κέκλοφα (κλέπτω), πέπομφα (πέμπω), πέπλοχα (πλέκω), ἦχα (ἄγω), τέτριφα (τρίβω), πέπρᾱχα (πράσσω) (earlier πέπρᾱγα).

Pluperfect

Originally the perfect was an isolated formation with no accompanying preterite. In Greek it was brought into the verbal conjugational system and provided with a past tense—the pluperfect. It has the augment and secondary endings. There is no difficulty about the terminations of the middle: they are identical with those discussed above.

In the active, three lines of development can be observed. In the most successful the endings go through two stages: 1, -η, -ης, -ει, -εμεν, -ετε, -εσαν; 2, -ειν, -εις, -ει, -εμεν, -ετε, -εσαν (the plural being levelled to -ειμεν, -ειτε, -εισαν in post-Classical times). In Homer by far the most frequent form is the third singular in -ει (ὀλώλει, βεβήκει, ἠνώγει, etc.). For οἶδα the most frequent form is third singular ἤδη with second singular ἤδησθα and ἠείδης. On the other hand the first singular ends in -εα: ἤδεα, πεποίθεα, ἠνώγεα, and similar uncontracted endings are found in Ionic (Herodotus) in 2, -εας. 3, -εε: the facts are difficult to interpret. A simple description of Attic-Ionic is that in 1, 2, 3 and 6 the endings of the s-aorist are added to a stem with suffix -ε. The origin of the suffix may be found in the conjugation of οἶδα, where ϝειδη-/ϝειδε- is surely ancient.

iv The Moods

Imperative – Active

In 2, the bare stem appears in the thematic verbs: λύε, λίπε.[1] For the athematics there are several possibilities: 1, the bare stem (ἔξ-ει, ἵστη, δείκνῡ, πίμπλη, etc.); 2, the locatival particle -θι (p. 284) is added (presents ἴθι, ἴσθι, δίδωθι, ἴληθι, etc.; aorists βῆθι, κλῦθι, γνῶθι, πῖθι, etc.; perfects ἄνωχθι, τέτλαθι, τέθναθι, (ϝ)ίσθι, etc.; in the -θη- aorists -θι > -τι (λύθητι, etc.). Interaction with the thematic class may be the explanation of Attic τίθει (< *τιθε-ε), δίδου (< *διδο-ε), (προσ-)ίστᾱ (<-ιστᾱ-ε). Unexplained is the origin of final -s which characterizes certain aorist imperatives of Attic (θές, δός, ἕς) and also appears in the thematic σχέ-ς and the Homeric ἐνί-σπες (< *sqʷe-). In 5, -τε is added to the stem, and the forms are identical with the unaugmented indicative with secondary endings—the so-called injunctive.

Injunctive forms are also basic to 3 and 6. In Sanskrit a particle -u is added (bhávat-u), and similar forms appear in Hittite eštu, Skt. astu. Sanskrit presents also the ending -tāt, which is used in 2, 3 and 5 in both active and middle. This corresponds to the future imperative of Latin in -tō(d) and the Greek -τω, which appears already in the earliest texts. Despite

---

[1] Attic aorist imperatives ἰδέ, λαβέ, εἰπέ, ἐλθέ and εὑρέ preserve the original accentuation.

the inherited indifference to person, number and voice, -τω became the mark of the third singular (ἔστω, ἴτω, etc., ἱστάτω, δότω, etc.). From this a second singular ἐλθέτως (Cypr.) was coined by addition of the -s characteristic of this person. For the third plural Greek evolved a number of solutions varying from dialect to dialect. 1, -ντω (particularly in Doric ἐντω after ἐντι, διαγνοντω, etc.); 2, -των (ἔστων, ἴτων); 3, -ντων (Hom. ἀγειρόντων, ἀγγελλόντων, etc.), the formation which is the normal one in Attic-Ionic (λυόντων, τιθέντων, γνόντων, etc.), but ἔστων is used in literature as against ὄντων elsewhere; 4, -σαν, originating in the s-aorist, becomes frequent in post-Classical times, though examples occur in Thucydides and Euripides (ἔστωσαν, λειπέτωσαν, etc.).

Imperative – Middle

In 2, the secondary ending *-so without augment (injunctive) is used (λύου < *λυε(h)ο, θοῦ < *θεσο, but with analogically restored or preserved -s- in τίθεσο, etc.). In 5, -σθε is likewise an injunctive form, and this was the basis for the analogically coined -σθω for 3, which in some dialects is also used for 6. The following pluralizing devices occur: (a) -νσθω sometimes with loss of -ν-, in the Doric dialects; (b) -σθων is the only form in Homer (λεξάσθων, ἐπέσθων, πιθέσθων, φερέσθων, etc.) and it is normal in Attic-Ionic; (c) -νσθων is rare; (d) recharacterization by -σαν becomes common in later Greek (φερέσθωσαν); (e) -εσθον in Lesbian (ἐπιμελεσθον).

In the sigmatic aorist the second active has the ending -ον (δεῖξον), which appears in other aorists in -α (εἶπον). The middle has -αι, which may be connected with the -αι which appears in -μαι, etc. of the finite verb. The resemblance to the aorist infinitive active is presumably coincidental (note the difference of accentuation in imperative τίμησαι, infinitive τιμῆσαι).

Subjunctive

Two main types can be distinguished: 1, with athematic verbs a short thematic vowel is used (ἴμεν/ἴομεν); 2, with thematic verbs the thematic vowel is lengthened (φέρομεν/φέρωμεν, φέρετε/φέρητε). Both types are IE: 1, Skt. ásti/ásati (in Latin *es-ō/es-et(i) survives as the future erō/erit); 2, Skt. bhávāni, *bhávās*(*i*), *bhávāt*(*i*). In Sanskrit the inflexions are partly primary and partly secondary, but the balance of the evidence points to the secondary endings for the IE system, of which Greek dialect forms like Arc. ἔχη (**eghē-t*) are survivals. Attic-Ionic changed **ἔχης, ἔχη to ἔχῃς, ἔχῃ under the influence of the indicative and also generalized the thematic type. Homeric examples of 1 are εἴδομεν, χεύομεν, φθίεται (indic. φθί-το), παύσομεν, τείσομεν, ἱλασόμεθα. Some are used as futures: ἔδομαι, πίομαι (on the middle see below). But even in Homer the thematic type encroaches (θήομεν/θήῃς, στήομεν/στήῃς, στήωσι, παύσωμεν) and in the verb 'to be' it is the only form found: ἔωμεν, contracted to ὦμεν. On the other hand, forms like θέωμεν may result from quantitative metathesis of θήομεν; later θῶμεν. Another evolution is possible: θήωμεν, θέωμεν (with shortening in hiatus), θῶμεν (contraction); thus οἶδα in Ionic has εἰδέω, εἰδέωσι < **εἴδη-ω, **εἴδηωσι, the forms with two long vowels being attested in other dialects, e.g. Delph. δωη.

In a few verbs the subjunctive stem is made simply by lengthening the vowel: Cret. δυνᾶμαι, Arc. -ιστᾶτοι. We may add the Ionic δυνεώμεθα, for this implies **δυνηωμεθα < **δυνᾱωμεθα.

Optative

There are two types: 1, the thematic verbs use the modal stem suffix **-jeH₁-/*-jH₁-* attached to the zero grade of the root with the secondary endings: e.g. from **es-* 'to be', **sjēm, *sjēs, *sjēt, *sīme, *sīte, *sijent*, best preserved in O.Lat. *siem, sīmus, sient* (Skt. *syām* has generalized the full grade of the modal suffix). In Greek the full grade of the root apparently occurs, but this may be the reflection of a laryngeal **H₁s-*: εἴην, εἴης, εἴη, εἶμεν, εἶτε, εἶεν. With ablauting verbal stems ending in a vowel the short vowel appears: τιθείην, θείην, διδοίην, δοίην, φαίην, δυναίμην: in -νῠ-verbs a few traces survive of **-nu-ī-to* > -νῦτο (p. 215); δαινῦτο (Hom.), πηγνῦτο (Attic), but here the thematic type has prevailed. The same phonetic development of **-ui-* appears in φῦμεν, δῦμεν. The short vowel also occurs in -η aorists, e.g. μιγείην, which may be simply due to the analogy of θείην or generalization of the regular development (Osthoff) of **μιγηι-μεν > μιγεῖμεν, this being less probable since the long vowel is retained analogically in καθήμην, μέμνητο, κέκτητο, etc.

In post-Classical Greek the full-grade suffix was generalized (εἴημεν, etc.), but there was a growing encroachment of the thematic type: ἴοιμι/ἴοις, εἴοις/ἔοι, κέοιτο, καθοῖτο and, as mentioned above, in the -νυ- verbs.

The thematic optative has the suffix -οι- which appears to be a combination of the thematic vowel -o- and the zero grade of *-jē-/*-jH₁-: φέροιμι, Skt. *bhareyam* < *bher-o-j-ṃ*. Greek has substituted the athematic primary ending for *-ṃ, but the expected -α appears in Arcadian ἐξελαυνοια. There has been some interaction between the thematic and athematic types. Thus Homeric φιλοίη, φοροίη anticipate the regular Attic optatives of such contracted verbs: φιλοίην, τιμῴην, the switch-point being plural forms like φιλοῖμεν (*φιλε-οι-μεν), which were equatable with διδοῖμεν (*διδο-ῑ-μεν). The composite stem-suffix -οιη- subsequently spread to the plural: e.g. σχοίησαν, where the dominant third plural -σαν may also be noted.

The sigmatic aorist is an athematic formation in Cretan δικακσιε̄ (third singular) and ϝερκσιεν (third plural). But generally the pseudo-thematic -α of this tense (p. 301) has been combined with -ι: λύσαιμι, λύσαις, λύσαι, λύσαιμεν, λύσαιτε, λύσαιεν. In Attic, however, 2 and 3 appear as λύσειας, λύσειε, and both types occur in Homer. Structurally, -ει- appears as an optative formant in the second and third singular and third plural of the sigmatic aorist. In Arcadian third singular διακωλυσει possibly appears. If these anomalous forms are old, we may postulate 1, *-sei-ṃ, 2, -sei-s, 3, -sei-t, 6, *-sei-ent > 1, *-σε(ι)α, 2, *-σεις, 3, -σει, -σε(ι)εν, 2 and 3 being transformed to -σειας, -σειε on the lines of the indicative -σας, -σε. The ultimate origin of -σει or -σ-ει remains an open question.

Future

Synchronically, the Greek future is a regular component of the conjugational tense system. It is discussed as a mood since IE lacked this tense, and in all the descendant languages it has developed mainly from the modal forms (e.g. Lat. *erō* from subjunctive *esō* (see pp. 308 f., where Hom. ἔδομαι, πίομαι, etc. are quoted). In a number of IE languages, however, there are resemblant future formations: Gk. λύσω, etc. (on more composite forms see below), Lat. *faxō*, Skt. *dāsyáti* 'he will give',

Lith. *dúosiu* 'I will give'. Latin *faxō* is explicable as the sub-junctive of an *s*-aorist (cf. 'optative' *faxim*), and the same origin has been mooted for the main Greek type. What gives pause is a fact of the synchronic structure: the future often has the *e*-grade against the zero grade of the aorist and, further, it often appears in the middle voice: πείσομαι (< *πενθ-σ-ομαι) *v.* ἔπαθον, πεύσομαι *v.* ἔπυθον, ἕξω (with *segh-) *v.* ἔσχον (with *sgh-), λήψομαι *v.* ἔλαβον. These are striking and anomalous features of the Greek future which are surely old, and it is no answer to say that Greek might once have had a suitable aorist, since we should have to posit aorists like *ἐ-πενθ-σα, precisely the type which was strongly expansive in Greek. The proposed explanatory hypothesis carries with it the assumption that the productive aorist, once having engendered the future, dis-appeared, leaving the anomalous pair *πενσομαι/ἔπαθον. It is preferable, therefore, to respect the given facts and retain the explanation that these futures are in fact, like Latin *quaeso*, *vīso*, desideratives. This is supported by the existence of re-duplicated futures like δεδέξομαι, going back to an IE type of intensive-desideratives (here with middle inflexions) like Skt. *bíbhitsa-* (*bhid-* 'split'), *yúyutsa-* (*yudh-* 'fight'), *vivits-* (*vid-* 'know),' with the proviso that these have the zero grade of the root. While these futures originally had no connection with the perfect, their reduplicated forms drew them into its orbit, so that futures came to be made from the perfect: κεκλήσομαι, γεγράψεται, etc. The active forms of earlier Attic ἑστήξω, τεθνήξω later give way to the middle ἑστήξομαι, τεθνήξομαι.

Other futures of this class have the stem of the reduplicated aorist: κεχάροντο/κεχαρήσεται, πεφιδέσθαι/πεφιδήσεται (φεί-δομαι 'spare'), πέπιθον/πεπιθήσω.

A third type appears with disyllabic bases in -α and -ε, that is with roots extended by laryngeal suffixation, -H_2 and H_1. The intervocalic -*s*- is lost so that the future appears as -άω (-ῶ), -έω (-ῶ), e.g. σκεδῶ, (ϝ)ερῶ. Prominent in this formation are verbs ending in nasals and liquids, and for verbs having asig-matic aorists it is the sole type: -θανέομαι (-ἔθανον), βαλέω (ἔβαλον), πεσέομαι (ἔπεσον); but both -έω/-άω and -ἐ(σ)σω/-ἀ(σ)σω occur in conjunction with *s*-aorists: καλέω/καλέσω (ἐκάλεσ(σ)α), δαμάω/δαμά(σ)σω (ἐδάμα(σ)σα). The types in -έω (-ῶ) and -άω (-ῶ) were particularly productive in Attic, those in -έω (-ῶ) being preferred by verbs ending in a liquid(and eventually verbs in -ίζω), while -άω was used only rarely in Attic with -άζω verbs: νεμῶ, μενῶ; κτεριοῦσι (Homer), νομιῶ, etc.; and finally βιβῶ, ἐξετῶ, such futures occurring with greater frequency in Ionic and the Koine, whereas Attic mostly has -άσω.

The so-called 'Doric future' in -σέω appears also in Homer (ἐσσεῖται) and in Attic (φευξοῦμαι), πεσοῦμαι, etc., but only in the middle, whereas West Greek has active forms (ποιησέω, κλεψέω, etc.). This type looks like a contamination of the two preceding classes, but Mycenaean has unexpectedly provided evidence of a type -*sĕs*-: *ewepsesomena* is most plausibly interpreted as 'to be woven' (see p. 50) and so represents the future participle (in a passive sense) of the verb 'to weave', which appears in alphabetic Greek only in the zero grade *wbh-: ὕφος, 'web', ὑφαίνω 'weave'. The full grade appears in other IE languages (cf. Engl. *web, weave*); there is no evidence for an initial laryngeal (p. 222). Thus the Myc. future is to be traced to *webh-sĕs-*, there being no evidence for the length of the vowel of the suffix. This supports the view that Myc. *asesosi* is the future of ἀσ- 'sate', 'fill with drink' (< *H_2es-) and is to be interpreted *as-sĕs-onsi*. Thus the 'Doric' future may be grouped with this type, i.e. with the phonetic development *-σεσ-ω > -σε(h)ω.

Future Passives

That the middle form could have passive meaning at an early date has just emerged, and Homer attests a similar usage: πέρσεται 'it will be destroyed'. Another passive type was based on the intransitive aorists in -η-, -θη- (p. 302). The only Homeric examples are δαήσεαι and μιγήσεσθαι, but there was considerable production in Attic from the fifth century B.C. on: τριβήσομαι, λειφθήσομαι, etc.

v VERBAL NOUNS AND ADJECTIVES

The IE verbal system comprised a number of adjectival forms, the 'participles'. The suffix -*nt*- is found in all IE languages, and these formations had an archaic type of declension: for instance, the participle of *es- 'to be' had the root in the zero grade, while the suffix had the Ablaut grades *-ōn/-ont-/-n̥t-:

singular nominative *sōn, accusative *sontm̥, genitive *sn̥tós, locative *sn̥tí, plural nominative *sóntes, accusative *sóntn̥s, genitive *sn̥tóm, locative *sn̥t-sú. The feminine was *sn̥tī (or *sn̥t-jH₂). Greek apparently has the full grade of the root (unless ἐ(σ)- represents *H₁s-) and has generalized the full grade of the suffix *-ont, with the exception of the vr̥ddhied nominative singular ἐών. This is so also in the feminine (ἐοῦσα < *H₁s-ont-jH₂), but there are dialect forms ἐασσα (Myc. and Arc.) which go back to *H₁s-n̥t-jH₂. Zero grade of the suffix is also indirectly attested in the Heraclean dative plural ἐντασσιν, which is a remodelling of *ἀσσι < *s-n̥t-si. Zero grade of the root must be postulated 1, for Attic ὤν/ὄν (since the neuter form cannot < *es-on) and 2, ἰών < *ei- 'go'.

Athematic stems ending in a vowel have the suffix -nt- (τιθείς, διδούς, ἱστάς, θείς, δούς, γνούς, etc.), and this group includes the sigmatic aorists (δείξᾱς, etc.). The thematic verbs also add -nt- to the stem, but the vowel is solely -o-: λύων, λύουσα (< *lu-ont-jH₂), etc.

The perfect participle active is formed with the suffix *-wŏs-/ *-us-, the corresponding feminine formant being *-us-jH₂. In Sanskrit the zero grade of the root appears both in the masculine vidvān (gen. viduṣas) and the feminine viduṣī. In Greek the feminine ἰδυῖα regularly < *wid-usjH₂, cf. further Myc. araruja. In the masculine, on the evidence of Gothic weitwoþs 'witness', the unreduplicated form (ϝ)εἰδώς will be ancient, but the Myc. presents widwoijo = widwo(h)ios, i.e. a derivative showing widwos-, the zero grade of the root. The conclusion is that in the IE declension the root had zero grade in the oblique cases; Greek generalized the full grade in the masculine/neuter and Sanskrit the zero grade, while the feminine, as a derived form, is based on the zero grade. In the reduplicated perfect the root was originally in the zero grade, e.g. Myc. tetukwo(ha) (later τετευχότα), Hom. γεγαώς, μεμαώς. As for the suffix in alphabetic Greek, except for εἰδώς/εἰδός and the feminine, all the cases have -wot- (εἰδότα, etc.). A dental stem appears also in the Sanskrit declension, e.g. singular nominative neuter vidvat, instrumental plural vidvadbhis, but the resemblance has been dismissed as accidental: Linear B allegedly proves that the Greek development was post-Mycenaean and so independent of the Sanskrit innovations. However, it would be hazardous to assume that the Linear B texts give us a complete picture of the Greek dialects of the Mycenaean age.

In the present participle middle the suffix is -μενο- for the present, the aorist and the perfect, except that the last has the accent -μένο-. If these were originally adjectives derived by means of the accented thematic vowel from verbal nouns in *-men, the suffix would be -mnó-, with the zero grade still preserved in Lat. *alumnus* and the substantivized βέλεμνον. Such an origin would imply that the insertion of the vowel in Greek -μενο- is an innovation, which appears to imply the attachment of the thematic vowel to a noun of the structure *φερεμεν-.

The adjectives in -tó- are not strictly speaking participles and have no connection with a tense stem, the suffix being added to the zero grade of the root: e.g. κλυτός (*klew-/klu-), τατός (*ten-/tn̥-). The meaning was not originally passive or active, but more generally 'susceptible to the action of the verb', so that, according to the context, such adjectives may be either active or passive or express possibility: βροτός (*mr̥-tó-s) does not mean 'dead' but 'susceptible to dying'. This word was probably created from ἄμβροτος 'immortal', since -tó- was used by preference in compound adjectives corresponding to simple adjectives in -μένο- (p. 257). The gerundive in -τέο-, on the Mycenaean evidence, is not to be connected with Skt. -tavya, but is a parallel formation from -ti- nouns, i.e. < *-tejo- rather than from -tu-/-tew- (p. 51).

Infinitives

These are, in origin, cases of verbal nouns which in IE had no systematic connection with the verbal conjugation. The underlying noun stems contained a general reference to the verbal event, but there was no connection with any 'tense'. The systematic development of present, future, aorist and perfect infinitives was a Greek innovation, as was the distinction of voice, for the verbal nouns were neutral in this respect. This state of affairs persisted in Vedic Sanskrit, which has a rich variety of noun forms in different cases (accusative, dative, ablative, genitive and locative) with infinitival function. Classical Sanskrit has only one infinitive in -tum, this being the accusative of a -tu- stem (like the Latin supine), whereas in Vedic the dative is by far the most frequent type of 'infinitive', this case having 'final' function. In Greek the dialectal distribution is the result of independent selection from a wide range of choice. In the active there is a preponderance of -n- suffixes, *-en-, *-sen-, *-men-, *-wen-, which appear to have been formally locatives with zero inflexion. The first two, -en- and -sen- (for the type *φερεσ-εν cf. Skt. ne-ṣáṇ-i 'to lead'), appear in the active infinitives of the thematic verbs: -εν is found in Arcadian and certain Doric dialects; -ehen in Myc. ekee = ekhehen; the contracted form -ειν or -ην in most alphabetic Greek dialects. The athematic verbs have -ναι in Attic-Ionic, Arcado-Cypriot and Homer (εἶναι < *es-nai, etc.); -μεναι in Lesbian and Homer (ἔμμεναι, etc.); and -μεν (δόμεν, ἴμεν, etc.) in West Greek, and in Boeotian, Thessalian and Homer (with secondary extension to thematic verbs). The last two recall the Vedic type dā́mane 'to give', while δοϝεναι (Cypr.) resembles dāváne 'to give' (cf. ἴδμεναι, Skt. vidmáne), but these are simply the datives of verbal nouns dā-man-, dā-van-, with -e from *-ei. Greek -αι, however, which is common to -ν-αι and -μεν-αι, is not equatable with any known IE case-ending, and it must be designated neutrally as a 'particle'. The same particle appears in the infinitive of the s-aorist -σαι, which may be based on s-stems (cf. Skt. áyase 'to go'), but it is open to equation with the Vedic type in -dhyai (duhádhyai 'to milk'), which would develop to -(σ)σαι in Greek: e.g. λοέσσαι.

In the middle only one suffix appears, -σθαι; there is a bare possibility that this is a remodelling of *-σσαι under the influence of the middle inflexions -σθε and -σθον (see above).

BIBLIOGRAPHY

GENERAL

Burrow, T., *The Sanskrit Language*, London (1973).

Chantraine, P., *Dictionnaire étymologique de la langue grecque: histoire des mots*, Paris (1968–).

Frisk, H., *Griechisches etymologisches Wörterbuch*, 3 vols., Heidelberg (1961–72).

Hiersche, R., *Grundzüge der griechischen Sprachgeschichte*, Wiesbaden (1970).

Hoffmann, O., and Debrunner, A., *Geschichte der griechischen Sprache*, I, 4th edn. by Scherer, A.; II, *Grundfragen und Grundzüge des nachklassischen Griechisch*, 2nd edn. by Scherer, A., Berlin (1969).

Householder, F. W., and Nagy, G., *Greek: A Survey of Recent Work*, The Hague (1972).

Kretschmer, P., *Sprache* in Gercke–Norden, *Einleitung in die Altertumswissenschaft*, I, 6, Leipzig–Berlin (1923), 64 ff.

Kretschmer, P., and Locker, E., *Rückläufiges Wörterbuch der griechischen Sprache*, 2nd edn., with additions by Kisser, G., Göttingen (1963).

Liddell, H. G., and Scott, R., *A Greek–English Lexicon*, 9th edn. by Jones, H. S., with the assistance of McKenzie, R., Oxford (1940). *A Supplement*, ed. by Barber, E. A., with the assistance of Maas, P., Scheller, M., and West, M. L., Oxford (1968).

Meillet, A., *Aperçu d'une histoire de la langue grecque*, Paris (1913); 8th edn. (with bibliography supplemented by Masson, O.) (1975).

Meillet, A., *Introduction à l'étude comparative des langues indo-européennes*, 8th edn., Paris (1937). Reprinted with a preface by Buck, G. C., Alabama (1964).

Palmer, L. R., *The Latin Language*, London (1954).

Pisani, V., *Manuale storico della lingua greca*, 2nd edn., Brescia (1973).

Schwyzer, E., *Griechische Grammatik*, I, *Lautlehre, Wortbildung, Flexion*; II (with Debrunner, A.), *Syntax*; III, *Indexes* by Georgacas, D. J.; IV, *Stellenregister* by Radt, F. and S., München (1939, 1950, 1953, 1971).

CHAPTER I

Hiersche, 13–39.

Hoffmann–Debrunner, I, 6–25.

Kretschmer, *Sprache*, 64–75.

Meillet, *Aperçu*, 3–76.

Schwyzer, *Gr. Gr.* 48–75.

Caskey, J. L., 'Greece and the Aegean Islands in the Middle Bronze Age', *Cambridge Ancient History*, 3rd edn., Cambridge (1973), II 1, Ch. iv (*a*), 117–40.

Chadwick, J. (1963), 'The Prehistory of the Greek Language', *Cambridge Ancient History*, 3rd edn., Cambridge (1975), II 2, Ch. xxxix (*a*), 805–19.

Crossland, R. A., 'Immigrants from the North', *Cambridge Ancient History*, 3rd edn., Cambridge (1971), I 2, Ch. xxvii, 824–76.

[316]

Kretschmer, P., *Einleitung in die Geschichte der griechischen Sprache*, 2nd edn., Göttingen (1970) (1st edn., 1896).

Laroche, E., 'Linguistique Asianique', *Acta Mycenaea* (ed. Ruipérez, M. S.), Salamanca (1972), I, 112–35.

Lewy, H., 'Anatolia in the Old Assyrian Period', *Cambridge Ancient History*, 3rd edn., Cambridge (1971), I 2, Ch. xxiv (*b*), 707–28.

Mellaart, J., 'Anatolia, *c.* 4000–2300 B.C.', *Cambridge Ancient History*, 3rd edn., Cambridge (1971), I 2, Ch. xviii, 373–416.

Mellaart, J., 'Anatolia, *c.* 2300–1750 B.C.', *Cambridge Ancient History*, 3rd edn., Cambridge (1971), I 2, Ch. xxiv (*a*), 681–706.

Palmer, L. R., *Mycenaeans and Minoans*, 2nd edn., London (1965), Ch. vi 'The Coming of the Greeks', 321–57.

Palmer, L. R., 'Linear B and the Anatolian Languages', *Atti e Memorie del 1° Congresso Internazionale di Micenologia*, Rome (1968), I, 339–54.

Vermeule, E., *Greece in the Bronze Age*, Chicago (1964).

CHAPTER II

Baumbach, L., *Studies in Mycenaean Inscriptions and Dialect*, Rome (1968).

Chadwick, J., *The Decipherment of Linear B*, 2nd edn., Cambridge (1967).

Dow, S., and Chadwick, J., 'The Linear Scripts and the Tablets as Historical Documents', *Cambridge Ancient History*, 3rd edn., Cambridge (1973), III, Ch. xiii, 582–626.

Hiller, S., and Panagl, O., *Die frühgriechischen Texte aus Mykenischer Zeit*, Erträge der Forschung Bd. 49, Darmstadt (1976).

Landau, O., *Mykenisch-griechische Personennamen*, Göteborg (1958).

Lejeune, M., *Mémoires de philologie mycénienne*, I, Paris (1958); II, Rome (1971); III, Rome (1972).

Morpurgo, A., *Mycenaeae Graecitatis Lexicon*, Rome (1963).

Olivier, J.-P., Godart, L., Seydel, C., and Sourvinou, C., *Index généraux du Linéaire B*, Incunabula Graeca LII, Rome (1973).

Palmer, L. R., *The Interpretation of Mycenaean Greek Texts*, 2nd impression with additions and corrections, Oxford (1969).

Palmer, L. R., and Boardman, J., *On the Knossos Tablets*, Oxford (1963).

Ruijgh, C. J., *Études sur la grammaire et le vocabulaire du grec mycénien*, Amsterdam (1967).

Ventris, M., and Chadwick, J., *Documents in Mycenaean Greek*, 2nd edn. by Chadwick, J., Cambridge (1973).

Vilborg, E., *A Tentative Grammar of Mycenaean Greek*, Göteborg (1960).

CHAPTER III

Hiersche, 39–71.

Hoffmann–Debrunner, I, 75–98.

Kretschmer, *Sprache*, 75–86.

Meillet, *Aperçu*, 77–114.

Pisani, 72–135.

Schwyzer, *Gr. Gr.*, I, 75–98.

Buck, C. D., *The Greek Dialects: Grammar, Selected Inscriptions, Glossary*, Chicago (1955).

Cowgill, W., 'Ancient Greek Dialectology in the Light of Mycenaean', *Ancient Indo-European Dialects*, Proceedings of the Conference on Indo-European Linguistics, held at the University of California, Los Angeles, eds. Birnbaum, H., and Puhvel, J., Berkeley and Los Angeles (1966), 77–95.

Risch, E., 'Die Gliederung der griechischen Dialekte in neuer Sicht', *Museum Helveticum*, 12 (1955), 61–76.

Schmitt, R., *Einführung in die griechischen Dialekte*, Darmstadt (1971).

Schwyzer, E., *Dialectorum graecarum exempla epigraphica potiora*, Leipzig (1923); reprinted Hildesheim (1960) (cited as *Del³*).

Szemerényi, O., 'The Attic "Rückverwandlung" or atomism and structuralism in action', *Studien zur Sprachwissenschaft und Kulturkunde*, Gedenkschrift für Wilhelm Brandenstein (1898–1967), ed. by Mayrhofer, M., Innsbruck (1968), 139–57.

Thumb, A., and Kieckers, E., *Handbuch der griechischen Dialekte*, I, 2nd edn., Heidelberg (1932).

Thumb, A., and Scherer, A., *Handbuch der griechischen Dialekte*, II, 2nd edn., Heidelberg (1959).

CHAPTER IV

Hiersche, 76–180.

Hoffmann–Scherer (1969), 60–114.

Kretschmer, *Sprache*, 89–94.

Meillet, *Aperçu*, 119–227.

Pisani, 136–210.

Schwyzer, *Gr. Gr.*, I, 100–12.

Aly, W., 'Herodots Sprache', *Glotta*, 15 (1927), 84–117.

Björck, G., *Das Alpha Impurum und die tragische Kunstsprache*, Uppsala (1950).

Breitenbach, W., *Untersuchungen zur Sprache der euripideischen Lyrik*, Tübinger Beiträge zur Altertumswissenschaft, Heft XX, Tübingen (1934).

Chantraine, P., *Grammaire homérique* I, 3rd edn., Paris (1958); II (1953).

Dover, K. J., 'The Poetry of Archilochus', *Entretiens sur l'antiquité classique* (Fondation Hardt), X (1964), 183–222.

Edwards, G. P., *The Language of Hesiod in its Traditional Context*, Publications of the Philological Society XXII, Oxford (1971).

Forssman, B., *Untersuchungen zur Sprache Pindars*, Wiesbaden (1966).

Hamm, E. M., *Grammatik zu Sappho und Alkaios*, 2nd edn., Berlin (1958).

Kirk, G. S., *The Songs of Homer*, Cambridge (1962).

Leumann, M., *Homerische Wörter*, Basel (1950).

Long, A. A., *Language and Thought in Sophocles*, London (1968).

Nöthiger, M., *Die Sprache des Stesichorus und des Ibycus*, Zürich (1971).

Page, D. L., 'Archilochus and the Oral Tradition', *Entretiens sur l'antiquité classique* (Fondation Hardt), X (1964), 117–79.

Palmer, L. R., 'The Language of Homer' in *A Companion to Homer* (eds. Wace, A. J. B., and Stubbings, F. H., London (1962), 75–178.

Parry, M., 'The Homeric Language as the Language of an Oral Poetry', *Harvard Studies in Classical Philology*, XLIII (1932), 1 ff.

Risch, E., 'Die Sprache Alkmans', *Museum Helveticum*, 11 (1954), 20–37.

Risch, E., *Wortbildung der homerischen Sprache*, 2nd edn., Berlin–New York (1974).

Scherer, A., 'Die Sprache des Archilochus', *Entretiens sur l'antiquité classique* (Fondation Hardt), X (1964), 87 ff.

Shipp, G. P., *Studies in the Language of Homer*, 2nd edn., Cambridge (1972).

Snell, Br., *Tyrtaios und die Sprache des Epos*, Hypomnemata 22, Göttingen (1969).

Troxler, H., *Sprache und Wortschatz Hesiods*, Zürich (1966).

CHAPTER V

Hiersche, 180–221.

Hoffmann–Scherer, I, 126–43.

Meillet, *Aperçu*, 229–46.

Pisani, 93–112.

Schwyzer, *Gr. Gr.*, I, 112–16.

Thumb–Scherer, I, 236–45, 302–5.

Aly, W., 'Formprobleme der frühen griechischen Prosa', *Philologus Supplementband*, 21, Heft III (1929).

Denniston, J. D., *Greek Prose Style*, Oxford (1952).

Drerup, E., 'Theodoros von Byzanz', *Jahrbücher für klassische Philologie*, Supplementband 27 (1902), 219–372.

Finley, J. H., 'The Origins of Thucydides' Style', *Harvard Studies in Classical Philology*, 50 (1939), 35–84.

Finley, J. H., *Thucydides*, Harvard (1947).

Grube, G. M. A., *The Greek and Roman Critics*, London (1965).

Kakrididis, J. T., 'Der thukydideische Epitaphios', *Zetemata*, 26, München (1961).

Norden, E., *Die antike Kunstprosa*, I, 3rd edn., Stuttgart (1915, reprinted 1971).

CHAPTER VI

Debrunner–Scherer, II (1969).

Meillet, *Aperçu*, 253–342.

Pisani (1973), 220–30, 238–45.

Schwyzer, *Gr. Gr.*, I, 116–37.

Bachkin, N., *Introduction to the Study of Modern Greek*, Cambridge (1935).

Blass, F., Debrunner, A., and Funk, R., *A Greek Grammar of the New Testament and Early Christian Literature*, a translation and revision of the 9–10th German edition, incorporating supplementary notes by Funk, R. W., Chicago (1961).

Browning, R., *Medieval and Modern Greek*, London (1969).

Chatzidakis, G. N., *Einleitung in die neugriechische Grammatik*, Leipzig (1892).

Costas, P. S., *An Outline of the History of the Greek Language, with particular emphasis on the Koine and the subsequent periods*, Chicago (1936).

Kapsomenos, S., *Die griechische Sprache zwischen Koine und Neugriechisch*, Berichte zum XI. internationalen Byzantinisten-Kongress, München (1958).

Mirambel, A., *La langue grecque moderne. Description et analyse*, Paris (1959).

Moulton, J. H., *A Grammar of New Testament Greek*, I, *Prolegomena*, 3rd edn., Edinburgh (1908); II (with Howard, W. F.) (1929); III (with Turner, N.) *Syntax* (1963).

Radermacher, L., *Koine. Sitzungsberichte der österreichischen Akademie der Wissenschaften*, Vienna (1947), 224, 5.

Thumb, A., *Handbuch der neugriechischen Volkssprache*, 2nd edn., Strassburg (1910); English translation by Angus, S., Edinburgh (1912).

CHAPTER VII

Allen, W. S., *Vox Graeca*, 2nd edn., Cambridge (1974).

Jeffery, L. H., *The Local Scripts of Archaic Greece*, Oxford (1961).

Pfohl, G. (ed.), *Das Alphabet*, Darmstadt (1968).

Sturtevant, E. H., *The Pronunciation of Greek and Latin*, 2nd edn., Philadelphia (Linguistic Society of America) (1940).

CHAPTERS VIII AND IX

Buck, C. D., *Comparative Grammar of Greek and Latin*, Chicago (1933).

Chantraine, P., *Traité de morphologie grecque*, 2nd edn., Paris (1961).

Kühner, R., Blass, P., and Gerth, B., *Ausführliche Grammatik der griechischen Sprache*, Hannover (1890–1904); reprinted Leverkusen (1955).

Lejeune, M., *Phonétique historique du mycénien et du grec ancien*, Paris (1972).

Meillet, A., and Vendryes, J., *Traité de grammaire comparée des langues classiques*, 3rd edn., Paris (1963).

Rix, H., *Historische Grammatik des Griechischen*, Darmstadt (1976).

Schwyzer, *Gr. Gr.*, I.

Szemerényi, O., *Einführung in die vergleichende Sprachwissenschaft*, Darmstadt (1970).

ABBREVIATIONS

(The usual abbreviations of Greek authors and
their works are omitted)

A	Attic	I	Ionic
abl.	ablative	IE	Indo-European
A-C	Arcado-Cypriot	impv.	imperative
acc.	accusative	indc.	indicative
act.	active	infin.	infinitive
Aeol.	Aeolic	instr.	instrumental
A-I	Attic-Ionic	Ir.	Irish
aor.	aorist		
Arc.	Arcadian	KN	Knossos
Arm.	Armenian		
Avest.	Avestan	Lat.	Latin
		Lesb.	Lesbian
Boeot.	Boeotian	Lett.	Lettish
Byz.	Byzantine	LH	Late Helladic
		Lith.	Lithuanian
C	consonant	LM	Late Minoan
C.Gmc.	Common Germanic	loc.	locative
Cret.	Cretan	Luw.	Luwian
Cun.	Cuneiform	LXX	Septuagint
Cypr.	Cypriot	Lyc.	Lycian
dat.	dative	masc.	masculine
decl.	declension	Meg.	Megarian
Delph.	Delphic	MH	Middle Helladic
Dor.	Doric	mid.	middle
		MnG	Modern Greek
E	English	MY	Mycenae
EH	Early Helladic	Myc.	Mycenaean
E.Thess.	East Thessalian		
		N	nasal
fem.	feminine	NE	New (Modern) English
fut.	future	NT	New Testament
		neut.	neuter
gen.	genitive	nom.	nominative
Gk.	Greek	NWG	North-west Greek
Gmc.	Germanic		
Goth.	Gothic	OCS	Old Church Slavonic
		OE	Old English
HH	Hieroglyph Hittite	OG	Old Greek
Hier.	Hieroglyphic	OHG	Old High German
Hitt.	Hittite	O.Hitt.	Old Hittite

O.Ice.	Old Icelandic	PY	Pylos
O.Ir.	Old Irish		
O.Lat.	Old Latin	*R*	resonant (sonant)
ON	Old Norse		
opt.	optative	*S*	sonant (resonant)
Osc.	Oscan	sing.	singular
O.Sl.	Old Slavonic	Skt.	Sanskrit
		subj.	subjunctive
part.	participle		
pass.	passive	Thess.	Thessalian
perf.	perfect	Toch.	Tocharian
Pers.	Persian		
pers.	person	*V*	vowel
plur.	plural	voc.	vocative
pres.	present	Vulg. Lat.	Vulgar Latin

SYMBOLS

---

*   reconstructed form, not directly attested.
>   becomes.
<   derives from.
[ ]   phonetic or allophonic transcription.
/ /   phonemic transcription.
ø   zero.

For transcriptions given in square brackets the symbols of the International Phonetics Association (IPA) are used (compare L. R. Palmer, *Descriptive and Comparative Linguistics*, p. 410).

SUBJECT INDEX

FGF

INDEX OF GREEK WORDS
AND AFFIXES

βιβλίδιον, 248
βίος, 234
βίοτος, 240
βιῶναι, 240
βλη-, 232
βλώσκω, 240, 263
βοάω, 265
βόειος/βόεος, 255
βοηθέω, 239
βοηλασία, 253
βολλομαι, 69
βολομαι, 69
βόλος, 232, 248
βοτήρ, 254
βοῦκλεψ, 260
βουκόλος, 259
βουλεία, 253
βούλευμα, 252
βουλευτήριον, 250
βουλλεύω, 193
βούλομαι, 234
βούπληξ, 260
βοῦς, 277
βραδινος, 114
βραχύνω, 264
βρίθω, 264
βροδον, 114
βροντή, 241
βροτός, 7, 314
βροχεως, 114
βροχυς, 68
βρώσιμον, 255
βρώσιμος, 255
βωμός, 252
βωτιάνειρα, 259

γάγγραινα, 249
γάλα, 228
γαλατᾶς, 250
γαμόροι, 146
γαργαίρω, 304
γάστρων, 250
γαυριάω, 266
γαυρόομαι, 266
γεγάτην, 305
γεγαώς, 313
γεγράφηκα, 306
γεγωνητέον, 257

γενᾶτος, 192
γενετήρ, 220
γένος, 216, 229, 235
γέντο, 300
γεραίρω, 274
γεραρός, 274
γέροντ-, 7
γηράσκω, 263, 301
γίγνομαι, 220, 262
γιγνώσκω, 214, 223, 229, 263
γλαφυρός, 258
γλυφευτής, 254
γλῶττα, 135
γνάθων, 250
γνήσιος, 220
γνύπετος, 220, 259
γόνιμος, 255
γόνος, 248
γόνυ, 229
γραία, 249
γραπτύς, 253
γραφεῖον, 250
γύναι, 272
γυναικεῖος, 255
γυνή, 233, 240

-δα, 284
δαήρ, 214
δαίμων, 273
δαινῦτο, 215, 309
δαιτρεύειν, 266
δακέθυμος, 129
δάκνω, 262
δαμαρτ-, 260
δαμνᾰ-/δαμνᾰ-, 262 f.
-δᾱν/-δην, 284
δασμός, 241
δασύς, 207
δαυχνα, 69
-δε, 284, 286
δέαμαι, 85
δέγμενος, 240
δεδέξομαι, 311
δείδιμεν, 305
δείδω, 95, 305
δεικνύᾶσι, 298
δείκνυμι, 214, 229, 263
δεικνύω, 185

INDEX OF LINEAR B WORDS